EMERGING ASIA
CHANGES AND CHALLENGES

ASIAN DEVELOPMENT BANK
1997

Published by Asian Development Bank, 1997
First printing, May 1997
Second printing, July 1997

The Asian Development Bank encourages the use of the material presented herein, with appropriate credit given to the published author. Please address inquiries for copies to the Chief, Information Office, Asian Development Bank, P.O. Box 789, 0980 Manila, Philippines.

Publication Stock Number: 010297

ISBN 971-561-105-2

CONTENTS

LIST OF TABLES

LIST OF FIGURES

LIST OF BOXES

FOREWORD

The emergence of Asia—or, more accurately, its reemergence—on the world economic scene has been a remarkable story. Today, several Asian economies have income levels approaching those of the industrial countries, and others are rapidly catching up. This does not mean that poverty has been eradicated from the region; on the contrary, there are still more poor people in Asia than in the rest of the world. Nor has economic success been an unmixed blessing: it has taken a heavy toll on Asia's natural environment. Nevertheless, the scale and pace of the transformation, especially in East Asia, remains a stunning achievement.

Small wonder, then, that Asia's growth has been the subject of much public discussion. Scholars argue over the sustainability of high Asian economic growth rates; development practitioners sift the evidence for pointers on what worked and what did not; and policymakers seek to adapt the lessons learned. And so the debate continues.

In this era of rapid transformation, the Bank needs a framework for the continuous evolution of its own strategic thinking. Our mission and development objectives must be continually aligned with the changing situations and requirements of member countries.

I hope that the present study, which examines the trends and assesses the outlook for Asia over the next three decades, will contribute to a better understanding of the issues, raise the level of policy debate, and encourage interest in the development prospects of this region. This study was prepared by a team of academic advisors and Bank staff under the overall direction of the Economics and Development Resource Center of the Bank. The perspectives and judgments expressed in the report do not necessarily reflect the views and policies of the ADB or its Board of Directors.

Finally, I wish to express deep appreciation to the four external advisors who provided guidance and counsel to the study team. They are Dr. Toyoo Gyohten, Senior Advisor, Bank of Tokyo-Mitsubishi, Ltd., Japan; Dr. Supachai Panitchpakdi, Member of Parliament, Thailand; Dr. Il SaKong, Chairman and Chief Executive Officer, Institute for Global Economics, Republic of Korea; and Dr. Manmohan Singh, Member of Parliament, India. The study benefited greatly from their comments and suggestions.

Mitsuo Sato
President
Asian Development Bank

ACKNOWLEDGMENTS

A team of academic advisors to and staff of the Asian Development Bank (ADB) prepared this study. Outside researchers and ADB staff wrote background papers commissioned for the study. The bibliographical note identifies these papers and their authors, as well as other resource materials used.

David Bloom and Jeffrey Sachs of the Harvard Institute for International Development (HIID) guided and coordinated the activities of the academic advisors and together drafted Chapter 1. Each of the subsequent chapters was prepared under the leadership of one or more theme leaders: Jeffrey Sachs served as the economics theme leader, and together with Steve Radelet of HIID drafted Chapter 2; David Bloom and Jeffrey Williamson (Harvard University) were the theme leaders for demography and human resource development and drafted Chapter 3; Theodore Panayotou of HIID was theme leader for the environment and drafted Chapter 4; and Michael Lipton (Sussex University) and Siddiqur Osmani (University of Ulster) were theme leaders for the quality of life and with the assistance of Arjan de Haan (Sussex University) drafted Chapter 5. Staff and editors at the ADB worked closely with the academic advisors to revise the drafts and finalize the study.

V. V. Desai was responsible for the overall direction and management of the study and headed a Bank team, comprising Jungsoo Lee, Bindu Lohani, M. G. Quibria, R. Swaminathan, and Jan van Heeswijk, that guided the study's design and advised on its contents. Frank Harrigan coordinated and substantially contributed to the study. David Edwards, Rajiv Kumar, Srinivasa Madhur, Elisabetta Marmolo, Sudipto Mundle, Ernesto Pernia, Nikhilesh Prasad, Pradumna Rana, Narhari Rao, Asad Ali Shah, Ricardo Tan, Graham Walter, and Christine Wong also provided valuable inputs. Vice-Presidents Bong-Suh Lee, Peter Sullivan, and Pierre Uhel gave advice and encouragement.

Zanny Minton Beddoes edited the study, Alice Dowsett and Judith Banning did the copy editing, and Stephen Banta advised on copy editing.

The production team consisted of Stella Alabastro, Laura Britt, Mercedita Cabañeros, Maritess Manalo, Edmond Pantilo, and Lea Sumulong. Ging Cuevas, Eva Olanda, and Beth Perez provided secretarial support. Chuckie Castillo, Helen Cruda, Ver Latay, and James Villafuerte provided additional production support and advice. Lily Bernal, Amy Bobis, Mercy Cano, Marina Galura, and Tess Redito helped with proofreading. R. Rajan and his staff prepared the report for publication.

At HIID, Sarah Newberry helped with editing, and Kelley Dwyer assisted with coordination and survey data tabulation. Administrative and secretarial support were provided at HIID by Alison Howe, Nancy Juskin, Angie Milonas, Faith Paul, Sabrina Putnam, Martha Synnott, and Jennifer Watts, and at Sussex by Eleanor Chowns and Hilary Cook.

ABBREVIATIONS AND ACRONYMS

ADB	Asian Development Bank
AFTA	ASEAN Free Trade Area
AIDS	Acquired Immune Deficiency Syndrome
APEC	Asia-Pacific Economic Cooperation Group
ASEAN	Association of Southeast Asian Nations
BAAC	Bank for Agriculture and Agricultural Cooperatives
BRAC	Bangladesh Rural Advancement Committee
EIA	environmental impact assessment
EPZ	export processing zone
FAO	Food and Agriculture Organization
GDP	gross domestic product
GNP	gross national product
HIID	Harvard Institute for International Development
HIV	Human Immunodeficiency Virus
ILO	International Labour Organisation
ISO	International Organization for Standardization
NGO	nongovernment organization
OECD	Organisation for Economic Co-operation and Development
PPP	purchasing power parity
PRC	People's Republic of China
RET	renewable energy technology
SITC	Standard International Trade Classification
TFP	total factor productivity
UN	United Nations
UNDP	United Nations Development Programme
WHO	World Health Organization
WTO	World Trade Organization

1

EMERGING ASIA

A sia is in the midst of an economic and social transformation unrivaled in history. In virtually every dimension, life in Asia is changing at a pace never seen before in any part of the world during a comparable period of time. The region is unrecognizable compared with only a generation ago. Not only have many Asians become richer, healthier, better fed, and more educated, but they have become so remarkably quickly. In large parts of Asia, the gap with industrial countries is closing rapidly.

Economic growth has driven this transformation. Asia's economic performance is best summarized by comparing its dramatic growth in gross domestic product (GDP) with that in other parts of the world. Between 1965 and 1990, the longest period for which comparable data exist, GDP in Asia as a whole grew by an annual average of 3.8 percent per person.[1] The East Asian subregion did even better, with average growth rates per person of 6.7 percent per year (Table 1.1).[2]

The result was a remarkable rise in prosperity. In 1965, Asia's average income per person was only 13 percent of the U.S. level, but by 1990 it had reached 26 percent. In East Asia, GDP per person rose from 17 percent of the U.S. level in 1965 to 57 percent of the U.S. level in 1990. The improvement is staggering. U.S. income per person was almost six times the East Asian average a generation ago. By 1990, it was less than double.

---

1. All GDP data, except as noted, are from Summers and Heston (1994) and are expressed in 1985 dollars, adjusted for purchasing power parity (PPP). PPP income is estimated at a common set of relative prices so that incomes in different places (and at different times) can be expressed in terms of their command over a common set of real resources. While far from perfect, economists generally consider the Summers and Heston data set to be the most suitable international one for making cross-country comparisons of income levels and growth. The most recent version (November 1994) has complete data through 1990 only, with data through 1992 for some countries.

2. The East Asian experience is extensively analyzed in the "East Asian Miracle," World Bank (1994).

Table 1.1 Growth in the Global Economy, 1965-90

Region/Economy	Average annual GDP growth per person (PPP adjusted)
East Asia	6.7
Hong Kong	5.8
Korea, Republic of	7.4
Singapore	7.4
Taipei,China	6.3
People's Republic of China	5.1
Southeast Asia	3.8
Indonesia	4.7
Malaysia	4.5
Philippines	1.4
Thailand	4.6
South Asia	1.7
Bangladesh	0.8
India	2.0
Pakistan	1.8
Sri Lanka	2.3
Pacific islands	
Papua New Guinea	-0.7
OECD	2.7
Middle East	2.5
Sub-Saharan Africa	0.7
Latin America	0.8

OECD = Organisation for Economic Co-operation and Development
PPP = purchasing power parity
Note: Growth performance has, in some cases, been uneven within the period. For example, between 1980 and 1990, growth in India was 3.7 percent, but was only 1 percent from 1970 to 1980.   See Chapter 2 and Appendix for details.

Some parts of Asia, however, have lagged seriously behind. Indeed, Asia is still home to most of the world's poor. In South Asia, for example, growth per person averaged just 1.7 percent per year. As a result, South Asia's average GDP per person was just 8.5 percent of the U.S. level in 1990, exactly the same as in 1965.

The years since 1990 have seen improvements in economic performance and prospects in some economies. In South Asia, policymakers have laid stronger economic foundations, and economic growth is beginning to respond. The Philippines, too, is now showing strong signs of economic improvement. At a regional level, however, broad trends remain more or less the same as in the previous quarter of a century, and growth in East and Southeast Asia is still rapid compared with that in other regions of the world.

In conjunction with this growth performance, Asia is also undergoing huge demographic changes. Death rates began to fall sharply a generation ago as medical advances began to conquer common diseases. Birth rates, too, have plummeted, but a little later than death rates. Birth rates began falling first in East Asia, earlier than in South Asia. The demographic transition—from high mortality and fertility rates to lower mortality and fertility rates—which took one or two centuries in Europe, is being compressed into a couple of generations. The impact on the age structure of Asia's population has been enormous.

Dramatic improvements in many other aspects of life have accompanied economic growth. In the 1960s, poverty throughout most of Asia was as bad as in Africa. Today, the scourge of poverty is receding. Virtually every indicator of public health has improved. An Asian born today can expect to live to more than 60, yet in 1960 life expectancy was less than 50. Access to education has improved, as has the availability of other basic goods, such as clean water, sewerage, and shelter. These improvements in Asia's quality of life are in large part a consequence of rising income levels, but the link goes both ways: a healthier and better educated population contributes to faster economic growth.

Unfortunately, improvements in the quality of life have been uneven across and within countries and not all change in Asia has been positive. Rapid social changes have created social and family stresses. While women have generally benefited, they have not always shared fully in rising prosperity. In South Asia, especially, they are less educated and often poorer than men. In addition, Asia's physical environment has deteriorated rapidly. The air and water in many parts of the region are among the most polluted in the world, resulting in serious diseases and loss of productivity. Enormous inconveniences and stresses in daily life are now increasingly apparent; for example, congestion in many of Asia's megacities has reached legendary proportions. These megacities are also home to many destitute pavement dwellers and contain some of the world's most deplorable slums. Environmental degradation is not an inevitable result of economic progress, but it is the price that Asia has paid through a combination of ineffective policies and lack of attention.

Asia in Perspective

This volume is a study of Asia's transformation: its causes, its future, and its challenges. These challenges will affect not only the more than 50 percent of the world's population who live in Asia, but emerging Asia will increasingly affect those who live outside the region. The study's approach is comparative, historical, and empirical. Historical analysis suggests that Asia is not simply emerging, but is reemerging to occupy the more prominent global position that it enjoyed for much of human history before a sharp relative decline after the industrial revolution. An international and comparative emphasis also helps clarify issues that cannot be clearly understood from studies based on the experiences of just one or two countries.

The international perspective also helps to illuminate the recent debate about Asia's growth prospects. Some observers have been almost euphoric about Asia's future prospects, giving rise to the notion of an endless growth miracle, especially in East Asia. A provocative opposing argument suggests that East Asia's growth record actually resembles that of the defunct Soviet Union, and by implication, is likely to collapse at some future date (Krugman 1994). International evidence points to a path in between these extremes. East Asia's growth is fundamentally different from Soviet-style growth and is vastly more sustainable. Indeed, the prospects for continued rapid growth in Asia are good, assuming that global economic conditions remain sound. However, international evidence also suggests that in some Asian countries, rapid growth will gradually taper off as they bridge the income gap with industrial countries.

This study is as much about the differences within Asia as it is about the contrasts between Asia and the rest of the world. Some parts of Asia, especially East Asia, have soared economically. Others, mainly in South Asia, have lagged behind, at least until recently. Most of Central Asia and parts of Southeast Asia are only now abandoning failed models of central planning, and therefore face the special challenges of economic transition. The Pacific island economies face the unique problems that come from having small populations and being located far from any major economic center (Box 1.1).[3]

The scope of this study extends well beyond economic growth. It is also concerned with demographic trends, the physical environment, urbanization, education, and other social conditions. The goal is to understand how the overall quality of life in Asia has changed, and to examine the challenges that Asian development—in its broadest sense—faces in the future. This multifaceted approach uncovers some of the more subtle aspects of Asia's growth experience and prospects. For example, demographic trends, especially changes in the population's age structure, help to account for a surprisingly large part of the differences in growth rates among Asian countries, and gave East Asia an advantage over South Asia in growth per person during the past 30 years. During the next 30 years, these same demographic factors are likely to work to South Asia's relative advantage.

To understand the broad differences in development patterns within Asia, a comparison of East Asia and South Asia is critical, given the economic significance of these subregions. Most of the analysis in this study therefore focuses on two broad groupings of countries: East Asia, including the People's Republic of China (PRC), and South Asia, including India.[4] Figure 1.1 shows the Asian and Pacific region. For some purposes, the groupings are adjusted to separately identify the two Asian giant countries, the PRC and India. At other times East Asia is divided into the four higher income economies (Hong Kong, Republic of Korea[5], Singapore, and Taipei,China) and the economies of Southeast Asia, which have begun to grow rapidly more recently. Occasionally, the study analyzes Asia's transitional economies (the Central Asian republics, Cambodia, Lao People's Democratic Republic (Lao PDR), Mongolia, Myanmar, and Viet Nam) as a group. This set of regional labels is, of course, imperfect. To account for differences in circumstances within subregions, the analysis will depart from the classification as necessary.

---

3. This study does not discuss the Pacific islands, but does refer to them as appropriate.

4. Japan is not one of the focus group of countries studied. However, where relevant, its experience is discussed.

5. Henceforth "Korea".

Box 1.1 The Future of the Pacific

The Pacific islands enter the next century with the most varied and uncertain prospects of the whole Asian and Pacific region. They recently emerged from colonial status to institutional arrangements that may be appropriate for much larger nation states, but that may be inappropriate when applied to remote island communities. Even though the Pacific islands have a relatively unspoiled physical environment and remarkably democratic political systems, they are handicapped by their small size and remote location. Unstable economic structures, financially and technically weak governments, and, in some cases, populations divided among themselves, exacerbate their natural handicaps. Income disparities are widening rapidly and traditional values are in disarray. Developments far outside the islands' influence are shaping their future.

The Melanesian states contain nine tenths of the land-based resources and population of the Pacific islands, but worsening terms of trade, combined with aid-induced complacency and rent seeking, have weakened their economic performance and eroded public services. Output growth has barely kept pace with population growth, open unemployment is rising, and the shock-absorbing capabilities of the subsistence sector are coming under increasing strain.

The Polynesian and Micronesian states have different resource endowments and closer social connections to the Pacific Rim. Large external financial transfers and remittance incomes have had a powerful effect on their recent economic performance. The vast fisheries, the few high islands, and human resources are unevenly distributed among these smallest of the Pacific island states. They also differ in the ability to manage their natural and human resources.

The high costs of inputs because of scale and distance factors, as well as international pressure on governments to dismantle protection, circumscribes the economic options for the Pacific islands. Fisheries, timber and tree crops, horticulture, tourism, minerals, and some transient niche markets based on these products in which they have a comparative advantage offer the most promise. While strains on the ocean's resources will increase as resident and migratory fish stocks are overfished, technology for recovering minerals from the seabed is advancing. Given the huge investments required for exploiting the ocean floor, the Pacific island states will come under enormous pressure to surrender any management rights they may claim to the ocean resources.

At the regional level, more cost-effective and more island-owned institutions will need to emerge to handle the interests of the Pacific islands. Substantial trade-offs of weak sovereignty for stronger mutual support will need to be negotiated. While the nation state will not disappear, and national identity will continue to have its uses, regional solidarity will become necessary for sustained management of the ocean. The forms of economic activity and modes of distribution that would come about with a successful mix of community, national, and regional governance should be capable of increasing output per person and distributing its benefits more equitably than is now the case.

Source: ADB (forthcoming).

Figure 1.1 The Asian and Pacific Region

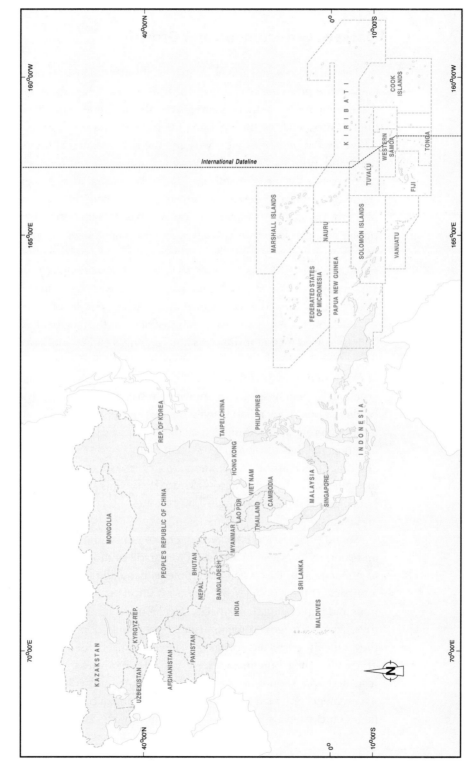

Asia 97-0319 HR

Markets, Government, and Growth

This study's central theme is that well-functioning institutions and markets are prerequisites for growth. The lessons of history and international comparison are that countries' growth rates depend partly on structural factors, such as their geography and resources, but primarily on differences in initial income levels and the performance of their institutions and policies. The concept of institutions is a broad one that encompasses the basic organizational and behavioral arrangements that shape the pattern of economic activity; for instance, the framework of property rights and commercial law is a basic institution. So too is a public bureaucracy or an education system. The concept of policies is narrower. A policy is typically expressed in terms of an objective and a set of procedures that is intended to achieve it; for example, promoting exports by lowering trade barriers is a policy, as is subsidizing children's school meals to encourage larger primary school enrollment.

Much of East Asia's success can be ascribed to the fact that East Asian countries used market institutions and openness earlier and much more than other developing economies. In particular, they adopted a strategy of export-led growth and stuck to the discipline that this imposed. Governments generally struck an appropriate balance between private and public actions. They relied heavily on the private sector as the engine of industrial growth, especially in the crucial area of export-oriented manufacturing, but they also provided selective support through directed credit and other mechanisms. A common error of less successful governments in South Asia and elsewhere was to try to do too much, not only providing public goods, but also trying to run bakeries, mines, steel mills, hotels, and banks.

Sound policies and effective government institutions helped nurture and support markets in East Asia. From trade or monetary management to public health, East Asian governments generally made good choices and backed their policies by strenuous efforts to foster sound institutions and implementation capacity. Unlike many other developing countries, East Asian governments usually got things done. In most cases, they quickly corrected mistakes. They organized their bureaucracies efficiently. Their bureaucrats were capable, motivated, and effectively insulated from short-term political pressures. At another level, East Asian governments provided a road map for development by forging and maintaining a consensus in favor of long-term growth. They supported private property rights through the law and markets through the provision of infrastructure, education, and other public goods.

One purpose of this study is to describe the kinds of institutional changes that are still needed in the slower growing countries to unleash faster economic growth. Another is to point out the institutional challenges—of which there are many—that the successful countries face. As income levels rise, East Asians' aspirations and expectations are changing. Political participation is rising; democracy is spreading. Such changes will broaden the political spectrum and increasingly preclude the kind of top-down policymaking that has characterized many countries in the region. The process of building consensus to support needed reform will assume greater importance. Governments will have to become more accountable and more transparent. The relationship between governments and the private sector will have to be based more on consultation and on mutual trust. Greater internationalization will also render old economic strategies redundant; for instance, international trading partners will no longer accept protectionist policies. Finally, greater global financial integration will complicate monetary management. In short, Asia's governments will face pressures from above and below. The strictures of greater international integration will limit all governments' room for maneuver, while increasing popular empowerment means that people will push harder to get things done. Navigating between these twin pressures will demand better governance than ever before.

Asia and the World

Asia's rising prosperity and trade will bring benefits far beyond Asia. A larger world market increases the scope for specialization and innovation, and thereby contributes to greater worldwide prosperity. Nonetheless, Asia's rapid reemergence also creates challenges well beyond its borders.

Increased affluence means that Asia's consumption, especially of food and energy, is rising fast. As agricultural production increases more slowly than in the past, the region will increasingly rely on imported food. Some commentators fear that increasing Asian food consumption will put unbearable pressure on world food balances. While this is unlikely, Asia will certainly have a much bigger impact on world food prices. By 2010 Asia's share of world cereal imports will rise to about 42 percent from its current level of 33 percent. Rapid growth will also raise Asia's energy requirements, with implications for global prices as well as for the environment. Asian demands for coal will double and its demand for liquid fuels may triple by 2010. Asian countries' choices about the types of energy they use will have implications far beyond their borders.

Rapid changes in trade patterns are also likely to demand significant adjustments on the part of some industrial countries. East Asia, for example, increased its exports to the rest of the world from $143 billion in 1980 to around $852 billion in 1995. Its imports also increased almost sixfold with increased demand for goods and services produced elsewhere in the world. While consumers and exporters in industrial countries have gained from this increased trade, labor-intensive sectors in Europe and North America have felt pressure from the competition of imports from East Asia. Such adjustment pressures are likely to intensify as India and other formerly inward-looking parts of Asia enlarge their roles in the world economy.

To manage such adjustments, international institutions such as the World Trade Organization will be vital for maintaining effective "rules of the game" for global economic interactions in the years ahead. Asia has an important stake in having its voice heard in and defining the directions of such global institutions. Both Asia and the rest of the world will have to play by well-defined rules if economic tensions are not to threaten global prosperity. The remainder of this overview provides a broad perspective on Asia's transformation, with detailed analysis left for later chapters. Thus the next section takes a historical perspective, examining Asia's past for clues about its current reemergence. The chapter moves on to look at the surge in Asian economic growth in the past 30 years, and then documents attendant changes in other dimensions of Asian society. Subsequently it highlights some of the main challenges that are likely to confront Asia during the next decades of rapid transformation. The final section makes some tentative projections about Asia's future prospects.

Asia in Historical Context

From a broad historical perspective, Asia is not emerging so much as reemerging. For much of human history, parts of Asia were the most economically advanced regions in the world. Technologically and economically, China was the world's leader during most of the period from 500 AD to 1500 AD. Only in the last half millennium did it lose preeminence to Europe, and later to the Americas and Oceania.

In 1820, at the beginning of the industrial age, Asia still made up an estimated 58 percent of world GDP. This share fell precipitously in the following 100 years, and by 1920 Asia accounted for only 27 percent of global GDP. By 1940 its share had fallen to a mere 19 percent, even though 60 percent of the world's population lived in Asia. Surging growth in recent decades brought Asia's share of world income back to around 37 percent as of 1992 (Maddison 1995). Looking ahead, fast growth will push this share up much further. Based on plausible assumptions, Asia could be back at around 57 percent of the world's GDP by 2025.

Asia's Rise and Decline

The roots of Asia's growth prospects lie in the distant past. Reflecting on the factors behind Asia's relative decline helps illuminate the reasons for its current ascendancy. As far back as 221 BC, China first unified politically, a remarkable feat that has remained intact. The early creation of a stable, centralized political administration, combined with good environmental conditions over much of the country, a temperate climate, alluvial agriculture, and fertile soils, led to rapid population growth and the early emergence of commercial society. By the time of the Sung Dynasty (960-1279 AD), China's commercial sophistication and technological advances had brought it preeminence in the world economy. The compass, gunpowder, the printing press, and paper currency are all Chinese innovations from this time.

After an interlude of Mongol domination, China's technological leadership was once again evident in the early years of the Ming Dynasty. Between 1405 and 1433, Admiral Cheng Ho led naval explorations to distant lands in the Indian Ocean, Arabia, and East Africa, proving that China could dominate long-distance ocean travel and trade. Suddenly, in 1433, the emperor suspended all future expeditions. Later governments prevented foreign travel and suspended much of foreign trade. China ceased to build ships and lost its technological lead in navigation.

Several scholarly studies have shown that between 1500 and 1800 or so, China lost its technological dynamism (Needham 1954). Nonetheless, as late as 1776, Adam Smith described China as "long one of the richest, that is, one of the most fertile, best cultivated, most industrious, and most populous countries in the world," and "a much richer country than any part of Europe." He noted, though, that "[China] seems, however, to have long been stationary." Significantly, Smith felt that China's neglect of foreign trade had imposed a heavy cost, writing that: "A more extensive foreign trade ... which to this great home market [of China] added the foreign market of all the rest of the world; especially if any considerable part of this trade was carried on in Chinese ships; could scarcely fail to increase very much the manufactures of China, and to improve very much the productive powers of its manufacturing industry." (Smith 1976) But that was not to be. By 1820, China's income per person had fallen to around half of the level in Western Europe.

A very different civilization developed in India across the same time span. Nevertheless, by the 15th century India had evolved into a sophisticated agrarian economy that sustained a large empire, a substantial preindustrial output of goods (particularly textiles), an impressive overseas trade, and an inquiring spirit that decimalized mathematics.

The rest of Asia also fell behind the West in relative terms after 1500. Japan, like China, largely closed itself off from the world during the military rule of the Tokugawa Shogunate (1603-1867). The policy of *sakoku*, implemented in stages around 1640, limited Japan's international trade to Dutch and Chinese traders in the single port of Dejima in Nagasaki. In India and various states in Southeast Asia, Western powers—Britain, France, Holland, and Portugal—used their naval superiority to wrest valuable trade from Asian hands and to secure it for Western monopolies, such as the Dutch East India Company and the British East India Company. These trading monopolies, backed by superior military power and mercantilist policies in Europe, contributed to the widening economic gap between Europe and Asia and the progressive loss of sovereignty of South and Southeast Asia.

While Asia was falling behind, parts of Europe were surging ahead, boosted by technological innovations combined with the economic dynamism of the emerging capitalist system. Between 1820 and 1870, Western Europe and its offshoots (Australia, Canada, New Zealand, and the United States) grew at an average annual rate of 1.1 percent per person, while Asia, Latin America, and Africa barely grew at all (their GDP rose around 0.1 percent per year). The resulting economic and military dominance of the ascendant Western powers gave them growing control over the non-Western world, either through direct colonial rule (as in India) or the imposition of unequal treaties in their favor (as in China).

The Meiji Restoration

Only Japan was able to make a dramatic institutional breakthrough to modern capitalism. Elsewhere in Asia, colonial rule or internal political barriers blocked or distorted institutional change, and hence faster growth. Even today, the character of the 1868 Meiji Restoration—which began a remarkable period of 20 years of dramatic institutional modernization—is relevant. Japan's leaders ended feudal privileges; created markets for land, labor, and capital; updated the taxation system from payment in kind to monetary levies; established a central bank with the gold standard as the basis of monetary management; introduced modern company law and a commercial code based largely on European models; and set up a political system based on constitutional rule and cabinet government. In short, they radically modernized virtually every economic and political institution in Japan.

One can draw many lessons from the success of the Meiji era. Even though debate about the relative importance of various aspects of the reforms continues, it embodied key features that would propel the rest of East Asia to rapid growth a century later. Agricultural reforms began early with government propagating the dissemination of best practice farming methods. Dramatic improvements in agricultural productivity followed, thereby releasing surplus labor for other activities. This laid the basis for labor-intensive manufactures, although much of the transformation remained related to the rural economy, was small in scale, and concentrated initially on traditional products.

As the state initiated a drive for larger scale, more pervasive industrialization, the authorities emphasized the promotion of international trade. Japanese industrialization under the Meiji era took place under nearly completely free trade, as unequal treaties imposed on Japan in the mid-1850s and later until the early 1900s held tariff rates below 5 percent. Government policy ensured export profitability. Even when cotton imports threatened domestic raw cotton producers, the government maintained free trade in raw cotton to preserve the profitability of cotton textile exporters. However, in the years up to 1900, and to a lesser extent in 1914, the scale of activity in the export sector was modest, though expanding rapidly. The share of exports in national output tripled to 15 percent between 1885-89 and 1910-14, and the share of imports expanded at a similar pace. Openness brought many benefits; for instance, many of Japan's early technological advances were based on imported technologies brought in through foreign machinery and foreign experts.

The government played an important role although the scope of government activity shifted over time. After a period of state-owned demonstration projects, which were privatized in the early 1880s as part of a program to consolidate state finances, private capital subject to the discipline of the international market overwhelmingly dominated Japan's export sector. The government focused on creating the conditions for modernization, especially by promoting export orientation and technological advances in industry through fiscal incentives and state-private partnerships, as well as more conventionally by building infrastructure and providing mass education.

The Early 20th Century

Few countries remained unaffected by the events of the first half of the 20th century. The period between 1914 and 1950 saw several global disasters, including two world wars, financial instability in the 1920s, and the Great Depression of the 1930s. World trade virtually collapsed under these shocks. National currencies became inconvertible, and the little trade that took place was mostly regulated by interstate agreements. The era of world markets of the late 19th century, in which the gold standard had linked virtually all parts of the world and trade had prospered, was a distant memory.

This period was especially disastrous for Asia. China suffered decades of internal turmoil, foreign invasion, civil war, and war-related hyperinflation. Japan's economic success was tempered by imperial ambitions and subsequent military disaster, and the country lay prostrate after its defeat in World War II. The confluence of political, military, and economic difficulties dragged Asia's living standards ever further behind the West. Asia's GDP per person in 1950 was virtually unchanged from its 1913 level. Western Europeans were by now almost seven times richer than Asians, while Americans were 12 times wealthier.[6]

The great opportunity for postwar Asia came with the renewal of political sovereignty. The colonial powers retreated from Asia, often peacefully, but in some cases only after an extended war or period of

---

6. According to Maddison's (1995) estimates, in 1950 Asia's GDP per person was $765 in 1990 PPP-adjusted dollars, Western Europe's was $5,126, and that of the Western offshoots was $9,255.

civil insurrection. Many of the new national governments came to power with the explicit goal of modernizing their economies and initiating rapid growth. The strategies many of these countries followed proved successful beyond their wildest expectations. East Asia's economic growth—and later Southeast Asia's—exploded, far exceeding the rest of the world's achievements. The fundamental question, however, is, Why?

Catalyzing Growth

Economic growth is a complex and much debated phenomenon. Scholars disagree not only on what influences economic growth, but also on the mechanisms through which it occurs. Chapter 2 interprets Asia's growth performance based upon a statistical and institutional analysis of differences in countries' growth performances. This section discusses the main themes.

There is no doubt that East Asia's relatively low income in the 1960s provided it with the potential to grow fast and catch up with richer countries. In poorer countries, with relatively lower stocks of capital, investment can generate higher returns than in richer ones. This allows the possibility of faster "catch-up." The world's long-standing technological leader, the United States, has seen average annual growth per person of around 1.6 percent per year for the past 175 years, with only modest variations over long subperiods. Other countries have exceeded that rate for long stretches only when they have lagged far behind the United States, and thus had opportunities to accumulate capital and technology more quickly. As the gap in income levels between poorer and richer countries closes, so too does the gap in growth rates. In Asia, Japan is the best example of how great success in catching up also leads to a tapering off in rapid growth. After its postwar reconstruction, Japan's growth rate soared to more than 9 percent a year and stayed that high until its income per person reached about half the U.S. level. During the 1970s and 1980s, as the income gap closed, Japan's growth rate slowed. By the early 1990s, as Japanese income per person reached 90 percent of the U.S. level, its rate of growth had slowed to about 2 percent, scarcely above that of the United States.

This process of catch-up growth is not an automatic one. Relative poverty provides potential, but nothing more—potential that geographic and other natural handicaps can prevent from developing. Landlocked countries, for instance, are burdened by the difficulty of reaching their markets. Trade is costlier and riskier than for those with access to the sea. Thus the Central Asian republics are at a natural disadvantage compared with the coastal economies around the South China Sea. In East Asia the physical environment broadly supported growth: the region has ample rainfall, fertile soils, natural harbors, and easy access to major shipping lanes.

The capacities of a country's population can also compromise economic potential, at least temporarily; for instance, lack of education and high morbidity rates will make rapid growth more difficult. Even though these capacities can, and do, change over time, they often put a temporary ceiling on a country's growth. Conversely, demographic trends can help growth. In East Asia, for instance, the relative share of the working-age population has been rising. If other policies are adequate, this can boost growth.

Above all, however, ineffective institutions and bad policies can squander economic potential. The defining characteristic of East Asia's governments was the successful institutional base they built for rapid growth and the subsequent policies these institutions supported. This combination was important in all areas of the economy, but the following six, in particular, stand out:

- *Export promotion.* East Asian governments put relatively open trade, especially export promotion, at the top of their agenda. They maintained a policy environment that supported exporters. Tariffs on intermediate and capital goods were low or moderate, and exporters were insulated from the negative effects of tariffs through specific institutions, such as export processing zones and duty rebate schemes. This institutional environment allowed the East Asian economies to export manufacturing goods successfully, even though they began from a low base of technology and industrialization. In turn, the rapid growth of manufactured exports allowed these countries to import productivity-enhancing capital goods and technology from abroad. Exports also provided an objective criterion for measuring the effectiveness of state support for industry.

- *Development led by the private sector.* As is now vividly clear, successful growth strategies have been built upon private ownership and market-based economic organization. Most East Asian economies hit upon a market-based strategy early in the postwar era. By contrast, many South Asian countries adopted far more statist strategies that resulted in slower economic growth. They are only now, in the 1990s, overcoming the consequences of these policies.

- *Agricultural transformation.* The growth in agricultural productivity was higher in East Asia than in other parts of the developing world. Unlike in many other developing countries, East Asian governments did not repress their agriculture sectors. With the exception of the two city states of Hong Kong and Singapore, most governments invested amply in agricultural research, local extension services, and rural infrastructure such as irrigation and electrification. This allowed rapid spread of the fruits of the Green Revolution. Food balances improved, as did standards of nutrition, and rising productivity in rural areas freed up labor for manufacturing exports, thereby allowing a rapid structural transformation of the economy.

- *High saving rates.* Public institutions supported high rates of national saving. The basic budgetary framework meant that East Asian governments were themselves large savers. They took in more revenues than they spent on current items, leaving plenty of money for public investment in basic infrastructure, such as roads and ports. They also kept social spending low, in turn allowing tax rates to stay low. For example, most governments, by avoiding ambitious publicly funded retirement schemes, not only kept public saving high, they also encouraged private thrift.

- *Skill accumulation.* East Asia's policies and supporting institutions led to rapid skill increases. This was not merely a matter of providing public education, although most East Asian governments did do that well. The broader upgrading of their skill base depended on more complex interactions; for example, exports accelerated the introduction and transfer of technology, creating a strong demand for skilled labor. This persuaded parents to invest in educating their children. Textiles, electronics, and other labor-intensive exports created a specific demand for female workers. As more young women began working, they married later and had fewer children. With fewer children, parents' investment in the health and education of each child rose.

- *Economic flexibility.* East Asia set up market-based institutions that allowed the economy to become more complex rapidly. Basic property rights existed and the rule of law was adhered to more closely than in most other developing countries. Contracts were enforced and legal institutions were set up to settle disputes. Legal stability fostered the rise of a vigorous private sector and gave long-term confidence to foreign investors. Governments relied mainly on private investors, both domestic and foreign, rather than on state enterprises, to organize manufacturing investments and production. Private firms generally built sophisticated production networks and linkages more successfully than state enterprises could. East Asian governments kept their labor markets flexible so that workers could readily shift between sectors as the economy's structure changed. Many governments also began farsighted programs of scientific and engineering upgrading that are now contributing to rapid technological development. Korea and Taipei,China, for instance, are now benefiting from their governments' earlier technological foresight.

Plainly, East Asia's catch-up had no single catalyst. Rather, it was the outcome of a fortunate combination of initial potential that capable governments harnessed through export promotion and increasingly effective market-supporting institutions. It might seem that the list of factors that contributed to rapid growth is so long and daunting that no other country could hope to follow in East Asia's wake. This would be a serious misunderstanding. East Asia was able to unleash rapid growth despite profound weaknesses in many key institutions. Not everything was in place at the start of the rapid growth era. The real achievement has been that governments and the private sector worked hard to keep pace with the changing needs and opportunities of a fast growing economy.

A stylized summary might be as follows. Governments turned to market forces and private ownership to underpin development. Exports provided the spark that set off rapid growth and paid for imports of world-class technologies and capital goods. Typically, agriculture provided an important initial underpinning. Frugal, high-saving governments helped to finance the growth and to provide conditions for private households and firms to save as well. Economic agility has been the key to sustaining growth, allowing the economy to progress from simple, labor-intensive operations to increasingly high-skilled, high-technology activities. The result has been rapidly rising prosperity and a profound change in Asia's quality of life.

A Changing Quality of Life

Economic indicators alone do not capture Asia's transformation adequately. Bare statistics of rising GDP cannot possibly document the extent to which life in Asia has changed. Some aspects of a changing quality of life can themselves be directly quantified. Life expectancy, literacy rates, and pollution levels, for instance, can all be measured, with improvements noted, deteriorations identified. Other aspects of life, however, remain less tangible. Measuring the stresses that rapid urbanization places on traditional families or the extent to which Asia's values are changing is impossible. In these areas, a more qualitative discussion must supplement statistical comparisons.

Overall, Asia's quality of life has improved dramatically during the past 30 years: people live longer, they are more literate, they eat better, and they go to school for longer. All these are powerful indications that living standards have risen. However, not everyone's life has improved equally. Countries, regions within countries, and particular demographic groups have been left behind. Life in Bangladesh or Nepal, for instance, has improved much less dramatically than in Korea or Taipei,China. Children in Thailand's northeastern frontier face greater risks of disease and fewer opportunities for education than those in Bangkok. Women, in general, have done worse than men. Nor has all change been positive. Ill-planned urbanization and the pollution of Asia's land, water, and air are all adversely impinging on the region's quality of life.

Rising economic prosperity has been, and will undoubtedly continue to be, the single most important determinant of improvements in Asian living standards. Economic growth provides the resources needed to finance better nutrition and housing; to build and staff clinics and hospitals; and to construct schools, pay teachers, and buy textbooks. But Asia's quality of life also has much to do with the strength of social and political commitments to improve living standards and the effectiveness of the institutions set up to implement them. The following sections document some of the main changes in Asia's quality of life.

The Demographic Transition

Asia's quality of life is powerfully connected to the size, growth, and structure of its population. The potential for better education or nutrition, for instance, depends in part on how many children a family must feed and educate relative to the number of working adults. In turn, improvements in the quality of life have direct demographic effects. Better educated women, for instance, tend to have fewer children, who in turn are better educated and nourished than the larger numbers of children in households where mothers are poorly educated.

The population of developing Asia is currently estimated at 3.0 billion.[7] This is about 53 percent of the world's population. Historical records suggest that more people have always lived in Asia than anywhere else. Demographers estimate that it took the world more than 1 million years to reach a total population of 1 billion people. Asia has added that many people during the past two decades alone.

During the past 50 years, Asia's population structure has also altered fundamentally. At the beginning of the postwar period, mortality rates, especially infant and child mortality rates, began dropping dramatically. Medical advances, such as the introduction of penicillin and streptomycin treatment for tuberculosis, together with disease control campaigns, better sanitation, cleaner water supplies, and improved nutrition, all meant that fewer Asians died in infancy and all Asians began to live longer. Nonetheless, there was, and continues to be, considerable variation within Asia. A newborn Japanese can expect to live to 80, whereas a newborn Cambodian or Nepalese is still not expected to reach 55.

Declining fertility followed declining mortality. As people's chances of survival improved, their need to have many children decreased. Government population policies to reduce family size strongly reinforced this trend in some countries, as did growth in formal sector jobs and incomes, which reduced children's economic value to parents. Between 1950 and 1990 the number of children a typical Asian woman would have fell from six to three, although once again, considerable diversity between countries is apparent. In nations such as Afghanistan, Lao PDR, and Pakistan six children is still the norm, while in Hong Kong, Japan, Korea, and Singapore women are having insufficient children to keep the population constant.

---

7. Aggregate mid-year population of the Asian Development Bank's developing member countries for 1995 (ADB 1996).

One of the most important consequences of a transition from high to low birth and death rates is a large, temporary bulge in the population's age distribution. In the years after mortality rates fall, fertility rates at first stay high, and the population growth rate rises rapidly. Subsequently, fertility rates and consequently population growth rates fall. Thus, early in the transition a country will have a relatively high number of young people, which is eventually attenuated, creating a well defined "bulge" in the age distribution. As the bulge generation ages, the proportion of the working-age population increases. Eventually, the bulge shows up as an increase in the relative number of old people, many of whom will live longer than the elderly used to in earlier times.

As Asia's demographic transition took place so quickly, it had major effects on the region's age distribution. For example, the share of Asia's population under 15 years old rose from 37 to 40 percent between 1950 and 1975, but then declined to 32 percent by the mid-1990s. Similarly, the proportion of the population who were of working-age (15 to 64) rose from 56 to 63 percent between 1975 and 1995.[8] In East Asia these patterns were even more dramatic, whereas in Southeast Asia, and particularly in South Asia, the changes have been less marked.

This transition has had a huge impact on Asian families, and especially on the position of women. It has also had several important economic consequences. In countries where an increasing share of the population is of working-age, economic growth per person tends to be highest and national saving rates tend to rise. In countries with a rising share of the young in the population, both economic growth per person and national saving rates are reduced. The fact that East Asia is further ahead in the demographic transition than South Asia has therefore helped East Asia's growth as well as boosted its saving rates. Looking ahead, however, South Asia will have a rising share of workers in the next 30 years. Although this does not guarantee higher growth, it does provide a potential boost. The challenge is to create sufficient jobs for the large numbers of labor force entrants. By contrast, the rising proportion of retirees in the total population will likely dampen East Asian growth and saving rates.

---

8. These numbers refer to all of Asia, not just the developing member countries of the Asian Development Bank.

Poverty in Asia

Poverty is perhaps Asia's largest, most urgent, and most fundamental problem. Almost 1 billion Asians, or roughly one third of the region's total population, live in absolute poverty.[9] This is a bigger share of the population than in Latin America (24 percent) and a smaller share than in Africa (39 percent). Although Asia's rapid economic growth has led to a significant drop in poverty, it remains a pressing concern. In terms of a straight headcount, South Asia has more people living in poverty than Latin America and sub-Saharan Africa together.[10]

The poverty rate is highest in South Asia where it is 43 percent. By comparison, in East Asia the poverty rate is 26 percent. Differences within subregions are also large. Within East Asia, Hong Kong and Singapore have virtually no poverty, while in the PRC the poverty rate is 29 percent. In Southeast Asia poverty rates vary enormously: from 6 percent in Malaysia to 27 percent in the Philippines. Within South Asia, most of the poor are in India, where the poverty rate is 52 percent. Because most Asians live in rural areas and rural poverty rates are typically much higher than urban rates, Asia's poverty is still primarily a rural phenomenon. The rural poor are usually landless farm or nonfarm laborers or farmers with very small plots of land. However, as urbanization increases, so do the number of urban poor. The urban poor are usually landless migrants or self-employed people in marginal occupations who are working in the informal sector.

Both international evidence and Asia's experience show that overall economic growth is a powerful remedy for poverty. An analysis of 61 countries' experience suggests that income growth for the population as a whole is tightly linked to income growth for the poor. Asia is no exception to this general conclusion. For most Asian countries for which statistics are available, income growth is evenly distributed across income groups, including the poor. However, some departures from this basic pattern are apparent, notably, the income of the poor grew

---

9. People who are malnourished, who have inadequate shelter, and who are deprived of the other basic necessities of life are "absolutely poor." A variety of ways to identify and count the number of people who are absolutely poor are available. This study measures the number of absolutely poor people in a country or region as the share of the total population whose consumption falls below a threshold level of real resources. This level is set at PPP $1 a day. While this measure, like others, is imperfect, it allows comparison of poverty incidence across countries and regions (see Chapter 5 for more details).

10. These poverty estimates are from World Bank (1997). They refer to PPP adjusted $1 a day poverty. Note that poverty estimates that draw on PPP income data may differ from national estimates for a variety of reasons (Chapter 5).

much faster than average income in Sri Lanka. In contrast, the average incomes of the poorest fifth of the population in Thailand have risen by less than the average incomes for the population as a whole (Chapter 5).

More than any other part of the population, the poor depend predominantly on raw labor power for their subsistence. Economic growth that increases the demand for labor, particularly unskilled labor, will therefore reduce poverty. But poverty can also be reduced by increasing the productivity of the poor, either by targeted expansion of education, especially at the primary level, or by expansion of their access to physical and financial capital. Growth strategies that focus on expanding labor-intensive manufacturing exports, on promoting rural development (especially improved agricultural productivity), and on increasing human capital among the poor will yield the largest poverty reduction benefits. In contrast, policies that discriminate against agriculture, including high taxation of agricultural inputs, tend to increase poverty.

While growth is the most effective long-term strategy for reducing poverty, eliminating poverty through growth takes time; however, people who are starving or malnourished do not have time. To deal with such situations, many Asian governments have set up a variety of direct support programs to protect the poor aimed mainly at rural areas, which account for the bulk of the poor. One can divide these types of programs into three broad categories: subsidized food or credit, microfinance programs, and transfer programs that are often linked to relief employment. The results have been mixed.

Subsidy programs have typically not worked well. Subsidized food deliveries are not easy to target, and the deliveries have often gone largely to the nonpoor in urban areas. Given the sensitivity of poverty incidence to food prices, the impact of this policy on poverty reduction has been indirect, through the moderation of food prices as additional food is supplied. However, these programs have often been inefficient, expensive, and are not a good way to stabilize food prices. Subsidized credit programs have been even less effective because the loans typically fail to reach the poor, are often used for consumption, and are not repaid. As a result, such programs become financially unsustainable relatively quickly. A good example is India's Integrated Rural Development Program, where about 60 percent of the loans are in default (UNDP and ILO 1993).

A second and more successful approach is microfinance. Virtually all poor households lack access to credit except from moneylenders at high cost. Microfinance schemes are a useful way to address this problem. They provide credit to the poor, without collateral, at market interest rates. Group liability for default ensures high rates of loan recovery that often exceed 90 percent. Indonesia has several such schemes at the federal as well as the provincial levels, including Badan Kredit Kecamatan and Badan Credit Desa. Grameen Bank in Bangladesh and the Bank for Agriculture and Agricultural Cooperatives (BAAC) in Thailand are two other well-known examples. Unfortunately, the scale of these programs has remained small relative to the total number of rural poor.

A third approach to poverty reduction is direct transfers of cash or food to landless agricultural workers with few or no productive assets. These programs can be well targeted if assistance is given in return for work, because those not in severe distress self-select themselves out of these programs. Such programs have sometimes reduced the incidence of poverty during periods of poor harvests, when the incidence of rural poverty normally increases sharply (UNDP and ILO 1993).

Unfortunately, like many other well-intended interventions, anti-poverty programs are subject to corruption and maladministration in countries with poor governance. This problem has no simple solution and points to the urgent need to improve the quality of governance.

Economic growth remains the most effective path to sustained reduction in poverty rates. Provided that Asia continues on a path of rapid growth, the incidence of poverty could be reduced sharply. A tentative projection, based on the analysis of future Asian growth presented in Chapter 2, is that three out of five of Asia's absolute poor could be lifted from poverty by the year 2025. Such an improvement would be remarkable. Whether it is achieved depends not only on continued growth, but also on the commitment of Asian governments to invest in health and education, as well as to expand the access of the rural poor to credit.

Nutrition and Health

Adequate health and nutrition are essential ingredients of human welfare. Hungry and unhealthy people are more vulnerable to disease and less able to work effectively. In recent decades, standards of health and nutrition have improved enormously in Asia, as in the rest of the developing world. In East Asia, where incomes have risen the fastest, many health and nutrition indicators are now comparable to those in countries of the Organisation for Economic Co-operation and Development (OECD). In South Asia, where incomes have risen more slowly and poverty is still widespread, indicators are similar to those for sub-Saharan Africa, and are sometimes worse.

The typical South Asian's daily calorie intake is 2,300 kilocalories, which is marginally higher than in sub-Saharan Africa (2,100 kilocalories). Nonetheless, a higher proportion of children in Asia suffer from malnutrition: 17 percent of children in South Asia suffer from wasting—that is, their weight is acutely low for their height—whereas in sub-Saharan Africa only 7 percent of children do. In addition, nearly 60 percent of South Asian children have their growth stunted from malnutrition, compared with 39 percent of children in sub-Saharan Africa (Rosegrant, Agcaoili-Sombilla, and Perez 1995).

Despite dramatic improvements, the health of children in particular is still relatively poor in parts of Asia, particularly in rural areas. In South Asia, for instance, 124 out of every 1,000 children still die before reaching their fifth birthday. In contrast, the under-five mortality rate in industrial countries is only 8 out of every 1,000 children. One third of Asians die from communicable diseases, such as pneumonia, diarrhea, cholera, and malaria. This is roughly ten times the proportion of deaths such diseases cause in industrial countries. However, virtually all these diseases are either preventable or curable. Treatments are generally inexpensive and belong to standard medical practice. Vaccines can prevent some diseases (for example, tetanus and typhoid), but in the case of India, for instance, six out of ten children receive no vaccines.

As Asia's economic transformation continues, so its health profile will change. Chronic, noncommunicable diseases and conditions, such as obesity, hypertension, diabetes, and heart disease, will account for a rising share of deaths. In many parts of Asia, the diseases of poverty and affluence already coexist. In addition, as more women work and traditional extended family ties are weakened, institutions outside the family will increasingly have to care for the elderly. Industrial country experience suggests that per person health care spending on the old is about three times that for the young. Asia's changing health and age profile implies a large rise in health expenditures. Conflicting demands on limited resources for health care will be accentuated even further in the future.

Public health provision in Asia will also face a particularly acute challenge from HIV/AIDS. Although the HIV epidemic arrived in Asia later than in other parts of the world, it is now expanding rapidly. Asia has more new infections than Africa. Largely because of its huge population, by the year 2000 most of the world's new HIV infections will be in Asia. With no cure or vaccine in sight, behavioral change is Asia's only defense against the HIV/AIDS epidemic. Initiating information and education campaigns, encouraging condom use, and screening blood supplies are all important in this regard.

Education

Asia has achieved a remarkable expansion in access to primary education during the past three decades. In two thirds of the Asian countries for which statistics exist, more than 95 percent of children between the ages of 6 and 11 now reportedly go to school. These include Asia's three most populous countries: PRC, India, and Indonesia. As a result, adult literacy has increased dramatically: eight out of ten people in East Asia can now read (if one excludes the PRC, 96 percent of East Asia's population is literate). In Southeast Asia, 86 percent of the population is literate; in South Asia, 50 percent is literate. Excluding the PRC, adult literacy rates in East Asia are now higher than in Latin America, though in South Asia they are still lower.

Secondary school enrollment has also risen. Nearly half the children aged between 12 and 17 in Asia attend school. Again, the improvements vary by region. In South Asia, where incomes grew more slowly, relatively fewer children go to secondary school. The exception is Sri Lanka, where, as in Korea and Taipei,China, secondary school enrollment rates are near 100 percent. In general, East Asian countries have seen the biggest increase in secondary school enrollments.

Some Asian countries have lagged severely behind this education push. In Pakistan the primary school enrollment rate is a paltry 44 percent; in Afghanistan it is even lower, 31 percent. In Bangladesh about eight out of ten children go to primary school. Throughout Asia more boys go to school than girls. In South Asia, especially, school enrollment rates for girls are well behind those of boys. South Asia also has the region's lowest adult literacy rates: 26 percent in Nepal, 30 percent in Afghanistan, 36 percent in Pakistan, 37 percent in Bangladesh, and 40 percent in Bhutan. Overall, South Asia has an estimated 420 million illiterate adults, most of them in rural areas, where both schools and teachers are most scarce. The expansion of education for girls, for poor groups, and in remote rural areas is key to increasing literacy and building for the future.

For these countries the major challenge remains increasing access to basic education, but for the more advanced Asian countries the biggest future challenge will be expanding higher education. Continued productivity improvements and technological progress will demand increasingly sophisticated education and training. Finance is the most critical issue involved in expanding higher education. Public spending on higher education rose nearly 7 percent a year in East Asia between 1980 and 1992, which was faster than in any other part of the world. Astonishingly, the amount spent per student actually fell during this time, as total enrollment soared. Government spending on higher education per student was lower in Asia than in Latin America, the Middle East, or sub-Saharan Africa.

Expanding Asia's tertiary education and improving its quality will place enormous burdens on government budgets, and governments will have to determine the appropriate balance between public and private provision. While governments do, and will, have an important role in supporting research, setting standards in higher education, and ensuring access for the needy, in the future individuals will have to take on a greater part of the cost of higher education. This means steering Asia's higher education systems in the direction of private financing. Even though this could prove politically difficult once people begin to view free tertiary education as an entitlement, it will be the only way to ensure continued quality improvements.

The Asian Family

Historically, a large proportion of Asians married, they married early, and they stayed married. Large households were traditionally the norm, not only because women had many children, but also because many generations and family branches lived together in an extended family. In India in the 1950s, for instance, around 95 percent of women married at the age of 15. Formal divorce was virtually nonexistent, and nearly one third of Indian families lived in households with one or more other families.

Asia's social, economic, and demographic transformation has altered the circumstances of Asian families, and done so in different ways in different places. However, there are some common threads. International comparisons show a strong negative relationship between rising income and household size. Asia is no exception. Women are having fewer children, and the practice of elderly parents living with their children is declining. As a result, average household size is falling. In Korea, for instance, more than 60 percent of households had five or more people in 1960. By 1990 the share was below 30 percent. During this period the size of the average household in Korea fell from 5.5 to 3.7. Given that average life expectancy increased so much over the same period, the rapid fall in household size is especially striking.

Another sign of the extent to which Asia's family structure is changing is Singapore's passage of the Maintenance of Parents Act in 1995. The objective of this act was to compel children to support their aging parents (those older than 60 years, or younger if infirm) if the parents were unable to support themselves. Legislation requiring parents to support their children was already in place. In traditional Asian families, filial piety provided substantial assurance that children would support their aging parents when necessary. The fact that the authorities considered this new legislation to be necessary may be a sign that this long-assumed obligation is breaking down.

Formal divorce rates are rising in Asia. In the early 1990s, the crude divorce rate, that is, the number of divorces every year per 1,000 people, was 1.48, almost triple the rate in the 1950s. Within Asia there are substantial differences in this rate. Japan's crude divorce rate was 1.51 in 1993, while in Sri Lanka it was 0.13 in 1985. Even though this is still substantially lower than the North American average (4.4 divorces per year for every 1,000 people), it is sobering to remember that the U.S. divorce rate doubled between the mid-1960s and the mid-1970s, a period of only ten years.

Family links are changing in other, less quantifiable, ways. Growing educational gaps between parents and children, for instance, can put pressure on family cohesion. As children migrate into cities, kinship ties with traditional villages are weakened. Long commutes into Asia's congested megacities separate parents and children for more hours during the day.

However, the existence of a threat to the "ideal" Asian family from development is not obvious. The 'ideal' itself is not widespread, and some changes are likely to be for the good. For example, whether unsanctioned abandonment of wives by their husbands is preferable to sanctioned divorce is questionable. Equally, educated children may be better able to support their elderly parents than when children assumed more direct responsibilities, but were less wealthy. Given the diversity in form of family structure and the difficulty in judging whether changes are positive or negative, offering a definitive assessment about the status of the Asian family is difficult.

Status of Women

Have women benefited from Asia's transformation? By most general measures, the answer is yes. To begin with, women now live much longer than they used to. Between 1970 and 1993, female life expectancy increased from 48 to 61 years in South Asia and from 60 to 71 years in East Asia. Women overall tend to live longer than men. In all parts of Asia other than the transitional economies, the percentage by which female life expectancy exceeds that of males is increasing. In the 1970s, women's life expectancy was only 1.4 percent higher than men's, but by 1993 women could expect to live 3.6 percent longer than men. Nonetheless, compared with the rest of the world this difference is small.

Progress in women's education has also been substantial, although much remains to be done, especially in South Asia. About 35 percent of adult women in South Asia are literate, up from only 17 percent in 1970. Eight out of ten girls in South Asia went to primary school in 1992, up from only five out of ten in 1965. In East Asia, female enrollment in primary education is over 100 percent, and East Asia has made great strides in increasing the equity of access to education. In parts of South Asia, the gap still remains large, however.

Declining fertility is both a cause and a consequence of improvements in women's quality of life. As noted earlier, fertility has fallen dramatically throughout most of Asia, and especially in East Asia. Declining fertility has also allowed women to participate more in the formal labor force. Women made up 42 percent of the labor force in East Asia in 1993 and 37 percent in Southeast Asia. Both rates are in the same range as in OECD countries. In contrast, formal labor force participation rates for women in South Asia are only 22 percent. Such simple comparisons, however, are fraught with difficulty. Cultural and religious factors, as well as income levels, also affect women's participation in the formal labor force. Also, if participation in the formal labor force doubles a woman's work day, formal labor force participation may not be a good guide to women's quality of life.

Thus while their quality of life has improved overall, women in Asia still face big challenges. One important issue is the practice of female infanticide and the neglect of girls, which means Asia has fewer women than would be expected statistically. This female deficit is known as the issue of missing women. In South Asia and the PRC, some 80 million to 100 million women are missing. Female infanticide is a concern in both places. Girls also suffer higher mortality rates in the first few years of life, and in some countries adult women also have higher than expected mortality rates. Possible reasons for this include inadequate access to health care and food, and cultural practices that place women under the control of their husbands' families. Women suffer more in this regard when they are from poor and lower middle-income groups.

The Environment and Natural Resources

Asia's environmental performance has not matched its remarkable economic progress during the past 30 years. Indeed, environmental quality has deteriorated rapidly, to the extent that Asia is now one of the world's most polluted regions. Of the world's 15 most polluted cities, 13 are in Asia, and Asian rivers contain three to four times the level of fecal pollutants than the world average. In addition, its natural resources are declining fast. During the last three decades, Asia has lost 50 percent of its forest cover and 50 percent of its fish stock.

Despite rapid and steady growth in income and wealth, at least one in three Asians still has no access to safe drinking water, and at least one in two has no access to sanitation services. Only in Africa is the situation worse. For those with access to public water supplies, service is intermittent and poor, with average system leakages exceeding 40 percent. Across Asia, at least one third of a billion tons of solid waste remains uncollected each year, attracting and promoting the breeding of insects, rodents, and pathogens that can cause and transmit diseases. At the same time millions of tons of hazardous waste are placed untreated in dumpsites, threatening groundwater and local food supplies.

Of course, environmental conditions are not the same everywhere. Pollution and resource depletion levels vary greatly, depending on a country's location, how many people it has, how many resources it started with, and how developed it is. The Pacific islands and the mature economies of Northeast Asia are the cleanest parts of Asia, but they are vulnerable to outside environmental influences. The Pacific islands, for instance, face the threat of rising sea levels brought about by global warming, while Korea and Taipei,China are vulnerable to acid rain from rising coal consumption in the PRC (Oogai and Tanaka 1994). Deforestation rates are highest in Southeast Asia. South Asia is already largely without forest cover and suffers from more serious land degradation problems. Growing levels of air and water pollution afflict both South and Southeast Asia.

Asia's cities present a particularly acute problem. The share of Asia's population living in urban areas will increase from 35 percent in 1995 to 55 percent in 2025. Of course, urbanization has its benefits: greater amenities, higher productivity, and a more sophisticated division of labor. Thus the close link between urbanization and development is not surprising. But Asia's style of urbanization—megacities as opposed to mid-sized cities—results in higher economic and environmental costs. Unlike in other developing countries, Asia's urban population is highly concentrated, with most people living in a country's largest city. Several factors lie behind this trend, including overcentralized national politics and underinvestment in intercity transport and communications. Some projections suggest that by the year 2000, 12 of the world's largest 25 cities will be in Asia.

Did economic growth cause these high rates of environmental degradation in Asia? International evidence suggests that the level of many pollutants does indeed become worse during the early stages of economic development; then when a country reaches higher income levels, it begins to decline again. Much of Asia has not yet reached this turning point; thus economic growth has to date been associated with worsening environmental conditions.

However, poverty is itself closely associated with environmental degradation. When poor people eke their living from open access natural resources, the imperative of survival sometimes leads to unsustainable behavior. To the extent that the share of open resources a family captures depends on its labor power, poor parents have a strong incentive to have more children. But higher population density puts greater stress on the resource base and, for the community as a whole, more children ultimately exacerbate rather than relieve poverty. These Malthusian dynamics mask the fact that poverty and population pressure are proximate rather than primary causes of environmental degradation. The underlying problems are ill-defined property rights and the institutional failures that cause poverty.

The observation that environmental quality eventually improves as incomes increase has led some to argue that environmental degradation is simply a passing stage of development, with little cause for worry. Proponents of this view sometimes cite the case of Japan as an illustration. During Japan's rapid growth in the 1950s and 1960s, air pollution went virtually unabated and the poor air quality in Tokyo and other major Japanese cities gained notoriety throughout the world. However, as Japanese income levels rose further, the demand for a cleaner environment also gained voice, to the point where air pollutants were significantly reduced and air quality was markedly improved.

Nevertheless, this perspective is much too fatalistic. Severe environmental degradation is not inevitable at low income levels, nor are improvements automatic at higher income levels. With better policies, countries can keep environmental degradation much lower at earlier stages of development, thereby mitigating its enormous social costs without jeopardizing growth.

Evidence documented in Chapter 4 shows that Asia has failed to find the mix of market forces, pricing policies, and governmental institutions that would most effectively combine economic and environmental concerns. For example, Asian governments have heavily subsidized extractive industries such as mining and logging, as well as polluting inputs, such as energy and agrochemicals. Thus they have harmed both the environment and their long-term growth prospects. Property rights for natural resources, such as forests, water, and fish stocks, are poorly defined or insecure; the environmental side-effects of economic activity, such as pollution, are often not priced or managed; and weak institutions have failed to enforce those environmental standards that are in place.

Asia's Future

Asia's transformation to date, although remarkable, is far from complete. The future will be different from the past. Emerging Asia is an important part of an increasingly integrated and rapidly changing world. Globalization brings opportunities, but also discipline. Asia must be capable of full integration in goods, services, and financial markets. It must meet international standards, from disposal of hazardous wastes to bank regulation. It must also prepare for the information revolution. Rapid technological change, especially in information technology, will benefit those with appropriate skills and infrastructure. In many of these areas, Asia is still lacking.

Asian governments will also face the changing demands of an increasingly affluent, aging, and politically active population. Pressures on government spending for health, education, and infrastructure will increase, as will demands for transparency and accountability. Governments themselves will have to change. The institutions that underlay East Asia's economic success need to be modernized and strengthened. In South Asia, the pressure for better government is even more pronounced. This section examines some of these important challenges.

Preparing for Globalization

The urgency of integrating national economies into the international economy will heighten in the coming years. No country can afford to ignore an increasingly globalized world. Ever bigger world markets will provide increasing gains from trade. Rapid technological change demands the ability to assimilate technological advances from abroad. Most technological innovations will have to be imported rather than produced domestically. Countries that are well integrated into international production networks and widely exposed to market trends abroad will be much better placed to benefit than those that remain isolated.

Firms themselves are becoming more international. As communication and transport costs fall, companies are increasingly relying on international joint ventures, strategic relationships, and information-sharing partnerships. This need for flexible partnering puts an increasing premium not only on open trade, but also on openness to foreign direct investment, and to open capital markets more generally. Free capital mobility allows firms to tap into funds from abroad and to create new and flexible capital structures with partners in other parts of the world. Thus, high-technology Korean firms, for example, are currently engaged in large-scale outward investment, not only to diversify production sites and to reduce production costs, but also to form partnerships with high-technology firms in other parts of the world.

In response to these trends, international standards for trade, taxation, and financial markets are being harmonized through a variety of institutions, including the World Trade Organization, the International

Monetary Fund, and the Bank for International Settlements. As the discipline and commitments made under these institutions are effectively enforced, the autonomy of national governments will be circumscribed for a whole range of policies, including monetary and fiscal management, trade, intellectual property rights, foreign investments, and banking regulations. Many kinds of national policies pursued in the past, such as trade protection for industry combined with subsidies for exporters and dual exchange rates, are now simply incompatible with international agreements. Asian economies have large stakes in ensuring that these institutions are strengthened and operate effectively to provide a level playing field for international trade and capital movements.

There is also a need to ensure that the evolution of international trading, monetary, and capital flow regimes under the changed rules of the game will be pragmatic and orderly. Adequate allowance should be made for differences in countries' circumstances. Graduated responses and some sharing of the costs of adjustment may be needed among countries to ensure that a backlash against globalization is avoided. At the same time, developing economies must make credible commitments to necessary reforms. Backsliding will ultimately be to their detriment.

In short, the process of globalization involves deepening four kinds of international economic linkages by means of international agreements: merchandise trade, financial flows, production networks, and shared institutions. To integrate effectively, economies must fulfill a number of specific conditions.

Strong and Transparent Legal Systems

International firms demand clear property rights and well-defined contractual relationships. Even if domestic firms can rely on personal relationships and their reputation, large international firms demand greater transparency. Cross-country evidence about legal systems, based on opinion surveys of entrepreneurs operating in various countries, shows a large gap between Asia and the industrial economies. (Chapter 2 discusses the impact of the rule of law on growth.) In only three Asian economies have legal systems reached the standards of industrial countries: Hong Kong, Japan, and Singapore. The rest of Asia lags behind. While South Asia has a comparatively well-developed legal system, it is poorly enforced and is not particularly conducive to growth. For example, rights over private property in India have been effectively eroded through a variety of measures, including rights given to squatters, ceilings on rentals, and laws that prevent firms from closing down, even when they are incurring losses.

Some argue that Asia is simply different from the West. While Western nations rely on law, the argument goes, Asian societies rely on informal relationships, and so do not need formal law to the same extent. This view is probably too simplistic. While law does not seem to play as big a role in much of Asia as it does in Western societies, part of the difference may be due to the current level of development rather than to different legal traditions. A broad comparative view suggests that when transactions between firms are simple and the division of labor in society is rudimentary, formal law is less important. Hence societies such as the PRC, which are still predominately rural and agrarian, have been able to develop rapidly without relying on formal law. However, as business transactions become more complex and, in particular, as they become more internationally integrated, a transparent, impartially administered, legal framework might be crucial.

Flexible Labor Markets

The ability to compete in the globalized economy depends on a flexible labor market. Companies must be able to alter their product mix quickly in response to changing consumer demands and workers must have the skills and flexibility to move between sectors. Labor market arrangements can promote, but can also undermine, this flexibility.

There is no single way to guarantee labor market flexibility. In different countries, flexibility has meant different things. Japan has had remarkable success in managing its labor relations: the number of days lost to industrial disputes fell from more than 8 million in 1975 to 85,000 in 1994. Many workers in Japan have traded job security for a moderation of wage demands and other fringe benefits. Hong Kong has followed a different model in which workers have had less job security, but have had much greater freedom to extract wage increases as productivity has risen. In contrast, India is an example of an inflexible labor market: job security and excessive wages for a comparatively small number of workers have conspired to exclude many people from jobs and formal sector employment.

The future of Asia's labor market institutions will not be like the past. State direction of, and interference in, labor relations will become less tenable as societies become politically more open and the state withdraws from production and trading activities. The state must focus more on framing labor laws that are sufficiently flexible to allow firms and workers to reach agreements that are mutually rewarding and do not contravene international law. Some concerns about existing labor market conditions should diminish. In particular, as incomes rise the value of child labor will naturally fall and health and safety standards improve.

In the future, however, occasions when jobs rather than wages will have to adjust to new conditions are bound to arise. Because unemployment erodes human capital and work habits, and may also threaten social cohesion, governments should support institutions that make labor markets work better. In particular, education and training programs will continue to be crucial in helping to match the supply of skills with demand. The reach of such programs must extend to experienced workers whose skills are threatened with obsolescence. This is one area where greater public-private partnership will be needed. In consultation with the private sector, Malaysia has already begun to develop schemes for the continuing vocational education of its workers. Other Asian countries should seriously consider such initiatives.

In South Asia and in the formerly centrally planned economies of Asia, the state sector still employs millions of workers, many of whom are engaged in inefficient activities. An orderly transfer of these workers to the private sector holds out the promise of substantial gains in national economic efficiency. Although some will migrate to the private sector naturally, many others face impediments; for instance, workers in state enterprises often have skills for which there is little demand. They may also be handicapped by a variety of other factors, including their location. In these circumstances, long spells of unemployment and job search are likely. While subsidized training and education programs are needed, governments must also consider how they might ameliorate the costs of adjustment through well-targeted and self-limiting safety nets.

Strong Financial Sectors

Globalization presents different challenges for financial sectors in different parts of Asia. To be able to compete effectively in global markets, many countries will have to invest a substantially larger proportion of their national income. Where government saving is low, as it is in much of South Asia, one of the best ways to raise national saving is for governments to increase their own saving (Chapter 2). Private sector resource mobilization can be encouraged by measures that inspire broad confidence in the banking system and related institutions. South Asia and the transitional economies still need to build the basic infrastructure for banking and nonbanking financial institutions.

International capital mobility requires strong, market-based financial institutions. Banks must be well-supervised and well-capitalized; equity and debt markets transparent and well-regulated. Efficient and well-managed financial systems must provide an adequate range of financial instruments, and ensure competition between providers. Many Asian countries are far from fulfilling these requirements. The ongoing process of financial sector liberalization and deregulation must be continued. In South Asia, there is still heavy state involvement in banking. In Korea and to a lesser extent in Taipei,China (both of which followed the Japanese "model" of tightly-controlled financial sectors), liberalization efforts remain unfinished. Elsewhere, the emphasis should be on improving the supervision of domestic banks, as well as strengthening their capital base. Prudential standards need to be effectively enforced and accounting practices, especially, must become more transparent.

There has been an explosion in security market capitalization in Asia in recent years. This has occurred, in part, because little more than a decade ago many Asian countries had only the most rudimentary stock market. As Asia develops, securities markets will continue to deepen. Trade in equities in Asian markets has grown especially quickly. Nevertheless, restrictions remain that inhibit competition and portfolio diversification. Debt markets have been slower to get off the ground. In some countries the regulation of interest rates and the absence of the necessary benchmark yields and maturities have further handicapped debt market development. Looking ahead, the process of financial market deregulation must continue as countries prepare themselves for the onset of even greater capital mobility and heightened competition from overseas financial institutions.

A strong financial system ultimately rests on sound monetary management. In the past, Asia's monetary authorities have been comparatively successful at managing foreign capital flows. To date, Asia's closer integration in world capital markets does not seem to have led to greater volatility in exchange or interest rates, but stock market valuations, especially in Malaysia and Thailand, did become more volatile in the wake of the Mexican crisis. Capital inflows in some countries have also created problems for monetary management. Thus in the future, monetary authorities will have to become even more adept. Prudent macro-economic policies will provide the best protection against volatile capital flows. Regional monetary cooperation through currency repurchase arrangements and other mechanisms may enhance the credibility of domestic policy and help to fend off speculative attacks on currencies.

Modernizing Government

Not all the challenges facing Asian governments come from outside. Increasingly complex economies demand more sophisticated forms of government. Asia's people are themselves demanding more and different things from their governments. Rising political participation and democratization are bringing new opportunities, but also new demands. In the future, governments will have to forge partnerships with the private sector in which mutual responsibilities are clearly set out and an appropriate balance is struck between private incentives and public interests.

In Southeast Asia and some of the transitional economies, societies are rapidly becoming more democratic and more pluralist. To date, this transition has often reinforced economic dynamism. Korea, Taipei,China, and Thailand have all, with varying degrees of smoothness, made the transition to democracy without losing their growth momentum. In the Philippines, growth has revived after years of stagnation, and social stability has risen. This bodes well for the future. Democracy creates institutions that endure under successive governments, thereby helping to dispel some of the uncertainty associated with authoritarian regimes. Nonetheless, the transition to a democratic government is accompanied by uncertainty and risk. For those Asian countries facing such transitions, their effective management will be an important concern.

While evidence from Asia indicates that policymakers can create consensus in favor of difficult policy changes within the parameters of electoral politics, South Asia provides a sober reminder that prudent government policies can be difficult to implement in a highly pluralistic society. The region's countries have recently begun to open up to the global economy, but too often they remain unable to curb the fiscal profligacy that limited growth in the past.

One of the biggest challenges facing Asia's governments in the future will be the ability to withstand pressures to increase spending. Another will be the need for successful decentralization. Asia's increasingly complex economies cannot be managed from the center alone, and their increasingly pluralist societies will not be content with top-down management.

Pressures on Government Budgets

Part of East Asia's success lies in low levels of government spending and modest rates of taxation. East Asia has maintained government spending at lower levels of GDP than South Asia, Latin America, Europe, and the industrial countries in the OECD (Table 1.2). In addition, East Asian governments have saved more and directed a larger fraction of overall spending toward investment. One reason is that many East Asian countries have low interest payments on public debt, the payoff from fiscal discipline in the past. More important, East Asia's economies have avoided large social expenditures. While they have, in general, directed their fiscal policy more toward growth than redistribution, growth has been shared remarkably evenly.

Globalization will increase the premium on fiscal prudence and moderate taxation, yet the pressures for government spending in Asia will rise. Rising public demands for spending on health, education, the

Table 1.2 Government Expenditure as a Percentage of GDP, 1975 and 1990

(unweighted averages)

Category of expenditure	Year	OECD	East and Southeast Asia	South Asia	Sub-Saharan Africa	Latin America
Education and health expenditure	1975	6.5	3.6	1.9	6.0	4.7
	1990	6.6	4.0	2.8	6.0	5.7
Defense expenditure	1975	2.8	3.0	2.8	1.1	1.9
	1990	2.0	2.2	2.4	2.9	2.5
Social security and welfare	1975	10.8	0.7	1.8	1.6	4.0
	1990	12.7	1.0	2.2	0.8	3.6
Public and economic services	1975	6.3	5.7	3.9	12.8	6.0
	1990	1.5	3.8	1.7	7.0	2.0
Interest payments	1975	1.4	1.2	1.8	0.8	1.3
	1990	4.7	3.5	5.2	2.5	3.9
Other expenditure	1975	3.8	3.1	3.0	3.4	3.1
	1990	6.2	3.9	1.7	6.1	5.0

Note: The results refer to a sample of economies in each region.
Source: World Bank (1995).

environment, and infrastructure are likely to accompany rising income levels. An aging economy will also promote higher demands for tertiary health and old-age economic security. As Asian countries become more democratic, demands for higher spending may become more vociferous and powerful. For instance, shortly after becoming democratic, Korea moved to introduce a European-style pension system based on payroll taxation. Democratization, of course, does not necessarily imply fiscal profligacy, simply the potential for greater budgetary pressure.

To avoid excessive burdens on the budget, Asian governments must be innovative in their provision of social welfare and learn from others' mistakes. Pension schemes provide a good illustration. Europe, Japan, and the United States dramatically expanded pay-as-you-go retirement schemes in the postwar era. These programs became a vehicle for large-scale fiscal transfers to the elderly. They have now built up enormous implicit liabilities that will be met only by steeply rising rates of taxation. As a result, they are in financial crisis. Asian countries can, and should, avoid this mistake.

The choices that Asian countries make about pension schemes in the coming years will have enduring fiscal repercussions. The defined contribution, self-funding, provident schemes that operate in many parts of Asia and the Pacific have much to commend them and deserve close attention. Malaysia and Singapore have set the pace with these arrangements, but provident funds also operate on a much smaller scale in India, Indonesia, Nepal, Sri Lanka, and much of the Pacific. The experience of both Malaysia and Singapore suggests that pension systems based on mandatory saving in individual accounts can help to raise national saving. As the population ages, provident fund balances can be drawn down without provoking fiscal crises. Other countries, such as Korea and the Philippines, that have adopted the pay-as-you-go approach to funding pension benefits will eventually face the choice of reneging on defined benefits or raising taxes as their populations age.

Equally innovative approaches will be needed to finance education. The case for public funding of primary and secondary education remains strong, as the benefits to society from primary and secondary education exceed those captured by the educated individual. At the level of tertiary education, however, this is less obviously the case. Nevertheless, public spending on higher education has increased enormously in Asia. The demand for university places is expected to more than triple during the next three decades. In the future, as governments' resources are squeezed, individuals, rather than the state, will have to bear much of the cost of higher education. Markets must be developed so that students can borrow against their future earnings to finance their education. A move toward private funding should help the education system respond better to the needs of industry and society more generally. In Hong Kong and Korea, student loans are already an important way in which students finance their tuition fees.

In many countries, however, steering higher education in the direction of private financing will require difficult reforms. Current and prospective students may regard free university education as an entitlement. In PRC, India, and Indonesia public funding of higher education still dominates. Moreover, private financing mechanisms must also be improved. The absence of secure loan collateral, for instance, hinders the development of student loan systems. Policymakers must also take care to ensure university access to needy, but capable, students. In short, a greater role for private financing is needed in tertiary education, but government involvement will still be necessary.

The provision of health care will pose similar financial challenges in the future. Aging populations, the increased prevalence of noncommunicable diseases, and expensive technological innovations in medicine will all put upward pressure on health care costs. Financing and controlling the rise of these costs demand a clear delineation of the limits of government responsibility. It also means creating efficient schemes of health insurance.

Like primary education, primary health care generates substantial social benefits. For this reason, close government involvement seems warranted, especially in lower-income countries and in the provision of targeted services for the poor. In other areas of health care, the optimal division between government and private financing is less clear.

Japan, Korea, and Taipei,China have compulsory social health insurance systems, funded from payroll taxes, that finance the private delivery of health care services. While these are more efficient than direct public provision, they are funded on a pay-as-you-go basis, and so will become fiscally onerous as populations age. With little incentive for consumers to monitor costs, social insurance schemes do little to control rises in health care spending. Despite these drawbacks, many Asian countries are actively considering social health insurance schemes.

Singapore follows a different, more innovative, approach. Under its Medisave program, individuals are compelled to save for their and their families' health care in personal accounts. Not only does this scheme reduce the fiscal burden of health care, it also provides an incentive for cost containment. In addition, a private medical insurance scheme (Medishield) provides coverage for catastrophic illness. Government involvement is limited to providing a suitable regulatory environment and ensuring medical coverage for the neediest. While such a system of medical finance may not be appropriate for countries with low administrative capacity and large informal sectors, it is an approach that many Asian economies would do well to examine.

Asia desperately needs expanded infrastructure in energy, roads, ports, telecommunications, and environmental control. Asia's accumulated infrastructure demands during the next 30 years are likely to exceed $10 trillion (Chapter 2). As with pensions, health, and education, policymakers will have to tap private markets as far as possible. Private sector investment has already made a significant impact in some countries; for instance, private sector investment by independent power producers in the Philippines quickly eliminated a power shortage that had crippled domestic industry and deterred foreign investment. Malaysia has made greatest headway in privatizing infrastructure and has already gained substantial budgetary savings as a result.

Despite these successes, private sector investment in Asian infrastructure still remains comparatively small in terms of total investment and is confined to a limited range of sectors and countries. Governments' capacity to create the necessary institutional and organizational conditions, including changes in their laws, to support private sector investment in infrastructure varies widely. In some countries, the regulatory framework is completely inadequate; dispute settlement procedures do not exist; public administration is inefficient; the law is unclear; the needed capital market infrastructure is absent; and governments have been reluctant to make the sectoral and other reforms that investors need for cost recovery. Public acceptance of appropriate reforms is still in doubt. Policymakers will have to remove these impediments to private infrastructure investment if countries such as the PRC and India—where projected infrastructure needs are massive, but public resources are limited—are to attract sufficient private investment in infrastructure.

Decentralization

Asia's economies are, in general, heavily centralized. Not only is political and economic decision making typically concentrated at the central government level, but the bulk of economic activity is often based overwhelmingly in a single urban center. (The PRC and India are, of course, important exceptions to this pattern.) Both these aspects of centralization will come under increasing pressure in the future.

The concentration of economic activity around single megacities will become increasingly costly. Industries located there already pay hefty premiums for labor and space, and environmental constraints are becoming increasingly apparent. Asia's megacities simply cannot continue growing. Further expansion will demand huge investments in supporting infrastructure and will also place enormous strains on public sector management. Economic and administrative imperatives during the next 30 years will therefore counteract earlier centralizing tendencies.

Greater pluralism will also promote decentralization of political and economic power. As political participation increases and civil society develops, so people will demand a greater say in all aspects of government, especially at the local level. In many areas, for instance, environmental concerns, this trend is already evident. In principle, it should also lead to better policy decisions, with local economic management becoming more responsive to local needs.

However, decentralization does not succeed automatically. Indeed, the outcome of decentralization efforts in Asia to date has been mixed, at best. In the Philippines, for instance, the political process has been decentralized, but without adequate devolution of financial responsibilities, which, among other things, prevents local municipalities from raising the capital they need to respond to local infrastructure needs. In other countries, such as Lao PDR, attempts at decentralization have faltered because of inadequate administrative capacity and a lack of accountability at the local level. Thailand is now also actively pursuing decentralization, both by providing better social and physical infrastructure in backward areas and by offering different investment incentives in different regions.

Effective decentralization is both necessary and possible in Asia, but it demands a two-pronged approach. Policymakers must complement economic decentralization with a devolution of political and fiscal responsibilities, and must also strengthen capacity at the local, municipal, and regional levels.

Managing Technology

For much of modern history, technological innovations have ushered in changes in patterns of global growth and the international division of labor. Until the 19th century, for instance, high transport costs meant that international trade was centered on high value-added goods, such as spices and precious metals. With the advent of ocean steamers in the mid-19th century, transport costs fell dramatically and trade in bulk commodities, such as wheat, increased.

In the late 20th century, the sharply falling costs of both transport and communications brought in a new international division of labor. Complex production processes are broken down into component steps that take place in different countries, even different continents. For instance, semiconductor wafer production, a highly capital-intensive process, is undertaken in Japan and the United States, while semiconductor assembly and testing, a labor-intensive step, is done in East Asia, where wages are lower. It was this new international division of labor that made possible the boom in electronics exports in Asia.

Technological change is also raising the demand for skilled labor relative to unskilled labor. Work that was previously performed by unskilled people is increasingly being carried out by labor-saving machines operated by skilled technicians. Assembly operations are being automated through the growing use of robotics, and computerization has replaced many clerical operations. As a result, skilled workers earn increasingly more relative to unskilled workers.

Countries with large shares of unskilled labor ignore these changes at their peril. The need to upgrade skills and technology is paramount. Without such upgrading, countries will find that they can compete in world markets only through a continuous decline in the price of their export goods. The result will be a steady loss of real incomes. Without a continued effort to expand access to education, especially higher education, Asian countries could see a rising gap between the more and less educated.

While all skills need to be upgraded, the need to prepare for the technological revolution in information and communications is particularly important. The information revolution in computerization, data management, and data transmission will have profound effects on the organization of business, government, and households in the future. High-speed digitized data transmission is already making possible new forms of service sector exports. Similarly, secretarial services, answering services, wholesale and retail trade operations, advertising operations, and financial services are now being traded across national lines. All these new forms of activities raise the possibility that lower-wage countries will find new export opportunities in information-based services.

The information industry itself will provide direct opportunities for work and international trade, but an economy's information infrastructure will define how that economy interacts with the rest of the world. As information is increasingly digitized and transmitted electronically, societies that are equipped to receive and manage large amounts of digitized information will have a much greater capacity to grow than countries that are excluded from these vast flows of global information.

To benefit from this information revolution, technology policy must become a critical component of economic policy for every country in Asia. One goal for technology policy is to create the technical and information infrastructure necessary to share in the global technical progress. Some Asian countries should aspire to become sources of innovation and technical advances, rather than merely imitators.

As with industrial policy generally, the design of appropriate technology policy depends on a country's stage of development. The richest Asian economies, such as Hong Kong and Singapore, which already provide advanced, high-technology services in finance, trade, and transport, need the most sophisticated information infrastructure. Economies such as Korea and Taipei,China require investments not just in information infrastructure, but also in basic scientific and technological development. Only then will they be able to move from importing technology to producing advanced technologies themselves. For the next tier of countries in Southeast Asia—Indonesia, Malaysia, and Thailand—the main goals will be to invest in physical infrastructure and the education of scientists and engineers. This will allow them to absorb global technologies and to innovate on the margin of these imported technologies. For countries still lagging behind in basic education and telecommunications, the struggle is primarily to promote mass literacy, basic access to telecommunication flows, and basic scientific and engineering capacity. India, finally, presents the most complex picture. It still faces the urgent task of establishing mass literacy and basic access to telecommunications, while at the same time it already hosts a world-class scientific and engineering community.

Governments can encourage technological capacity through a wide range of policy instruments, including establishing government laboratories and scientific institutes, creating national science councils to give grants to universities and industry, and setting up science parks to encourage investment in high-technology ventures. Korea and Taipei,China have led the way among Asian developing economies, partly emulating Japan's experience. In Korea, the Korean Institute for Science and Technology, which was established in 1966, has played a clear and important role in upgrading the country's scientific and technical capacity. Similarly, Taipei,China created scientific institutes in various fields, such as the Industrial Technology Research Institute to develop information technologies. In addition, both Korea and Taipei,China have instituted special industrial zones for high-technology firms. The most successful of these has been Hsinchu, an industrial park in Taipei,China modeled on Silicon Valley, which draws upon Chinese scientists and engineers who have worked in Silicon Valley.

To build technological capacity, Asian governments will also need to upgrade their tertiary education in general, and their science and engineering courses in particular. Korea has already demonstrated that a country can nurture private universities to meet the needs of a rapidly growing cohort of students, and that private financing is compatible with a dramatic increase in university enrollments. Interestingly, the Korean government has directed relatively little research funding toward universities compared with funds allocated for government research institutes and industry.

International openness of an economy, both in trade and in finance, is also an important aspect of technology policy. To an increasing extent, high-technology firms must rely on joint ventures, strategic alliances, and other forms of international networking to remain at the cutting edge of rapidly changing technology. Previously, strategies of "doing it alone" were merely ineffective. Today, such strategies would be suicidal for Asian countries aspiring to keep up with global technological advances.

Finally, Asia should not neglect agricultural research. A substantial proportion of world cereal production is expected to come from Asia in the next 30 years, but without continued public and private support for agricultural research and development, future productivity growth will not match past accomplishments. It is worrying to note that Asian countries' interest in and expenditure on agricultural research has weakened in recent years.

Improving Environmental Management

While the extent of Asia's environmental problems is obvious, the environment is a particularly difficult area for government policy. Evaluating the trade-offs and opportunities involved in environmental management is not easy, and reaching consensus on which trade-offs to make is more difficult still. In other areas of the economy, markets can efficiently allocate resources between sectors and between the present and the future. But in the case of the environment, markets are not likely to function well unless governments create special legal and regulatory underpinnings for them. Markets fail because most environmental goods—such as clean air and water or the preservation of forests and fisheries—do not have market prices. A factory that fills the air with a dangerous chemical or that dumps polluted wastewater in the city's reservoirs of drinking water is not faced with an automatic market price.

A perception exists among Asian policymakers (shared by policymakers in other developing regions) that this type of market failure is unavoidable. Markets, so the argument goes, cannot be created for environmental goods. Inappropriate policies and regulations are then adopted. For example, it is often argued that private investors are unwilling to invest in certain types of infrastructure (such as a household water supply system). It is also argued that people are simply not willing to pay for environmental improvements, even for such basic services as access to safe drinking water. Consequently, water is often publicly supplied at subsidized prices. These subsidies, financed from general taxation, are often enjoyed by the better off. The attendant difficulties of cost recovery that subsidization creates leads to serious underinvestment in water supply and management. However, accumulating evidence from surveys and observed behavior suggests that most Asian households, including the poor, are willing to pay the costs of, for example, improved municipal water supply and indoor sanitation. With no access to reliable and safe public water supply, millions of Asians are already buying water from vendors at five to ten times the price of metered tap water. Underestimating willingness to pay for safe drinking water thus prevents governments from satisfying households' actual demands.

One goal of improved environmental management must therefore be to establish institutions that can register public demand for an improved environment and generate an appropriate supply response. Government monopolies over drinking water, sewerage, and clean air do not do this. A much greater role for the private sector and civil society is needed in areas where government bureaucracies have dominated.

At the same time, governments still have an important role to play in that they must clarify property rights and create the institutional underpinning for markets. Without a much stronger attempt to establish property rights and markets for key environmental goods, Asia faces serious problems ahead in cross-border disputes about scarce water supplies, energy, and other natural resources. Apparent shortages of such resources largely reflect the lack of market pricing. Rationing by administrative fiat and political strong-arming rather than by markets is an invitation not only to economic inefficiency and environmental degradation, but also to resource battles and international tensions.

In some areas, direct regulation will still be required, and Asian governments must improve their capacity to implement such regulation. Increased public investment will also be necessary. Most important, however, Asia's governments need to combat environmental problems by thinking about them entirely differently.

Estimating Asia's Income in 2025

Predicting the future is a hazardous endeavor. Unforeseen calamities can strike; the pace of change can surpass all expectations. Even as recently as 15 years ago, few foresaw the speed and strength of the information revolution. Fifty years ago, few in Asia foresaw the dynamism that lay ahead. One cannot use the past to predict the future. Nonetheless, a careful analysis of the catalysts of Asian growth so far allows us to make some tentative projections.

The growth framework summarized in this chapter and discussed in detail in Chapter 2 provides the foundation for such projections, and international comparisons that analyze the determinants of growth provide a reasonable basis for looking ahead. Historical experience provides some guidance about a country's potential for growth given its income level, structural features, and policy choices.

Figure 1.2 presents baseline projections of PPP-adjusted income. These forecasts assume that government policies remain similar to those in the mid-1990s. So, for instance, open economies do not return to protectionism and high-saving governments do not become profligate.

The analysis of Chapter 2 shows that, all else being equal, economies that start from a lower income base have greater potential for growth.

Figure 1.2 Baseline Income Projections

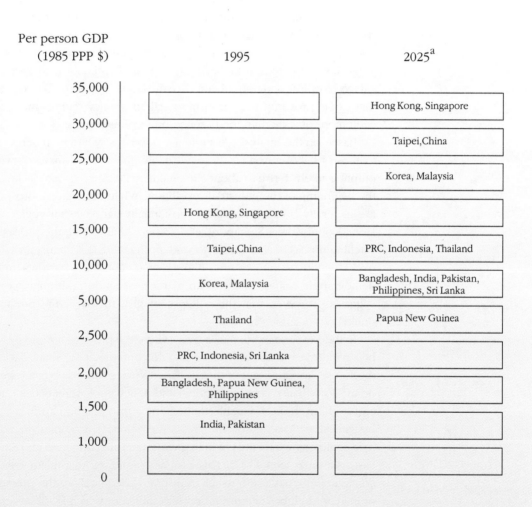

Per person GDP (1985 PPP $)

Per person GDP (1985 PPP $)	1995	2025[a]
35,000		Hong Kong, Singapore
30,000		Taipei,China
25,000		Korea, Malaysia
20,000	Hong Kong, Singapore	
15,000	Taipei,China	PRC, Indonesia, Thailand
10,000	Korea, Malaysia	Bangladesh, India, Pakistan, Philippines, Sri Lanka
5,000	Thailand	Papua New Guinea
2,500	PRC, Indonesia, Sri Lanka	
2,000	Bangladesh, Papua New Guinea, Philippines	
1,500	India, Pakistan	
1,000		
0		

PPP = purchasing power parity
a.   Projected per person GDP levels in 2025 assume that all economies maintain the same natural and policy conditions as in 1995. To impute GDP levels in 2025, per person GDP in the U.S. is assumed to grow at 1.47 percent per year between 1995 and 2025.
Note: The economies selected were based on the availability of complete data from 1965 to 1995. See Chapter 2 and the Appendix for details.

It also shows that circumstances beyond governments' control, such as structural and geographical factors, influence this potential, along with events that are already in progress, such as the demographic transition. For example, incomes per person grow more slowly in economies with adverse geographical circumstances and more quickly in those with a rising share of workers to total population. However, variables that are under governments' control are more important in determining outcomes. Thus those economies with the best policies and institutions are projected, subject to other conditions, to advance most quickly. Of course, countries that can improve upon their institutional and policy settings may grow even more quickly than the baseline projections suggest.

Based on this analysis, Asian living standards will draw much closer to those of the currently advanced economies. Asia's share of world output is likely to rise to about 57 percent by 2025, a return to its level at the beginning of the industrial revolution. While the region's prospects are generally bright, they differ substantially across its subregions. In Hong Kong, Korea, Singapore, and Taipei,China, where the process of catching up has been especially rapid during the last 30 years, growth is likely to slow as the gap with high-income economies narrows and as demographic changes lead to an aging population. The analysis also suggests, however, that the collapse of growth that some predict is unlikely to occur.

In the PRC and in Southeast Asia, where the process of rapid growth began later, economic expansion should continue at the same pace for the foreseeable future. South Asia is well placed to accelerate its economic growth as recent institutional and policy improvements bear fruit and it enjoys more favorable demographic trends. The gap in growth between East Asia and South Asia is therefore likely to narrow. South Asia could enjoy the kinds of high growth rates that only East and Southeast Asia have seen so far. This assumes, however, that major reforms continue, and that South Asia can respond adequately to the pressures of increased globalization. Central Asia, much of which is still in transition from central planning, can achieve increased economic growth, but the region will be hindered by difficult structural conditions, such as partially mountainous terrain, deserted steppe, and large distances from international markets, as well as by the landlocked circumstances of most of these countries.

Of course, such optimism should not be delivered or accepted uncritically. At other key moments of history, for example, the eve of

World War I, many supposedly careful observers could see nothing but a continuing era of peace and prosperity. Instead, the world descended into 30 years of war and economic collapse. As the 20th century draws to a close, Asia does, of course, face risks. Two classes of risk, in particular, stand out: external risks and internal risks.

Assessing External Risks

If the world's economic system closes up, as it did after World War I, Asia is unlikely to continue to enjoy rapid growth. How might such a collapse occur? One possibility involves a surge in protectionism in the industrial countries or a more general retreat into regional trading blocs. Some economists believe that heightened competition from producers in Asia and in other developing countries will exacerbate unemployment in the industrial countries and will increase the wage gap in favor of skilled workers. The balance of evidence suggests that to the extent that such effects exist, they are comparatively small (Chapter 2). In any case, trade is a two-way process. If the industrial countries import more from developing Asia, they must export more to pay for these imports. Inevitably, income growth in the developing economies will increase demand for the products of industrial countries. Indeed, over the next 30 years, exports from the industrial countries to Asia are projected to grow at a rate 50 percent faster than their exports to any other region (Chapter 2). Nevertheless, policymakers in the industrial countries may erroneously perceive strong growth in Asia as a threat rather than as an opportunity and intensify calls for the protection of "sunset industries." To the extent that such demands are met, Asia's terms of trade would suffer and its growth prospects would be damaged.

Despite repeated warnings about the risks of renewed protectionism, the actual trend in trade policy has continued to move in the direction of greater openness for goods, services, and capital. There seems to be a broad recognition that economic growth in Asia and the expansion of world markets will bring an enormous opportunity for the industrial countries, not a threat. Therefore, a retreat toward protectionism seems unlikely, unless a deep economic crisis caused by something other than trade leads to a spiraling of nationalism and isolationism. Thus a second risk to the global economy is a financial calamity that contributes first to the breakdown of international financial flows, and then to trade flows. This century has seen one such episode: the Great Depression. The period between world wars is both a warning and an illustration of how a seemingly robust global trading system can come crashing down in just a few years. In large part, the turmoil of the interwar period was itself the result of the cataclysmic dislocations of World War I.

Some see risks in the competition for global resources. As Asia's vast population becomes more prosperous, its diet will change. In particular, its demand for grain used as cattlefeed will also grow as its meat consumption expands. Warnings of a pending crisis in global grain markets are, however, exaggerated. The best available estimates suggest that world grain markets will be able to cope with Asia's growing demands, but will require a renewed commitment to agricultural research and finding solutions to a number of environmental threats to agricultural productivity (Chapter 4). Experience shows that, given sufficient time, markets do a good job in aligning demand with supply. Trade rather than self-sufficiency remains the best form of food security.

Asia is likely to become an energy deficit region in the next 30 years. There will be a many fold expansion in energy demand. Asia will become much more dependent on the Organization of Petroleum Exporting Countries for its oil supplies. Asia's emergence as a major oil customer could have implications both for volatility in oil markets and for longer term movements in energy prices. However, earlier experience, particularly that of Japan, has shown that the capacity for substitution in energy consumption is large.

Assessing Internal Risks

Short of a global crisis, the major kind of risk facing Asia's long-term growth lies within Asia itself, and involves the region's ability to adjust its politics, policies, and basic institutions. As Asia becomes richer and more deeply integrated in the world trading system, its policies and institutions must evolve. They must respond to the process of democratization and increased public participation, while at the same time they must resist populist pressures on budgetary spending that may accompany rising expectations and an aging population.

Latin America's economic experience during this century is a sober warning to emerging Asia. After World War II most observers judged that Latin America's growth prospects were better than Asia's. Widespread optimism prevailed. Yet gradually, in the following years, mass politics interacted with disastrous policy choices—especially protectionism and statism—to result in populist budgetary excesses, political instability, and ultimately a crushing debt crisis that lasted for longer than a generation.

Much of Asia has not yet experienced mass democratic politics. The early results of democratic transitions in Korea and Taipei,China are promising, in that both economies have made a peaceful transition to broad political participation while also preserving economic dynamism. However, the future likely holds greater challenges.

Navigating the transition to a market economy will also be difficult for those countries facing such a prospect. The PRC, for example, faces numerous profound and unique challenges. Merely running a country of 1.3 billion people is not easy. Growing inequalities of income within the PRC, including the widening gaps between urban and rural households and between coastal and inland provinces, will add further problems. The natural advantages of the seaboard, combined with the special trading advantages granted to the coastal regions, have led to massive internal migration, perhaps 100 million strong (known in the PRC as the floating population). This mass migration is straining local finances, infrastructure, and political relationships between regions. In addition, the state enterprise sector loses large amounts of money, saddled as it is with 25 million excess workers. Farmers in the PRC lack the ownership rights in land that are needed to promote long-term investments in their farms; and much of the nonstate sector lacks the clarity of property rights needed for long-run efficiency.

India has been able to manage a complex federated democracy and to implement deep economic reforms in the 1990s. However, as a democratic polity emerging from decades of statism, labyrinthine legal and bureaucratic structures have slowed India's reforms. In addition, the Indian government carries a heavy burden of indebtedness, the result of a long period of deficit financing. Vast regional differences in growth prospects, income levels, and cultural and ethnic traditions make governance in India especially difficult. Ethnic conflicts have spilled over into violence and confrontational politics that have often left economic reforms on the back burner. Thus, while India has made substantial progress on reform since 1991 and has accelerated its growth, the reforms remain partial, hamstrung by the financial and legal inheritance from the past, and subject to complex and shifting coalition politics. Despite these difficulties, recent bold measures signal the continuation of the reform process.

The impact of Asia's growth on its environment is a serious concern. The point may not be too far off when Asia's polluted environment will act as a brake on its growth. In particular, heavy dependence on dirty coal-based technologies threatens to exacerbate already unacceptable levels of pollution, particularly in the PRC, India, and neighboring economies. Not only does a poor environment exact a toll on workers' health and productivity, it may actively discourage foreign investors. Transboundary air pollution is also likely to meet with growing opposition from its victims in other countries, who may increasingly demand retaliatory action. Asia's water supply is also approaching a crisis point (Chapter 4). Certainly, if Asia continues to squander its water resources, this will act as a strong damper to its economic growth. Agricultural productivity will suffer, and both industrial and domestic water supply in Asia's megacities will be threatened as their water tables become more contaminated and sink further.

Asia Emerging

This chapter has argued that much about Asia's future can be gleaned from its recent past. The underpinnings of economic success are identifiable and are potentially durable and replicable. The combination of open economies and effective institutions will provide much of the momentum for catch-up growth in South Asia, as they have already done in East and Southeast Asia. The dynamics of economic growth will be similar. The rising share of the working-age population has the potential to lead to further economic growth in Southeast Asia in the near future, and more so in South Asia but somewhat later. Even for the successful East Asian economies, the path to greater prosperity remains the same, although much of the boost resulting from demographic change has already occurred. Open markets, effective institutions and continued emphasis on education and skill upgrading are the best ways to ensure East Asia's future growth.

But the future will, of course, be more than a replay of the past, and much remains to be done. Asia is part of a global economy that is barely recognizable from that of even a generation ago. In virtually all economic dimensions the world has become more integrated. International trade has grown far faster than global output; cross-border capital flows are rising inexorably; information flows across borders almost instantaneously. This integration provides greater opportunities for open economies, but it also brings the hard discipline of market forces. Global capital markets, for instance, do not eliminate the power of national governments entirely, but they punish mistakes severely. Populist policies that lead to fiscal or monetary instability will increasingly provoke a quick and hard-hitting response from the global investment community. International standards and policy harmonization will become increasingly important in many areas of economic life. Asian countries will no longer have the freedom for domestic protectionism, or other unilateral economic policies that were tried in the past. Asian governments must support competitive markets, and promote greater integration in global goods and capital markets. Otherwise, sustained growth may prove elusive.

Continued growth in Asia will be linked to growth in the OECD economies. Equally, the economic prospects of industrial countries will be strengthened by Asia's prosperity. Asia can best contribute to a mutually beneficial relationship with its global partners by playing an active role in the WTO and other institutions that set the rules of international commerce and trade. Asian countries will sometimes participate most effectively in these international arrangements by acting collectively. In particular, joint action by Asian countries may be needed to ensure that international rules governing trade are not interpreted or their reach extended to their disadvantage. However, exclusive regional clubs would likely worsen future growth prospects for all.

Open and outward oriented regional cooperation, in contrast, has much to offer. Cooperation between regional partners offers practical benefits on many issues, from technology development to coordination of monetary arrangements. Indeed, broad economic and political cooperation at the regional and subregional level is likely to be necessary to safeguard peace and stability. Asia has innovative forms of subregional cooperation, in the Mekong area and elsewhere. These could usefully be replicated. On a larger scale, organizations such as the ASEAN Free Trade Area (AFTA), the Asia-Pacific Economic Cooperation (APEC), and the South Asian Association for Regional Cooperation (SAARC) Preferential Trade Arrangement should evolve in ways that promote greater openness between their members as well as greater openness to the world.

Just as Asia will have to respond to external changes, it will also have to manage internal change. A more affluent and more politically aware population will demand more democratic governance. An older and richer population may also demand more public spending, on health care, say, or on pensions. As these demands rise, Asia's governments will have to be both innovative and prudent. From environmental protection to health care, merely copying the advanced industrialized economies would be a mistake. In pushing the pace of technological and structural change, increased globalization will also require policy adeptness at the domestic level. Asian countries will need to find their own, new solutions. In many areas, the failure to innovate would almost certainly result in fiscal profligacy, and thus threaten the foundations of economic success.

Asian countries face a double squeeze: greater demands on government and yet greater need for fiscal restraint in the face of discipline from both international and domestic market forces. In the future it will be even more critical for government to concentrate its energies on what it does best, and on what the private sector cannot do. Government, for example, has a central role in developing, together with the private sector, a long-term vision of the economy and cultivating broad acceptance of it among its citizens. Likewise, government must also determine when regulation is needed and what form it should take. More generally, governments have the responsibility for the rule of law and its fair application. Across Asia, governments must become less concerned with the appropriation and direct use of resources, and more concerned with supporting the legal and institutional arrangements that determine efficient resource allocation.

For some countries in Asia reforms need to be substantial. These may involve social costs that will make their implementation politically difficult. Statist policies and institutions have left a complicated political and social legacy, particularly in India and the PRC. Some groups may lose out from liberalization and may attempt to obstruct its progress. Successful reform demands well informed, pragmatic, and determined governments. Within budgetary means, reform may require social safety nets and other forms of interim support to protect those who are most vulnerable and those who are hit hardest by change. Social protection measures, which may help catalyze support for reforms, are best designed as an integral part of a reform package and should aim at ensuring that as many as possible can access the benefits of growth. Successful economic reform soon creates a social consensus behind it. But even in the interim, governments cannot afford to ignore those who lose out from change.

Many governments in Asia must forge a new kind of relationship with the private sector. Mutual trust and dialogue must replace suspicion and diktat. Greater openness and disclosure is also needed to ensure that the interests of regulated enterprises do not take precedence over those of the communities they are intended to serve. Relationships between the public and private sector should be based on clearly demarcated responsibilities and the rule of law. Private-sector involvement in areas that have traditionally been dominated by governments, such as infrastructure, will require transparency and accountability. Governments must draw up the rules of the game, and play by them. Regulation must assist, not obstruct, the process of efficient private sector resource allocation.

But for government to succeed in these areas, the reform of government itself is necessary in many parts of Asia. Even good policies can fail if they are not effectively implemented. Government institutions must be made more accountable and run by committed professional staff who are appropriately rewarded. Countries that persist with bad governance will have to endure slower growth.

In the next 30 years, the promise of growth is perhaps greatest in South Asia, which has two enormous advantages. First, it can draw on the previous experience of East Asia as well as on its own past disappointments. Second, South Asia will benefit from a favorable change in its demographic circumstances. But if South Asia backslides on reform, it may yet again squander its promise. The lessons of the past 30 years show that slow growth is likely to mean slow progress in poverty reduction and in improvement in other dimensions of the quality of life.

In East and Southeast Asia, the challenges are somewhat different. In the economic sphere, East and Southeast Asia must continue their process of engagement with the international economy. To meet this challenge, they will have to remove barriers to trade, upgrade their technological capacity, liberalize their financial regimes, and more generally support competitive markets and human resource development. East and Southeast Asia should take care to avoid the adoption of the institutional structures that have led to sclerosis in maturing industrial societies. In the years ahead, growth is likely to slow down in Hong Kong, Korea, Singapore, and Taipei,China, but not precipitously so, and populations will inevitably age. In Southeast Asia, growth rates are likely to continue at about the pace of the recent past. In the past, the benefits of growth in East and Southeast Asia have been spread widely. In the future, these countries must continue to strive to avoid the social distress that co-exists with prosperity in many industrial countries. The design of institutions and policies that will maintain social cohesiveness and mitigate the stresses of rising prosperity without threatening sound economic management will be a challenge of enormous proportions.

In the PRC, the greatest challenge is continuing the process of economic reform that began in 1978. The reforms to date have brought about vast improvements in the quality of life. Yet the process is far from complete, and the partial nature of the reforms imposes high costs throughout the economy. The relatively poor performance of the state enterprise sector slows the pace of reform in other sectors, and inflicts large financial and allocative costs that slow the pace of overall growth. Similarly, the underdeveloped legal system acts as a drag on the economy. Growing disparities in incomes across regions should be addressed by speeding the pace of reforms in the inland provinces, which have so far received less favorable policy treatment than coastal provinces. The future of Asia, and for that matter, the future of the world, will be influenced enormously by the PRC's success in meeting these challenges.

Finally, across all regions of Asia, environmental distress is already at a critical level. The point has been reached where further environmental neglect will inflict economic as well as social costs of increasing proportions. A well designed and resolute attack on the policy and institutional failures that have led to environmental degradation is now overdue. There is an urgent need to develop an institutional and regulatory setting in which the private sector and civil society can participate in environmental monitoring and enforcement, in the provision of environmental infrastructure, and in the conservation and management of natural resources. It is equally critical to strengthen the capacity of governments to set environmental priorities and to enforce them efficiently.

It will take determined and disciplined governments and mature societies to rise to the various challenges that Asia faces. But there is, in the final analysis, sound reason for optimism. Asia is thinking ahead to a remarkable extent, producing bold but realistic visions of what it can achieve in the coming quarter century. Asian countries have glimpsed the future of prosperity and open societies, and have unleashed a positive economic dynamism befitting the region's grand history. Indeed, the next 30 years have the extraordinary promise to bring durable improvements in the quality of life to many more Asians.

References

ADB (Asian Development Bank). 1996. *Key Indicators of Developing Asian and Pacific Countries,* electronic data. Manila.

_____. Forthcoming paper on the Pacific island countries (title to be announced). Manila.

Gang, Fan, Dwight Perkins, and Lora Sabin. 1996. "China's Economic Performance and Prospects." Background paper for *Emerging Asia: Changes and Challenges.* Asian Development Bank, Manila.

IMF (International Monetary Fund). 1996. *International Financial Statistics.* Washington, D.C.

Krugman, Paul. 1994. "The Myth of Asia's Miracle." *Foreign Affairs* 73(6):62-78.

Maddison, Angus. 1995. *Monitoring the World Economy 1820-1992.* Paris: Organisation for Economic Co-operation and Development.

Needham, Joseph. 1954. *Science and Civilization in China.* Cambridge, U.K.: Cambridge University Press.

Oogai, Okihiro, and Akira Tanaka. 1994. "Sources of Funds for Environmental Management." In *Financing Environmentally Sound Development.* Manila: Asian Development Bank.

Rosegrant, Mark W., Mercedita Agcaoili-Sombilla, and Nicostrato D. Perez. 1995. "Global Food Projections to 2020." *Food, Agriculture, and the Environment* Discussion Paper No. 5. Washington, D.C.: International Food Policy Research Institute.

Smith, Adam. 1976. *The Wealth of Nations.* Chicago: University of Chicago Press.

Summers, Robert and Alan Heston. 1994. *The Penn World Table,* Mark 5.6. (website version). Philadelphia: University of Pennsylvania.

UNDP and ILO (United Nations Development Programme and International Labour Organisation). 1993. *Employment and Poverty and Economic Policies.* New Delhi: Asian Regional Center for Employment Promotion.

World Bank. 1994. *The East Asian Miracle.* New York: Oxford University Press.

_____. 1995. *World Data 1995* (website version). Washington, D.C.

_____. 1997. *World Development Indicators.* Washington, D.C.

2

ECONOMIC GROWTH
AND TRANSFORMATION

Asia's record of economic growth during the past three decades is one of great accomplishments and contrasts. The region has been home to the world's most dynamic economies, but also to many less successful ones. The eight best performing economies—People's Republic of China (PRC), Hong Kong, Indonesia, Korea, Malaysia, Singapore, Taipei,China, and Thailand—grew at an average annual rate of more than 5.5 percent per person between 1965 and 1990. Sustained growth rates of this magnitude for a generation are virtually without parallel in either the industrial or developing world. Unfortunately, this record was not repeated throughout the region. In South Asia, for instance, income per person grew only 1.7 percent a year during the same period. Thus while Asia's sluggish economies did see reasonably rapid growth at times, they could not sustain it for long periods.

The result of such varied growth has been a huge divergence of income levels among the countries of Asia. In just one generation, Singapore has transformed itself from a struggling ministate to one of the richest, most dynamic economies in the world. Korea, a country that was widely viewed in the early 1960s as having less development potential than most of Africa, now has an income per person of $10,300 and has just joined the Organisation for Economic Co-operation and Development (OECD). At the other extreme Bangladesh, Myanmar, Nepal, and Viet Nam are among the world's poorest nations. Once exchange rate differentials are taken into account, the three highest income economies in Asia (Hong Kong, Japan, and Singapore) are, on average, 17 times richer than the three poorest (Bangladesh, India, and Nepal). This is the largest such gap of any region in the world, and is far higher than it was 30 years ago.[1]

While average growth performances provide an important insight into Asia's diversity, they mask a number of important nuances. Even among the successful economies, growth rates have not been uniform over time. Hong Kong, Korea, Taipei,China, and Singapore were the first economies to take off, but in some of them, particularly Hong Kong and Taipei,China, trend growth rates seem to be slowing down. Other economies, especially in Southeast Asia, started to grow rapidly later and still continue to see high rates of growth. For example, the PRC's extraordinary growth performance began in the late 1970s with the liberalization of its agriculture sector and the opening to world markets. Other economies have accelerated their growth rates even more recently. Viet Nam, newly emerged from the strictures of central planning, has surged ahead in the past few years. Growth there reached 9.5 percent in 1995, although its sustainability is far from certain. Other slow movers have also made promising progress in recent years: India's annual growth rate has averaged 5 percent per person between 1994 and 1996.

Asia has also seen a remarkable diversity of growth within countries. The remote western provinces of the PRC, for instance, have been left behind as the eastern coastal regions have boomed. In many parts of Asia, economic activity is heavily concentrated in urban centers: almost 40 percent of Thailand's gross domestic product (GDP) is generated in Bangkok, and Metro Manila contributes 30 percent of the output of the Philippines. Rural hinterlands remain mired in poverty, while the metropolises prosper.

The first purpose of this chapter is to examine the reasons underlying these divergent growth performances. Why did some Asian economies do so well, and others so badly? Why did some countries begin rapid growth sooner than others? These are not easy questions. At first sight, Asia's successful economies are themselves surprisingly diverse. They differ enormously in size, natural resource endowments, and culture. With 1.2 billion inhabitants, the PRC is the world's most populous country. Hong Kong and Singapore, in contrast, are tiny city states. Indonesia and Malaysia are both rich in natural resources, while

---

1. These data are based on gross domestic product per person converted on a purchasing power parity basis from World Bank (1995a). The ratio of the richest three countries to the poorest three for various regions are as follows: Asia 17.5; Africa 13.9; the Middle East 4.3; Latin America and the Caribbean 4; Eastern Europe 3.4; and Western Europe, North America, and Australasia 2.1.

Taipei,China and Korea have few natural resources. Nor can economic success be attributed to similar economic and political systems. The PRC still espouses socialist principles and much of its industry sector is state-owned, while Korea's government intervened extensively in the country's economy. In contrast, Hong Kong has arguably been the freest market economy in the world in recent decades. This chapter attempts to identify common threads among the successful economies to find out what set them apart from the laggards.

Equipped with an understanding of what lay behind the rapid and sustainable growth in those economies where it occurred, the analysis can then look forward. Two questions are key to the future of emerging Asia. First, are the ingredients of growth replicable in other parts of the region? Second, are they sustainable in the successful countries? The answers to these questions are important not just for Asia, but also for the rest of the world. Rapid growth in emerging Asian economies has already changed global patterns of trade and investment. Thirty years ago, Asian trade made up only 6 percent of world trade, yet now it accounts for almost 17 percent. Nearly 20 percent of global foreign direct investment now flows into Asia, up from only 6 percent two decades ago. Continued momentum in Asian economies will have enormous implications for world patterns of production, consumption, and trade. For this reason, understanding the potential for Asian growth, as well as the attendant risks, is important for non-Asians and Asians alike.

Economic Growth Across Countries

The sources of economic growth have been much debated in recent years within the economics profession. There are many ways of thinking about growth. This chapter concentrates on three broad models that attempt to account for differences in economic growth and living standards across countries.

The classical theory of economic growth follows Adam Smith in emphasizing that high levels of national income depend on the division of labor within an economy, as well as the division of labor between the national economy and the rest of the world. As Smith emphasized, market-based trade allows an economy to reap the benefits of labor specialization. The gains from specialization depend on an intricate web of market relationships, especially on low transaction costs in domestic and international trade. Thus Smith and many scholars after him highlighted the following factors as ingredients of rapid growth: open international trade, low transport costs (obtained, for instance, from access to favorable sea-lanes and good port facilities), and well-functioning markets in which property rights are well protected and contracts can be enforced at reasonable cost.

The neoclassical theory of economic growth is based on the important contribution of Robert Solow, and emphasizes that economic growth depends on capital accumulation. The neoclassical theory attributes rising income per person to a rising stock of capital per person. While the theory originally stressed the rising stock of physical capital (buildings and equipment), it has long since been extended to include the accumulation of human capital (schooling and on-the-job training). As economic growth proceeds, the ratio of capital to labor rises in the economy until a steady-state level is reached. Neoclassical theory predicts that the rise in the capital stock per worker is associated with a fall in the rate of return to capital. As an economy becomes richer, the returns to new investments diminish. The theory assumes that poor countries differ from rich countries mainly because they start out with lower stocks of capital per person. As a result of this capital scarcity, the rate of return to capital should be higher. Poorer countries should therefore grow more rapidly than richer countries because they have a higher return to investment, and because the proportional growth of the capital stock is faster.

Poorer countries also have another route to faster growth. They can borrow and adapt technology and production techniques from richer countries without paying the full costs of research and development. Similarly, poor countries can learn from the richer countries' successes and mistakes. They can copy good (and bad) ways to manage factories, organize institutions, and run economies. Alexander Gerschenkron referred to potential of this kind as "the advantages of backwardness" (Gerschenkron 1962).

Endogenous growth theory stresses new ideas and new products as the engine of long-term growth, rather than capital accumulation. Following Romer (1986), endogenous growth theory focuses on the economy's human resources (such as scientists and engineers) and on specific institutions (such as patent laws) that give rise to technological innovations, and thus to improved living standards. Endogenous growth theory builds on the notion that knowledge begets knowledge in a kind of chain reaction process. Just as in a chain reaction, an economy might have to acquire a critical mass of scientists and engineers before an economic take-off can occur. Unlike the neoclassical assumption about a decline in the rate of return to investments, endogenous growth models stress that investments in knowledge might have a constant, or even rising, rate of return. The theory assumes that new knowledge opens the way for further breakthroughs rather than exhausting the opportunities for new ideas. Thus according to this model, rich countries could grow just as fast or faster than poor countries.

These three approaches make quite different predictions about economic prosperity and growth across countries. The classical theory suggests that poor countries may be poor as a result of policies and institutions that inhibit the division of labor in the society. The classical theory also draws attention to geography. Landlocked countries or countries far away from major market economies are less able to benefit from the global division of labor. The neoclassical theory, in contrast, argues that high saving and investment rates, combined with a low initial level of capital per worker, are the key to rapid growth. As the neoclassical theory pays little heed to natural differences in geography or technology across countries, it is rather optimistic that poorer countries will catch up with richer countries through faster capital accumulation. For poorer countries, the endogenous growth theory is probably most problematic. It suggests that if rich countries are ahead of poor countries because of a higher stock of knowledge, they might well be able to maintain or widen their lead, because a higher knowledge base in rich countries is likely to generate even more innovations in the future.

Growth Theory and Asia

Naturally, the general debate about sources of economic growth has spilled over into the debate about Asia. The three approaches offer different explanations for East Asia's rapid growth during the past 30 years, and yield different predictions about the future. The classical theory stresses East Asia's outward orientation and relatively strong protection of property rights. According to the classical approach, East Asian countries have benefited from a high degree of specialization in international trade and an increasingly sophisticated internal division of labor. Moreover, with its fine natural ports and easy access to major markets through sea-based trade, East Asia's geography is favorable.

In contrast, the neoclassical theory emphasizes East Asia's rapid capital accumulation. In the mid-1960s, the East Asian countries had low stocks of capital per person. Hence, the rates of return to investment have been high, as have rates of capital accumulation. Neoclassical theory predicts that East Asian countries will succeed in narrowing the gap in income levels with richer countries. As they do so, however, the rate of economic growth will slow down, because the rate of return to new investments will decline as the ratio of capital to labor rises.

The endogenous growth theory tends to treat East Asia's rapid growth not as a matter of catching up, but as a reflection of superior economic institutions that have led to successful innovation and product development. For example, one possibility is that East Asia's particular institutions and values (such as Confucian loyalty to superiors, lifetime employment, and consensus-building institutions) may have enabled the subregion's economies to be especially dynamic in technological innovation. If this is the case, and if endogenous growth theory is correct that knowledge leads to more knowledge without decreasing returns to investment, then the theory predicts that East Asian countries will eventually overtake richer countries. (This prediction, of course, also assumes that slower growth in richer countries is evidence of poorer institutions for generating new knowledge.)

None of the three main theories, however, attaches sufficient importance to the role of demography as a factor in explaining cross-country patterns of growth. This is unfortunate. Changes in population dynamics—including life expectancy, the age structure of the population, dependency ratios, and overall population growth rates—have important effects on the growth of the labor force, the ratio of workers to the total population, national saving rates, and other potential determinants of growth. As the subsequent analysis points out, demographic differences between East and South Asia do much to explain the differences in economic growth between the two subregions.

Sometimes economists regard the alternative approaches to understanding economic growth as tenets of faith. This study's approach is to subject the various theories to empirical testing. The goal is to highlight the testable implications of the different theories and to analyze whether international comparisons support or refute them. The analysis begins with formal statistical models of cross-country growth, and then looks more closely at specific aspects of the growth process.

For convenience, the findings are summarized at the outset. These conclusions are based on empirical analysis. The evidence best supports a synthesis of the classical and neoclassical approaches, augmented by demographic considerations. East Asia has benefited from rapid capital accumulation (as the neoclassical approach would suggest), an increasingly sophisticated internal and international division of labor supported by good policies and institutions (as the classical approach implies), and a rapid demographic transition. These findings suggest that most of Asia has the potential for rapid growth in the future and can further narrow the gap with richer economies. Nonetheless, as the countries reach higher income levels, economic growth will gradually slow down as the ratio of capital to labor rises and rates of return to new investment decline. An aging of the population will reinforce this tendency for growth to slow.

Growth rates will slow first in the high-income economies of East Asia (Hong Kong, Korea, Singapore, and Taipei,China). Growth rates in poorer South Asia are likely to rise rather than fall during the next 30 years. In short, the predictions of endogenous growth theory do not seem to apply. Most important, the idea that East Asia's high performers owe their success to a superior system for innovation seems erroneous. While Asia has accomplished important technological advances, most of the rapid growth has come through capital accumulation. However, this should not be a cause for panic. There is still considerable scope for growth in Asia in the years ahead.

Models of Cross-Country Growth

This section undertakes a statistical analysis of differences in growth rates across a large set of countries to try to isolate some of the factors that distinguish fast and slow growing countries. Such models provide a powerful organizing framework within which one can test the veracity of different ideas about growth. But by definition models are a stylized simplification of reality. Many factors that may influence growth are not easily observed or measured, and so cannot be incorporated into a cross-country model. Moreover, the model's results do little to explain the mechanisms through which particular factors affect growth. Hence the cross-country models should be seen as a useful first step toward understanding the determinants of growth, not a complete explanation.

The basic approach is as follows. Economic growth rates between 1965 and 1990 are analyzed for a large sample of industrial and developing countries. The analysis takes into account the countries' initial income level in 1965 and several other variables, which according to the various theories of growth, might explain economic growth. These variables include trade policies, fiscal policies, geography, demographic trends, and the quality of market institutions. The results of this analysis permit an evaluation of alternative theories of growth. For example, the neoclassical theory predicts that, all other things being equal, poorer countries will grow faster than richer ones. The endogenous growth theory, in contrast, predicts that poorer countries will not grow faster than richer ones, and may even grow more slowly if their poverty reflects a smaller stock of knowledge. The statistical analysis will show which theory is more in tune with the evidence. One can also measure the relative importance of different factors that might influence growth. For instance, the analysis will show whether "classical" considerations (such as openness to trade) or "neoclassical" factors (such as saving) explain relatively more of the differences in growth performances between countries.

The analysis examines a number of explanatory variables, including the following:

- *Trade policy.* Is an economy open to trade? Assuming that a greater division of labor is a source of economic efficiency, autarkic countries should have lower levels of income in the long run than open, export-oriented economies. This means that countries that open themselves to trade have greater income potential and grow more quickly as they reap the gains from added efficiency. An aggregate measure of economic openness created by Sachs and Warner (1995a) captures this factor in the analysis. A country is said to be open if four conditions apply: tariffs on intermediate and capital goods are low or moderate; quantitative restrictions on imports of intermediate and capital goods are also limited; the exchange rate is (nearly) convertible, in that the gap between the official rate and the black market rate averages less than 20 percent; and the state does not monopolize the export of key commodities.

- *Government saving.* Neoclassical growth theory suggests that an increase in the national saving rate will raise the rate of growth associated with any initial level of income. Higher rates of government saving should promote higher rates of national saving, and thereby higher rates of growth.

- *Quality of government institutions.* Is growth fostered by a government that respects property rights, enforces contracts, and avoids corruption? The classical theory stresses that the division of labor depends on the institutions of private property, as enforced by the state. This theory of growth is examined using internationally comparable indicators of the quality of these institutions based on surveys of the business community.

- *Demography.* Changes in the age distribution of the population and in life expectancy might both affect economic growth. A rise in the proportion of working-age people, for instance, could boost the rate of growth of GDP per person, and higher life expectancy indicates a healthier, and thus potentially more productive, labor force.

- *Schooling.* Is growth faster in a country that begins with a higher average level of schooling? A better educated workforce should support a higher level of productivity and be better able to adapt to new technologies. However, a low initial level of schooling would offer a greater opportunity for rapid increases in schooling in later years, and thus a chance for faster growth later.

- *Geography.* Is a country landlocked? Is it in the tropics? Classical theory suggests that landlocked countries will have lower growth than coastal economies, because of the increased difficulty of engaging in sea-based trade. Tropical countries may have slower growth than non-tropical countries, because of the higher incidence of infectious diseases and the lower average quality of soils.

- *Resources.* Does a country have abundant natural resources? Recent research (Sachs and Warner 1995b) suggests that the relative endowment of natural resources may affect a country's growth rate. Diversity in natural resource endowments can lead to a different sectoral allocation of resources. The political economy of managing resource-rich and resource-poor economies may also differ.

Explaining Variations in Growth Across Countries

The Appendix presents the econometric details of the analysis. The subsequent sections simply summarize and interpret the main findings. Initial income is the factor analyzed first. The analysis of other factors begins with those variables that a government can most easily influence, including trade policy, the rate of government saving, and the quality of institutions. Next come variables that governments can alter, but are more difficult to influence quickly, including educational standards and demographic factors. Finally, this section examines the importance of immutable structural factors, such as geographic location.

Initial Income

An important first result is the evidence on initial income. Once all the other variables are taken into account, there is an inverse relationship between initial income in 1965 and subsequent growth between 1965 and 1990. Countries that had high incomes in 1965 grew more slowly than countries that began with low incomes. In other words, the empirical evidence strongly supports the neoclassical interpretation of growth rather than the endogenous approach. Much of the variation in cross-country growth is the result of poorer countries catching up with richer countries, and much of East Asia's rapid growth, in particular, is due to this catch-up factor. The analysis suggests that the catch-up factor boosted growth in East Asian countries by 3.5 percentage points a year relative to the United States between 1965 and 1990.

Remember that catch-up in this analysis occurs once all the other factors that might influence growth are included. When the analysis does not take these other factors into account, poor countries do not show a general tendency to grow faster than rich countries, but once important structural and policy variables are taken into account, poor countries indeed grow faster than rich countries. A considerable body of empirical evidence exists to support this result (Barro 1991; Barro and Lee 1994; Barro and Sala-i-Martin 1992; Mankiw, Romer, and Weil 1992; Sala-i-Martin 1996; Sachs and Warner 1995a). The outcome has become known as conditional convergence.

Research has found, for example, that poor but open economies tend to grow faster than rich, open economies. Countries that isolate themselves are in a much weaker position to make use of "the advantages of backwardness," and therefore show less tendency to catch up.

Figure 2.1 shows the basic relationship between the initial level of income and the subsequent rate of economic growth for the subset of countries that have been most open to the global economy during the last 25 years (specifically, where the openness variable has a value of 0.8 or higher on a scale of 0 to 1, with 1 being the most open). In this set of open countries, the poorest countries exhibit the highest growth rates and the richer countries record slower growth rates, as indicated by the downward-sloping relationship. In all but one of these open economies,

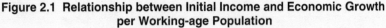

Figure 2.1 Relationship between Initial Income and Economic Growth per Working-age Population

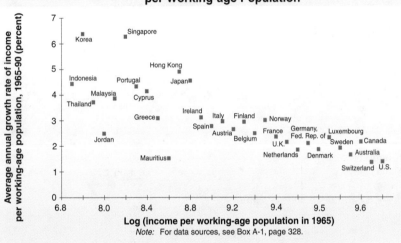

Note: For data sources, see Box A-1, page 328.

the level of income relative to the United States in 1990 was higher than it was in 1965 (see Table 2.1). Switzerland, the one exception, was the country closest to the U.S. average in 1965, and thus the one with the weakest tendency for further catching up.

The tendency for poor countries to grow faster than rich countries has two important implications in the Asian context. First, it provides one piece to the puzzle of explaining East and Southeast Asia's rapid growth during the last 30 years, as the low levels of income of the countries in these subregions in the 1960s provided the potential for rapid growth. This reasoning also implies that some of the Asian countries currently growing only slowly have the capacity for more rapid growth in the future. Second, as East Asian countries become wealthier, their growth rates are likely to slow. Japan is a clear example of this pattern:

Table 2.1 Relative Incomes of Open Economies, 1965 and 1990
(GDP per person relative to the United States)

Economy	1965	1990
Industrial economies		
Australia	0.76	0.80
Austria	0.53	0.70
Belgium	0.58	0.73
Canada	0.74	0.95
Denmark	0.72	0.77
Finland	0.56	0.78
France	0.63	0.77
Germany, Federal Republic of	0.68	0.79
Italy	0.49	0.69
Japan	0.38	0.79
Luxembourg	0.74	0.90
Netherlands	0.63	0.72
Norway	0.60	0.83
Spain	0.39	0.53
Sweden	0.81	0.82
Switzerland	0.96	0.91
United Kingdom	0.66	0.73
United States	1.00	1.00
Asian low- and middle-income economies[a]		
Hong Kong	0.30	0.82
Indonesia	0.05	0.11
Korea	0.09	0.37
Malaysia	0.14	0.28
Singapore	0.16	0.65
Taipei,China	0.14	0.45
Thailand	0.10	0.20
Non-Asian low- and middle-income economies[a]		
Barbados	0.28	0.40
Cyprus	0.24	0.46
Greece	0.26	0.37
Ireland	0.34	0.51
Jordan	0.14	0.16
Mauritius	0.27	0.32
Portugal	0.21	0.41

a. Those with 1965 per person income of $4,000 or less in 1985 purchasing power parity prices.
Note: Open economies are those with openness value greater than 0.8 on a scale of 0 to 1. For data sources, see Box A-1, page 328.

its expansion slowed considerably during the 1980s after sustained rapid growth between 1950 and the mid-1970s.

Of course, there is much more to the process of economic growth than simply how rich or poor a country happens to be. Many of the world's poorest countries are growing extremely slowly or not at all, especially in sub-Saharan Africa. Rather than catching up with the world leaders, these countries are falling further behind. The main reasons for this poor performance lie in the differences in other characteristics— government policies, institutional effectiveness, demography, and geography—that determine a poor country's ability to exploit its potential to catch up.

Openness and Growth

A strong and positive relationship exists between integration with the global economy and economic growth. Countries that were consistently open to trade between 1965 and 1990 grew about 2 percentage points faster per year, on average, than countries that were consistently closed to trade. The East and Southeast Asian countries were among the most open of all developing countries during the period under review, which helps to account for their better growth performance. Following an initial stage of modest import substitution, most of the fast growing Asian countries lowered their import tariffs and export taxes, removed quantity restrictions on trade, and reduced barriers to international flows of capital. In a critically important move, East and Southeast Asian countries ensured high profitability for their exporters of manufactured goods by giving them easy access to inputs at world market prices by following prudent exchange rate policies, and by developing new institutions, such as export processing zones (EPZs), to support export-led growth. Issues pertinent in this context are discussed in more depth later in this chapter.

The PRC transformed itself from one of the most closed economies in the world in the 1960s to a moderately open one in the mid-1990s. After breaking off ties with the Soviet Union in 1960, the PRC sealed itself off almost completely from the rest of the world. When it began its program of economic reforms in the late 1970s, total trade was the equivalent of an astonishingly low 1 percent of gross national product (GNP). The PRC's trade policy changes were gradual. For many years it continued to maintain dual exchange rates, controls on capital movements, high tariffs, and other trade restrictions. Even today, the economy is far from fully open. However, like the East and Southeast Asian countries, the PRC introduced facilities to help exporters circumvent these distortions and to compete in world markets. The first step was the establishment of four special economic zones early in the reform program, with trading privileges that were later extended to many more regions.

Other Asian countries have remained more closed to trade. South Asian countries generally isolated themselves from the global economy by imposing high tariff rates and a plethora of controls on imports to protect their domestic industries. Only recently have these countries, led by India, begun to open themselves to the global economy. Lao People's Democratic Republic, Cambodia, and Viet Nam were nearly autarkic throughout the period. Of the three, only Viet Nam has taken substantial steps toward opening in recent years. The Central Asian republics were also closed, except for bureaucratically determined interstate trading relationships with the socialist bloc. These countries face the challenge of finding a whole new set of trading partners.

Saving

Countries with a higher rate of government saving relative to GDP have grown more rapidly in recent decades. The analysis finds that a 10 percentage point increase in the rate of government's saving (that is, current revenues minus current expenditures) is associated with an increase in growth of about 1.2 percentage points per year. The fast growing Asian countries tended to have smaller governments, with correspondingly lower levels of expenditure and taxation and higher levels of government saving and investment. Between 1965 and 1990 government saving rates in East and Southeast Asia averaged 3.5 percent of GDP, more than double the level recorded in South Asia and other developing regions. In the 1990s government saving rates have been even higher, averaging 5 percent of GDP.

Government budget policies support growth through two distinct channels. First, the more governments save, the more the nation as a whole saves (although the relationship is not one to one). This adds to the pool of finances available for investment. Second, higher government saving tends to be indicative of sound overall macroeconomic management, including low rates of inflation, prudent exchange rate policies, and capable monetary management. Stable economies, in turn, lower the risks for investors, and therefore lower the cost of capital for long-term investments.

Institutional Quality

Countries with more constructive interactions between the government and the market tended to record faster economic growth. The measure of these interactions used in the analysis is drawn from the work of Knack and Keefer (1995) and is based on surveys of business communities' attitudes about various aspects of the institutional framework underpinning governments and markets. These include the perceived efficiency of the government bureaucracy, the extent of government corruption, the efficacy of the rule of law, the presence or absence of expropriation risk, and the perceived risk of repudiation of contracts by the government. The overall measure aims to gauge the security of property and contractual rights, the efficiency of the government's intervention in markets, and the allocation of public goods. The analysis finds a strong, positive statistical relationship between this measure of institutional quality and rates of economic growth in recent decades. East Asian economies scored particularly highly on this index, especially Hong Kong and Singapore. The quality of government-market interactions tended to be more constructive in East Asia than in other developing regions of the world. Generally speaking, property and contractual rights tended to be more secure, government bureaucracy less intrusive, and corruption less extensive.

Schooling

The analysis shows a moderately positive association between initial levels of education in 1965 and economic growth between 1965 and 1990. Adults in East and Southeast Asia had, on average, about one year of secondary education in 1965. This was about twice the average for South Asia and other developing regions. Literacy rates were also much higher in East and Southeast Asia: about 73 percent of the adult population met minimum standards of literacy in 1970, compared with 43 percent in South Asia and 30 percent in sub-Saharan Africa. By 1990 literacy rates had reached 87 percent in East and Southeast Asia, compared with just 52 percent in South Asia.

The relationship between growth and education is statistically somewhat weaker than with the other variables. One possible explanation is measurement problems. For example, the best available statistics do not make any adjustment for the quality of schooling. Arguably, it is the quality of schooling that matters most. It is also possible that low levels of schooling in 1965 implied faster increases in schooling after 1965, and therefore a faster improvement in human capital in the subsequent 25 years. Chapters 3 and 5 look at the role of education in Asia's development in greater depth.

Demography

Demographic factors have had an important impact on growth rates. Life expectancy (measured at birth) has a nonlinear relationship with economic growth. At low levels of life expectancy, further increases in life expectancy are strongly associated with more rapid economic growth, probably because higher life expectancy boosts growth by increasing the supply of working-age labor (as a result of lower morbidity), by raising labor productivity (as a healthier population is also a more productive one), by raising the rates of human capital accumulation (as people are more likely to invest in skills and education if they live longer), and by promoting more saving for retirement. East Asia's higher life expectancy of 63 years in 1965 gave the subregion a greater growth potential than South Asia, where life expectancy was just 49 years. However, the positive effect on growth diminishes as life expectancy increases, and once it passes 68 years, the analysis shows that further increases have a negative effect on growth, as beyond this point, increased life expectancy is associated with a longer life span for those who are retired and consuming out of their lifetime savings.

Changes in the population's age structure also affect the rate of growth of GDP per person. For a given population growth rate, relatively fast growth in the working-age population (aged between 15 and 64) increases the size of the workforce relative to the overall population, and therefore the rate of economic growth per person. Part of East Asia's rapid growth in income per person between 1965 and 1990 is due to the rising share of the working-age population relative to the total population. During these years, the working-age population grew almost 1 percentage point faster than the total population in East Asia, a far larger gap than in other developing regions. Chapter 3 discusses these demographic factors at length.

Geography

Once other factors affecting growth are taken into consideration, landlocked countries grew about 0.6 of a percentage point per year more slowly than countries with direct access to the sea between 1965 and 1990. Landlocked countries have enormous cost and risk disadvantages that they must overcome to compete on world markets. Thus it is much more difficult for manufacturing firms located in landlocked countries such as Kazakstan, Kyrgyz Republic, Mongolia, Nepal, and Uzbekistan to be competitive in world markets, unless they are processing domestic natural resources.

A country's location also seems to affect its potential for economic growth. Countries situated in temperate climatic zones grew, on average, 1.3 percentage points faster every year between 1965 and 1990 than countries located in the tropics (controlling for other factors). Countries located in the tropics tend to face a wide variety of parasitic diseases that are much less prevalent in the temperate zones. Tropical soils also tend to be more fragile. In addition, typhoons and other natural disasters are more frequent in the tropics.

Resource Base

Somewhat paradoxically, countries with abundant natural resources grew much less rapidly than resource-poor countries between 1965 and 1990. Each 10 percentage point increase in the share of primary product exports in GDP in 1970 was associated, on average, with a decline in growth per person of just less than half of 1 percentage point. The statistical relationship is strong (Figure 2.2). Countries with primary product exports valued at 0 to 5 percent of GDP recorded growth per person of more than 3.2 percent between 1965 and 1990. At the other extreme, countries with primary product exports equivalent to more than 20 percent of GDP grew just 0.8 percent per person per year. This pattern continues to hold once other variables, including initial income, geography, and government policies, are taken into account.

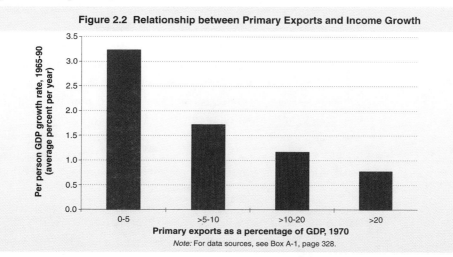

Figure 2.2 Relationship between Primary Exports and Income Growth

Per person GDP growth rate, 1965-90 (average percent per year)

Primary exports as a percentage of GDP, 1970

Note: For data sources, see Box A-1, page 328.

This negative relationship seems odd. Natural resource exports can provide foreign exchange earnings and give a direct income boost to developing countries. If used judiciously, the receipts from natural resource exports can finance investments in infrastructure, health, and education, thereby supporting long-term growth. Indonesia and Malaysia are examples of how governments can use the revenues earned from natural resource exports to boost incomes and improve welfare. During the last century, exports of natural resources also played a critical role in supporting sustained growth and development in several countries, including Argentina and the United States.

During the last 30 years, however, many countries with abundant natural resources have performed poorly. In Mexico, Nigeria, Venezuela, Zambia, and a host of other countries, long periods of stagnation, or even decline, followed the initial fillip to income from natural resource exports. This poor performance has several possible explanations. Natural resource exports lead to a strong currency, which makes manufactured exports (and perhaps manufacturing production itself) uncompetitive. The resultant shift of resources out of manufactures—a phenomenon known as the Dutch disease—may have adverse consequences, especially if manufacturing generates important benefits for the rest of the economy.[2]

In addition, resource-abundant economies provide greater opportunity and incentive for rent seeking and corruption, particularly if the resources are government owned or heavily taxed. Government officials, the armed forces, and private businesses often vie for economic and political power to gain access to the wealth generated by the resources. Entrepreneurs focus their energies on obtaining a larger piece of the existing economic pie, rather than on enlarging the pie. In addition, resource-abundant countries tend to follow boom-and-bust cycles in line with sharply fluctuating prices of their export commodities. Export receipts and government revenues are subject to sharp increases and declines, which complicate macroeconomic management, create uncertainty, and undermine long-term investment.

Finally, long-term structural trends in commodity markets may put primary producers at a disadvantage. Prebisch (1950, 1959) argued that secular declines in commodity prices would doom exporters of primary

---

2. The Dutch disease derived its name from the experience of the Netherlands after 1960, when major reserves of natural gas were discovered. The ensuing export boom sparked inflationary pressures, raised wages, and undermined the competitiveness of other export sectors.

products to slow growth. Nurske (1961) concluded that because of technological innovations, world demand for primary products would grow slowly at best. Although debate about these trends continues, the evidence appears to support both a gradual decline in commodity prices and slower growth in demand for primary products.

Nonetheless, the negative relationship between resource abundance and growth is a tendency, not a straightjacket. Natural resource abundance does not necessarily impede growth, but it creates economic management challenges that many countries have had difficulty coping with. As a result, resource-abundant countries have tended to grow more slowly than others.

Putting the Pieces Together:
Explaining East Asia's Rapid Growth

The preceding sections show that initial conditions, policy variables, demographic characteristics, and geographic and other structural variables are all associated with economic growth, but which of these factors are most important in accounting for the large differences in growth rates across developing regions? The analysis demonstrated that policy variables account for the main differences. For example, Table 2.2 shows the contribution of each variable to the difference in growth rates between South Asia and selected East and Southeast Asian economies.

In South Asia, annual growth rates per person were, on average, about 2.9 percentage points lower than in East and Southeast Asia between 1965 and 1990. South Asia's initial conditions—that is, the level of income and education—do not account for this difference. Indeed, initial conditions favored slightly faster growth in South Asia. South Asia started with a lower income per person in 1965 that, all else being equal, gave the subregion the potential to grow about half a percentage point per year faster than the East and Southeast Asian countries. South Asia also started with slightly lower average years of schooling, which somewhat tempered the "advantage" of lower income.

Similarly, structural characteristics—geography and natural resources—gave South Asia a small edge. For example, South Asia has fewer natural resources than several of the Southeast Asian countries (Indonesia and Malaysia in particular), a factor that has been associated with faster growth. The South Asian countries are also located in slightly more temperate zones than the Southeast Asian countries. Together, the

Table 2.2 Contribution of Selected Factors to Growth Differentials between East and Southeast Asia and Selected Regions, 1965-90
(percent)

Factor	Contribution of each variable to the difference in annual per person growth relative to East and Southeast Asia		
	South Asia	Sub-Saharan Africa	Latin America
Initial conditions	0.3	0.7	-1.2
Initial GDP per person	0.5	1.0	-1.2
Schooling	-0.2	-0.4	-0.1
Policy variables	-2.1	-1.7	-1.8
Government saving rate	-0.4	-0.1	-0.3
Openness	-1.2	-1.2	-1.0
Institutional quality	-0.5	-0.4	-0.5
Demography	-0.9	-1.9	-0.2
Life expectancy	-0.5	-1.3	0.1
Growth in working-age population	-0.3	0.1	-0.2
Growth in total population	-0.2	-0.7	-0.1
Resources and geography	0.2	-1.0	-0.6
Natural resources	0.1	-0.2	-0.2
Landlocked	0.0	-0.3	-0.1
Tropics	0.5	-0.2	0.0
Ratio of coastline distance to land area	-0.3	-0.3	-0.3
Difference in			
Predicted growth	-2.5	-3.9	-3.8
Actual growth	-2.9	-4.0	-3.9

Note: The ten economies in our sample from East and Southeast Asia are PRC, Hong Kong, Indonesia, Korea, Malaysia, Papua New Guinea, Philippines, Singapore, Taipei,China, and Thailand.
Source: Radelet, Sachs, and Lee (1996).

net effect of initial conditions, natural resources, and geography gave the South Asian countries the potential to grow about 0.2 of a percentage point faster per year than the East and Southeast Asian countries. Thus geography and natural resources actually accounted for only a small amount of the differences in growth rates across regions.

Demographic characteristics underlay a significant portion of South Asia's weaker growth performance. South Asian countries recorded shorter average life expectancy, which reduced growth by about half a percentage point. Moreover, the changing structure of the population worked against South Asia. The growth rate of the working-age population was slower than in East and Southeast Asia, and the growth rate of the dependent population was faster. Thus, South Asia recorded a rising share of the dependent population relative to the number of workers, which created a drag on growth per person.

The impact of policy choices, however, made the most difference. South Asian governments generated smaller government saving, were less open to world trade, and created weaker institutions than their neighbors to the East. The combined effect of the differences in these three variables was to reduce South Asia's growth rate by 2.1 percentage points relative to East and Southeast Asia. South Asia's relative isolation from world markets played an especially large role: its high tariff and quota coverage accounted for 1.2 percentage points of slower growth.

The key lesson from this exercise is that initial and resource conditions account for only modest differences in growth rates across regions. Policy variables play the major role with demographic characteristics also making an important contribution. The most important factors behind East Asia's rapid growth during the last three decades have been its openness to the world economy, especially its export orientation; maintenance of good institutions; and implementation of prudent fiscal policies. Similarly, these policy variables account for a lion's share of South Asia's lower growth performance.

This analysis of cross-country growth performance provides a useful starting point for exploring the past and projecting the future of Asia's developing economies by furnishing a framework that identifies some of the most critical factors that account for differences in growth performance across regions and countries. Obviously, this framework does not by itself fully explain the process of economic growth. It does not, for example, capture the complex relationships between policy choices, institutional settings, and economic outcomes in their entirety, nor does it highlight the importance of high-quality economic leadership and skillful policymaking. In addition, the analysis omits some important considerations, such as environmental degradation, because of the lack of sufficient data across a broad range of countries. The aggregate cross-country analysis may also obscure important conditions that are specific to individual countries or groups of countries. This simple framework must therefore be complemented by a more detailed analysis of how the fast growing Asian economies either resembled or differed from other developing economies, and how these factors might have affected Asia's economic performance.

More Evidence on How East Asia was Different

Another way to gauge Asia's distinctiveness from an international perspective is to analyze how much Asia's subregions differ from other industrial and developing countries on a broad range of economic indicators, such as trade ratios, industrial shares, and government spending. One way to do this is to compare the average values of these variables in Asia with averages for other regions. Simple averages can be misleading, however, because differences across regions might themselves be due to other factors, such as levels of income or geography. For example, the relatively high trade ratios in Korea and Singapore may simply be due to the fact that they have smaller populations and higher incomes than most developing countries. A more informative approach would be to determine whether these two countries record unusually high trade ratios once these structural factors are taken into account. Table 2.3 presents the results of this type of analysis for several economic indicators for a broad sample of 77 countries from all income levels around the world. The analysis is conducted first for average values for 1969-71 and then for 1989-91.

As Table 2.3 shows, the more advanced East Asian economies—which include Hong Kong, Korea, Singapore, and Taipei,China—differed from other countries in several important respects. First, exports and imports in the advanced East Asian economies accounted for a significantly larger share of GDP in 1970 than in other countries of the same size, income level, resource abundance, and demographic structure. Manufactured exports, in particular, were substantially more important than elsewhere. In contrast, the share of primary product exports was significantly smaller in East Asia. The same basic pattern held in 1990. Second, saving and investment rates in East Asia were well above the average of other countries in 1990, and marginally so in 1970. The advanced East Asian economies also had slightly larger central government budget surpluses and slightly lower rates of spending on social security, compared with other countries at similar income levels. Third, the average number of years of school attendance was unusually high in East Asia. Finally, the advanced East Asian economies were also more urbanized than other developing countries, a result that reflects the presence of Hong Kong and Singapore in the group.

Notably, the structure of the advanced East Asian economies—the division between agriculture, industry, and services—was not significantly different from that of other countries. In particular, the share of manufacturing in GDP was not different, although the share of manufactured exports was much larger. What set the East Asians apart was not manufacturing as such, but manufactured exports.

Southeast Asian countries differed from other countries in only a few dimensions in 1970: they had higher exports, more years of schooling, slightly higher literacy rates, and lower social security expenditures. By 1990, however, the Southeast Asian countries followed a similar pattern to that of the more mature East Asian economies in that they had higher shares of imports and higher shares of exports, especially manufactured exports (but not manufacturing production) relative to GDP than other developing countries. They saved and invested more relative to GDP and, in particular, had higher rates of central government saving.

South Asia, in contrast, followed a different pattern. South Asian countries did not have unusually high or low shares of trade in GDP in 1970, nor did their investment and saving ratios stand out. By 1990, their saving and investment rates were significantly lower than was typical for other countries of the same size and at the same income level, as were their literacy rates. South Asian countries also had unusually high levels of agricultural production and lower shares of industry and manufacturing in GDP.

This analysis of controlled averages across countries, combined with the earlier cross-country growth regressions, points to four areas that are associated with rapid growth across all countries, and in which East and Southeast Asia differed from others. These are openness and the growth of manufactured exports, strong macroeconomic management, higher saving and investment, and more education. Chapters 3 and 5 discuss the role of education at length. A discussion of the other components of Asian distinctiveness follows, along with a discussion of the role of agriculture in Asia's development.

Table 2.3 Differences in Economic Variables between Asia and a Selected Group of Countries Worldwide, 1969-71 and 1989-91

Variable	Period	Number of countries	East Asia	Southeast Asia	South Asia
Exports/GDP	1969-71	77	+*	+***	—
	1989-91	76	+*	+*	—
Manufacturing exports	1969-71	71	+*	—	—
	1989-91	73	+*	+*	—
Net primary exports	1969-71	72	-**	—	—
	1989-91	63	—	—	—
Imports/GDP	1969-71	77	+*	—	—
	1989-91	76	+*	+*	—
Resource balance	1969-71	77	—	—	—
	1989-91	76	-***	—	—
Investment/GDP	1969-71	77	+***	—	—
	1989-91	76	+**	+*	-***
Domestic saving/GDP	1969-71	77	—	—	—
	1989-91	76	+*	+*	-**
National saving/GNP	1969-71	77	—	—	—
	1989-91	76	+***	+**	—
Agriculture/GDP, value added	1969-71	67	—	—	+*
	1989-91	69	—	—	+*
Industry/GDP, value added	1969-71	66	—	—	-**
	1989-91	69	—	—	-**
Manufacturing/GDP, value added	1969-71	63	—	—	-***
	1989-91	65	—	—	-*
Services/GDP, value added	1969-71	66	—	—	—
	1989-91	69	—	—	—
Government total expenditures	1969-71[a]	69	—	—	—
	1989-91	62	—	—	—

Variable	Period	Number of countries	East Asia	Southeast Asia	South Asia
Government current expenditures	1969-71[a]	64	—	—	—
	1989-91	59	—	—	—
Social security expenditures	1969-71[a]	59	-*	-***	—
	1989-91	47	-**	—	—
Tax revenue (percentage of GDP)	1969-71[a]	68	—	—	—
	1989-91	62	—	—	—
Central government balance	1969-71[a]	64	+****	—	—
	1989-91	59	—	+***	—
Primary school enrollment	1969-71	73	—	—	—
	1989-91	72	—	—	—
Secondary schooling enrollment	1969-71	72	—	+**	+***
	1989-91	66	—	—	—
Secondary years of schooling	1969-71	69	+*	—	+***
	1989-91	68	+*	—	+**
Total years of schooling	1969-71	68	—	+**	—
	1989-91	68	—	—	—
Literacy rate	1969-71	64	—	+***	—
	1989-91	76	—	—	-***
Life expectancy	1969-71	77	—	—	—
	1989-91	73	—	—	—
Urbanization	1969-71	77	+*	—	—
	1989-91	76	—	-**	-***

* = level of significance of 1 percent; ** = level of significance of 5 percent; *** = level of significance of 10 percent;
— = no significant difference
a.   These variables refer to 1974-76 due to missing data problems.
Note: A plus (minus) sign in a cell indicates that the average for the subregion was statistically significantly higher (lower) than that of the other countries after controlling for several structural variables, including log of GDP, log of GDP squared, log of population, log of population squared, log of land per person, log of shipping distance to a major industrial center, lower and upper dependency ratios, and a dummy variable for Asian countries.
Source: Radelet, Sachs, and Lee (1996).

Manufactured Exports and Growth

Rapid growth of manufactured exports boosts overall economic growth in several ways: it accelerates economic specialization and fosters technological progress by allowing exporting firms to learn by doing, it promotes higher rates of capital investment in profitable export sectors, and it provides the foreign exchange needed to finance imports of capital goods. No country can generate all the sophisticated capital goods needed for high-quality investment projects by itself. Countries that can pay for imported capital goods with export earnings are therefore in a better position to tap into world-class technologies.

Manufacturing export growth also confers a range of other benefits on an economy, in particular, success in exporting has important spillover and demonstration effects on other sectors of the economy. Exporters compete with other firms for resources, especially labor, and labor practices in internationally competitive export firms often serve as a model for others to follow. Exporters are also more likely to demand high standards of service from their suppliers and to exert pressure for improved infrastructure provision, maintenance, and management. Positive spillovers such as these have helped to modernize the economies of East Asia and sustain their growth.

The cross-country growth analysis described earlier provided circumstantial evidence of the close links between manufactured exports and overall growth. There is also direct evidence of the strong link between manufactured export growth and overall economic growth. In recent years, those countries that have been most successful at expanding their manufactured exports have achieved the highest rates of economic growth. This relationship is especially strong for manufactured goods that do not derive directly from natural resources, such as polished diamonds, plywood, and processed mineral manufactures.[3] Relatively complete disaggregated trade data are available for the group of low- and middle-income countries with a population greater than 1 million in 1994 and an income per person of less than $15,000 for the years 1970-90. Table 2.4 divides these countries into fast and slow growers in two ways: based on growth of GDP per person and based on growth of the share of manufactured exports in GDP.

---

3. Specifically, Standard International Trade Classification (SITC) (Revision 1) 0-4, 61, 63, 66, 68, and 9 are excluded.

Table 2.4 Manufactured Exports and Economic Growth, Selected Low- and Middle-Income Countries, 1970-90

		Growth of GDP per person, 1970-90		Total number of countries
		Growth > 3%	Growth < 3%	
Weighted nonresource-based manufactured export growth	Growth > 1 %	PRC Portugal Hong Kong Singapore Ireland Taipei,China Korea Thailand Malaysia Tunisia Mauritius	Israel	12
	Growth < 1 %	Indonesia Jordan	64 countries	66
Total number of countries		13	65	78

Note: Includes 78 countries with a population greater than 1 million in 1994 and GNP per person of less than $15,000 (or income adjusted for purchasing power parity of less than $16,000). The weighted nonresource-based manufactured exports growth rate is equal to the annual growth rate of those exports times their share in GDP averaged over 1970-90. Pearson chi-squared statistic = 53.82, with probability = 0.000.
Source: Radelet, Sachs, and Lee (1996).

The results are revealing. Only 12 countries saw their share of nonprimary manufactured exports rise by an average of more than 1 percent per year between 1970 and 1990. Almost all these countries also experienced rapid overall economic growth: 11 of the 12 recorded an average annual growth in GDP per person of 3 percent or more during the period. Of the 12 countries where manufactured exports rose rapidly, 7 were in Asia. Only two countries, Indonesia and Jordan, achieved rapid economic growth without rapid growth in nonprimary manufactured exports. Indonesia's high rates of economic growth were due to unusually skilled management of its natural resource base. Moreover, when Indonesia began to shift toward manufactured exports in the mid-1980s, its growth rate accelerated. Conversely, Jordan's economy slowed significantly in the late 1980s and early 1990s, hence it is not really an outlier. Israel is the only country in the group where rapid export growth did not coincide with annual economic growth above 3 percent per person. At 2.2 percent per year, its growth rate was hardly dismal, however, and has risen significantly in the 1990s. In short, the relationship between fast growth of nonprimary manufactured exports and overall GDP growth is strong and highly statistically significant.[4]

What factors determine a country's ability to compete in nonprimary manufactured exports? Statistical analysis by Radelet, Sachs, and Lee (1996) shows that five factors are critical: trade policy, natural resource endowments, geography, quality of government institutions, and size of the domestic market. First, not surprisingly, trade openness is strongly associated with faster growth of nonprimary manufactured exports. Low tariff rates (especially on capital goods and intermediate inputs), the absence of trade quotas, and the ease with which international financial transactions can be undertaken are all likely to support the competitiveness of manufactured exports. Second, a relative scarcity of natural resources is positively associated with the growth of manufacturing exports. Resource-rich countries tend to export their natural resources, while resource-poor countries tend to export manufactured goods. Third, physical proximity to major markets (Japan, North America, or Western Europe) gives exporters of manufactured goods an advantage. Fourth, countries with higher quality government institutions have also recorded faster growth in manufactured exports. Finally, countries with smaller domestic economies have had more success in expanding nonprimary manufactured exports. A greater share of manufactured products is sold on the domestic market in larger countries, with a correspondingly smaller share sold as exports. It used to be thought that a large domestic market is necessary to support the division of labor required for advanced manufacturing processes. The evidence suggests otherwise. Even small, open economies can engage in advanced manufacturing for the export market. These economies rely on imported inputs rather than domestic production to achieve the necessary degree of specialization.

Export Growth and Technological Development

One of the lessons of recent history—highlighted by the previous analysis—is that very poor countries, even those that are poorly endowed with skilled labor, can achieve international competitiveness in manufactures, something that was widely doubted 50 years ago. Indeed, the basic motivation underlying countries' import substitution strategies in their attempts to achieve industrialization was the belief that industrial-

---

4. A chi-square test easily rejects (at the 0.01 percent level) the null hypothesis that the distribution of the number of countries in each cell in the table is random.

ization would be possible only in a protected, closed market. Few economists dreamed that poor developing countries would be able to achieve rapid export growth in manufactures.

The main reason for the success of developing country exporters is that they can participate in global production and distribution systems using their comparative advantage in labor-intensive operations. For example, Malaysia was able to build up an electronics sector in the early 1970s almost from scratch, because U.S. manufacturers moved the labor-intensive parts of their production process there. Even though Malaysia could not design nor produce computer chips, it was able to assemble and test them, operations that are labor-intensive. When Intel invested in Malaysia in 1972, the country was quickly brought into a world-class production system that drew on its comparative advantage.

Rapid growth in manufacturing exports requires close links with multinational firms that provide intermediate inputs, technology, capital goods, and export markets. There is no realistic chance of this occurring if a country is cut off from world markets through severe restrictions on trade and capital flows. From an early stage, East and Southeast Asian firms bought most of their machinery and equipment abroad. For example, in 1970, capital goods imports accounted for about 50 percent of total investment in East and Southeast Asia, compared with 17 percent in South Asia and about 35 percent in Latin America and sub-Saharan Africa. Imported capital goods were a primary channel through which Asian countries gained access to leading edge technologies, thereby enabling their firms to compete in world markets.

Although several East Asian countries went through a phase of import substitution for consumer goods, they did not attempt to provide protection for domestic producers of capital goods. Even today in Korea—which produces more capital-intensive exports than any other Asian country—these exports are chemicals, ships, and automobiles, not machinery. For example, between 1991 and 1994, imported capital goods accounted for 73 percent of all equipment investment in Korea (IMF 1995). This indicates the country's continued heavy reliance on imported foreign technology.

Foreign direct investment provided an important link to global markets for Hong Kong and Singapore, but played a more limited role in Korea and Taipei,China. Both countries actively discouraged, and even prohibited, some types of foreign investments until the 1980s. They chose instead to import technology under licensing agreements and as part of original equipment manufacturing arrangements. These allowed Asian exporters to produce goods under the brand names of U.S. and Japanese firms. Southeast Asian countries, especially Indonesia and Thailand, also limited foreign investment in manufacturing (although they were more welcoming in minerals) until the 1980s, or even the 1990s. South Asia, too, severely limited foreign investment until recent years. Notably, where foreign investment has taken place, it has been heavily export-oriented.

Despite the modest flows of foreign direct investment, at least in earlier years, East Asian firms developed strong links with multinational firms. For example, most finished consumer goods exports were produced to precise specifications from overseas buyers' orders. In most cases, the buyers were either importer-wholesalers or overseas manufacturers subcontracting to local firms. The first buyers to operate in the developing countries of East and Southeast Asia were from big Japanese trading houses, which in turn often sold in North American markets. Major U.S. trading firms followed.

To establish relationships with reliable, stable suppliers, these overseas buyers often provided instruction and advice to exporting firms on virtually all aspects of business (Kessing 1983). The successful Asian firms learned quickly and developed the flexibility and acumen to manufacture a variety of constantly changing designs. Some firms gained specialized knowledge of particular markets, others became skilled at quickly producing "knock-off" copies of samples, and still others specialized in producing higher quality niche products. Successful firms also often took the initiative to send representatives to major industrial country markets to visit actual and potential buyers, thereby enriching their knowledge of business practices in industrial countries. Each of these activities allowed exporting firms to become better positioned than domestic-oriented firms to enhance their skills, adapt new technologies, and expand their production.

The Composition of Asian Exports

Most manufacturing exporters in Asia export a completely different range of products than they did 30 years ago. Broadly speaking, changes in export products have followed changes in comparative advantage. Initially, most East Asian exporters concentrated on primary products. For example, primary products (including primary-based manufactures) accounted for more than 90 percent of exports in 9 of 15 Asian econo-mies for which data are available for 1970 (Table 2.5). Labor-intensive goods—especially textiles and clothing—accounted for 25 percent or more of exports in only five economies (Bangladesh, Hong Kong, India, Korea, and Pakistan). Capital- and technology-intensive products (including electronics, machinery, scale-intensive, and other human capital intensive exports) were much less common. Only in Hong Kong, India, Korea, and Singapore did exports of these products account for more than 10 percent of exports, and only in Hong Kong did the share reach 20 percent. Even these small shares are seriously overstated, as some of these products, especially electronics, are actually little more than labor-intensive assembly in which the final output is technology intensive.

By the 1990s the picture had changed dramatically. Primary products accounted for more than 70 percent of exports in only 3 of the 16 Asian countries for which data are available. Several countries had shifted their export base toward labor-intensive products, including Bangladesh, Fiji, Indonesia, Pakistan, and Sri Lanka, although the size of the structural change was smallest for the relatively closed economies of South Asia. In the most advanced Asian countries, exports have continued to move toward skill-intensive and technology-intensive products, including more sophisticated electronics in some countries (Lall 1997). In Malaysia and Singapore, for example, capital- and technology-intensive products accounted for more than 50 percent of exports (although labor-intensive assembly operations remained important in these high-tech sectors). PRC, India, and Philippines are moving in that direction, with capital- and technology-intensive products accounting for 20 to 25 percent of exports by the 1990s. These newer exports continue to be based on comparative advantage, although that advantage is quickly shifting from labor-intensive to skill-intensive goods in many countries.

Two manufactured product sectors have dominated Asia's exports in recent decades: textiles and electronics. South Asia, of course, has been exporting textiles to the world for centuries. In East Asia, as with so many other manufactured products, textile exports have their origins in Japan. In the 19th century Japan exported raw and spun silk, and then moved into cotton textiles. In the early years of the 20th century Japanese entrepreneurs helped to organize and expand the textile industry in Shanghai, which then thrived for several decades. Following the 1949 Chinese revolution, much of Shanghai's textile industry moved to

Table 2.5 Composition of Asian Exports, 1970 and 1994
(percent)

Economy	Year	Primary products	Textiles	Other labor-intensive items	Electronics	Machinery	Scale-intensive items	Other human capital-intensive items	Other manufactures	Total manufactures
							Manufactures			
Bangladesh	1977[a]	55.4	43.0	0.0	0.1	0.0	0.7	0.5	0.3	44.6
	1994	22.3	14.8	58.8	0.1	0.8	0.2	0.2	2.8	77.7
PRC[b]	1994	20.3	9.7	34.9	10.4	4.2	7.2	8.4	4.8	79.7
Fiji	1970	98.3	0.0	0.3	0.0	0.0	0.6	0.5	0.3	1.7
	1994	68.1	1.2	26.5	0.6	0.1	1.5	1.3	0.6	31.9
Hong Kong	1970	4.8	10.4	49.8	10.5	0.8	1.3	8.0	14.5	95.3
	1994	5.2	6.8	36.5	16.0	9.3	3.2	15.5	7.4	94.8
India	1970	58.2	22.9	3.0	1.1	1.8	9.1	3.1	1.2	42.2
	1994	42.0	13.2	19.3	1.5	2.8	10.3	5.4	5.8	58.0
Indonesia	1970	98.6	0.2	0.0	0.0	0.0	0.0	0.3	0.7	1.2
	1994	60.7	6.4	16.4	3.6	1.2	3.8	6.4	1.4	39.3
Korea	1970	35.2	10.6	29.0	5.3	1.0	3.5	1.7	13.8	64.9
	1994	8.1	12.0	10.2	25.6	8.9	24.4	8.1	2.7	91.9
Malaysia	1970	94.7	0.4	0.5	0.3	0.7	1.4	0.8	1.2	5.3
	1994	29.4	1.5	6.8	32.8	11.6	6.7	8.7	2.6	70.6
Myanmar	1970	99.9	0.0	0.0	0.0	0.0	0.0	0.0	0.0	0.0
	1994	91.6	0.8	3.5	0.0	0.0	0.1	1.7	2.2	8.4
Pakistan	1970	47.8	46.1	2.6	0.2	0.2	0.3	0.9	2.0	52.3
	1994	16.7	53.1	26.6	0.0	0.1	0.2	0.6	2.6	83.3
Papua New Guinea	1971[c]	99.2	0.0	0.0	0.0	0.0	0.0	0.2	0.6	0.8
	1994	96.3	0.0	0.1	0.1	1.1	2.0	0.1	0.3	3.7
Philippines	1970	96.8	0.5	0.4	0.0	0.1	1.4	0.2	0.7	3.3
	1994	22.6	1.4	13.1	18.2	2.2	2.9	1.6	38.0	77.4
Singapore	1970	71.2	3.5	3.3	4.0	4.0	5.3	3.4	5.3	28.8
	1994	17.1	1.5	3.4	28.3	29.4	6.7	8.6	5.0	82.9
Sri Lanka	1970	99.0	0.0	0.5	0.0	0.0	0.1	0.3	0.0	0.9
	1994	33.7	4.1	52.1	1.3	0.9	2.6	1.8	3.5	66.3
Thailand	1970	94.0	1.2	0.2	0.1	0.0	0.4	0.5	3.5	5.9
	1994	31.1	3.9	19.9	15.5	12.2	6.1	7.8	3.6	68.9
Western Samoa	1970	93.5	0.0	0.4	0.0	0.0	0.0	0.1	6.0	6.5
	1994	96.5	0.0	1.2	0.0	0.0	1.9	0.3	0.0	3.5

a. Data shown are for 1977, not available for 1970.
b. Data for the PRC for 1970 are not available.
c. Data shown are for 1971, not available for 1970.
Note: Primary exports include SITC (Revision 1) categories 001-265, 267-431, 611-3, 661-3, 671, and 68. Manufactures include SITC1 categories 266, 511-599, 621-9, 641-657, 664-6, 672-9, and 691-961.
Source: UN (1995).

Hong Kong, and Taipei,China. In the 1960s, direct foreign investment from Japan into Taipei,China's textile industry reinforced this trend. Since the 1970s the textile industry, especially its ready-made garments component, has moved progressively to East Asia, to Southeast Asia, and in more recent years to the PRC and Viet Nam. The search for cheaper labor by the textile producers and exporters drove these movements initially, but they received a substantial boost as a device to overcome quota restrictions imposed under the Multi-Fiber Arrangement.

More recently, an export common to the fastest growing Asian countries has been electronics products. Some countries, like Malaysia, started their export drive almost exclusively in electronics. Electrical machinery alone made up more than 20 percent of total exports in Korea, Malaysia, and Singapore between 1990 and 1994. In Hong Kong, Philippines, and Thailand the share was 15 percent. Electronics exports also grew rapidly in the PRC and Indonesia. In the Philippines, electronics exports expanded from near zero in the late 1980s to 40 percent of all exports in 1995.

Why are electronics exports so heavily concentrated in Asia? The seeds of Asia's electronics industry germinated in the late 1950s, when U.S. firms began searching for offshore production locations. Although Latin America and the Caribbean basin were an obvious choice, the region's political instability, inward orientation of many of the countries, and record of expropriation of foreign capital deterred U.S. firms. While many Asian economies were equally uninviting, there were exceptions. Hong Kong, in particular, proved to be an attractive location for U.S. firms. The Hong Kong economy was as open as any in the world and had a surfeit of low-wage workers. Perhaps most important, Hong Kong's status as a British territory provided some assurance of political stability, a relatively well-functioning legal system, and little risk of expropriation. No other developing country could compete with this environment. Thus in the late 1950s, U.S. semiconductor and other electronics firms looking for low-wage locations for product assembly established themselves in Hong Kong. The success of these firms led others to follow, first from the United States, and later from Europe and Japan. In this initial success, Hong Kong did not attempt to "pick winners." Rather, the winners picked Hong Kong!

This initial success encouraged other Asian economies to copy Hong Kong's approach. Korea, Malaysia, Singapore, and Taipei,China all tried to establish more open trading regimes—especially regimes of free trade for exporters—with an eye toward attracting electronics firms. They were extremely successful. Table 2.6 shows that in 1971, 17 of the world's 21 offshore electronics operations were located in East and Southeast Asia, and in 1974 the figure stood at 51 of 53 firms. Almost all the European, Japanese, and U.S. electronics firms that invested offshore in the early 1970s did so in Asia. While the number of electronics firms in Asia tripled between 1971 and 1974, the number of employees nearly quadrupled. Meanwhile, the four firms that were located in Mexico in 1971 had ceased operations there by 1974.

Table 2.7 suggests why electronics firms were so attracted to Asia. Statistics drawn from an early study of electronics firms (UNCTAD 1975) show the estimated costs of producing radio receivers for the European market in 1974. Asian firms could produce 1,000 receivers for $12,849, below the cost of European producers and far below the costs of African producers. Asia's advantage over Europe was its access to cheaper material (from Japan) and its lower wages. As a result, Asian firms could produce less expensively than European firms, even after paying 14 percent duty to sell the products in Europe. Two important differences become apparent when one compares Asian firms with the least

Table 2.6 Location of Offshore Operations of Major Electronics Component Manufacturing Firms, 1971 and 1974

Location	1971		1974	
	Number of firms	Number of employees	Number of firms	Number of employees
East and Southeast Asia	17	19,600	51	77,337
Singapore	10	7,300	12	22,400
Hong Kong	2	5,000	6	8,250
Korea	2	4,800	7	17,300
Taipei,China	3	2,500	3	5,500
Malaysia	0	0	18	17,387
Indonesia	0	0	3	2,500
Thailand	0	0	1	2,000
Philippines	0	0	1	2,000
Rest of the world	4	2,361	2	2,650
Mexico	4	2,361	0	0
El Salvador	0	0	1	1,800
Mauritius	0	0	1	850
World total	21	21,961	53	79,987

Source: UNCTAD (1975).

Table 2.7 Price Comparison for Annual Production of 1,000 Radio Receivers for the European Market, 1974
($ per 1,000 sets)

Cost item	Manufactured in Western Europe, source of material = Western Europe	Manufactured in Far East, source of material = Far East	Manufactured in Africa	
			Source of material = Western Europe	Source of material = Far East
Production				
Material	7,490	6,554	7,491	6,554
Handling, freight, insurance	375	562	1,423	1,498
Duties 20%	—	—	1,783	1,610
Cost of production, of which	3,552	1,831	2,151	2,119
Direct personnel	1,723	562	468	468
Indirect personnel	974	421	381	381
Expatriate personnel	—	187	262	262
Depreciation	252	104	159	159
Repair and maintenance	45	22	26	26
Utilities	22	7	7	7
Loss of material	39	43	75	68
General expenses	82	109	112	112
Interest	379	352	621	599
Insurance	35	23	39	37
Running-in expenses	562	562	562	562
Coverage for research and development	936	936	936	936
Ex-factory delivery price	12,915	10,446	14,346	13,279
Transport to European commercial stores				
Interest goods in transit	26	120	176	161
Handling, freight, insurance	388	818	839	828
Duties 14%	—	1,466	2,008	1,859
Price in European market	13,329	12,849	17,369	16,127

— = not applicable
Source: UNCTAD (1975).

expensive African firms (which purchase their materials in Asia). First, freight charges (including handling and insurance) for imported inputs were far lower for Asian firms, because they were located much closer to their source of materials. Second, African countries charged their firms an average of 20 percent in duties on the imported inputs, while Asian firms paid no duties. These costs more than offset Africa's advantage of lower wages. These two differences alone ensured that African firms could not compete in the European market.

Government Institutions and Exports

Success in manufactured exports depends on two elements of government policy: open trade (especially for exporters), and government institutions that help markets to work effectively. Many commentators have argued that one element or the other is the more important. The evidence suggests, however, that exporting success depends on a combination of the two.

The growth of manufactured exports in East and Southeast Asia during the past three decades cannot be reasonably portrayed as the product of generalized free and open markets throughout the region. Only Hong Kong, with perhaps the most open market in the world, can truly be classified as a laissez faire economy. Singapore is in many respects also a very open economy, but it still has significant state involvement and ownership. Without question, other Asian countries often strayed far from the neoclassical ideal of competitive free markets and limited government interventions. Korea and Taipei,China intervened in credit markets, as did most Southeast Asian countries. While average import tariff rates were lower than in most other parts of the developing world, they were still far from zero, and governments regularly used tariffs and quotas to protect favored industries.

Nonetheless, one common pattern exists across the region: the most successful Asian economies all established free and flexible markets for exporters. The common element between the open markets of Hong Kong and Singapore; the more interventionist governments of PRC, Korea, and Taipei,China; as well as the more state-centered, natural resource-abundant economies of Indonesia, Malaysia, and Thailand, was their orientation toward world markets and their overriding goal of expanding exports of manufactured goods.

To succeed, exporters must be free to sell in world markets. They must also have access to imported inputs unhindered by tariffs or quotas, because imported inputs typically constitute a significant proportion of production costs, except for the low-technology items. Labor-intensive manufactured exports, especially, tend to have a high import content, that for electronic goods, for example, reach as much as 85 percent of their export value. Under these circumstances, even an import tariff as low as 18 percent can effectively wipe out the potential profitability from such exports. Competition in world markets for manufactured products is so intense that even moderate barriers to trade can spell the difference between profitability and loss for exporting firms.

Asian countries have understood this better than other developing countries, and have kept their import tariffs relatively low (typically at zero) for the intermediate and capital goods exporters' use. They have also limited the use of quantitative restrictions on such imports. Table 2.8 shows average tariff rates on capital and intermediate goods,

Table 2.8 Tariff Rates and Quantitative Restrictions on Imported Capital Goods and Intermediate Goods, 1985

(percent)

Region/economy	Tariff rate	Share of imports covered by quantitative restrictions
World	17.0	19.0
East Asia	5.7	12.0
Hong Kong	0.0	0.0
Korea	13.7	1.0
Singapore	1.6	0.5
Taipei,China	7.3	37.5
PRC	25.4	29.1
Southeast Asia	18.5	16.7
Indonesia	13.7	10.1
Malaysia	8.7	4.5
Philippines	22.1	46.7
Thailand	29.4	5.5
South Asia	50.5	31.7
Bangladesh	40.9	49.7
India	132.0	88.8
Nepal	10.4	4.5
Pakistan	41.1	7.5
Sri Lanka	28.0	8.0
Papua New Guinea	10.6	0.2
Sub-Saharan Africa	22.5	20.5
Latin America	19.5	21.8
OECD	3.9	8.8

Source: Barro and Lee (1994).

as well as the share of imports of these goods covered by quantitative restrictions in 1985. The eight fastest growing economies charged an average tariff on these goods of 12.5 percent. Hong Kong's tariff was zero, and Singapore's was 1.6 percent. Only two of the fast growing economies—the PRC and Thailand—imposed tariffs greater than 14 percent. Even these figures overstate the actual tariffs charged to exporters, because almost all these countries provided facilities under which exporters could receive capital goods and imported inputs duty free. In contrast, the tariff on imported capital and intermediate goods averaged 51 percent in South Asia, 23 percent in sub-Saharan Africa, and 20 percent in Latin America.

Other elements of open and flexible markets for exporters were just as important. For example, the successful Asian exporters generally allowed firms free entry into and exit out of export manufacturing activities, which helped to ensure that the most productive and efficient firms would succeed. Governments maintained prudent exchange rate policies and avoided costly overvaluations that could have rendered exports unprofitable. They established relatively flexible labor markets (albeit sometimes with heavy-handed interventions against organized labor) in which the market determined wages, and in which firms were able to hire and fire workers when conditions warranted. Asian governments also generally imposed relatively low taxes, especially for exporters. All these factors reduced costs, lowered risks, and enhanced exporting firms' competitiveness on world markets.

Export Facilitation

The process of establishing free markets for exporters was far from automatic. Asian governments had to play an active role in encouraging and supporting exporters. Many factor and product markets were (and still are) highly distorted as a result of trade quotas, high and uneven average tariff rates, administratively determined prices on domestic markets, and controlled credit markets. In purely theoretical terms, the best way to address these distortions would have been for governments to attack them directly by removing price and quantity controls and reducing tariff rates. Hong Kong and Singapore basically followed this prescription with their extremely open trade regimes. For a variety of reasons, however, most other Asian governments either could not or would not remove these distortions directly. In some countries, this reluctance came from initial apprehension about the wisdom of an export-led strategy; in others, it was driven by the desire to protect vested economic and political interests.

As a second-best solution, governments in East and Southeast Asia created several innovative programs and institutions to provide the means by which firms could become competitive exporters. The range of facilities included subsidized credit, tax breaks, EPZs, bonded manufacturing warehouses, duty drawback programs, privatization of customs administration, and direct export subsidies. A common element in each country was at least one facility that allowed exporters access to reduced or zero duties on capital and intermediate goods imports. Most countries introduced more than one facility or program to support exporters. Three of these facilities were particularly important in several Asian countries: EPZs, bonded manufacturing warehouses, and duty drawback systems.

EPZs are special industrial areas located physically or administratively outside a country's customs barrier and designed for firms producing manufactured export products. Imports by firms located inside EPZs are not subject to duties or other restrictions. EPZs normally provide firms with higher quality infrastructure compared with that available outside the zone. They are normally situated within easy access of ports and other industrial facilities, so that firms are subjected to fewer administrative delays in receiving imports and shipping exports. EPZs have had a mixed record in other parts of the world, but they generally have been quite successful in Asia. In Malaysia, for example, exports from EPZs accounted for 74 percent of total exports of manufactured goods in 1980, and in 1990 EPZ exports still accounted for 57 percent of the total (Sivalingam 1994).

Bonded manufacturing warehouses are essentially single-factory EPZs designed for larger firms producing exclusively for export markets. Approved warehouses, with a customs officer stationed at the site, can receive duty free imports of capital and intermediate goods and bypass other customs procedures. Firms post a bond as a guarantee against any duties that might be applicable to imports that are diverted to the domestic market.

Duty drawback (or exemption) systems are a broader method of assisting exporters. Exporting firms, regardless of where they are located, pay duties on imported inputs, but these duties are reimbursed when the final product is exported. In some cases, firms with a strong history of compliance are exempted from paying duties on imported inputs as long as they continue to provide proof of exports. The main advantage of a duty drawback system is that a firm can choose its location, rather than being confined to a predetermined geographical area. This allows the firm greater flexibility in its operations, helps encourage links with the rest of the economy, and saves the government the cost of establishing a special zone. However, duty drawback mechanisms can be difficult to administer, and sometimes the system has been abused, for example, when duty free imports leak to the domestic market. Despite these difficulties, Indonesia, Korea, Malaysia, and Singapore have successfully used well-designed duty drawback programs.

East and Southeast Asian countries have used a combination of specific facilities to support exporters. Korea provides a good example. Korea had high and uneven tariff rates on imports in the 1960s and 1970s, and continues to do so today, especially for agricultural products. However, early in its postwar development process, the Korean government ensured that these distortions did not affect export competitiveness by establishing a complex system of export subsidies, cheap credit, and access to controlled imports. From the early 1960s, exporters could import raw materials and capital goods duty free. In the early 1970s the government complemented these facilities by opening two large EPZs. In addition, by 1981, exporters were operating more than 200 bonded warehouses. Exports from EPZs and bonded warehouses accounted for 15 percent of total Korean exports in 1981 (Rhee 1994). Exporters located outside the zones used duty exemption and drawback facilities. The Korean system also provided access to duty free imports to indirect exporters (domestic firms that do not export directly, but sell all their output to exporting firms). This helped to deepen the backward linkages of exporting firms by allowing indirect exporters to compete more readily with international suppliers.

In Taipei,China the shift toward export promotion began in earnest in 1957, when the government started offering subsidized credit to firms that were attempting to penetrate export markets. In 1959 the government unified the exchange rate, shifting incentives markedly away from import substitutes and toward exports. It also began to reduce tariffs and relax controls on imports of capital and intermediate goods used by exporters. In 1966 the government established the Kaoshing EPZ, the world's first EPZ for manufacturing, and opened two other EPZs in the early 1970s. In addition, by 1981 Taipei,China had well over 300 bonded manufacturing warehouses. Together, exports from the EPZs and warehouses accounted for more than 20 percent of total exports in 1981 (Rhee 1994). Almost all other exporters took advantage of a well-functioning duty drawback system.

Indonesia used a three-pronged approach to support exporters when it began its deregulation program in the mid-1980s. First, a wide range of tariff cuts reduced the cost of imported inputs for all domestic producers, including exporters. Second, the government introduced a successful duty drawback system that was widely used by many manufactured exporters. Third, when weak customs administration threatened the export promotion strategy and undermined the government's revenue collection efforts, the government effectively privatized customs administration by hiring a private firm to take over responsibility for many of the functions of the customs authorities.

Although EPZs, bonded manufacturing warehouses, duty drawback systems and other facilities are only second-best solutions to removing trade distortions, they have played an important role in accelerating the process toward openness to free trade in Asia. In each of the countries where these facilities were most successful, governments have subsequently introduced more broadly based tariff and quota reform. Although the link from successful EPZs and drawback facilities to trade reform is impossible to prove, at least three indications suggest that this pattern is more than a coincidence. First, successful EPZs and drawback systems demonstrated that exports can be profitable, reassuring those who doubted the potential for developing countries to successfully compete in global markets for manufacturers. Second, these systems created a political interest group that supported exports. Third, some duty free imports intended for use in EPZs and drawback systems inevitably leaked to the domestic market, undermining the high tariff walls protecting inward-oriented industries. A tempting speculation is that as the effective levels of tariffs are eroded, it eventually becomes easier for governments to lower the actual tariff rates. In any case, EPZs, bonded manufacturing warehouses, and duty drawback systems have become less important over time in countries that have eventually undertaken broader trade liberalization.

Industry Policy

Not all forms of government intervention in Asia contributed to the success of exports and growth. Although some scholars have argued that the promotion of heavy industry through industrial policies was critical to rapid growth of East Asian economies (Amsden 1989; Wade 1990), careful international comparison does not fully support this view. Three of the most successful economies in East Asia—Japan, Korea, and Taipei,China—certainly intervened heavily to promote specific industries. Singapore also did so, albeit to a much lesser extent.

Effective rates of protection in Korea, while moderate on average, were highly dispersed, and an elaborate web of trade associations had informal, but effectively exclusive, rights to import certain goods (Luedde-Neurath 1988). Taipei,China applied restrictions to more than half of its imports as recently as 1984 (Wade 1990). In financial markets, Korea controlled both the allocation of credit and the interest rate through its state-owned banking system. The largest conglomerates, or *chaebol*, had access to subsidized credit, while smaller firms were forced to borrow in informal markets at much higher rates (Roemer 1994). The government leaned heavily on the *chaebol* to meet export targets, and during the 1970s pressured them to invest in infant heavy industries. Taipei,China also directed credit toward favored industries, although the government used subsidized credit less extensively. Credit markets did not fully clear, and many small firms, by contrast, had to borrow in informal markets.

Were these policies at the core of Korea and Taipei,China's success? Did they give these countries an extra push that would not have been possible otherwise? Some of the favored industries were clear success stories. Advocates of strong industrial policies, for example, point to the accomplishments of Korea's Pohang Iron and Steel and Hyundai Motor Company, but Korean industrial policy also had its failures, such as Korean Heavy Industries and Okpo Shipbuilding (Stern and others 1995).

Many of the best-known studies of industrial policies in Korea and Taipei,China focus heavily on specific case studies of the successes, but pay far less attention to the costs of the failures. To evaluate the impacts of interventionist industrial policies the appropriate measure is the net effect of both success and failures (Perkins 1994). Studies that have looked at cases of both success and failures have cast doubt on the overall effectiveness of the interventionist strategies (Smith 1995; Stern and others 1995). Once one considers the full range of impacts, whether Korea and

Taipei,China would have done better or worse in the absence of these interventions is not clear.

Perhaps more important, this strategy clearly was not central to the success of Hong Kong, Indonesia, Malaysia, Singapore, and Thailand. State intervention in industrial policy was minimal in Hong Kong. Singapore's strategy has been close to the free market approach, albeit with several important and successful state-owned enterprises and selected interventions in support of high technology. In Indonesia, Malaysia, and Thailand, governments ruled the markets with a much heavier hand, and not always in support of export markets. Sometimes, policymakers designed interventions to provide economic favors for important individuals, families, and firms in return for political support, and these interventions have failed to support broader development objectives (Hill 1996; Roemer 1994). Efforts to promote heavy industry in South Asia have been equally unsuccessful. In short, while the promotion of heavy industry may have been beneficial in some cases, it was not the common denominator that accounts for the rapid growth across almost all the countries of East and Southeast Asia. Instead, that denominator was manufactured exports.

Despite analysts' divergent views about the effectiveness of industrial interventions in East Asia, they appear to agree on a number of points (Roemer 1994). First, government trade and industrial policies should be geared toward removing existing biases against exports and ensuring the competitiveness of exporters. Amsden (1989) argues that a critical aspect of Korean industrial policy was that export targets were "an objective, transparent criterion by which firm performance is easily judged."

Second, government policies may be effective in pushing the pace of change in comparative advantage, but they will not be effective if they stray too far from the basic direction of market forces. Korea's heavy and chemical industry drive and Singapore's attempt to move quickly into high-wage exports are two examples of the problems that can arise when governments try to force the pace of change too far.

Third, government interventions of the type employed in Korea and Taipei,China could only succeed in countries with an effective and disciplined civil service, thus the potential for replicability to other countries is limited, as indicated by the failure of these types of policies in most countries that have tried to adopt them.

Fourth, Korea and Taipei,China's example is probably not relevant in today's international trading environment. When these two countries employed interventionist strategies, few competitor countries paid close attention. However, with the establishment of the World Trade Organization (WTO) and the associated agreements reached in the Uruguay Round of the General Agreement on Tariffs and Trade, developing country governments today would be much more circumscribed in their ability to use such policies as subsidized and directed credit for exporters.

Agricultural Development and Growth

East and Southeast Asia's economic success was not confined to manufactured exports. Agricultural growth was also unusually high compared with other developing countries.[5] In both Korea and Taipei,China, for instance, agricultural production grew by an average of 4.1 percent per year between 1960 and 1975, the period when aggregate economic growth began to accelerate. In the PRC, Indonesia, Malaysia, and Thailand agricultural growth averaged 4.2 percent per year between 1970 and 1990. In contrast, agricultural growth averaged just 2.7 percent per year in Bangladesh, India, Pakistan, Philippines, and Sri Lanka during the same period. In Latin America and sub-Saharan Africa, agriculture grew by an average of 2.8 percent per year and 1.7 percent per year, respectively, between 1970 and 1990.

While in all these cases the agricultural sector grew less rapidly than overall GDP, it provided an important initial underpinning to rapid economic growth throughout East and Southeast Asia (Goldman 1997). East Asia's superior agricultural growth had several positive consequences: rural poverty was sharply reduced; and rising agricultural incomes improved the health, longevity, and productivity of the rural poor. In the early 1960s per person caloric intake was below minimum nutritional standards in all Asian economies except Hong Kong, Malaysia, and Singapore, but by 1990, only one Asian country, Bangladesh, remained seriously below the standard. In most Asian countries, increases in domestic food production, rather than imports, account for the bulk of the improvement. Higher rural incomes also made it much easier for the rural poor to invest in more education, and thereby to enter the nonagricultural economy. Productivity improvements released labor to

---

5. Hong Kong and Singapore are excluded from the discussion about agriculture, because the agriculture sectors in both economies are tiny.

work in nonfarm employment. In urban areas, reduced food prices helped increase the value of real incomes. Strong agricultural production helped stabilize prices, which enhanced both economic and political stability. Thus agriculture provided an important foundation for the transition to modern, industrial societies.

Asia's relatively strong performance in agriculture during the last three decades is due largely to appropriate government policies. Several Asian governments, on the whole, supported agriculture, while other governments, though not overly supportive, did far less damage to their agriculture sectors than did governments in other developing regions. Green revolution breakthroughs, mainly in wheat and rice production, were the result of public investments and management reforms in national agricultural research systems and public support for cooperative arrangements with key international agricultural institutes. The initial introduction of high-yielding varieties often simply involved a transfer of technology from international centers, but this was followed by adaptive research and extension activities organized nationally that were vital for deepening and sustaining the green revolution process. In addition, investments in irrigation and other rural infrastructure (both public and private) in South and much of Southeast Asia were critical to the historically rapid growth rates in food production, as were the trade, commercial, and industrial policy reforms that resulted in less expensive and more efficient fertilizer use.

While some countries, such as Indonesia, provided net subsidies to their agricultural sectors, several others imposed net taxes. Korea, Pakistan, Taipei,China, and Thailand all taxed agricultural exports as a way of transferring some resources to their growing urban industrial sectors. However, the tax burden in these countries was never large enough to undermine agricultural growth, and cost-reducing technological innovations and publicly supported irrigation compensated somewhat for the negative effects. As capacity became fully used and farmers faced diminishing returns, however, the disincentive price policy effects began to dominate. Other countries, such as India, taxed agriculture indirectly by following policies that kept agricultural output prices below their world levels.

Agriculture's share in total output will fall substantially during the next three decades, and thus its impact on income and welfare will be reduced. Nevertheless, agriculture will continue to play a vital role, especially in South Asia, in the transitional economies of Central Asia and Indochina, in the rapidly growing countries of Southeast Asia, and in the PRC. In all these countries, the influence of agricultural growth on rural incomes and food availability will continue to have substantial impacts on rural poverty. In Bangladesh and India, agriculture still accounts for more than a quarter of GDP, and its performance will strongly affect overall economic growth. A key determinant of future agricultural growth in Asia will be increased funds and management resources for agricultural research.

Saving and Growth

Another critical area in which Asian countries have differed from other developing countries is saving. Saving rates in Asia were not unusually high 30 years ago, but they have risen substantially and are now among the highest in the world. Between 1965 and 1969, national saving as a share of GNP averaged 19.7 percent in East Asia, 17 percent in Southeast Asia, and 9.5 percent in South Asia, compared with 16.2 percent in Latin America. However, these simple averages disguise substantial differences across economies. In Hong Kong, for example, the saving rate averaged 25 percent, even during this early period, and PRC, Malaysia, Taipei,China, and Thailand all recorded saving rates greater than 20 percent. In contrast, Singapore saved only 13 percent of GNP in 1965 and Korea saved just 9 percent. India recorded the highest rate in South Asia at 14 percent, with Nepal reaching just 3 percent.

These patterns began to change during the 1970s, when national saving rates rose across East and Southeast Asia, as well as in the PRC. Between 1970 and 1979, national saving rates rose above 20 percent throughout East and Southeast Asia and exceeded 27 percent in PRC, Hong Kong, Malaysia, Singapore, and Taipei,China. The spectacular rise in saving rates in Singapore—from 13 percent in 1965, to 30 percent in 1975, and more than 40 percent in 1982 and each year thereafter—is especially noteworthy. Similarly, Indonesia's saving rate jumped from 5 percent during the political and economic chaos of the mid-1960s to 25 percent in 1976. Only in Hong Kong did saving rates not rise substantially—they simply maintained their previous high rates of 25 to 30 percent.

In South Asia, India's saving rate climbed steadily to 19 percent during the 1970s, Sri Lanka's grew slightly to 13 percent, and Nepal's reached

8 percent. However, in all the other South Asian countries, saving rates stagnated or fell, and averaged just 10 percent across the region. Nevertheless, statistical analysis suggests that by 1990 saving rates for all of developing Asia were about 8 percentage points higher than the average for the rest of the world, once differences in income, population, and other structural characteristics are taken into account.

High national saving rates in Asia are due to higher rates of both government and private sector saving. Government saving is defined as the surplus on the government's current revenue and expenditures, which means that it excludes government investment expenditures and capital revenues. Ideally, all state and local governments, as well as all public sector enterprises, should be included in this definition. Unfortunately, comparable statistics across countries are not available on this basis, so the following analysis concentrates on central government saving.

Central government saving rates have been especially high in Indonesia and Singapore, averaging between 9 and 11 percent of GNP. Taipei,China's government saved nearly as much, on average, between 5 and 7 percent of GNP. In Malaysia and Thailand, government saving reached 6 to 7 percent of GNP in the early 1990s. All the other countries in East and Southeast Asia consistently maintained government surpluses of between 1 and 3 percent of GNP. In contrast, government saving rates were close to zero, or even negative, for all the South Asian countries.

Private sector saving in Asia have generally followed the same basic patterns as national saving, with smaller differences across regions. India's private saving rate, for example, has hovered around 20 percent of GNP since the 1970s, and rose to an average of 22 percent between 1990 and 1993. This latter rate is higher than in the Philippines during this period, and comparable with that in Indonesia. Pakistan's private saving rate has been above 15 percent since 1983. On the whole, private saving rates across Asia have exceeded those in Latin America, and been more than double the average rate recorded in sub-Saharan Africa.

Why have national saving rates in Asia exceeded those in other developing countries, and why have they increased so rapidly since the 1960s? How are Asian saving rates likely to change during the next 30 years? The determinants of saving are not fully understood, but four broad groups of variables appear to play an important role: demographic factors (including dependency ratios and life expectancy), government policies (broadly including central government saving, credit to the public sector, social security expenditures, and inflation), economic growth, and financial sector development (Table 2.9).

Can these variables account for the high and rising saving rates in Asia? The analysis that follows suggests that they can. Table 2.10 shows the results of a statistical examination of the relationship between these variables and national saving rates for a group of 75 countries between 1970 and 1992. Details of this analysis can be found in Radelet, Sachs, and Lee (1996).

Table 2.9 Summary of Saving Variables by Region, 1970-92

Saving variable	All countries	East and Southeast Asia	South Asia	Sub-Saharan Africa	Latin America	OECD
Saving rates (percentage of GNP)						
Private	14.9	20.9	14.5	7.5	14.9	22.5
National	16.9	24.9	12.8	9.9	16.0	23.0
Demographic factors						
Young-age dependency ratio (percent)	65.3	63.7	70.9	85.7	72.4	34.7
Life expectancy (log years)	4.1	4.1	4.1	3.9	4.2	4.3
Government policies						
Central government saving (percentage of GNP)	2.5	4.3	0.8	3.7	1.0	0.0
Government social security expenditure (percentage of GNP)	4.9	1.0	2.1	0.8	3.8	12.4
Credit to the public sector (percentage of GDP)	15.4	1.7	23.3	11.8	15.6	18.1
Inflation rate (percent)	57.4	8.2	10.8	20.7	196.2	8.2
Economic growth						
Growth in per person income (lagged percentage)	2.1	4.1	1.8	1.0	1.1	2.7
Financial sector development						
Money supply (M2) (percentage of GDP)	46.1	55.1	35.1	26.8	33.7	70.6

Note: Values are unweighted averages from five-year averages panel.
Source: Radelet, Sachs, and Lee (1996).

Table 2.10 Determinants of National Saving: Results of Random-Effects Generalized Least Squares Regression

Independent variable	Coefficient	
	I	II
Young-age dependency	-19.39	-18.80
	(-4.36)	(-3.93)
Life expectancy	1.82	1.60
	(3.24)	(2.66)
Life expectancy (squared)	-0.01	-0.01
	(-2.63)	(-2.25)
Lagged growth rate	0.35	0.31
	(3.33)	(2.99)
Central government saving	0.59	0.59
	(6.51)	(6.51)
Social security expenditure	-0.42	-0.45
	(-3.40)	(-3.22)
Credit to the public sector	-0.82	-1.88
	(-3.44)	(-3.14)
Threshhold inflation	-1.99	-1.88
	(-2.35)	(-2.13)
Money supply	0.05	0.04
	(2.25)	(1.90)
East Asia		0.39
		(0.18)
South Asia		-3.97
		(-1.57)
Sub-Saharan Africa		-3.39
		(-1.49)
Latin America		-1.34
		(-0.71)
Constant	-30.70	-20.60
	(-2.10)	(-1.27)
R^2	0.64	0.65
Number of observations	285	285
Number of countries	75	75

Note: t-statistics in parentheses. R^2 is the percentage of the variation in the dependent variable explained by the independent variables. Column I shows results from the model which excludes regional variables in the regression.

Demography

Most research has found that saving rates increase along with the relative size of the working-age population (Chapter 3). Workers earn more than they spend, which generates most of an economy's savings. Children who have not reached working age (birth to 14 years of age) do not generate saving, and instead consume out of their parents' earnings. Similarly, those of retirement age (65 and over) tend to earn less and consume out of their accumulated savings.

The demographic composition of the countries of East and Southeast Asia has clearly been an important factor in their relatively high saving rates. The statistical analysis shows a strong, negative relationship between the share of the young dependent population and the saving rate. In the 1970s and 1980s, East and Southeast Asia had relatively fewer young people than other parts of the world (64 percent, compared with 70 percent in South Asia, 72 percent in Latin America, and 87 percent in sub-Saharan Africa). Each working-age individual in East and Southeast Asia had fewer young dependents to care for than workers in other regions, which allowed them to save more of their incomes.

Life expectancy is another powerful determinant of saving. Low life expectancies tend to indicate high rates of infant mortality, widespread disease, and short time horizons, and saving tends to be quite low. Rising life expectancies are associated with higher personal saving rates, but once life expectancy reaches 68 years, further increases are strongly associated with lower saving. At this stage, higher life expectancy indicates the presence of a larger population of retirement age and that retirees are living longer. Because retirees are consuming out of their lifelong savings, national saving declines.

As Chapter 3, which discusses this issue in greater depth, points out, these demographic characteristics are likely to change dramatically in the next 30 years, with corresponding impacts on saving. Populations in East Asia are aging, and the rising share of the population reaching retirement age in East Asia in the coming decades will dampen further increases in saving. In South Asia, demographic change is more likely to work in the opposite direction. A shrinking population of young people is likely to outweigh a slowly growing retired population, giving a positive impetus to saving rates.

Government Policies

Government policies can influence national saving, both directly through the rate of government saving, and indirectly through the government's retirement pension system. Some recent studies (Edwards 1995; Masson, Bayoumi, and Samiei 1995) have found that an increase in government saving of 1 percent of GNP is associated with a decline in private saving of much less than a percentage point of GNP.

The analysis in this study suggests that an increase in government saving of 1 percentage point in GNP raises total saving by 0.6 percent of GNP. East and Southeast Asia's fiscal prudence has therefore been an important factor in the region's high saving rate, because they recorded much higher rates of government saving than other regions of the world. Government saving rates in East and Southeast Asia were about 4 percentage points higher than in the industrial countries between 1970 and 1992, which explains about 2.5 percentage points of the differences in saving rates between the regions.

Available information on government saving is limited to central governments—few countries regularly report data on provincial and local governments or state-owned enterprises. To incorporate the effect of these entities on national saving, this study examined the relationship between national saving and outstanding credit from the banking system to the entire public sector. The analysis found a strong negative relationship, which suggests that larger public sector borrowing and losses by state-owned enterprises (at least to the extent the banking system finances them) are associated with lower national saving.

Government policies will also affect the saving rate to the extent that they influence the inflation rate. Inflation erodes real returns on financial assets, thereby undermining incentives to save. Perhaps more important, high rates of inflation (20 percent or more) are indicative of wider macroeconomic stability, which can lead to capital flight and lower national saving.

The size and nature of government pension programs can also influence saving. Many economists (for example, Feldstein 1980) have argued that pay-as-you-go pension programs are likely to imply lower overall rates of private saving, as households rely on future government transfers rather than on their own saving for retirement purposes. Unfunded social security programs can also reduce government saving. The analysis confirms this view. The size of the government's social security (pensions) program has a highly significant negative impact on saving. A 1 percentage point increase in the share of social security spending in GNP is associated with a fall in the rate of national saving of 0.73 percentage point.

Between 1970 and 1992, social security expenditures in East and Southeast Asia averaged just 1 percent of GNP, compared with 2.1 percent in South Asia and 3.8 percent in Latin America. Thus if Asian countries were to rely more on Western-style pension programs in the future—and Korea appears to be moving in this direction—their saving rates might decrease more than they would otherwise. Note, however, that individualized pension schemes, such as the provident fund systems of Malaysia and Singapore, would not reduce private saving, as households remain responsible for saving for their own retirement. (Chapter 3 discusses the advantages and disadvantages of pension schemes in more detail.)

Economic Growth and Saving

The relationship between economic growth and saving works in two ways. Higher saving raises growth, but faster growth also tends to raise saving rates. In a fast growing economy, increased saving from the working-age population is likely to outweigh the dissaving of the non-working population. Another possibility, however, is that economic growth could also lead to lower saving. If individuals expect their income to continue to grow during their lifetime, they may adjust their current consumption upward, thereby reducing saving rates. Most research (Carrol and Weil 1993) has found a positive relationship between income growth and saving rates, but the evidence is not overwhelming.

The possible two-way relationship between economic growth and saving creates difficulties in interpreting statistical results if both current saving and current growth are included in the analysis. To avoid this problem, this analysis also examined the relationship between the average growth rate of the previous five years and current saving. The results show a strong relationship between lagged growth and saving: for each 1 percentage point increase in the growth rate, the saving rate increases by about one third of a percentage point of GDP.

Financial Sector Development

The development of financial systems is also likely to affect saving. In countries with rudimentary banking systems or artificially controlled interest rates, the incentive to save is lower. In contrast, countries with well-functioning and profitable banking systems, active and efficient stock and bond markets, and well-developed insurance systems offer individuals and businesses a wider array of remunerative mechanisms by which to save.

In practice, the relationship between saving and financial market development is difficult to capture, not only because finding a good measure of financial market depth for many countries is difficult, but also because higher saving might itself promote deeper financial markets. A crude measure of financial depth—the ratio of broad money (M2) to GDP—is positively associated with higher saving.

Governance, Leadership, and Economic Management

There is little question that governments in East and Southeast Asia have successfully managed their economies during the course of several difficult decades (Stiglitz 1996). These governments have maintained low inflation rates, even when inflation skyrocketed elsewhere in the world, and kept budgets roughly in balance. Policymakers deftly managed exchange rates, by-and-large avoiding major overvaluations and moving quickly to restore stability when imbalances arose. With the exceptions of Indonesia, Korea, and Philippines, governments did not rely heavily on foreign borrowing, and only in the Philippines did foreign debt service become a problem. Macroeconomic management was especially challenging for the resource-rich countries of Southeast Asia, which had to maintain stability through several commodity boom and bust cycles. Less obvious, however, is how these governments have managed their economies so successfully. What sets these governments apart? Why have they been better able than other governments to promote macroeconomic stability and long-term development?

The reasons are not fully understood, but several factors appear to have made a difference. To begin with, sustained political stability in most of these countries enabled governments to be consistent in their approach and to implement longer term strategies (Lindauer and Roemer 1994). Almost all the successful Asian economies had stable political leadership, with few changes in heads of state and little shift in underlying economic direction. Thailand's frequent changes in political regime make it an exception, but even there, economic policymakers remained in their positions even when the political leadership changed, providing continuity to economic policy. However, stable political leadership is far from sufficient for sustained economic development. The Democratic People's Republic of Korea, Myanmar, and several other countries in Asia, as well as many countries in sub-Saharan Africa, with long-lived governments have had poor economic performance.

To a large degree, one can differentiate between Asia's successful governments and other long-standing governments by their ideas about development strategy. Governments must have an approach for economic management and development that can be implemented and that will ultimately succeed in achieving sustained economic growth. During the past several decades, many, perhaps well-meaning, governments followed misguided development paradigms: extensive central planning with nonmarket allocation (in Eastern Europe and the former Soviet Union, for instance), long-term and widespread import substitution (throughout Latin America), or the extraction of resources from the agriculture sector to support urban industry (in many countries of sub-Saharan Africa). Numerous countries withdrew at least partially, if not wholly, from the world trading system in an attempt to develop more self-sufficient production systems.

In Asia, these ideas were manifested in their most extreme form in the communist regimes of the PRC until 1978; in the Central Asian republics; in the Democratic People's Republic of Korea; and later in Cambodia, Lao People's Democratic Republic, and Viet Nam. In South Asia, although ideas about the state's role in the development process were far less extreme, they had a profound impact on government strategy and policy choices. India, after its independence in 1947, followed the Fabian socialist ideals of its leaders to a planned and regulated economy. Other countries in the subregion broadly followed India's lead. Market pessimism was also influential in East Asia in the 1950s, as exemplified by Korea's and Taipei,China's early import substitution strategy.

By the early 1960s, however, Japan's success with a more outward-oriented strategy based on labor-intensive exports began to exert a strong influence on East Asian ideas about development strategy. Governments in Hong Kong, Korea, Taipei,China, and later Singapore all faced small domestic markets and were wary of the centrally planned, nonmarket approach the PRC advocated. They could not help but notice Japan's success based on manufactured exports. Exports became even more appealing when U.S. foreign aid began to dry up in Korea and Taipei,China in the early 1960s. Moreover, for strategic reasons the United States took special measures to ensure market access to East Asian exporters. In addition, East Asia's leaders were strongly committed to their strategy of stimulating exports and supporting rapid economic growth.

Various analysts have argued that economic policymakers and government leaders in some East Asian countries may have put an unusually high premium on rapid economic growth, because they saw it as essential to the survival of their regimes (Perkins and Roemer 1994). In the 1950s and early 1960s, many observers questioned whether such small and unstable economies as Korea, Singapore, and Taipei,China could survive in the face of external threats. Failure to grow rapidly and distribute the gains relatively equitably might have doomed the existence of these governments, or even of these nations. National survival was less of an issue in Southeast Asia, but leaders nevertheless seemed to understand that political legitimacy and stability depended in part on a well-managed and growing economy, and in some cases, on improving the welfare of the rural poor.

To implement their development strategies, the successful Asian economies consistently placed well-trained, able economic technicians in charge of macroeconomic management. In at least some of the more successful countries, a competent civil service aided policy implementation. Korea upgraded the quality of economic analysis available to its policymakers by establishing the Korea Development Institute in 1971, which could attract well-qualified technicians without directly hiring them into the civil service. Civil servants were generally well paid, both to enable the government to attract top talent and to diminish the incentives for corruption. However, civil service performance still lags in some countries.

Some governments also backed their commitment to long-term growth by providing strategic direction and support for technological development. With active participation by the private sector, governments forged long-term goals for economic development that were often expressed in terms of a vision of the desired social and economic order and included targets of annual growth rates to be achieved over the long term. These exercises helped build a broad consensus on major policy initiatives. A number of institutions and forums in which public sector agencies engaged in dialogue and information sharing with the private sector and with the research and scientific communities fostered active participation. These mechanisms deepened governments' understanding of the practicalities of policymaking and strengthened their implementation capacity.

East Asia's Distinctiveness: Does the PRC Fit?

This study argues that market competition, openness, and export orientation were indispensable ingredients of East Asia's rapid growth and were key determinants of East Asia's distinctiveness. But if this is the case, then the PRC's experience since the onset of market reforms in 1978 cries out for explanation. How has a country that is still pursuing a socialist model, albeit one with "Chinese characteristics," achieved such rapid growth? Unlike the other East Asian economies, the PRC has retained a major role for the state in guiding investment, and the state still owns many enterprises. Is the PRC an exceptional case in East Asia, or is it an exception that proves the rule?

In reality, it is both. While the PRC has protected its large, state-owned industrial sector, the source of dynamic growth in the PRC lies in its nonstate sector, which has operated much closer to market forces (Gang, Perkins, and Sabin 1996). Indeed, outside the state enterprise sector, the PRC's economy has much in common with the other East Asian economies, especially when those other economies were at an earlier stage of development. While the nonstate PRC economy operates without many of the legal underpinnings of a more advanced market economy, the nonstate sector is subject to the strong market competition, international trade, and low taxation that are the hallmarks of the fast growing market economies of East Asia.

The key to understanding the PRC's economic success lies in an appreciation of the limited role of the state-owned sector. The nonstate sector now accounts for more than half of industrial output, two thirds of GDP, and 80 percent of jobs (including farm employment). The PRC's "gradual" reforms after 1978 have involved liberalizing the nonstate part of the economy while preserving the socialistic character of state-owned enterprises.

Considerable evidence confirms that the PRC's nonstate sector, rather than its state sector has been the source of the country's dynamism. First, despite more than ten years of active experimentation by the government with alternative incentive schemes for management and workers, the state-owned sector has continued to incur large losses. Second, productivity growth in the state-owned sector has lagged far behind productivity growth in the nonstate sector. Third, the nonstate sector accounts for the explosive rise of the PRC's manufacturing exports. For example, the share of small-scale, rural enterprises (the so-called township and village enterprises) in total exports grew from 16 percent in 1980 to around 44 percent in 1993.

Special economic zones, coastal open cities, and economic and technological development zones, all designed to encourage manufacturing exports, have also contributed another large share of exports. These special areas have received various kinds of favorable tax and regulatory treatment, such as tax holidays and duty free access to imported inputs and capital goods needed for export production. The special economic zones and other special areas are akin to the EPZs other Asian countries used as part of their initial export-led growth. Fourth, overall GDP growth has been much faster in regions with a high proportion of employment in nonstate enterprises (Xiao 1991) and in the special economic zones (Wei 1995).

An important aspect of the PRC's dynamism is the low rate of taxation of nonstate enterprises. As already noted, many nonstate enterprises are almost completely exempt from taxation, at least in their first few years of operation, because of tax privileges associated with special economic zones.

The PRC's labor markets are also highly flexible in the nonstate sector. While workers in the state sector are accorded generous job guarantees, workers in the nonstate sector do not receive guaranteed employment. One result has been the rapid growth of employment in the PRC, as firms can hire workers without fear of being stuck with unwanted labor in the future because of restrictions on dismissals. Formal sector employment increased dramatically, from 95 million people in 1978 (9.7 percent of the economically active population) to 148.5 million in 1994 (19.2 percent of the economically active population). Most of the rest of the labor force is still engaged in peasant agriculture. The dynamic growth of formal sector employment has not been without social cost. The PRC has a "floating population," estimated to exceed 100 million people, made up of mostly rural immigrants, who take whatever jobs are available.

In short, the PRC is the outlier that proves the importance of East Asian policies. Economic growth has been export-led, generated by firms operating in an environment conducive to exporters.

Nonetheless, the PRC continues to face a serious need for market reforms. The state enterprise sector is running up large losses, and therefore poses a chronic threat to macroeconomic stability. The agricultural sector is also lagging in growth, partly because of the absence of secure private property rights in landholdings. The leasehold system in peasant agriculture was a vast improvement over the commune system, but it is still a far cry from private landownership. Recent evidence suggests that farmers are indeed reluctant to invest in land improvements, because of the unreliability of their claims to their farmland. Overall, much remains to be done to ensure that the PRC maintains its growth rates.

The Future

What are Asia's future growth prospects? Is East and Southeast Asia's growth performance sustainable or replicable? For Asia's 3 billion inhabitants, few questions are more fundamental. For the global economy overall, much will depend on future patterns of growth in Asia.

The overall picture that emerges from the analysis in this study is an optimistic one. East Asia's growth rates are largely the result of economic catch-up, catalyzed by open, export-oriented economic policies and boosted by demographic trends. As the richer countries in East Asia catch up with the income levels in the advanced industrial economies, so their growth rates are likely to fall over time. They will not, however, fall precipitously or suddenly. Most of Asia, however, still has much catching up left to do. South Asia, in particular, has great potential with the right kind of economic reforms. Not only is it still relatively poorer, but it also has favorable demographic trends to come.

The remainder of this chapter takes a more detailed look at the future. First, it analyzes two common arguments against the sustainability of Asian growth: that it is based on flawed foundations, just as the former Soviet Union's growth was; and that manufactured exports cannot continue to form a central tenet of growth strategy for all countries in Asia.

Then the analysis looks forward. Based on the cross-country analysis developed earlier, the chapter makes some tentative projections about Asia's future and looks at the attendant risks.

Is East Asia's Growth Sustainable?

Krugman (1994) recently began a lively debate about East Asia's future by implying that the region was following a flawed growth strategy. He argued that East Asian growth had been based exclusively on the accumulation of capital per worker, rather than on increases in the productivity with which it was used. He likened the approach to that of the former Soviet Union, and suggested that East Asia might face a collapse in growth similar to that the former Soviet Union experienced.

The argument is partly true, but also seriously flawed. Much of East Asia's growth was due to a rising share of capital to labor in the economy. As these economies accumulate more capital, so the marginal productivity of capital will fall over time and growth will slow. One way to assess the extent to which this is occurring is to disaggregate increases in output per worker into the share accounted for by rises in capital per worker and the share accounted for by pure productivity increases. Technically, the term total factor productivity (TFP) is used as the measure of pure productivity once the inputs of capital per worker are included.[6]

Many researchers (Kim and Lau 1994; Young 1995) have concluded that TFP growth accounts for a relatively modest share of overall economic growth in East Asia, with much larger shares attributable to the accumulation of physical and human capital. Nonetheless, between 1970 and 1992 average TFP growth in Asia was higher than in any other region of the world, including the industrial countries. Moreover, TFP growth seems to have been rising in many countries in East and Southeast Asia in recent years (Bosworth, Collins, and Chen 1995). This suggests that the more advanced Asian economies are getting a rising growth fillip from productivity growth in addition to capital accumulation. Nonetheless, the bulk of Asia's rapid growth has come from accumulation. For the more mature economies, this means that growth will inevitably slow.

The comparison to the Soviet Union is, however, mistaken. The Soviet growth strategy was based on nonmarket allocation of capital under

---

6. Note that TFP must be measured indirectly. It is the amount of measured overall GDP growth per worker that cannot be explained by factors such as capital deepening. As such, what we label as TFP is actually a combination of errors in the data, omissions of other factors that should be included in the growth accounting framework, and pure technological progress.

conditions of virtual autarky. As a result, the Soviet economy was inflexible and inefficient. The authorities allocated capital administratively to areas of the economy that had low, or even negative, productivities of capital. The conditions for investment in East Asia are completely different. To a large degree, investment is allocated under conditions of market competition and—especially in industry—with an eye toward market conditions. That is, in East Asia investment is subject to a market test.

Although no internationally comparable statistics on rates of return on capital are available for a large number of countries, partial information exists for Hong Kong, Korea, Singapore, and Taipei,China. According to OECD data, the rate of return on capital in Korea declined gradually from around 22 percent in the mid-1980s to about 14 percent in 1994. In Singapore, a comparable indicator—the rates of return on U.S. foreign direct investment—fell from 27 percent in the late 1980s to 19 percent in the mid-1990s. In Hong Kong and Taipei,China rates of return fell from around 21 percent to 15 percent during the same period. While these declines confirm the neoclassical prediction of declining returns to investment, the important point is that they are still well above the worldwide average return on U.S. foreign direct investment of 11 percent. In contrast, the Soviet Union's rates of return on investment fell from 26 percent in the 1950s to just 5 percent a decade later and to zero by the mid-1970s (Easterly and Fischer 1995). Hence the flawed nature of the Soviet analogy. East Asian growth will not go the way of Soviet growth, because it is sustained by high profitability and flexible markets rather than by bureaucratic fiat.

The Future of Manufactured Exports

A second popular pessimistic scenario for Asian growth is that the engine of its growth—manufactured exports—will fail. Surely, the argument goes, countries around the world, including large countries such as the PRC and India, cannot simultaneously adopt an export-oriented strategy. The evidence suggests that they can.

Since the 1950s, world trade has grown much faster than world income, and world trade in manufactures has grown especially quickly. These trends are likely to continue for the foreseeable future, and there should be plenty of room for world markets to expand to accommodate new entrants. As transportation and communication costs continue to fall and more countries open themselves to global production and consumption markets, the opportunities for specialization will continue to grow. Global production networks will increasingly allow firms in developing countries to specialize in one particular phase of the production process, such as electronics assembly, while others specialize in parts production, testing, or packaging. Similarly, firms in one country will be better able to serve niche markets in several different countries for specialized consumer goods.

As world trade grows, new exporters will not have to rely exclusively on traditional industrial countries for their main markets. The growing economies of Asia will themselves provide new markets for manufactured exports. Trade in manufactured products is growing rapidly within Asia, as well as between Asia and other growing regions of the world, for instance, Latin America. Concerns about whether global markets can accommodate new entrants tend to overlook the fact that trade is a two-way process. For example, while the PRC's share of the world's manufactured exports will continue to grow in the coming decades, its imports will grow just as rapidly. Thus the PRC will provide an enormous market for capital goods, raw materials, agricultural products, and consumer goods.

Prospects for Growth

The analytical framework described earlier can be used to construct long-term forecasts of economic growth for individual countries. Table 2.11, for instance, gives an indication of what selected Asian economies could achieve in terms of growth during the next 30 years, based on their 1995 income levels, policy stance, and structural conditions.

Of course, these projections are meant to be indicative rather than precise. Many factors will influence growth rates in ways that cannot possibly be foreseen or predicted accurately. The projections have not allowed for the possibility of wars, breakdowns of open trade, substantial changes in world commodity prices (such as the oil price shocks of the 1970s), financial crises, or significant technological breakthroughs that could fundamentally alter the global division of labor. Nor can important changes in individual countries be foreseen. The estimates are simply an attempt to highlight broad current trends that have an important bearing on growth. The precise estimates of each country's growth rates are less important in this exercise than the broad direction of change over time. These estimates are much better than simple extrapolations of recent growth in that they explicitly take into account

Table 2.11 Growth Prospects for Selected Asian Economies, 1995-2025
(percent)

| Region and economy | GDP per person relative to the U.S. | | Per person GDP growth rate, 1965-95 | Projections | | | | |
| | 1965 | 1995 | | Baseline[a] | | East Asian standard[b] | Inward policies[c] |
				GDP per person relative to the U.S. in 2025	Per person GDP growth rate, 1995-2025	Per person GDP growth rate, 1995-2025	Per person GDP growth rate, 1995-2025
East Asia	17.3	72.2	6.6	98.5	2.8	2.8	1.2
Hong Kong	30.1	98.4	5.6	116.5	2.1	2.1	0.5
Korea	9.0	48.8	7.2	82.6	3.5	3.5	2.0
Singapore	15.9	85.2	7.2	107.0	2.5	2.5	0.9
Taipei,China	14.2	56.2	6.2	88.0	3.1	3.1	1.4
PRC	3.2	10.8	5.6	38.2	6.0	6.6	4.4
Southeast Asia	10.0	21.2	3.9	45.7	4.5	5.1	2.9
Indonesia	5.2	13.1	4.7	35.8	5.0	5.6	3.5
Malaysia	14.3	36.8	4.8	71.2	3.9	4.1	2.2
Philippines	10.7	9.4	1.2	28.5	5.3	6.5	3.7
Thailand	9.7	25.6	4.8	47.4	3.8	4.0	2.1
South Asia	8.5	9.2	1.9	21.3	4.4	6.9	3.3
Bangladesh	9.9	8.5	1.6	17.2	3.9	7.3	3.3
India	6.5	7.8	2.2	24.4	5.5	6.9	3.9
Pakistan	7.7	7.7	1.6	18.1	4.4	7.9	3.8
Sri Lanka	10.1	12.6	2.3	25.3	3.9	5.3	2.3
Papua New Guinea	14.5	10.0	0.4	10.1	1.5	4.7	0.9

a. Baseline projection assumes that all countries maintain the natural and policy conditions recorded in 1995.
b. East Asian standard projection assumes that all countries adopt the same policies as East Asia in 1995.
c. Inward policies assume openness changes from 1 to 0.5, and that central government saving declines 5 percentage points.
Note: 1995 per person GDP levels are based on 1992 values from Summers and Heston (1994), extrapolated forward with growth rates from IMF (1996). For data sources, see Box A-1, page 328.

the implications of conditional convergence, therefore building in the proposition that countries tend to grow more slowly as they rise in income levels relative to the income leader (assumed to be the United States).

In comparing these projected growth rates to actual growth during 1965-90, three forces are at work. First, for most countries longer life expectancy, more extensive education, and improved policies lead to increased growth rates. Second, operating in the opposite direction, as incomes rise, growth rates fall in accordance with convergence. Third, in some countries demographic trends will speed growth (as the working-age population makes up a greater percentage of the population), while in others demographic tendencies will slow economic growth (for example, as the share of the retired population grows).

The results suggest that Hong Kong, Korea, Taipei,China, and Singapore will continue and largely complete the process of rapidly catching up with the world's income leaders during the next 30 years. Whereas incomes in these four economies averaged about 72 percent of U.S. income per person in 1995, projections indicate that they will reach the equivalent of about 98 percent of U.S. income per person by 2025. Average incomes in Hong Kong and Singapore may surpass the U.S. average, which is consistent with the pattern for many large modern cities in industrial countries. Not surprisingly, as these economies continue to catch up, their growth rates will slow. Although these economies now have somewhat more favorable education indicators than they had in the past, their dramatically higher initial income levels as of 1995 suggest that their growth rates will be lower in the next 30 years than in the past 30 years. In addition, the favorable demographic trends of the last several decades that led to a rising share of workers in the population will change as the population ages and more workers reach retirement age. The average growth rate of income per person will slow to around 2.8 percent per year, down from the 6.6 percent recorded between 1965 and 1995. The projected slowdown in growth is similar to the pattern Japan has displayed in recent decades: its growth rate per person fell from an annual average of 9 percent during the 1960s to 3.5 percent in the 1980s and 2.0 percent in the 1990s.

In PRC, Philippines, and much of South Asia, however, improved initial conditions and better economic policies dominate the convergence effect. The average growth rate between 1995 and 2025 is likely to be higher than during 1965-90. South Asian countries should receive an additional boost from demographic trends that are leading to a rising proportion of those of working age in the overall population. In the PRC, income per person is expected to reach the equivalent of about 38 percent of average U.S. income in 2025, about the same relative level Korea reached in 1990.

Income levels in the four South Asian countries should reach about 21 percent of the U.S. level. Of course, more rapid growth will not come automatically in South Asia and other countries that currently lag. In South Asia, and in other places where the reform process is still uncertain, maintaining the momentum of current growth is likely to require further progress on liberalization, market opening, and institutional upgrading. In the absence of continued reform, future growth is likely to be slower than these projections indicate.

The analysis projects that in Indonesia, Malaysia, and Thailand growth rates will remain roughly the same as they have been in the recent past, as improved initial conditions and policies offset the impact of convergence almost exactly. With continued rapid growth, average incomes in these three countries should reach about 51 percent of the U.S. average. Malaysia will lead the way, with its average income expected to be more than 70 percent of average U.S. income by 2025.

With additional policy reforms, however, the South and Southeast Asian countries can achieve even higher growth rates. For illustrative purposes, assume that all Asian countries adopt the policies of the fast growing East Asian countries, including higher government savings, higher quality institutions, and increased openness. With these optimistic policy projections, growth is likely to be much faster during the next 30 years, with far higher incomes in 2025.

The transitional economies face a more difficult and complex set of tasks to initiate the process of sustained economic growth (Box 2.1). These countries must build entirely new government institutions to support trade, finance, and the government budget. Countries dependent on the former Soviet Union must find new trading partners, authorities must create whole new tax systems to replace governments' dependence on state enterprises, and new commercial banks must spring up to support private sector entrepreneurship.

Such an optimistic forecast is not, of course, the only possibility. A turn toward protectionist policies around the world and a reduction in the growth of world trade could derail Asia's rapid growth. Similarly, if Asia were to follow the path of much of Europe and of the United States

Box 2.1 The Future of the Central Asian Republics

The Central Asian republics face a difficult and complex set of tasks to initiate the process of sustained economic growth. The governments must manage a dual transformation, in which they must restructure the countries' political and economic institutions. The political aspect of this transformation stems from when they ceased to be political regions within the Soviet Union and became independent. Within a short period, one characterized by political uncertainty, the new governments had to create public institutions to take decisions formerly made in the Soviet Union. Most of the republics accomplished this by using institutions that had previously been regional offices of former central government agencies.

Economic management after independence was complicated by the need to cope with the still strong influence of the overhang from the past integration in the former Soviet Union. At the outset, moreover, the authorities lacked complete autonomy over a few key areas of economic management. The role of government also had to be redefined to make it more appropriate for a market-oriented economy than a command economy.

The new governments also had to undertake certain prominent administrative tasks, namely, to (a) strengthen their independent fiscal systems and institute alternative budgetary resources; (b) develop monetary and credit systems, and after establishing their own currencies, set up appropriate instruments of monetary policy and control; (c) redefine and redesign their social protection systems; (d) develop viable trade regimes and external payment systems; (e) establish the capability to administer and control external assistance and foreign investment; and (f) establish the capacity to manage external debt.

The shift from a centrally controlled economy to one in which market forces set prices and allocate factors of production required the development of new organizational structures and new behavioral modes. Particularly important in this connection is establishing private property rights and appropriately enforced contractual law in support of markets, initiating privatization, fostering a private sector, and setting up an environment conducive to foreign direct investment.

In addition to these institutional requirements, the Central Asian republics face several extremely difficult challenges. For example, these countries that were formerly dependent on the Soviet Union need to find new trading partners. One fundamental problem in this regard is geographical: they tend to be far from other economic centers, and as landlocked countries their transport costs are high. As a result, the Central Asian republics are likely to find it more difficult to replicate the East Asian model of labor-intensive, export-led growth. Central Asia, as well as Mongolia, also faces another challenge unique among the developing countries of Asia at this stage of their development: rebuilding agricultural systems that in most of the countries all but collapsed following the dissolution of the Soviet Union.

toward higher government spending and increased social welfare programs, growth would slow. A pessimistic scenario for the future would therefore include reduced economic openness and decreased government saving. If, for instance, the average level of openness in Asia contracted substantially and the average rate of government saving fell by 5 percentage points of GDP, future growth rates in almost all Asian countries would be lower than those recorded during the last quarter of a century. The only exception might be in South Asia, where the effects of the continuing demographic transition are likely to boost growth per person. Even here, however, future growth will depend on the continuation of current reform programs.

Such an inward turn with slower growth is not only feasible, but has several precedents in world history. Latin America's growth, for instance, was interrupted by fiscal mismanagement and inward-looking industrial policies, and economic growth around the world stagnated with the collapse in world trade in the 1930s during the Great Depression. Clearly, continued rapid growth in Asia is not assured, especially if conditions in the world trading system deteriorate significantly.

In addition to these general concerns, the PRC and India will have an enormous influence on Asia's future during the next 30 years. These countries are so large that their progress will have profound effects on both the rest of the region and on the global economy. Each has initiated a fundamental reform program; at this stage, the PRC's is far more advanced than India's. Many observers have raised questions about the sustainability of these reforms and about their potential impact on Asia's future.

Assuming no major periods of political uncertainty, the PRC's economic future is likely to follow one of two scenarios, one optimistic and the other pessimistic. Under the optimistic scenario, the country will continue along the path of economic reform and keep productivity and capital formation growth relatively high. The PRC could maintain growth at around 7 to 8 percent per person per year for the next decade, with the rate gradually falling closer to 5 to 6 percent in the 2020s as dependency rates rise and saving falls.

Under the pessimistic scenario, the PRC will fail to make essential reforms and sectoral bottlenecks will inhibit growth throughout the economy. For example, increased losses by the state sector could lead to some degree of financial destabilization, which would hamper future growth. Reforms could also be derailed by the growing divergence of incomes, both within urban areas and between the rapidly growing coastal regions and the more slowly growing interior. Even in this case, however, the reforms that have already taken place should allow the PRC to achieve growth rates of 4 to 5 percent per person in the future (Gang, Perkins, and Sabin 1996).

Which of these paths of development the PRC will actually take during the next three decades will depend partly on reforms within the country, but perhaps equally important will be what happens in the rest of the world. Only a world economic system open to expanding international trade shares will be able to accommodate the kind of trade expansion that the PRC anticipates.

India has had much less economic success than the PRC in recent years, and has lagged behind the countries of East and Southeast Asia in both growth and poverty alleviation. Historically, India's economic strategy differed widely from that of its East and Southeast Asian neighbors, with much greater state control of production and distribution. Low investment productivity resulted from India's planning strategy, which was characterized by a distrust of the price mechanism, a preference for administrative controls, and a belief in self-reliance that negated the efficient use of foreign trade and technology. The results of this strategy were slow growth, little job creation, and continued mass poverty (Joshi and Little 1996).

India's reform process began in 1991 and initially focused on achieving macroeconomic stabilization through fiscal adjustment and improved balance of payments management. To this end the authorities have eased financial sector controls, strengthened prudential regulation, and reduced trade restrictions; however, in each of these cases, the reforms have been modest at best. Markets for land, labor, and capital are still highly distorted; many government officials continue to be lukewarm about foreign investment; and the transaction costs for investors remain high. Much more comprehensive reforms are necessary for Indian firms to be able to compete in world markets. In addition, the sustainability of the reform process is far from clear: India still lacks the consensus for open markets and integration with the world economy that is required for more rapid growth.

Thus, as with the PRC, the outlook for India's future depends on the extent to which the reform process continues. The most optimistic scenario foresees continued banking and financial sector reform, more extensive trade liberalization, and increased government saving. If the authorities implement these and other reforms, more rapid growth is possible as India's millions of workers gain the opportunity to compete in world markets. However, if the reform process stagnates or, is reversed, the increased growth rates recorded since the initiation of the reform process could decline to the rates seen in the 1970s and early 1980s (Joshi and Little 1996).

Asia's Integration into the World Economy

The countries of East and Southeast Asia are far more integrated with the global economy than they were 30 years ago. A strategy of export-led growth has greatly increased trade links: Asian exports have soared, as have imports of capital and intermediate goods from the rest of the world. More recently, capital markets have become far more integrated as East and Southeast Asian countries have begun to deregulate their domestic financial markets and liberalize many kinds of capital account transactions. In South Asia, ties to global markets have only recently begun to strengthen, but they too are already significant.

In the coming decades several forces will combine to continue the process of integration, for instance, continued change in communications and transportation technology. Further reductions in transport costs, the diffusion of "real time" trading systems, videoconferencing facilities, and other kinds of large-scale electronic data transmission will make conducting business across national borders easier, cheaper, and presumably less risky. Language barriers are likely to become less of an impediment to international commerce, thereby facilitating greater trade and investment flows within Asia and between Asia and the rest of the world.

Increased integration with global markets has numerous benefits, but it also entails risks. Economic disturbances can be transmitted more easily from one country to another. For instance, a sudden reduction in industrial country demand for developing country exports will immediately reduce output and incomes in producer countries. As exports from Asia, Eastern Europe, Latin America, and sub-Saharan Africa grow, global markets will become increasingly competitive. Firms that are unable to adapt quickly will face declining profitability and will lose markets.

Fiscal or monetary policy shifts in industrial countries are now more likely to affect Asian investment through global capital markets than in the past. The combination of enormous advances in communications technology and deregulation of capital markets has brought about a huge increase in international capital movements. Asian capital markets are still relatively thin and are vulnerable to rapid swings in capital. Thus prudent macroeconomic management is more important and more difficult than before. Policymakers must be able to distinguish between short- and long-term capital flows and must ensure that large capital inflows do not lead to overvalued exchange rates. In short, exchange rate, fiscal, and monetary policies must be more coordinated than ever before.

Although the trend toward greater integration is universal, the extent of integration differs. One way to gauge the degree of integration is to measure the links between growth in the industrial countries and growth in Asia. These links vary widely in nature and strength: they tend to be strongest in the most advanced, fastest growing economies; slightly weaker in Southeast Asia; and weaker still in South Asia. A simple analysis of the association of changes in growth rates in the Group of Seven (G7) and in Asian growth rates indicates that a 1 percent permanent increase in G7 growth rates has been associated with a 0.5 percent increase in growth in East Asia and a somewhat smaller fillip to growth in Southeast Asia (Harrigan and Sumulong 1996).

Institutions for Integration

The pace and scope of Asia's global integration during the next 30 years will be profoundly influenced by its participation in, and the development of, international economic institutions. Perhaps the most important of these is the WTO. Roughly half of the economies in emerging Asia are already members of the WTO in 1997, and most of the rest have either already applied for membership or are intending to.

WTO membership will set the rules of the game for international trade and will affect Asian as well as other countries far more than previous multilateral trade regimes. All WTO members have agreed to the "single undertaking" of accepting all membership obligations, including agreements on trade in services and on intellectual property rights. The organization also has an ambitious agenda for future negotiations on trade reform. Negotiations on telecommunications were completed in early 1997 and have started on financial services and maritime transport. Negotiations in other areas are likely in the near future.

Not only will trade barriers be reduced over a much broader set of transactions, but the WTO has far less room for special exemptions than previous arrangements. Most developing countries, including those in Asia, sought and received special exemptions under the General Agreement on Tariffs and Trade (the WTO's predecessor). These are now much less likely. Far fewer quantitative restrictions will be allowed, and all member countries will have to negotiate schedules to allow greater market access for their goods and services.

At one level, the WTO provides significant promise that global markets for trade and services will be far more integrated in the early 21st century than they are now. This offers Asia enormous opportunities. But at another level it demands discipline, in that many of East Asia's protectionist trade policies will no longer be permissible.

The Asia-Pacific Economic Cooperation (APEC) group will reinforce the tendency toward more open trading arrangements. Although APEC is not a trading block, the group has committed itself to free trade within the region by 2010 for higher income member countries and by 2020 for all member countries. APEC is committed to "open regionalism," which although not precisely defined, is generally taken to mean adopting a nondiscriminatory stance toward nonmembers. Although this cannot be guaranteed, APEC represents a strong commitment in Asia to continue integration in the global economy during the next three decades. The South Asian Association for Regional Cooperation could potentially fulfill a similar role in South Asia.

Southeast Asian countries have their own subregional commitments. The ASEAN Free Trade Area (AFTA) accords call for free trade between ASEAN's seven members (Brunei Darussalam, Indonesia, Malaysia, Philippines, Singapore, Thailand, and Viet Nam) by 2003. This agreement is perhaps of larger political than economic significance, because trade between the member countries is relatively low, and the agreement for "free" trade contains many important exceptions. Nonetheless, ASEAN has helped to deepen the dialogue between these countries on a wide range of issues, and may act as an additional stimulus toward trade reform in some countries.

The general enthusiasm and support for the WTO and APEC agreements in East and Southeast Asia is as much a reflection of these countries' moves toward trade liberalization during the 1970s and 1980s as it is a push toward continued reform today. Each of the rapidly growing Asian countries undertook major trade reforms of its own volition and on its own schedule, and these countries wish to continue to control the pace and extent of their reforms. This desire to maintain independence in their reform schedules is reflected in Asian countries' resistance to making APEC a formal trading block, and instead pushing for a strategy of "concerted unilateralism" as APEC's approach to freer trade in the early 21st century. Domestic resistance to the liberalization of certain sectors has been and continues to be strong. Korea fought hard against WTO accords on liberalizing rice trade, and Indonesia and Malaysia are strongly resisting opening the market for automobiles. Asia is likely to see a pattern of gradual opening in the future, as in the past, but the international trade agreements set a clearly defined framework within which it will occur.

Asia's rapid growth and its integration with the global economy creates challenges and opportunities for the rest of the world. The region's reemergence as a world economic power is reshaping global economics and geopolitics, with consequences that are difficult to foresee, but important to anticipate.

Trade-Induced Adjustment

As Asia will have to restructure in the process of global integration, so too will the industrial countries. Trade between regions with abundant skilled labor (most industrial economies) and those with abundant unskilled labor (most developing economies) may exert downward pressure on the wages of unskilled labor in industrial economies. As developing economies continue to upgrade their capital stock and skills, they may start to produce the higher technology goods currently exported by industrial economies. This trend is exemplified by the rise of Japanese automobile production in the 1960s and 1970s and by similar trends currently under way in Korea and Taipei,China. This process of capital and skill deepening in developing economies could affect incomes in industrial economies unless they move further up the technology ladder. Moreover, with increased globalization capital can flow more easily from advanced to developing economies to take advantage of lower wages. Returns on mobile capital rise and immobile workers' wages in the capital exporting country fall. This process is already under political attack, particularly by trade unions in the United States (known as outsourcing) and in Europe (where it is widely disparaged as social dumping).

The overall impact of internationalization is, however, hard to measure. Relative wages of unskilled workers in industrial economies may fall due to other reasons as well. Technological change is also working against unskilled workers. While computers, new forms of telecommunications, automated production processes, and other technological advances increase the productivity of and create new jobs for those skilled workers who know how to use them, they reduce the demand for many unskilled jobs.

One way to gauge the consequences of increasing trade between Asia and the rest of the world is to simulate likely future trade patterns. Given the baseline growth projections described earlier, Harrigan and Sumulong (1996) used a version of the Global Trade Analysis Project model (Hertel and Tsigas 1996) to project patterns of trade flows between 11 Asian countries and major regions of the world. They also used the model to calculate the investment rates, and changes in both economic structure and terms of trade that are consistent with the growth projections.[7] Four clear conclusions emerge from this exercise.

First, fast growth in Asia provides larger markets for exports from industrial countries. Indeed, the model projects that a bigger share of exports from Japan, North America, and Western Europe will find their way to East and South Asian markets in the future. Trade is a two-way process. Both North American and European exports to Asia grow about 50 percent more quickly than their exports to any other region of the world.

Second, the locus of future global trade will shift toward Asia, because Asian countries will, in general, be growing more quickly than other countries. Fast growing incomes within Asia will increase the demand for exports other Asian countries are producing. In particular, as the PRC and India grow, new market opportunities will arise for other, smaller Asian countries. As intra-Asian trade shares increase, the share of Asian exports destined for industrial countries will decline.

Third, induced terms of trade changes are likely to benefit industrial countries. Residents of these countries will enjoy larger real incomes as the cost of the goods they import falls relative to the price of the goods they export. The other side of this is that Asia's terms of trade are likely to deteriorate. Projected terms of trade deteriorations are modest, but are most pronounced for the three largest Asian countries, PRC, India, and Indonesia, whose joint share in total world trade is expected to rise

---

7. To achieve baseline growth rates, domestic saving rates of between 35 to 40 percent of GDP are projected for both the PRC and India. While these saving rates are in line with those currently recorded in the PRC, they are well above those recorded in India. As Chapter 3 argues, however, India may benefit from favorable demographic circumstances in the years to come. India's saving would also rise if fiscal imbalances were corrected. Total investment needs for developing Asia are projected to be around $40 trillion (1992 prices, not adjusted for purchasing power parity), of which between $7 trillion and $9 trillion would be for infrastructure, depending on the share of infrastructure investment in aggregate.

from 5 percent to around 16 percent during the next 30 years. In the more advanced Asian economies, terms of trade deteriorations are likely to be negligible, and in both Hong Kong and Singapore a terms of trade improvement is projected.

Fourth, while trade raises aggregate income, it will also change its distribution. As Asia's share of manufacturing exports that make intensive use of low-skilled labor increases, this will exert downward pressure on the wages of low-skilled and immobile labor in the industrial countries. The model's projections suggest that Asian growth will require moderate, but not radical, structural adjustment in the rest of the world. If these adjustments are spread out over time, as seems likely, their impact will be more easily absorbed. In the United States, for example, projected changes in global economic structure would require that about a quarter of 1 percent of the labor force shift jobs in any one year (Harrigan and Sumulong 1996). Similarly modest adjustments would be needed in Europe.

Other evidence broadly corroborates these findings of only modest adverse effects resulting from expanded trade. A number of studies has stressed that the increasing gap in wages between skilled and unskilled workers in Europe and the United States is the result not only of trade pressures, but also of technological changes, which tend to favor skilled workers relative to unskilled workers (see, for example, Krugman and Lawrence 1994; Sachs and Shatz 1996). Apportioning the change in overall wage inequality that is due to each of these factors is extremely hard, as is, therefore, making precise predictions about future changes in wage inequalities that will result from expanded trade. Most studies suggest that both trade and technology have played a role in widening inequalities, but almost all studies attribute half or more of the widening of wage inequalities to technological trends and somewhat less than half to trade. Note that even if imports from developing countries have heightened wage inequality or caused unemployment of low-skilled workers, this does not make the case for protection. Rather, industrial countries should respond by investing in upgrading their labor or devising mechanisms that "insure" unskilled and immobile labor against some of the risks which they cannot "insure."

Projected fast export growth from Asia will generally have a positive effect on other regions. Asia will import more as it grows, and it will probably do so at less advantageous terms of trade. Both these trends will help increase incomes in industrial countries. However, these conclusions rest on a number of important conditions being met. Most important, they assume that future international trade in goods and services proceeds unimpeded, in particular, that the provisions of the Uruguay Round, including the dismantling of the Multi-Fiber Arrangement, are duly implemented. They also assume that developing and industrial countries alike can facilitate orderly structural change in their economies. While the industrial economies will undoubtedly face challenges, the magnitude and pace of structural transformation is likely to be most pronounced in the developing economies.

Asia and World Food Markets

A recent study by the World Watch Institute (Brown 1995) has focused attention on the implications for world trade in cereals of Asia's economic and demographic transition. The study projects that in the early 21st century, food prices will rise substantially as world production falters and the demand for cereals rises, especially in Asia. In particular, the institute anticipates that extremely large cereal imports by the PRC will put intensive upward pressure on world food prices.

Without question, Asia will have a growing impact on global food balances in the coming decades. The general view is that agricultural productivity in much of the region is likely to grow more slowly than in recent decades (Goldman 1997). At the same time rising affluence and greater meat consumption will increase the demand for cereals in parts of Asia, particularly the PRC, although slower population growth in the region will partially offset the rise in demand. Asia's share of the world's cereal trade is likely to increase from just over 25 percent to about 40 percent. The PRC and Pakistan, for example, are expected to account for a third of world wheat imports by the year 2020. Small changes in supply or demand conditions in Asia will have increasingly large spillover effects into the world market as Asia becomes an increasingly pivotal player in world cereal markets.

Nevertheless, the World Watch Institute's projections are overly pessimistic. More systematically constructed projections by the World Bank, the International Food Policy Research Institute, the Food and Agriculture Organization of the United Nations, official PRC sources, and most recently, the U.S. Department of Agriculture all project a substantially smaller cereal trade imbalance for the PRC than does the World Watch Institute (Goldman 1997). Both the World Bank and the International Food Policy Research Institute believe that world cereal prices will not change significantly (in real terms), and may even continue to decline slowly as they have done throughout much of the 20th century. Nevertheless, these outcomes will not be achieved automatically. To attain even modest growth in cereal production, Asia's governments will have to invest in agricultural research and improve the efficiency of irrigation.

Conclusion

The main conclusion in connection with economic growth in Asia is that one can explain Asia's growth patterns in an international comparative context. A special theory of Asian growth is unnecessary, as Asia fits well within international experience. East Asian countries grew faster than the rest of the world for two main reasons: there was substantial room for catching up, as these countries entered the 1960s with extremely low income levels; and these countries took advantage of key opportunities that most other developing countries neglected or rejected. Most important, the high-performing East Asian countries recognized the imperative to join the world economy by promoting labor-intensive manufacturing exports. These economies promoted exports through a combination of policies—free trade for exporters, relatively convertible currencies, macroeconomic stability, selective subsidies—and through a set of innovative institutions, such as EPZs, duty exemption schemes, and incentive packages for foreign direct investment.

Export-led growth is only part of the story, however. Key demographic developments, favorable trends in literacy and education, public health policies that raised life expectancy, government attention to the agriculture sector, high levels of budgetary saving, and the protection of private property rights also supported rapid growth in East Asia. Even salutary geographic considerations, such as favorable natural harbors and proximity to major sea lanes, have played a role. In quantitative terms, however, economic institutions and policies have been the most important factors differentiating the performance of fast growing and slow growing economies.

These basic lessons have profound implications for the next 30 years. The fast growing countries of East Asia still have the opportunity to continue to grow rapidly, though at rates that are likely to be somewhat slower than in the past, precisely because they have been so successful at catching up to date. Yet future growth will require successful

institutional adaptation to new challenges, including an aging population, increased urbanization and political participation, and pressures
related to increasing integration of the world economy. As a result, these
countries will face greater stresses on public sector budgets; pressures
for continued reforms of the legal system; and the need for flexibility
and adjustment of political institutions, including the decentralization of
powers to local governments.

For countries that grew more slowly during the past 30 years, the
main message is that faster growth is possible, and indeed likely, as these
countries adopt market-based strategies and increase their openness to
world markets. Projections show that South Asia has the opportunity for
the kind of dynamism previously displayed in East Asia. However, such
good performance will depend on continued institutional and policy
reforms in trade; the budget; and the social spheres, especially health
and education.

Finally, continued rapid growth in Asia will challenge the rest of the
world as the balance of economic activity increasingly shifts toward Asia.
Trade flows between Asia and the rest of the world will continue to
increase rapidly, posing significant, but manageable, shifts of employment and production within the advanced economies. Indeed, both Asia
and the rest of the world stand to benefit in important ways from Asia's
continuing economic dynamism and increasing integration with the world
economy. The best hopes for successful global adjustments to Asia will
be for all the major countries in both Asia and the rest of the world to
maintain flexibility in their domestic markets, while adhering to shared
rules of the game in international trade and finance under the framework of the WTO and other international organizations and agreements.

References

Amsden, Alice H. 1989. *Asia's Next Giant: South Korea and Late
    Industrialization.* New York and Oxford: Oxford University Press.
Barro, Robert. 1991. "Economic Growth in a Cross-Section of Countries."
    Quarterly Journal of Economics 106(2):407-43.
Barro, Robert, and J. W. Lee. 1994. "Sources of Economic Growth."
    Carnegie-Rochester Conference Series on Public Policy 40(2):1-46.
Barro, Robert, and Xavier Sala-i-Martin. 1992. "Convergence." *Journal of
    Political Economy* 100(2):223-51.

Bosworth, Barry, Susan M. Collins, and Yu-Chin Chen. 1995. *Accounting for Differences in Economic Growth*. Brookings Discussion Papers in International Economics No. 115. Washington, D.C.: The Brookings Institution.

Brown, Lester. 1995. "Who will Feed China? Wake up Call for a Small Planet." The World Watch Institute, Washington, D.C.

Carrol, C., and D. Weil. 1993. "Savings and Growth: A Reinterpretation." Working Paper No. 4470. National Bureau of Economic Research, Cambridge, Massachusetts.

Easterly, William, and Stanley Fischer. 1995. "The Soviet Economic Decline." *World Bank Economic Review* 9(3):341-71.

Edwards, S. 1995. "Why are Latin America's Saving Rates So Low? An International Comparative Analysis." The World Bank, Washington, D.C.

Feldstein, Martin. 1980. "International Differences in Social Security and Saving." *Journal of Public Economics* 14(2):225-44.

Gang, Fan, Dwight Perkins, and Lora Sabin. 1996. "China's Economic Performance and Prospects." Background paper for *Emerging Asia: Changes and Challenges*. Asian Development Bank, Manila.

Gerschenkron, Alexander. 1962. *Economic Backwardness in Historical Perspective*. Cambridge, Massachusetts: Harvard University Press.

Goldman, Richard. 1997. "Agriculture and Growth in Asia." Background paper for *Emerging Asia: Changes and Challenges*. Asian Development Bank, Manila.

Harrigan, Frank, and Lea Sumulong. 1996. "Aspects of Asian Macroeconomic and Structural Interdependence." Background paper for *Emerging Asia: Changes and Challenges*. Asian Development Bank, Manila.

Hertel, Thomas W., and Marinos E. Tsigas. 1996. "Structure of the GTAP Model." In T. Hertel, ed., *Global Trade Analysis: Modeling and Applications*. Cambridge, U.K.: Cambridge University Press.

Hill, H. 1996. "Indonesia's Industrial Policy and Performance: "Orthodoxy" Vindicated." *Economic Development and Cultural Change* 45(1), October, pp. 147-74.

IMF (International Monetary Fund). 1995. "Korea: Statistical Tables." IMF Staff Country Report No. 95/137, Washington, D.C.

_____. 1996. *International Financial Statistics Yearbook*. Washington, D.C.

Joshi, Vijay, and Ian Little. 1996. "India." Background paper for *Emerging Asia: Changes and Challenges*. Asian Development Bank, Manila.

Kessing, Donald B. 1983. "Linking up to Distant Markets: South to North Exports of Manufactured Consumer Goods." *American Economic Review* 73(2):338-42.

Kim, Jong-Il, and Lawrence J. Lau. 1994. "The Sources of Economic Growth of the East Asian Newly Industrialized Countries." *Journal of the Japanese and International Economies* 8(3):235-71.

Knack, Stephen, and Philip Keefer. 1995. "Institutions and Economic Performance: Cross-Country Tests Using Alternative Institutional Measures." *Economics and Politics* 7(3):207-27.

Krugman, Paul. 1994. "The Myth of Asia's Miracle." *Foreign Affairs* 73(6):62-78.

Krugman, Paul R., and Robert Z. Lawrence. 1994. "Trade, Jobs, and Wages." *Scientific American* 270(4):44-9.

Lall, Sanjaya. 1997. "Coping with New Technologies in Emerging Asia." Background paper for *Emerging Asia: Changes and Challenges*. Asian Development Bank, Manila.

Lindauer, David, and Michael Roemer. 1994. "Legacies and Opportunities." In David Lindauer and Michael Roemer, eds., *Asia and Africa: Legacies and Opportunities in Development*. San Francisco: Institute for Contemporary Studies.

Luedde-Neurath, Richard. 1988. "State Intervention and Export-Oriented Development in South Korea." In Gordon White, ed., *Developmental States in East Asia*. New York: St. Martin's Press.

Mankiw, N. G., D. Romer, and D. N. Weil. 1992. "A Contribution to the Empirics of Economic Growth." *Quarterly Journal of Economics* 107(2):407-37.

Masson, P., T. Bayoumi, and H. Samiei. 1995. "International Evidence on the Determinants of Private Saving." Working Paper WP/95/51. International Monetary Fund, Washington, D.C.

Nurske, Ragnar. 1961. *Equilibrium Growth in the World Economy*. Cambridge, Massachusetts: Harvard University Press.

Perkins, Dwight. 1994. "There Are at Least Three Models of East Asian Development." *World Development* 22(4):655-61.

Perkins, Dwight, and Michael Roemer. 1994. "Differing Endowments and Historical Legacies." In David Lindauer and Michael Roemer, eds., *Asia and Africa: Legacies and Opportunities in Development*. San Francisco: Institute for Contemporary Studies.

Prebisch, Raul. 1950. *The Economic Development of Latin America and its Principal Problems*. New York: United Nations.

_____. 1959. "Commercial Policy in the Underdeveloped Countries." *American Economic Review* 49(2):251-73.

Radelet, Steven, Jeffrey Sachs, and Jong-Wha Lee. 1996. "Economic Growth in Asia." Background paper for *Emerging Asia: Changes and Challenges*. Asian Development Bank, Manila.

Rhee, Yung Whee. 1994. "Managing Entry into International Markets: Lessons from the East Asian Experience." In Shu-Chin Yang, ed., *Manufactured Exports of East Asian Industrializing Economies*. Armonk, New York: M. E. Sharpe.

Roemer, Michael. 1994. "Industrial Strategies: Outward Bound." In David L. Lindauer and Michael Roemer, eds., *Asia and Africa: Legacies and Opportunities in Development*. San Francisco: Institute for Contemporary Studies.

Romer, Paul M. 1986. "Increasing Returns and Long-Run Growth." *Journal of Political Economy* 99(3):500-21.

Root, Hilton. 1996. *Small Countries, Big Lessons: Governance and the Rise of East Asia.* Oxford, U.K.: Oxford University Press.

Sachs, Jeffrey, and Howard J. Shatz. 1996. "U.S. Trade with Developing Countries and Wage Inequality." *American Economic Review* 86(2):234-39.

Sachs, Jeffrey, and Andrew Warner. 1995a. "Economic Reform and the Process of Global Integration." *Brookings Papers on Economic Activity* 0(1):1-95.

_____. 1995b. *Natural Resource Abundance and Economic Growth.* Discussion Paper No. 517A. Cambridge, Massachusetts: Harvard Institute for International Development.

Sachs, Jeffrey, and Wing Thye Woo. 1994. "Structural Factors in the Economic Reforms of China, Eastern Europe, and the Former Soviet Union." *Economic Policy: A European Forum* 9(18):101-45.

Sala-i-Martin, Xavier. 1996. "The Classical Approach to Convergence Analysis." *Economic Journal* 106(437):1019-36.

Sivalingam, G. 1994. "The Economic and Social Impact of Export Processing Zones: The Case of Malaysia." Working Paper No. 66. Multinational Enterprise Programme, International Labour Organisation, Geneva.

Smith, Heather. 1995. "Industry Policy in East Asia." *Asian-Pacific Economic Literature* 9(1):17-39.

Stern, Joseph J., Ji-Hong Kim, Dwight H. Perkins, and Jung-Ho Yoo. 1995. "Industrialization and the State: The Korean Heavy and Chemical Industry Drive." In *Harvard Studies in International Development.* Cambridge, Massachusetts: Harvard Institute for International Development.

Stiglitz, Joseph E. 1996. "Some Lessons from the East Asian Miracle." *The World Bank Research Observer* 11(2):151-77.

Summers, Robert, and Alan Heston. 1994. *Penn World Table,* Mark 5.6 (website version). Philapelphia: University of Pennsylvania.

UN (United Nations). 1994. *World Population Prospects 1950-2050: The 1994 Revision,* electronic data. New York.

_____. 1995. *Commodity Trade Statistics,* electronic data. New York.

UNCTAD (United Nations Conference on Trade and Development). 1975. *International Subcontracting Arrangements in Electronics between Developed Market Economy Countries and Developing Countries.* Report No. TD/B/C.2/144 Supp 1. New York.

Wade, R. 1990. *Governing the Market: Economic Theory and the Role of Government in East Asian Industrialization.* Princeton, New Jersey: Princeton University Press.

Wei, Shang-Jin. 1995. "Attracting Foreign Direct Investment: Has China Reached its Potential?" *China Economic Review* 6(2):187-99.

Wong, Christine. 1996. "Transition Economies of Asia." Background paper for *Emerging Asia: Changes and Challenges*. Asian Development Bank, Manila.

World Bank. 1995a. *World Development Report 1995*. New York: Oxford University Press.

_____. 1995b. *World Data 1995*. Socioeconomic Time Series Access and Retrieval System, Version 3.0, electronic resource. Washington, D.C.

Xiao, Geng. 1991. "Managerial Autonomy, Fringe Benefits, and Ownership Structure: A Comparative Study of Chinese State and Collective Enterprises." *China Economic Review* 2(1):47-73.

Young, Alwyn. 1995. "The Tyranny of Numbers: Confronting the Statistical Realities of the East Asian Growth Experience." *Quarterly Journal of Economics* 110(3):641-80.

3

DEMOGRAPHIC CHANGE AND HUMAN RESOURCE DEVELOPMENT

The economic changes that Asia is experiencing are taking place in a demographic context that contains both perils and opportunities. This chapter discusses Asia's rapidly changing demography and examines its implications for economic growth and human resource development.

Why Demography Matters

In 1950, 1.5 billion people lived in Asia. In 1975, 2.5 billion people lived there. By 1995 Asia's population had reached almost 3.5 billion people.[1] Thus in roughly two generations, the region's population has grown by 2 billion—about the same number of people that currently

---

1. Regions for the purpose of this chapter are defined as follows. References to Asia include East Asia, South Asia, Southeast Asia, Central Asian republics, Pacific islands, and the rest of Asia. Note, therefore, that Asia's total population is larger than that of the developing member countries of the Asian Development Bank by about 0.5 billion people. References to East Asia include People's Republic of China, Hong Kong, Japan, Republic of Korea, Mongolia, Singapore, and Taipei,China. References to South Asia include Afghanistan, Bangladesh, Bhutan, India, Maldives, Nepal, Pakistan, and Sri Lanka. References to Southeast Asia include Cambodia, Indonesia, Lao People's Democratic Republic, Malaysia, Myanmar, Philippines, Thailand, and Viet Nam. References to the Central Asian republics include Kazakstan, Kyrgyz Republic, and Uzbekistan. References to Pacific islands include Cook Islands, Fiji, Kiribati, Marshall Islands, Federated States of Micronesia, Nauru, Papua New Guinea, Solomon Islands, Western Samoa, Tonga, Tuvalu, and Vanuatu. References to the rest of Asia include Armenia, Azerbaijan, Bahrain, Brunei Darussalam, Cyprus, East Timor, Georgia, Iran, Iraq, Israel, Jordan, Democratic People's Republic of Korea, Kuwait, Lebanon, Oman, Qatar, Saudi Arabia, Syrian Arab Republic, Tajikistan, Turkmenistan, Turkey, United Arab Emirates, and Yemen.

live in all the industrial countries combined. Population increases of this magnitude are difficult to comprehend, but they certainly appear to be alarming. Asia has more mouths to feed, more families to house, more children to educate, and more people searching for productive employment. Millions are moving from one country to another; millions more are migrating from the countryside to cities in search of jobs. Rising pressure on the environment and natural resources seems inevitable.

However, these trends hide more promising developments. In parts of Asia, rapid demographic change in recent decades has been accompanied by an even more remarkable rise in prosperity. The rapid and sustained economic growth in East Asia—and more recently in Southeast Asia—is the envy of the developing world. Careful analysis suggests that this is no coincidence. Rising prosperity has come about in no small measure because of demographic change.

Asia has seen a dramatic and rapid demographic transition from high fertility and mortality rates to low fertility and mortality rates. In nearly all Asian countries, mortality rates began to fall sharply soon after World War II. Of this mortality fall, 60 percent is attributable to a fall in infant and child mortality. Somewhat later, fertility rates also declined. These asynchronous changes in mortality and fertility substantially altered Asia's age distribution. The population of young people bulged temporarily after mortality rates had fallen and before fertility rates fell. This population bulge has started working its way through the age distribution: after the bulge of young people, the share of the working-age population rose, and eventually the share of old people will grow.

The analysis in this chapter shows that a surprisingly large part of East Asia's spectacular economic growth derives from a working-age population bulge. This bulge represents a demographic "gift," because it carries with it the potential for an increased pace of economic growth. East Asia has had relatively more workers (and savers) and relatively fewer nonworkers (and nonsavers) compared with earlier periods, with other parts of Asia, and with the rest of the world. More recently, Southeast Asia has begun to benefit from the same bulge in the working-age population. The analysis suggests that South Asia, too, will receive this demographic gift, though with some delay.

Eventually, however, the demographic gift becomes a burden. As the population bulge ages, the relative share of old people increases, but the rising prosperity that a large fraction of working-age people can spur will make this burden less onerous than it might have been. After the entire demographic transition—both gift and burden—has passed, Asia's total population and age distribution will stabilize and will no longer affect growth.

While the demographic transition provides an opportunity for increasing prosperity, it does not guarantee it. Whether increased prosperity actually occurs depends on whether countries can mobilize sufficient capital and use it, together with their human resources, efficiently. This, in turn, depends largely on government policies. If, for example, a government chooses trade and macroeconomic policies that encourage job creation, the country is more likely to realize the potential beneficial effect on growth of having a large share of the population of working age. If the workforce is better educated, it will be better placed to contribute to economic growth. If, however, governments mismanage their economies, the large workforce can become an army of unemployed.

This chapter explains both the origins and the effects of Asia's demographic transition. Demography influences, and is influenced by, economic change through several channels. The size and structure of the labor force, expansion of education, and saving and investment rates are all affected by demographic factors. In turn, they all affect economic growth. Higher life expectancy and rising income themselves create demand for more and higher quality education and health services, which again contribute to future economic growth.

This chapter concentrates on five policy areas that will be especially important in Asia: population policy, health care financing, higher education provision, pension policies, and labor market policy. The goal is to suggest ways that Asia can obtain maximum benefit from its demographic transition and minimize the subsequent burden.

Understanding Asia's Changing Demography

Asia has long been the most populous region of the world. Until recently, the rate at which its population grew was moderate. This situation changed, however, in the years following World War II.

Historical Context

In the preindustrial period, high fertility rates, but also high mortality rates, were the norm. Although historical population statistics are sketchy for many parts of Asia, reasonably reliable estimates exist for the People's Republic of China (PRC), India, and Japan (Wilson 1996). In all three countries, the average rate of population growth between 1880 and 1950 was less than 1 percent a year. In the PRC it was only about 0.2 percent a year.

Beginning in the early 1950s, this changed dramatically as falling mortality rates boosted population growth rates. During the past 45 years, the average population growth rate in Asia has been just over 2 percent a year, peaking at 2.4 percent a year between 1965 and 1970. Since then, birth rates have decreased more rapidly than death rates. As a result, the rate of population growth has now fallen to 1.6 percent per year. In the future it is likely to decline even more, to around 0.8 percent per year by 2025 (UN 1994). Today, however, 30 percent of Asians are still under the age of 15. This large group of young people means that Asia's population growth rate will probably remain above 1 percent per year until 2015. As a result, Asia's population is likely to rise by a further 800 million people in the next 15 years and 700 million more in the 15 years thereafter.

Today, Asia's population is still growing much more quickly than that of Europe or North America, but is growing more slowly than that of either Africa or Latin America. Fertility rates are similar to those in Latin America, much higher than in Europe or North America, but much lower than in Africa. Mortality rates in Asia are higher and life expectancy still lower than anywhere but Africa. Table 3.1 compares the

Table 3.1 Growth Rates for Different Population Groups and Regions, 1965-90
(percent per year)

Region	Total population	Economically active population	Economically dependent population
Asia	2.13	2.63	1.41
East Asia	1.58	2.39	0.25
Southeast Asia	2.36	2.90	1.66
South Asia	2.27	2.51	1.95
Africa	2.81	2.78	2.85
Europe	0.49	0.68	0.15
Latin America	2.25	2.64	1.77
North America	1.69	2.21	0.91

Source: World Bank (1995) and calculations based thereon.

evolution of Asia's population age structure with that in other parts of the world. As the table shows, from 1965-90 the working-age population grew at a similar rate in Asia, Africa, and Latin America, but more slowly in North America and much more slowly in Europe. Meanwhile, the economically dependent population in Asia has grown more slowly than in any other part of the developing world. The divergence between the growth rates of the working and the nonworking population is especially pronounced in East Asia. This divergence has been the region's demographic gift.

Asia's Demographic Transition

Nearly all countries in Asia have experienced—or are currently in the midst of—a demographic transition from high fertility and high mortality rates to low fertility and low mortality rates (Figure 3.1). A stylized description of the transition is as follows. In general, mortality rates fell before fertility rates, and infant and child mortality fell earlier and faster than mortality rates in other age groups. The result was the surge in population growth already described and a dramatically larger share of young people in the population.

To get a sense of the dimensions of this change, consider that the infant mortality rate for Asia as a whole has dropped by more than two

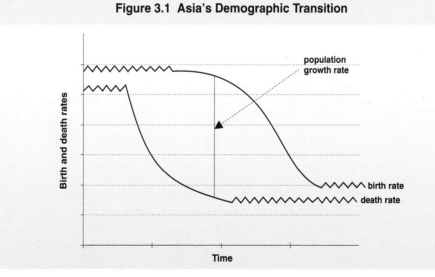

Figure 3.1 Asia's Demographic Transition

thirds: in 1995 an average of 52 babies out of every 1,000 born died before their first birthday, down from 175 in 1950. The crude death rate, that is, the number of overall deaths per 1,000 people, has dropped by the same proportion. The typical Asian born today can expect to live until the age of 67, 60 percent longer than an Asian born in 1950. Most of the reduction in mortality rates had taken place by the early 1970s. Since then, fertility rates have also plummeted: the typical Asian woman now has about three children, down from six in 1970. The crude birth rate, that is, the number of births per 1,000 population, has also fallen by one third.

Not only have these changes been profound, they have taken place remarkably quickly. In Western Europe a similar demographic shift took more than two centuries to complete. The improvements in basic sanitation, solid waste management, clean drinking water provision, and nutrition that underpin lower mortality rates developed over many generations in Europe, but in the postcolonial era Asia was able to benefit remarkably quickly from what more developed countries had already learned. Moreover, investment in the projects and infrastructure that improved public health was heavily financed with external assistance that was not available to 19th century Europe. Hence, Asian health standards could catch up quickly, and the demographic transition could be compressed into a couple of generations.

The Decline in Mortality Rates

Although the statistics are incomplete, mortality rates seem to have begun to fall in a large number of Asian countries at around the same time—roughly the late 1940s. This suggests one or more common causes. Levels of income cannot be a common cause, because they varied so significantly across Asia. A more likely explanation is that many Asian countries gained political sovereignty at the same time as the global economy slowly recovered from two world wars and the Great Depression. This ushered in an era of health technology transfer and the diffusion of new public health programs and techniques throughout Asia.

The medical advances that were implemented in Asia at this time stemmed from the introduction of sulfa drugs and powerful antibiotics, such as penicillin and streptomycin, which changed the potential for health care in Asia. Diseases such as scarlet fever, pneumonia, tuberculosis, malaria, and diarrhea became treatable. These were diseases that had once killed hundreds of thousands, and even millions, of people.

The impact on children's survival was particularly large, because infectious diseases were a prime cause of death at birth and in childhood. The effect on maternal health was also significant, as until effective antibiotics were available, maternal mortality during childbirth was high.

Another factor that may have helped to precipitate the sharp decline in Asian mortality rates in the late 1940s was the use of DDT, which became available in 1943. Between 1949 and 1952 malaria control demonstrations were carried out in Afghanistan, Bangladesh, Cambodia, India, Indonesia, Myanmar, Taipei,China, Thailand, and Viet Nam. DDT spraying in Sri Lanka in the late 1940s reduced the incidence of malaria dramatically: the crude death rate fell from 21.5 to 12.6 per 1,000 population between 1945 and 1950, with the most precipitous drops in the areas most severely affected by malaria (Livi-Bacci 1992). Some diseases also became less common as countries grew wealthier. Tuberculosis, for example, subsided as crowding and malnutrition eased.

With the steep fall in mortality rates, births outstripped deaths and population growth accelerated. Because infant mortality fell fastest and earliest, these demographic events produced rising numbers of young people. The share of the dependent population (children and the elderly) rose, while the share of the working-age population (aged 15 to 64) fell during the 1950s and 1960s. Beginning in the 1970s, as these young people grew up, the share of the working-age population rose, and rose especially steeply in East Asia.

The Decline in Fertility Rates

Some time after mortality rates began to fall, Asian countries experienced a relatively brief rise in fertility rates. This was probably because more pregnancies came to term as maternal health improved. Thereafter, fertility rates began a sustained decline. While the timing of the fall in mortality rates was remarkably similar across rich and poor countries in Asia, the lag between the drop in mortality rates and the changes in fertility rates, as well as the size of the ensuing fertility drop, varied. In countries such as Korea, Malaysia, and Singapore, fertility began to fall about 15 years after the mortality drop. Elsewhere, in Thailand, for example, the delay was closer to 25 years. Nonetheless, East Asia overall completed this shift to low fertility remarkably quickly.

One factor that greatly influences fertility rates is the extent to which contraceptives are used. Table 3.2 shows how widely contraceptive use rates vary across Asia. (Note that the table does not take into account the use of abortion for fertility control, which is high in both the PRC and Japan.) Government intervention accounts for some of the variance. National family planning programs have been central to the decline in Asian fertility, beginning with India in 1951. These programs typically involve setting up government centers for delivering information as well as contraceptive services and supplies.

People have traditionally married young in Asian societies. Thus women have usually started having children early in life. Led by East Asia, the practice of early marriage is beginning to change. In Southeast Asia and Sri Lanka, too, fewer women are marrying early. The PRC and Viet Nam both have encouraged later marriages, with some success. Yet in Bangladesh, India, Indonesia, and Pakistan at least half of all women

Table 3.2 Contraceptive Use Rates in Selected Asian Economies, 1988-92

Economy	Percentage of population employing contraception[a]	Contraceptive method (percentage of total population employing the method)[b]	
		Most common	Next most common
PRC	83	Sterilization (44)	IUD (33)
Hong Kong	81	Condom (26)	Sterilization (24)
Korea	79	Sterilization (47)	Condom (9)
Singapore	74	Condom (24)	Sterilization (23)
Thailand	66	Sterilization (29)	Pill (19)
Japan	64	Condom (48)	Nonsupply (17)
Sri Lanka	62	Sterilization (30)	Nonsupply (22)
Viet Nam	53	IUD (33)	Nonsupply (15)
Indonesia	50	Pill (15)	Other supply (15)
Malaysia	48	Nonsupply (17)	Pill (15)
India	43	Sterilization (30)	Condom (5)
Philippines	40	Nonsupply (15)	Sterilization (12)
Bangladesh	40	Pill (14)	Sterilization (10)
Nepal	23	Sterilization (18)	Other supply (2)
Pakistan	12	Sterilization (4)	Condom (3)

IUD = intrauterine device
a. Excludes abortion.
b. Sterilization is of either partner. Other supply methods include injectables, implants, spermicides, diaphragms, and caps. Nonsupply methods include abstinence, rhythm, withdrawal, and douche.
Source: Caldwell and Caldwell (1996).

are married by the age of 20 (Caldwell and Caldwell 1996). Historically, a high proportion of Asian women marry. Even by the late 1980s, more than 95 percent of women in PRC, Indonesia, Pakistan, Sri Lanka, Thailand, and Viet Nam were married. However, there are some signs that the share of women who never marry is rising.

More important, fertility within marriage has declined significantly. The expansion of primary health care and improvements in water and sanitation provision have both helped to increase life expectancy and reduce mortality rates. As life expectancy increases and infant mortality falls, couples can wait longer to have children and still achieve desired family size. Additionally, families may desire fewer births, because the children are more likely to survive. Urbanization and industrialization contribute to the fall in fertility rates. To families living in rural areas, children are an important asset: they help tend crops and cattle, and can provide care and companionship in old age; often parents do not need to make child care arrangements when they are working nearby in the fields. In contrast, children are often a financial burden for families living in the city. They have no fields and herds that can make children economically productive and, in addition, they cannot take their children to work, so families must provide care for young children during working hours. Finally, increased schooling reduces the net benefits of having a household full of children. As mothers' education rises, the costs of the time they devote to raising children also rises. Increased educational attainment also increases out-of-pocket costs of raising children and diminishes the income generated by children.

Intraregional Differences

The pattern of demographic change has not been uniform across Asia. East Asia saw the earliest and sharpest increases in life expectancy and the earliest and most dramatic falls in infant mortality rates. South Asia has been at the opposite end of the spectrum, but has nonetheless made much progress in raising life expectancy and reducing infant mortality.

While fertility rates began to fall throughout Asia beginning in the latter half of the 1960s, East Asia experienced by far the most precipitous drop (Figure 3.2). By the early 1990s, the total fertility rate in East Asia had leveled out at around 2 births per woman. South Asia now has the highest fertility in the region, but projections indicate that the large gap between East and South Asia will disappear during the next 30 years.

Figure 3.2 Total Fertility Rate by Subregion, Actual and Projected 1950-2020

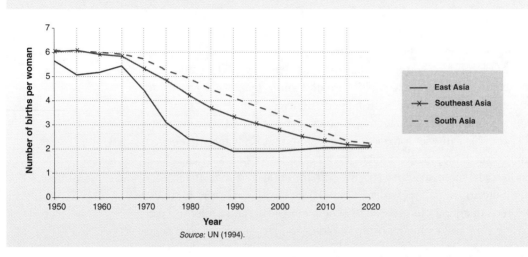

Source: UN (1994).

Ten Asian economies, mostly in East Asia, already have fertility rates that will, over the next generation or two, mean their population size will stay constant.[2] Taken together, these countries make up nearly half of Asia's total population.

These diverging fertility rates have directly influenced differences in Asia's population growth rates. Population growth rates in the three sub-regions (Figure 3.3) were approximately equal from 1965 to 1970

Figure 3.3 Population Growth Rate by Subregion, Actual and Projected, 1950-2025

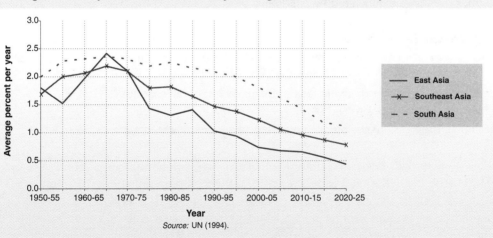

Source: UN (1994).

2.   The economies are PRC, Hong Kong, Japan, Kazakstan, Korea, Democratic People's Republic of Korea, Singapore, Sri Lanka, Taipei,China, and Thailand.

(between 2.2 and 2.4 percent per year). Thereafter, they began to diverge, with East Asia's population growth rates falling most rapidly and South Asia's least rapidly. Although all regions now have declining population growth rates, the relative rates among the regions have maintained their long-standing pattern, with South Asia's population still growing the fastest and East Asia's the slowest.

The age distribution of the population follows a similar pattern. East Asia has the lowest proportion of people under age 15 (25 percent in 1995), South Asia has the highest (37 percent), and Southeast Asia is in between (35 percent). As concerns the share of older people, East Asia has the highest share of population over the age of 64 (7 percent), while in South and Southeast Asia the share is much lower, 3.5 and 4 percent, respectively (calculations based on UN 1994).

Figure 3.4, which shows the proportion of the working-age population (aged between 15 and 64) for each subregion, illustrates the importance of the demographic transition. The share of the working-age population fell everywhere in Asia between 1950 and 1970 and then rose everywhere. Since 1950 the proportion of working-age people has been considerably higher in East Asia, and that proportion rose faster in East Asia after 1975. This caused the gap in the proportion of the working-age population between East Asia and both South and Southeast Asia to rise dramatically until 1990, but by 2025 or thereabouts, this gap will have disappeared. In short, East Asia has already experienced an

Figure 3.4 Share of the Working-Age Population by Subregion, Actual and Projected, 1950-2025

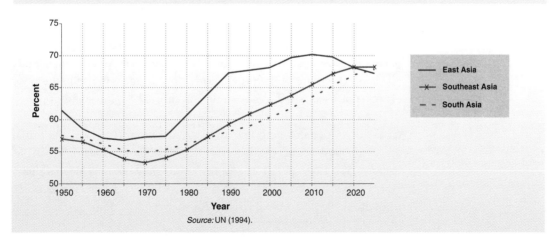

Source: UN (1994).

enormous boom in the fraction of its population that is of working age. This boom is just beginning in Southeast Asia, and will follow later in South Asia as the demographic transition takes further hold.

Dependency Rates

For much of the postwar period, the fraction of the population under age 15 (called the youth dependency rate) was much higher in developing Asia than in the industrial countries (Table 3.3). During the baby boom in the 1950s, the share of young people in the populations of countries of the Organisation for Economic Co-operation and Development (OECD) averaged about 26 percent.[3] In Asia, the peak youth dependency rates were in many cases 20 percentage points higher. In Bangladesh and Pakistan, for instance, the share of people under 15 in the population peaked at about 46 percent. In short, Asia was carrying heavy youth dependency burdens during the 1950s and 1960s.

Table 3.3 also shows the large decline in Asia's youth dependency rate from its peak to the early 1990s. The biggest declines have occurred in East and Southeast Asia. In Korea, for instance, the youth dependency rate fell by a phenomenal 18 percentage points, and in Japan it fell by 17 percentage points. Dependency rates in Southeast Asia have also fallen, but by less than in East Asia. The smallest declines have occurred in South Asia. India's youth dependency rate in the early 1990s was only 4 percentage points below its peak in the 1960s, and Pakistan's fell by less than 1 percentage point. Sri Lanka is the lone exception to the South Asian pattern.

This decline in youth dependency in Asia was compressed into two or three decades, half the time it took industrializing Europe to record far less substantial reductions a century ago. Similarly dramatic changes are likely in the future. The prime-age population projections in Figure 3.5 imply considerable demographic convergence in Asia during the next 30 years. The share of the population of prime age will rise in the poorest parts of Asia. Bangladesh is a typical case. There the share of people of prime age will rise from 31 to 46 percent from 1990 to 2025, an increase of 15 percentage points over a generation. However, the prime-age share will begin to fall in the richest parts of Asia. In Japan, for instance, it is likely to fall by around 5 percentage points. Meanwhile, in Korea it will peak around 2005 and then fall by 3 percentage points through to 2025. Southeast Asia will see a period of demographic catch-

---

3. This figure is for all OECD members as of 1992.

Table 3.3 Dependency Rates in Asia, Selected Economies and Periods

Economy	Peak period of youth dependency and recent period	Percentage of the population		
		Young (age 0-14)	Prime (age 25-59)	Old (age 65+)
East Asia				
Hong Kong	1960-64	40.7	40.9	3.0
	1990-92	20.1	50.8	9.3
Japan	1950-54	34.7	38.1	5.1
	1990-92	18.0	48.9	12.4
Korea	1965-69	42.8	34.6	3.3
	1990-92	24.8	47.3	5.0
Taipei,China	1960-64	45.2	34.8	2.6
	1990-92	26.4	45.5	6.5
PRC	1965-69	40.0	35.5	4.4
	1990-92	26.4	43.7	6.0
Southeast Asia				
Indonesia	1970-74	42.2	34.4	3.1
	1990-92	34.9	37.7	4.1
Malaysia	1960-64	45.6	31.8	3.3
	1990-92	38.0	37.2	3.8
Myanmar	1965-69	41.1	34.2	3.6
	1990-92	36.8	36.2	4.2
Philippines	1965-69	45.2	30.7	2.8
	1990-92	39.6	35.3	3.4
Singapore	1960-64	43.5	35.1	2.4
	1990-92	23.3	51.8	5.9
Thailand	1965-69	46.2	31.5	3.0
	1990-92	31.5	40.6	4.1
South Asia				
Bangladesh	1975-79	46.0	29.6	3.5
	1990-92	43.3	31.4	2.9
India	1965-69	40.4	35.8	3.6
	1990-92	36.3	37.3	4.6
Nepal	1975-79	42.2	34.9	3.2
	1990-92	41.9	34.1	3.2
Pakistan	1965-69	46.3	31.1	3.4
	1990-92	45.9	31.3	2.7
Sri Lanka	1955-59	41.7	34.3	3.7
	1990-92	31.8	41.1	5.4

Note: Figures for 1990-92 are estimates.
Source: UN (1991).

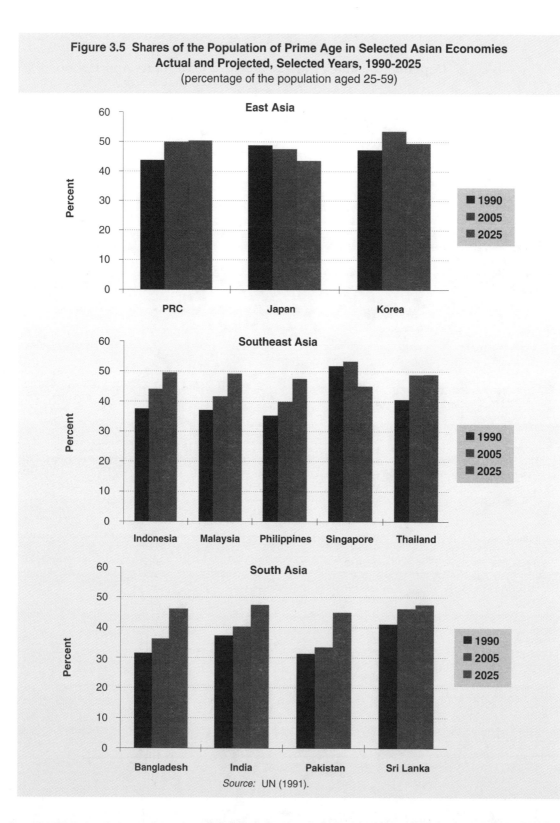

**Figure 3.5 Shares of the Population of Prime Age in Selected Asian Economies
Actual and Projected, Selected Years, 1990-2025**
(percentage of the population aged 25-59)

Source: UN (1991).

up ahead, especially between 2005 and 2025, and this will be even more pronounced in South Asia. In other words, the supply of labor will boom in South and Southeast Asia and slump in East Asia. As South Asia sees its demographic gift, the burden of an aging population will become increasingly apparent in East Asia.

Demography and Economic Growth

There is a long-standing debate as to whether population growth helps or hinders economic growth (Coale and Hoover 1958). At one extreme, population pessimists assert that rapid population growth increases the dependency burden imposed by having a high fraction of young people in the population. This reduces rates of saving and investment, and so reduces the rate of economic growth, thereby aggravating underemployment, unemployment, and poverty (Ehrlich 1968; Meadows and others 1972). At the other extreme, population optimists argue that rapid population growth stimulates both technological change and the adoption of techniques that realize economies of scale, thereby promoting economic growth (Boserup 1981; Simon 1981).

Both views are too simplistic. Income growth has many more determinants than just population growth. One can estimate the independent influence of population growth on economic performance by using the empirical growth model presented in Chapter 2. The model accounts for several possible determinants of growth, including initial income, education, life expectancy, characteristics of the physical environment, and the extent of government involvement in and support for growth. Once these factors are taken into account, no clear relationship is apparent between population growth and the growth of gross domestic product (GDP) per person. In keeping with many other studies, the analysis finds no evidence to support the view that countries with higher rates of population growth experience either higher or lower rates of income growth per person (Bloom and Freeman 1986). Thus the population neutralist view appears to be the most reasonable. (The Appendix presents a detailed explanation of the results discussed here.)

This approach does not explain, however, whether the underlying mechanisms proposed by either the population optimists or pessimists have any validity. For example, it does not show whether fertility and mortality changes have different effects on economic growth that correspond to their different effects on the population's age structure. (The short-term impact of fertility declines is to reduce the share of young dependents, while the effect of mortality declines is spread throughout the age structure.) Nor does it show whether the changes in the population's age distribution that occur during the course of a demographic transition correspond to changes in the pace of economic growth.

A larger working-age population enhances an economy's productive capacity. A larger nonworking population that nonetheless consumes reduces an economy's per person productive capacity. Thus distinguishing between the components of population change is essential when analyzing the impact of demography on economic growth (Bloom and Freeman 1988; Coale 1986; Kelley 1988; Kelley and Schmidt 1996; Meltzer 1995; Williamson 1993). Hence, a recurrent theme in this study is that the effects of a growing working-age population differ from those associated with the growth of the dependent population, that is, individuals younger than 15 or older than 64 (see the Appendix for details).

The results suggest that if the share of the population of working-age is growing, this stimulates the growth rate of income per person. The correspondingly slower growth of the dependent population presumably frees up resources that would otherwise be devoted to the rearing and maintenance of children (especially schools, hospitals, food, clothing, and housing). Hence, it permits higher rates of saving and higher rates of investment in physical capital. In East Asia, the subregion in which the share of the working-age population has risen most dramatically, this effect has been particularly pronounced.

Dependency and Growth

One issue to be considered within the context of dependency is whether the type of dependency matters. In particular, do the shares of young dependents or old people have different impacts on growth? The analysis shows that increases in the growth rate of the population under age 15 are associated with decreases in the economy's growth rate, that is, the population under the age of 15 contributes negatively to current production. In contrast, no significant association exists between economic growth and growth of the elderly population, perhaps because the elderly (especially the younger among them) in many cases continue to work or enable others to work, for example, by providing child care, and may continue to save as well. However, as the elderly population swells to unprecedented levels and their average age rises, this relationship may exert a significant drag on economic growth, an effect that could be mitigated somewhat by raising the mandatory retirement age. As for the effects between 1965 and 1990, because the elderly population made up a small minority of the total dependent population in Asia (11 percent in 1990), the negative relationship between the share of the younger population and economic growth dominates the overall results.

The positive impact of the changing population structure on economic growth has been bigger in East Asia than in Southeast and South Asia. In East Asia, the working-age population grew by 2.4 percent per year between 1965 and 1990, much faster than the rate at which the dependent population grew, which was a mere 0.3 percent a year (Table 3.4). The working-age population also grew faster than the dependent population in Southeast and South Asia, but the differences, 1.2 percentage points in Southeast Asia and 0.5 percentage points in South Asia, were much smaller. These differences help explain part of the disparity in growth across Asia. In East Asia, 1.2 percentage points of economic growth are attributable to differential growth rates of the working-age and dependent populations. In Southeast Asia, where the fertility decline took place somewhat later, the changing age structure of the population

Table 3.4 Average Population Growth Rates by Subregion, Actual 1965-90 and Projected 1995-2025
(percent per year)

Subregion	Period	Economically active population	Economically dependent population
East Asia	1965-1990	2.4	0.3
	1995-2025	0.5	1.1
Southeast Asia	1965-1990	2.9	1.7
	1995-2025	2.0	0.8
South Asia	1965-1990	2.5	2.0
	1995-2025	2.3	1.2

Source: World Bank (1995) and calculations based thereon.

accounts for about 1 percentage point of annual income growth per person. In South Asia, the incipient demographic transition accounts for 0.7 of a percentage point of economic growth per person.

The Size of Asia's Demographic Gift

How large are the overall contributions to economic growth from demographic change? Based on a variety of analyses, demographic change in Asia accounts for between 0.5 and 1.3 percentage points of the annual growth rate of GDP per person. That represents about 15 to 40 percent of the average annual growth rate of 3.3 percent between 1965 and 1990.

In absolute terms, East Asia gained the most from the demographic contribution: demographic factors can explain between 0.9 and 1.5 percentage points of its average annual growth rate of 6.1 percent per person. Assuming that Asia's long-term sustainable growth rate is around 2 percent and that 4.1 percent of East Asian growth is attributable to transitional catch-up factors, then up to a third of the transitional growth is attributable to demographic change. Hong Kong, Korea, Malaysia, Singapore, Taipei,China, and Thailand benefited the most from this transitional boost. In each of these economies the demographic transition accounted for more than 1.5 percentage points of GDP growth per person. South Asia has benefited the least from favorable demographic contributions, gaining only between 0.3 and 1 percentage point.

Compared with other parts of the world, the demographic factors were particularly powerful in East Asia between 1965 and 1990. In Europe, where the demographic transition had long ended, demographic factors contributed only a small amount to overall growth per person (0.2 to 0.4 of a percentage point a year). This was largely because of a further decline in fertility rates in Europe. In Africa demographic factors accounted for zero to 0.9 of a percentage point of the region's growth, and in Latin America the impact was between 0.5 and 1.2 percentage points—smaller than in East Asia, but close to that of Asia as a whole.

The future, however, will look quite different. The rate of income growth attributable to demographic influences in East Asia is likely to fall, from a gain of between 0.9 and 1.5 percentage points between 1965 and 1990 to a loss of between 0.1 and 0.3 of a percentage point between 1995 and 2025. Hong Kong and Japan will feel the negative impact of an aging population most strongly. Demographic change will detract 0.3

of a percentage point from the rate of economic growth in Hong Kong and 0.5 of a percentage point in Japan. It could also induce declines in the growth rate of GDP per person of between 1.3 and 1.9 percentage points in Hong Kong, Korea, and Singapore, between 1965-1990 and 1990-2025. Meanwhile, Southeast Asia should also experience a loss associated with the demographic transition. Growth rates could fall between 0.2 and 0.6 of a percentage point during the next 35 years. In contrast, South Asia can look forward to a boost of up to 0.25 of a percentage point in its rate of economic growth based solely on projected demographic change, taking the overall contribution to a maximum of 1.35 percentage points, which is close to what was recorded in East Asia in past decades. Of course, if South Asia could accelerate its demographic transition—its fertility decline in particular—it could expect to enjoy an even larger demographic gift.

Impact of Demography on the Labor Force

Labor's contribution to economic growth does not depend only on the share of the total population that is of working-age. The growth of overall labor inputs per person also plays a role. Labor inputs can be separated into three parts. First, as discussed earlier, overall labor input depends on the share of the working-age population, which is the purely demographic effect. Second, it depends on how many of these potential workers actually work (the labor participation effect). Third, it depends on how hard they work (the input per worker effect).

How have each of these components of overall labor input fared in Asia? As already noted, the growth in the relative share of working-age people could account for between 15 and 40 percent of Asia's economic growth. By looking only at working-age shares, however, the analysis assumed that the share of potential workers actually working and the amount they worked had stayed constant, but this has not been the case. Labor participation rates for those of working-age were declining throughout the developing world between 1965 and 1975. Asia did not start with higher labor participation rates than other regions, and they declined most dramatically in Asia in the 1960s and 1970s. This fall was big enough to offset the rise in the working-age share of the population up to 1975, but between 1975 and 1990, the increased size of the working-age share of the population more than offset the effects of declining participation rates for those of working age.

Whether Asians added to overall growth by working ever harder is more difficult to calculate. The only relevant internationally comparable statistics measure the average number of hours worked per week in manufacturing industries. Of course, this is not an adequate gauge of how hard people work across the labor force, but it provides some basis for comparison. With minor exceptions, workers in Asian countries work longer hours per week than elsewhere in the world. The impact on growth, however, comes not from the number of hours that people work, but from the increase in hours worked. Only by working harder and harder can individual workers boost growth rates. Have Asians worked harder and harder? Between 1975 and 1990 they did, but they are unlikely to continue to do so in the future. If Asian countries behave like all industrial countries, the rise in working hours per person will stop at some point and will then begin to fall. This will put downward pressure on the growth of GDP per person. In East Asia this turning point could occur very soon.

In short, demographic factors point to a convergence of growth rates in Asia during the next three decades. The rise in the working-age share of the population and longer life expectancy will tend to raise South Asia's growth rate of income per person substantially, but will have much smaller effects elsewhere. Indeed, in some cases in East Asia, a declining working-age share will slow down growth. These purely demographic effects are unlikely to be offset by East Asians working harder or by higher rates of labor force participation. Hours worked per worker in Asia as a whole will probably decline, just as has happened in more mature economies. Labor participation rates are also likely to fall. With earlier retirement, longer spells of schooling, declining farm employment shares, and rising incomes, fewer prime-age Asians are likely to work. Both these changes will further temper GDP growth per person.

Impact of Demography on Education

Asia has invested heavily in education since the 1950s, a commitment that has doubtless contributed to economic growth. The impact of such investment, however, depends in large part on demographic changes. When a country has more children to educate, a particular level of investment in education achieves less than when it has fewer children to educate. Enrollment rates and expenditure per child tend to fall when the share of the population to be educated rises, if the number of schools is insufficient, and if schools have inadequate resources. When the share of the population to be educated falls, the opposite occurs.

Because a large and rising fraction of Asia's population was of school-age in the 1950s and 1960s, Asia had a more difficult task in providing its children with an adequate education than other parts of the world. However, a falling share of school-age children can strengthen the impact of investments in education. In East Asia, for example, the fraction of the population that was of secondary school-age fell sharply after the early 1970s. This demographic shift had some impact on the effect of educational investment: the decline in relative cohort size of school-age children from the previous decade explains between 3 and 4 percent of the rise in secondary school enrollment rates since the mid-1970s and between 10 and 13 percent of the rise in expenditure per child.

In short, the amount that a country can achieve with a particular level of educational investment depends on the relative size of the school-age population. Recent research (Card and Krueger 1992; Schultz 1987; Williamson 1993) has found a link between the level of school expenditure per child and the quality of education received. Smaller class sizes, for instance, make for a better learning environment. This means that the decline in Asia's youth dependency rates that is predicted for coming decades should improve educational quality, because more resources should be available per child. In turn, improved quality of education should have a positive impact on growth potential. Moreover, it will contribute to economic convergence within Asia as dependency rates decline in poorer South Asia.

Impact of Demography on Saving and Investment

The analysis in Chapter 2 showed that high saving rates have been a fundamental contributor to East Asia's rapid economic growth. Average saving rates in East Asia have been consistently above 30 percent of GDP in recent decades. In Japan and Singapore, the average saving rate exceeded 40 percent of GDP at various times. In the early 1960s, before the demographic transition got underway, the saving rate was much lower. Much of the rise in East Asia's saving rate is attributable to the region's demographic transition.

In the 1950s and 1960s a rising dependent share of the population depressed Asia's saving rates. Families with young children face large expenses for child care and may have only one wage earner per family.

This usually results in lower disposable income and lower saving rates. A similar phenomenon took place at the government level. Diminished tax revenues and the cost of educational and other expenses implied by a large dependent population lowered public saving rates. In both cases, however, the effect was only temporary. By 1980 most of the children who had been the cause of the lower saving rate had entered the workforce, and aggregate saving rates increased substantially. In Singapore, the change was particularly striking. The share of the working-age population rose from 55 percent in the 1960s to 70 percent in the 1980s, while saving rates rose from 24 to 42 percent of GDP during the same period.

This sharp rise in saving rates has two components, one permanent and one transitory. The permanent component is the impact of a declining fertility rate. As fertility rates drop, parents can save money that they would otherwise have used to take care of their children. The transitory effect comes from the demographic transition. The decline in saving rates that comes from a bigger share of young dependents in the population reverses as this bulge of people enters the workforce and begins to save. Government saving, too, can increase, because more people working means more taxpayers. Some researchers have suggested that the entire change in saving associated with this demographic transition is as high as 20 percent in Singapore (Bercuson and others 1995). The emerging consensus is that the average increase in Asia's saving rate brought about by demographic factors is closer to 5 percentage points (Collins 1991; Harrigan 1996; Higgins forthcoming; Kang 1994; Kelley and Schmidt 1996; Lee, Mason, and Miller 1997; Mason 1987; Williamson and Higgins 1996). Singapore's exceptional increase also reflects policy decisions, including mandatory personal saving requirements.

Shortly after the age of 40, people's saving rates peak, although the exact timing varies by Asian country. Thereafter, people begin to spend their accumulated assets rather than saving further. As the demographic bulge progresses through Asia's age distribution, the transitory rise in saving rates will be partially reversed. Saving rates will decrease as fewer people are able or willing to save as much, and as governments (with a relatively smaller tax base) and families (with relatively lower incomes) have to divert resources to care for an aging population. While ways to mitigate this trend exist, for example, by raising retirement ages, they will not compensate for the decrease in saving that is inevitably associated with a fall in the fraction of the population that is of working-age.

Without doubt, East Asia's saving rate will fall as the elderly dependent population swells.

The demand for investment also fluctuates with shifts in the age distribution associated with the demographic transition. As the share of young dependents rises and the working-age share diminishes at the beginning of a demographic transition, investment demand falls relative to its long-term trend. Only when the disproportionately large population of young people matures and enters the workforce does investment demand rise again. This is mainly because new members of the workforce need to be equipped with capital, must be transported to work, and need homes built as they form new families. While dependent populations, young or old, generate some investment demand for schools, hospitals, nursing homes, and so on, this demand is lower than that of a working-age population.

Some evidence indicates that the demand for investment exceeds the supply of savings until workers reach their peak saving years. Thereafter, the reverse holds true (Williamson and Higgins 1996). Thus, as the saving rate in a country rises as young workers move into their years of higher saving, the country is able to finance more of its own rising investment demand. This helps to explain why some countries in East Asia have made the transition from being net international debtors to net international lenders during the past three decades (Taylor 1995; Taylor and Williamson 1994; Williamson and Higgins 1996).[4]

Challenges of Changing Demography

Demographic change does not occur spontaneously, nor do countries reap its potential benefits automatically. The speed of Asia's demographic transition had (and will continue to have) much to do with policy choices. Policy decisions can also ensure that the demographic gift is maximized and the subsequent burden minimized. This section analyzes some of the most important policy challenges that changing demography poses.

---

4. In this context, East Asia refers to Hong Kong, Korea, Taipei,China, and Singapore.

Population Policy

Population policy had an important impact on the speed of the demographic transition in Asia. At one level, in some countries family planning programs were a powerful instrument for triggering fertility decline (see Box 3.1). In Korea, for instance, estimates indicate that contraceptives supplied by family planning programs accounted for 40 percent of the fertility decline between 1963 and 1973 (Khoo and Park 1978). At another level, fertility reduction has also received an enormous boost from the development process itself. As education becomes

---

Box 3.1 Fertility Decline in Asia: The Role of Family Planning Programs

Public policies that can accelerate the demographic transition have been the focus of debate for many years. A widely accepted view is that the main cause of fertility decline is the falling demand for children in response to economic and social changes. This view holds that once demand for fertility regulation exists, wide availability of, and access to, contraceptives can influence the timing and speed of the demographic transition. The experience of East and Southeast Asia seems to support this view. A sharp fertility decline in Thailand in the early 1970s and later on in Indonesia, Kerala (India), and Sri Lanka coincided with improved health and educational attainments and the emergence of effective family planning programs.

The example of Bangladesh shows that well-designed family planning programs can reduce fertility even in the absence of extensive socioeconomic development. In this context, a comparison of the demographic experiences of Bangladesh and Pakistan is illustrative. Before 1971, Bangladesh and Pakistan were a single country with a common family planning program and similar levels of contraceptive prevalence and fertility. However, since the split into two countries in 1971, they have followed quite different demographic paths. Bangladesh has achieved rapid increases in contraceptive use and an impressive decline in fertility, while surveys in Pakistan repeatedly show a huge unmet need for contraception, that is, a large percentage of sexually active women want to avoid or postpone their next pregnancy, but currently do not use contraceptives. Estimates indicate that contraceptive prevalence in Bangladesh is currently 46 percent, compared with only 12 percent in Pakistan. Differences in socioeconomic development do not explain these divergent paths, because Pakistan ranks well above Bangladesh in almost all socioeconomic indicators. The major explanation lies in Bangladesh's well-designed family planning program. The country has successfully increased access to family planning services through a village-based cadre of women workers who have been able to overcome social barriers and provide appropriate information, counseling, and contraceptives in a largely traditional society.

Source: Robey, Ross, and Bhushan (1996).

more widespread, as health indicators improve, and as incomes rise, people tend to want fewer children. A successful population policy must take both these levels into account (Sen 1994).

The structure of the costs and benefits involved influences the demand for having children. For instance, investments in health care that reduce the rate of infant mortality can lower the number of children a family desires. Policies to raise the status of women—such as increasing education levels and improving employment possibilities—also influence family size. Better educated mothers invest more in their children's education and health, and hence desire fewer children.

Once the widespread desire to limit family size promotes the use of contraception, and when higher levels of income allow people to pay for contraception, government involvement in family planning can decrease. In many parts of Asia, however, this is not yet the case. Fertility rates in Asia, particularly in South Asia and parts of Southeast Asia, are still high compared with rates in industrial countries. The extent of poverty implies that governments seeking to decrease fertility levels further will need to remain involved in family planning programs in the medium term.

Large proportions of married women of reproductive age in Asia do not want to have any more children or want to space their children, but are not using any method of birth control. The goal of family planning programs is to reduce this unmet need, which is particularly common among the poor, the less educated, and those living in rural areas. Because this unmet need is so large, family planning programs could have a major impact on fertility in Asian countries (Bongaarts 1994; Boulier 1985; Caldwell and Caldwell 1996). Table 3.5 shows by how much selected Asian countries could lower their fertility rates if they satisfied the unmet need for family planning. In the Philippines, for example, women have had an average of 4.1 births when they only wanted, on average, 2.9 births. Eliminating the unwanted births entirely would represent a substantial decline in overall fertility. In contrast, the potential effectiveness of family planning programs in Pakistan is much more limited, given the fertility levels currently desired. An appropriate policy response in these circumstances might be to influence desired fertility through education.

To be effective in a democratic setting, family planning programs must empower couples to make decisions about the timing of having children, the number of children they have, and the spacing between

Table 3.5 Effectiveness and Potential Effectiveness of Family Planning Programs in Selected Asian Economies, Selected Years

Economy	Unmet need for family planning[a] (percent)	Fertility rate (number of births per woman)			Proportion of progress toward replacement level (2.1) that could be achieved by reducing fertility rate from total to wanted (percent)
		Total	Wanted[b]	Unwanted[c]	
Bangladesh, 1993/94	19.4	3.4	2.1	1.3	100
Indonesia, 1994	10.6	2.9	2.4	0.5	62
Pakistan, 1990/91	28.0	5.4	4.7	0.7	21
Philippines, 1993	26.2	4.1	2.9	1.2	60

a.   Unmet need is defined as the percentage of currently married women who either do not want any more children or want to wait before having their next child, but are not using any method of family planning.
b.   A birth is wanted if the number of living children is less than or equal to the current ideal number of children. Wanted fertility rates express the level of fertility if all unwanted births were prevented.
c.   Unwanted fertility is total fertility minus wanted fertility.
Source: Macro International (1990-94) and calculations based thereon.

them. Programs that help people to exert control over their fertility are likely to have a lasting effect, especially if they result in a tangible improvement in living standards. Some family planning programs in Asia have had a significant coercive element. Increased political participation in the region means that such programs will be increasingly difficult to implement.

The exact mix of strategies varies by country, but successful family planning programs ensure the wide availability of a large range of contraceptive techniques and combine the provision of contraception with well-designed communication and information programs. The limited success of India's family planning program, for instance, is partly due to its heavy reliance on just one method of contraception—sterilization. The availability of additional contraceptive methods can increase contraceptive use considerably.

The extent of government involvement in family planning differs substantially within Asia. In Malaysia and the Philippines, for instance, public expenditures on family planning amount to 0.03 percent of gross national product (GNP). Bangladesh, in contrast, spends 0.41 percent of its GNP on family planning. The availability of financial resources alone, however, does not imply effective family planning programs. One important ingredient of success is understanding why individuals who want to limit their family size do not use contraception. Possible answers could be that they lack knowledge about contraceptive techniques, they lack access to contraceptive services, they cannot afford to pay for contraceptive services, they fear side effects, they fear the effects of sterilization surgery, they face religious restrictions, or they fail to obtain their partner's cooperation. The more successful family planning programs explicitly address these issues.

Education on family planning issues should extend beyond the dissemination of information about contraceptive devices. For instance, some women do not know that breast feeding is moderately effective in preventing conception. Spreading such knowledge is useful in limiting fertility.

Family planning and reproductive health programs have generally been independent of each other, but there are gains to coordinating these efforts. Specifically, many countries—PRC, India, Korea, Nepal, Pakistan, Sri Lanka, and Thailand (Table 3.2)—rely on surgical sterilization of either men or women as the primary means of birth control, because it is relatively inexpensive and is permanent. This practice, however, offers no protection against sexually transmitted diseases. At a time when sexually transmitted diseases, particularly HIV/AIDS, are rampant throughout the region (Bloom 1995; Box 3.2), governments can address this problem and provide effective birth control by focusing on condoms as an effective solution. In countries where condoms have not previously been widely used, conveying the importance of condoms for control of sexually transmitted diseases may present significant challenges to family planning programs and to public health education programs. Coordination between such programs will be important for the success of changing attitudes and practices regarding the use of condoms. Of course, among truly monogamous couples with long-term relationships, other means of birth control may be preferable.

In countries where fertility rates have fallen to a level that ensures that the population stays constant, much of the population not only desires contraception, but is willing and able to pay for it. In these countries government resources are best targeted toward those who still need to be convinced of the benefits of limiting family size and to those who want to use contraception, but cannot afford to pay for it. For many

Box 3.2 AIDS in Asia

The spread of HIV, the virus that causes AIDS, is one of the most ominous developments in Asia. Even though the HIV/AIDS epidemic began later in the region than elsewhere, it has spread rapidly: today more people in Asia are infected with HIV every year than in any other part of the world. Already 23 percent of all individuals living with HIV are in Asia, and by the year 2000 more than half of those living with HIV will live there (Mann and Tarantola 1996). In Cambodia, parts of India, Myanmar, and Thailand more than 2 percent of the adult population is infected. In Indonesia, Malaysia, and Viet Nam the number of HIV infections is rising fast. No country in the region remains unaffected. The large number of projected AIDS cases, the relatively high cost of caring for people with HIV and AIDS, and the concentration of the disease among individuals in their prime productive years all suggest that the social and economic impacts of the epidemic are potentially staggering (Bloom and Mahal 1997).

Asia is particularly vulnerable to the AIDS epidemic for several reasons. For instance, labor migration, both within countries and internationally, tends to encourage the growth of the commercial sex industry and is an avenue for spreading HIV. Social and demographic changes have also resulted in an increase in the size of the sexually active single population. In addition, in many Asian countries other sexually transmitted diseases, which enhance HIV transmission, are widespread and often untreated (Bloom and Godwin 1997).

Asian policymakers are generally unprepared for the spread of AIDS (Bloom and Godwin 1997). Only Thailand has taken early and aggressive action to confront the epidemic and reduce its impact. This effort has led to substantial success in slowing the spread of the disease. Nonetheless, by the year 2000 close to 1 million Thai children will have at least one parent with HIV (Brown and Sittitrai 1995). In many other countries, AIDS is not a policy priority despite its devastating potential. Unless this attitude changes, Asian countries will not be able to undertake timely and effective action to prevent the spread of HIV/AIDS or to deal with its consequences.

In the absence of either a vaccine or affordable, effective treatment for HIV infection and AIDS, preventing infection is vital. How well prevention programs work depends on how well they educate the general population about HIV prevention,

couples, however, willingness to pay for contraception depends almost entirely upon the man's willingness to pay. In situations where the man is unwilling to pay for contraception, even though the couple would generally be considered able to pay, governments will need to continue supplying contraceptive services.

In some countries religious concerns hamper the potential for family planning programs. The Philippines' 1987-92 health plan, for example, specified family planning as a central element of its approach for promoting health and socioeconomic development. Because of the opposi-

how well they identify and work closely with vulnerable populations, and whether they are customized to suit local conditions. Current knowledge of HIV/AIDS prevention varies considerably among Asian countries, as does the willingness to work with particularly vulnerable populations, such as commercial sex workers, active male homosexuals, injecting drug users, and commercial blood donors.

Health care systems face particular challenges from AIDS. The disease has a long gestation period during which infection is largely invisible. Unless testing and counseling are readily available, individuals may unknowingly infect others. The spread of AIDS also portends the resurgence of other diseases, particularly tuberculosis, the latent presence of which is extremely widespread in Asia, and incidence of which increases with the spread of HIV infection. The appropriate medical response for infected individuals will necessarily depend on the resources available. Where affordable, of course, the new "drug cocktails" are currently the best treatment; however, the reality in many Asian countries is that little or no treatment will be available to most of those with HIV/AIDS. Possible alternatives

to be explored in this context include identifying less expensive (but also less effective) prophylactic regimens, developing outpatient care facilities, and expanding home-based service delivery and family-based care.

Many Asian countries will need to bolster the social protection mechanisms afforded to those infected with or affected by HIV/AIDS, either directly because they live with HIV/AIDS, or indirectly because they have depended on individuals who have died of AIDS or who can no longer work because of it (Pitayonon, Kongsin, and Janjareon 1997). Possible policy responses include improving the poor's access to free or subsidized health care and basic social services and initiating government-sponsored campaigns against discrimination.

As the burden of HIV/AIDS infection grows, government resources alone may be insufficient to meet the needs. Community resources will then need to be mobilized to provide social and financial support for those with HIV/AIDS and their families. Throughout Asia, an effective response to the epidemic will depend greatly on building support and compassion in the community.

tion of the Roman Catholic Church, however, the government reoriented the family planning aspect of the program to focus on maternal and child health, with no specific focus on reducing fertility (National Statistics Office of the Philippines and Macro International 1994). In some countries, Islamic groups have shown similar opposition to family planning programs. These kinds of religious sensitivities will remain important in the future, and population programs will continue to have to take them into account.

Table 3.6 Health Care Cost Projections, Selected Asian Economies

Economy	Health expenditure per person (1985 $)			Share of GDP (percent)			Annual growth of health expenditure per person 1992-2025 (percent)	
	1992	Current policy 2025	East Asian policy 2025	1992	Current policy 2025	East Asian policy 2025	Current policy 2025	East Asian policy 2025
East Asia								
Hong Kong	539	1,393	1,393	3.3	4.1	4.1	2.9	2.9
Korea	166	711	736	2.2	2.9	3.0	4.4	4.5
Singapore	381	1,165	1,165	3.0	3.7	3.7	3.4	3.4
PRC	15	212	271	1.0	1.9	2.0	8.0	8.8
Southeast Asia								
Indonesia	28	206	254	1.3	2.0	2.0	6.1	6.7
Malaysia	124	567	621	2.2	2.7	2.8	4.6	4.9
Philippines	32	166	251	1.9	2.0	2.1	5.0	6.3
Thailand	104	352	379	2.6	2.5	2.5	3.7	3.9
South Asia								
Bangladesh	24	97	299	1.6	1.9	2.1	4.2	7.6
India	25	135	212	2.0	1.9	2.0	5.1	6.5
Pakistan	14	92	323	1.0	1.7	2.1	5.7	9.5
Sri Lanka	41	154	232	1.8	2.1	2.1	4.0	5.3

Note: All figures are in 1985 purchasing power parity (PPP) international dollars. The estimated equation is

$$\ln(health) = -3.44 \ln(gdppc) + 0.241 \ln(gdppc)^2 + 0.012\,time + 16.71$$
$$(-1.94) \qquad (2.23) \qquad\qquad (2.07) \qquad (2.27)$$

with country specific fixed effects (t-statistics in parentheses). $\ln(health)$ is the natural logarithm of health care spending per person, $\ln(gdppc)$ is the log of PPP GDP per person, and *time* is a year indicator with 1970 = 0. There are 187 observations from 66 countries with an overall R^2 of 0.76. Predictions for 1992 and 2025 used actual GDP (1992) or projected GDP (2025) from projections of economic growth in this study. Predictions were adjusted by adding the prediction error from the last year with data (usually 1985).
Source: health care expenditure as a share of GDP: World Bank (1995); GDP per person: Summers and Heston (1994); and calculations based thereon.

Health Care

Asia faces a substantial rise in health care expenditures during the coming decades. A more affluent population will demand higher standards of health care, an increasingly aged population will be more prone to expensive and chronic diseases, and further advances in medical technology will raise the potential for treatment. Moreover, Asia is in the midst of an epidemiological transition. The prevalence of infectious diseases such as malaria or tuberculosis is declining, and health is improving overall. At the same time, the prevalence of noninfectious and more costly diseases, such as heart disease and diabetes, is increasing. All these factors together imply that Asia's health care expenditures will rise, both absolutely and as a share of national income.

International comparisons suggest that health expenditures per person increase more or less in proportion with average income (Gerdtham and others 1992; Hitiris and Posnett 1992; Newhouse 1977). In addition, statistics from industrial countries show that health care costs per person are roughly three times higher for the elderly than for the nonelderly (Waldo and others 1989). Table 3.6 shows projections of health care costs in selected Asian countries under two scenarios for economic growth. One assumes a continuation of current policies, the other assumes the adoption of high-growth policies throughout Asia (shown in the table as East Asian policy). (These scenarios are discussed in greater detail in Chapter 2.) Plainly, health care costs are set to rise dramatically. Under a high-growth scenario, for instance, the real cost of health expenditures per person could increase tenfold in some countries between 1992 and 2025. In the PRC they could increase by a factor of nearly 20 under a similar scenario.

The increased importance of the expensive noncommunicable diseases that are accompanying Asia's epidemiological transition account for much of the upward pressure on health care costs. As these diseases become increasingly common, more individuals will seek insurance to cover the risk of high health care costs for both acute and chronic illnesses.

Japan, Korea, and Taipei,China currently rely on compulsory social health insurance systems, funded primarily from payroll taxes, to finance private sector delivery of health services, which economists generally regard as more efficient than public provision. These insurance systems initially focused only on the formal wage sector, but have since expanded their coverage. They all operate on a pay-as-you-go basis, which makes insurance premiums highly sensitive to changes in the age distribution of the population. For example, projections indicate that the proportion of the elderly in the population will approximately double in Japan between 1995 and 2025, making the elderly roughly one fourth of the total population. Under the current insurance financing scheme, the maintenance of existing benefit levels will impose a sizable tax burden on the workforce.

Nonetheless, social health insurance is either planned, has been recently legislated, or is under active consideration in a number of other Asian countries, including PRC, Indonesia, Malaysia, Mongolia, Philippines, Thailand, and Viet Nam (Gertler 1995). The introduction of social health insurance involves many important decisions. Among other things, countries must decide who is covered, what benefits are covered, how well they are covered, what form of tax will be used to finance the insurance, whether the insurance system will operate on a pay-as-you-go or provident fund basis, whether benefit coverage will start immediately or be phased in, whether flexible mechanisms for expanding benefit coverage will be available, how providers will be paid, and whether beneficiaries can supplement the insurance with private insurance. In each of these areas the potential for making mistakes and ending up with a poorly designed system is great. Most Asian countries that are currently considering such schemes are also at far earlier stages of development than Japan, Korea, Singapore, and Taipei,China were when they introduced compulsory social health insurance systems.

Despite their drawbacks, such systems do have advantages, in particular, they can correct the underprovision of health insurance in private markets that may arise from adverse selection. This occurs because individuals may be able to hide information about their health from insurers, and as those with the greatest health risks have a strong incentive to insure themselves, this leads insurers to impose conditions, which, although intended to screen out bad risks, will also exclude some genuine demands.

However, successful social insurance schemes demand strong administrative capacity and a strong rule of law to guard against corruption and allow just resolution of disputes. Moreover, social health insurance requires the population as a whole to be willing and able to pay for health care.

Most social insurance programs go far beyond preventing and curing infectious diseases, the main set of health problems for which a public good justification can be claimed. They usually include a strong element of pure public subsidy to the poor, the elderly, and rural residents. Health costs overall tend to rise under such schemes, largely because patients do not bear the full cost of treatment, which in turn encourages the use of costly, new treatments (Newhouse 1993). This has certainly been the experience of Japan, Korea, and Taipei,China; however, these economies have also shown how the use of deductibles, copayments, coverage limits, fee regulation, and prescribed treatments can help limit rising health care costs.

Singapore provides an unusually innovative model of health financing that is designed to limit the level and growth of health spending and intergenerational transfers (Gertler 1995; Hsiao 1995). Under this system, workers and their employers must contribute equally to place between 6 and 8 percent of workers' monthly incomes into a medical savings account known as a Medisave plan. The money in this account accumulates and earns a return over time. Workers can draw down their medical savings account to cover the costs of hospital care for themselves or members of their immediate family. Medisave is thus designed to give health care consumers an incentive to keep the costs of care down even after they are insured. Medisave also tries to control physician-induced demand by limiting reimbursement to prescribed treatments in some instances. Although comparing Singapore's health care costs with costs in other countries is difficult, Singapore reports that its health care expenditures in 1991 were less than 3 percent of GDP. Nevertheless, despite its measures to control costs, health care costs have grown sharply under the Medisave program. In 1993, in an effort to control costs, the government began to regulate both the price and quantity of hospital and physician services covered under Medisave.

Medisave provides little insurance against costly catastrophic illnesses, a situation mitigated somewhat by the introduction of Medishield in the 1990s. A voluntary private insurance plan against catastrophic illness, Medishield allows individuals to insure themselves against the risks of such illness. Ninety-seven percent of people eligible for Medishield have chosen to participate in the program. The government also funds medical care for the demonstrably poor under the Medifund scheme.

Singapore's health financing institutions present a unique approach to addressing the key goals of a health system: universal access to good-quality health care, insurance against large health costs, intergenerational equity, and cost containment. Of course, the Singapore model cannot simply be exported to other Asian countries. It is less appropriate in countries that are growing less rapidly and have smaller formal wage sectors, a less educated population, and weaker administrative capacity. Nonetheless, the system's basic tenets and Singapore's experience with it offer valuable lessons.

Higher Education

Asia has achieved a remarkable and widespread expansion in access to education during the past three decades. Although access to primary education is far from universal for everyone in Asia—countries in South Asia, especially, lag behind, as do women and those living in rural areas—the improvements have been enormous. They have been similarly striking in secondary education. In both areas, future efforts must concentrate not only on continuing to widen access, but also on providing more and better trained teachers and improved learning materials. Chapter 5 discusses primary and secondary education in Asia in more detail. This section concentrates on the policy challenge that derives directly from the demographic transition: how to finance and improve the quality of higher education. The combination of large numbers of school-age children and higher rates of secondary school enrollment will create enormous pressure for expanding higher education. This, in turn, raises difficult financing issues that will be exacerbated by the expected rise in the share of university students who study science and engineering, fields that are particularly expensive.

Projections indicate that the demand for university enrollments in Asia will nearly triple during the next two decades. Partly because of the difficulty of securing admission to local universities and partly because of the superior knowledge and skills attributed to foreign universities, a large and increasing share of Asians attend universities abroad, usually at considerable cost. Universities in Australia, Europe, and the United States frequently vie for tuition-paying Asian students.

Public spending on higher education has been rising rapidly in Asia. Between 1980 and 1992 it grew at nearly 7 percent per year in East Asia, faster than in any other Asian subregion and in all other parts of the world. This growth in total spending took place despite a decrease in spending per student. Larger total enrollments account for the growth in expenditure. In 1992 public spending per student in higher education was lower in Asia than in Latin America, the Middle East, or sub-Saharan Africa.

Total spending by Asian countries as a whole on higher education is projected to increase sharply between 1992 and 2002, growing at an annual rate of 7 percent. Total annual expenditures will reach approximately $58 billion by 2002. These projections are based on expected increases in the population of university-age people, expected future enrollment ratios, and expected changes in spending per student. Spending on higher education is likely to rise twice as fast in East and Southeast Asia as in South Asia (Bloom and Rivera-Batiz 1996).

Financing Higher Education

The case for public funding of primary and secondary education is strong. Education at these levels brings benefits to society as a whole that exceed the private benefits generated (Psacharopolous 1994). East Asia's main educational achievement in the past three decades has been the dramatic expansion of primary education. During the next three decades, similar gains in primary education are likely to occur throughout South Asia. A correspondingly large government-led expansion of secondary education is likely to be the main educational achievement in Asia as a whole during the next three decades.

The case for public funding of higher education is far less compelling. Although the social returns to higher education are not small, they are lower than the social returns to primary and secondary education. Higher education also has a smaller impact on the nonincome dimensions of the quality of life than primary and secondary education. In addition, the long-standing pattern of children from well-to-do and predominantly urban families attending universities at considerably higher rates than children from poor and rural families is unlikely to change significantly in the foreseeable future. Therefore, unless they were specifically targeted toward the needy, public subsidies of higher education would disproportionately benefit already well-off families living in urban areas.

The rapidly growing Asian economies generally finance a larger portion of higher education expenses from private sources than do Asian countries as a whole. In East Asia 50 to 60 percent of higher education expenses are privately funded. In Asia overall the share is about 33 percent. Moreover, the unit costs of privately funded higher education in Asia are considerably lower than the unit costs for publicly funded institutions (Mingat 1995).

Nonetheless, steering higher education systems further in the direction of private financing will require difficult reforms in many countries that have already embarked on a system of public financing. These reforms will be politically contentious, because many who currently enjoy publicly provided higher education or are likely to in the near future may see it as an entitlement. Any substantial privatization may well provoke student unrest, which has at times contributed to political instability in Asia. Governments that seek to move away from public funding of higher education must therefore convince their constituencies that public funds have better or more equitable uses.

A private system of higher education must ensure access to promising students from poor families. Although government scholarship and loan programs are natural devices for providing this access, the administration of such programs has proven difficult. Finding effective ways to conduct means tests and enforce loan repayments is not easy. Part of the problem lies in the absence of collateral generated as part of an education loan. Students gain new skills, but this does not guarantee their ability to repay. Alternative funding mechanisms include fixing tuition at levels high enough to allow some subsidies to demonstrably needy students.

Recent years have seen a wave of new, private centers of higher education that focus on a narrow set of topics. In many cases, these institutions provide effective vocational training, although others appear to be diploma mills. The proliferation of such institutions raises questions of accreditation and standards that policymakers need to address. Distance learning—whereby students pursue advanced-level correspondence courses—is another interesting approach to higher education that has been gaining ground in Asia. Such courses are much less expensive to run than on-campus courses, but whether they can offer the quality required to educate students for participation in a global economy remains to be seen.

Improving the Quality of Higher Education

Higher education in Asia, as elsewhere, has three broad goals: it trains students in the skills needed to run a modern society, it promotes the study and preservation of a society's culture and values, and it promotes the generation of new ideas and provides a setting for discussing such ideas (Rosovsky 1990). Given these purposes of higher education, Asia offers few models of world-class universities. This is particularly distressing given the strong demand among prospective students for good quality higher education and the strong demand among prospective employers for well-trained and innovative graduates. Several policy changes could address these issues and greatly improve the quality of higher education in Asia (Box 3.3). One such policy is decentralization, which can promote a strong spirit of competition among universities. This competition for faculty, for resources, and for students can lead to a system that strongly rewards merit and performance. For example,

Indonesia's recent adoption of a competitive system for awarding research grants has led to highly relevant research into the development
of new varieties of food crops, biofertilizers, bacterial isolates for industry, prototypes of machines, and concrete (Koswara 1996).

Academic excellence cannot be centrally decreed. However, it can
be promoted by institutional autonomy, which can give universities a
relatively free hand to exploit their strengths and to overcome their weaknesses. At the same time, unless autonomy is instituted within a system
that monitors the educational and research achievements of both faculty
and students and holds the administration accountable for the outcomes,
it can become an invitation to poor performance. By itself, autonomy is
clearly an insufficient guarantee of improved quality.

Effective governance within universities can help create high-quality
institutions. A chief operating officer who has incentives to make good
decisions and who can be held accountable for bad decisions sets the
tone for governance that is oriented toward high quality. Deans and
department chairs can be appointed by their superiors in the university
administration and can be either dismissed or not reappointed if they
fail to fulfill their responsibilities adequately, much like the management
in a commercial enterprise. Similarly, peer review and peer pressure can
be important mechanisms of accountability that help to promote quality. University administration and faculty at all levels need incentives to
ensure that they are working effectively to help students emerge from
their education with the skills and knowledge that a growing economy
requires (Rosovsky 1990).

A multitiered system of higher education can provide a useful means
of achieving both excellence and widespread access to universities. An
upper level dedicated primarily to achieving excellence across-the-board
can complement lower tiers aimed at providing large numbers of students with a more basic educational experience.

One additional point deserves mention, namely, that academic excellence has a long gestation period. In other words, abundant financial
resources, autonomy, and effective governance are all necessary conditions for excellence, but they cannot transform a mediocre university
into an excellent university overnight. Thus for Asia to improve the
quality of its university systems, which will play a crucial role in its
continuing growth and development, it will take great leadership and
sustained commitment (Rosovsky 1990).

Box 3.3 Reforming Higher Education in the PRC

During the 1950s and 1960s, higher education in the PRC was based on the Soviet model. The government managed the system with the aim of training higher-level personnel to serve the needs of the socialist state. Students were selected and funded primarily by the State Education Commission, or sometimes by a sponsoring ministry, province, or municipality. Administrative and faculty appointments required central approval, as did new academic programs. University graduates were usually assigned jobs by their sponsors after graduation.

The Cultural Revolution demolished this system. Universities closed and students were exiled to rural areas for "re-education." Reconstruction of the system began in 1978 and proceeded rapidly. By 1994, 2.8 million full-time students were enrolled in courses offered by more than 1,000 public higher education institutions. Graduate programs, unknown in 1978, enrolled an additional 130,000 students in 1994.

Despite this recovery in student numbers, a far smaller proportion of people aged 20 to 24 are enrolled in higher educa-

tion in the PRC than in most other Asian countries. In 1994, just 2.4 percent of this age group attended higher education institutions, which barely exceeds the enrollment ratio in 1960. Including all institutions of tertiary education, the enrollment ratio rose to 4 percent, still much lower than in other Asian countries. For example, enrollment rates were 10 percent in Indonesia, 19 percent in Thailand, and 51 percent in Korea. Even India, a far poorer country than the PRC, enrolled 8 percent of its 20- to 24-year-olds in higher education.

Since 1978 the PRC has made considerable progress in reforming higher education. Central control of appointments is now generally limited to university presidents, and job assignment for graduates has virtually disappeared. Universities have been encouraged to widen their income sources and all students are now expected to pay some fees, which are gradually being raised.

Nonetheless, educational and economic considerations demand further reform. The government will need to limit itself to defining policies, setting standards, and regu-

Paying for Pensions

Asia's populations are young now, but are aging rapidly. Over time, rising life expectancy and falling fertility create a population structure with relatively few young people and a large elderly population. The demographic transition is one reason for the rising number of elderly: the bulge generation eventually works its way through to augment the elderly's share of the population. Falling death rates among the elderly reinforce the trend, as today's old people live longer than yesterday's. However, lower fertility means that there are relatively fewer new workers to support them.

lating educational institutions, while granting individual institutions substantial financial, managerial, and pedagogical autonomy. Despite its low enrollment ratio, the PRC's higher education system is enormous and cannot be managed effectively on a centralized basis. The government needs to encourage regional and private initiatives, and perhaps open the door to twinning arrangements with foreign universities, which some other Asian countries have encouraged as being less expensive than sending students overseas.

Demand for higher education is almost certain to grow rapidly in the coming years. A significant increase in the quality of the education offered will need to accompany the required expansion of the university system. However, pursuit of both these goals at once is difficult. To do so, accountability and competitiveness must become the touchstones of the recommended decentralized structure. University autonomy will encourage individual universities to raise the quality of their offerings and attract more students. Students, trustees, and public officials can all hold universities

accountable for the quality of their graduates. Universities that effectively train students in how to run a modern society will see more students flock to them. Those that fall short will not.

Like other developing economies, the PRC needs skilled individuals at many levels of responsibility throughout society. Elite institutions that succeed in marshaling sufficient academic and financial resources can train a new generation of leaders. At the same time, lower-level institutions can specialize in a narrower range of needed skills. Transforming provincial universities (which enroll more than half of all students) into high-quality institutions will require major governmental assistance. None of this will be easy, but unless the PRC dramatically raises its stock of highly skilled people, its capacity to compete effectively in international markets and manage its own increasingly complex economy will diminish greatly.

Source: Brooks and Thant (1996); Gannicott (1996); Harman and Selin (1991); Lewin (1996); Silverman and Saywell (1996); World Bank (1996).

Throughout Asia, elderly populations will grow relatively larger. How much larger they become depends on how far the demographic transition has advanced in each country. The biggest changes will occur in PRC, Hong Kong, Singapore, Sri Lanka, and Taipei,China, where those aged 65 or more will make up more than 10 percent of the population by 2025. These countries will have between two and five people of working age for every old person. Elsewhere the effect will be similar, but less pronounced. For example, India, Malaysia, and Thailand will have six working-age people per elderly person in 2025. Well over half the elderly will be women, as women tend to live longer than men. Over time, a rising proportion of the elderly will be extremely old—aged 85 and over (Figure 3.6).

Ensuring financial security for the elderly thus presents an important challenge in Asia. Traditionally, Asian families provide for their elderly relatives, but dramatic social changes are weakening filial ties. Families are more mobile. Many young people have moved from rural to urban areas, so fewer children live close to their parents. In addition, as more women seek outside work, the tradition of staying at home to care for both children and the elderly is diminishing.

Given these trends, pension financing is increasingly becoming a matter of public policy. Government involvement in pension provision can take two broad forms. The most common form of pension scheme in industrial countries is a pay-as-you-go pension system, where today's workers pay for the pensions of today's retirees, usually through a pay-roll tax. The alternative is a fully funded system whereby individuals are forced to save for their own retirement in specific, and regulated, pension funds. Pay-as-you-go systems normally guarantee a specific level of benefits upon retirement. In defined contribution plans, the amount of benefits participants receive depends on the amount they contribute and the rate of return their contributions earn. Asia has both types of systems. Japan pioneered a pay-as-you-go system in Asia, and Korea and Taipei,China have recently adopted such systems. In contrast, Hong Kong, Malaysia, and Singapore all have fully funded systems known as provident funds, and Thailand has recently elected to follow this model. Under these systems contributions are required both from employers and employees. The contributions deposited in the provident funds earn a return until retirement, when they become available to the individual. If contributors withdraw funds for allowable investments, such as buying a house, they must repay the fund with interest on disposal of the asset.

Pay-as-you-go pension schemes can work in a rapidly growing economy with a constant number of elderly. They also allow for an element of redistribution between rich and poor and permit coverage for those who never enter the formal labor market. If, however, economic growth slows or the relative number of old people rises, pay-as-you-go systems rapidly create a fiscal burden as pension commitments rise and the relative number of workers to pay them falls. As Chapter 2 argued, this can reduce government saving, and may even precipitate a fiscal crisis. The evidence from industrial countries suggests that pay-as-you-

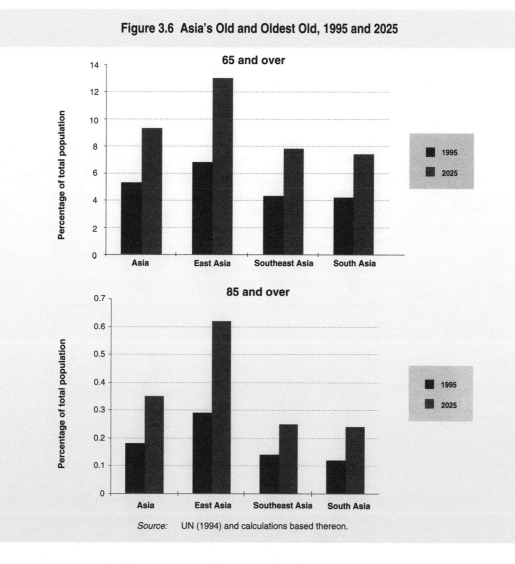

Figure 3.6 Asia's Old and Oldest Old, 1995 and 2025

65 and over

Source: UN (1994) and calculations based thereon.

go pensions, especially during a time of demographic change, eventually become unsustainable (Auerbach, Kotlikoff, and Leibfritz forthcoming; Leibfritz and others 1995).

In contrast, defined contribution pension schemes have much to commend them. To the extent that they succeed in raising the saving of the myopic and ill-informed, they raise national saving, thereby making resources available for needed investment. As long as provident funds are invested in a sufficiently diversified portfolio, they avoid the perilous fiscal dynamics of pay-as-you-go schemes. Indeed, for an aging population (such as Asia faces), this is the only approach to pensions that ensures fiscal prudence. Thus Asian countries would do well to consider defined contribution schemes.

The design of provident funds involves four critical issues: their coverage, the rates at which contributions are levied, the permissible uses of provident fund assets, and the regulatory framework that governs their management.

Provident fund coverage is usually limited to those in formal sector employment. A significant share of the population therefore falls outside their reach. This means that publicly funded safety nets may be needed for those elderly that are demonstrably needy, some of whom may never have held a formal sector job. Also, the regulatory framework governing entitlements should afford protection to fund members' spouses and dependents in the event of death or marital breakdown.

Singapore has opted for higher contribution rates than Malaysia and other countries. In Singapore, workers must pay 40 percent of their wages into their provident fund accounts, of which employers pay half. These levies have potentially complex implications for labor costs. In some circumstances, workers may effectively bear the entire incidence of their employer's contribution through lower wages. High contribution rates are also likely to "tax" employment more severely than lower rates. In an increasingly integrated world, surcharges that significantly raise labor costs may deter investment.

As saving is effectively forced under provident fund arrangements, high contribution rates are more likely to lead to inefficiencies. Even those who would otherwise have made adequate provision for their retirement may be forced to save too much. If high rates of provident fund contributions are levied, efficiency is promoted if greater flexibility is permitted in the use of fund balances by, for example, allowing people before retiring, to make withdrawals for certain approved investments. Singapore is moving in this direction. While this makes economic sense, it can greatly complicate the management of a fund. Withdrawals, say to purchase approved securities, have to be repaid with interest when they are liquidated. Therefore, to ensure that balances are maintained, the provident fund must monitor, record, and audit a whole panoply of financial and other transactions by its members. This creates an administrative burden that is ultimately paid for by provident fund members themselves. Where this monitoring capacity does not exist or its costs are excessive, more moderate levies and narrower uses for fund balances may be preferable.

Two important issues arise in connection with the regulatory framework surrounding provident fund management. First, what should fund managers be able to invest in, and second, should funds be privately or publicly managed? In the absence of appropriate disclosure and supervision, mismanagement and malfeasance can occur in both the public and private sectors. Public management of a fund is no guarantee of good stewardship. Governments may renege on earlier promises and tax away accumulated contributions by a variety of means. In any case, in practice, the distinction between private and public management of funds is not clear cut. In Malaysia, where a statutory body manages the Employees' Provident Fund, private fund managers are entrusted with investment. In Singapore, the Central Provident Fund's board invests in government bonds and these receipts are reinvested in both domestic and foreign capital markets (Asher and Shantakumar 1995). In Chile, provident fund assets are privately managed.

While adequate stewardship of provident funds is possible under public and/or private arrangements, greater choice is probably afforded where there is competition between private sector pension managers whose earnings are related to their performance. Appropriate prudential safeguards must, of course, be in place in cases where funds are privately managed. In addition, provident fund assets should not provide a captive market for government debt, as has been the case in some countries. If the rate of return on government bonds is below the rate of return on alternative investments, this effectively taxes pension benefits. One possible drawback of having the private sector compete for the management of provident fund accounts is that more resources may be diverted to marketing and other uses that increase charges on fund balances.

Labor Markets

Economies will not be able to realize the potential benefits of the demographic transition unless their labor markets are flexible. Workers must have the opportunity and incentives to shift between jobs and sectors as the economy's structure changes. If workers are unemployed or underemployed because they lack skills, because the minimum wage is too high, or because wage increases significantly outstrip productivity gains, this limits the potential for rapid economic growth.

At early stages of development, most of an economy's workers are involved in agriculture, and formal government involvement in the labor market is scant. As the share of industry and services in the economy increases—as it has throughout Asia—the share of people working in the formal sector grows, and government decisions about labor markets become increasingly important. For instance, in East Asia only 24 percent of the workforce is currently involved in agriculture, with 46 percent in services and 30 percent in industry. In contrast, 65 percent of the labor force in South Asia still works in agriculture, and only 14 percent works in industry. Southeast Asia lies in between: its industry sector is proportionately as small as South Asia's, but more people are employed in services and fewer in agriculture.

Government involvement in labor markets is primarily through the creation, design, and regulation of labor market institutions, such as establishing the role of unions, setting minimum wages, providing unemployment insurance, and regulating employment contracts. The fastest growing Asian economies have had relatively fewer labor market regulations. In contrast, sclerotic labor practices have hobbled some of the slower growing economies, especially those in South Asia. In India, for instance, complex procedures and regulations about worker dismissal have dampened employment creation.

Employers' ability to hire and dismiss is, of course, not the only component of labor market flexibility. In fact, some Asian economies have been remarkably flexible with systems that guarantee employment. Japan, for instance, has a well-known system of lifetime employment for part of its workforce. Flexibility instead comes in wage and bonus packages (Freeman and Weitzman 1987). If the firm makes less money, workers' jobs are safe, but their pay packets are cut. Such security of employment has advantages: workers are more likely to develop company-specific skills and may contribute ideas to the firm that enhance its productivity. In turn, the development of company-specific skills, which were themselves promoted by the need to adapt quickly to rapid technical change, reduces turnover (Mincer and Higuchi 1988).

Powerful unions are often blamed for labor market ills. By demanding excessive wage rises, the argument goes, they price people out of work. This is too simplistic. The fast growing economies of East Asia have quite a high degree of unionization. In Taipei,China, for instance, 35 percent of the workforce belong to a union. Such formal labor organizations were widely used to gain support for national development goals. A union's impact on flexibility depends in part on how countries conduct wage bargaining as well as on the laws governing union behavior. In most rapidly growing East Asian economies other than Hong Kong, wage bargaining is done collectively at the factory level. This promotes flexibility, because pay rises can be tailored to productivity improvements in the firm. In India collective bargaining occurs at the industry level in organized, mostly government-owned, industries, making it difficult to arrive at settlements consistent with productivity gains. This hampers competitiveness and employment growth, even though only 7 percent of the Indian workforce is unionized. In India's private sector, factory-level bargaining is the norm.

In general, labor market flexibility is best guaranteed by a government approach that is relatively hands-off. Too many government regulations and restrictions tend to impede firms' decisions. Calls for direct government intervention in labor markets become more plausible when free markets have negative social consequences, say in the case of child labor (Box 3.4) or inadequate health and safety conditions at work. Child labor is pervasive in some Asian countries. Estimates of the number of child laborers in Asia range from 50 million to 100 million (Grootaert and Kanbur 1995; UNICEF 1996). As children are unable to protect themselves from the pressures put on them by factory owners to work long hours, a case for regulation exists. Often, however, the basic reason for child labor is poverty. Families push their children to work to supplement the family's income. Legislative bans on child labor—which exist in many Asian countries, but are ignored—are therefore unlikely to be effective. Addressing the root cause, poverty, is far more important. This is best done by, among other things, improving access to education and ensuring a safety net for the poorest of the poor.

Health and safety at work is also of concern. If workers do not realize that the conditions in which they are working may be dangerous, they cannot exercise informed choices about where they work. This provides a rationale for regulation. However, policymakers must carefully weigh the costs and benefits of greater regulation.

International labor migration is an important dimension of labor market flexibility. In 1991, nearly half a million workers left the Philippines, nearly two-thirds of them headed for the Middle East (Bloom and Noor forthcoming). For countries that supply labor, such as India, Indonesia, Pakistan, Philippines, and Sri Lanka, emigration relieves unemployment and is often a source of significant financial flows in the form

Box 3.4 Child Labor

Upon ratification, the International Labour Organisation's (ILO's) Minimum Age Convention of 1973 commits member countries to set a minimum age for work that is not less than the age of compulsory schooling and, in any case, is not less than 15 years, or 14 in developing countries. The convention does not, however, set a blanket prohibition, and authorizes some exemptions, usually of a temporary duration. However, as of mid-1996, fewer than one third of member countries had ratified the convention, of which just over 20 were developing countries (ILO 1996a,b).

The ILO takes child labor to encompass all economic activities regardless of occupational status, such as wage earners, own-account workers, and unpaid family workers. In general, household work in the parents' home is not included, except as such work can be identified with an economic activity. Given the breadth of this definition, the extent of child labor is difficult to gauge. Almost all available data concern the 10- to 14-year-old age group, yet the number of child workers under ten years of age is not negligible, nor is adequate account taken of full-time domestic work by girls. In addition, wide variations exist in the limited country-level data. ILO surveys are important in measuring the extent and incidence of child labor; however, UNICEF (1996) estimates the number of

child workers in Asia to be at least double the ILO estimates cited below. Accordingly, some caution should be exercised in interpreting the data.

The ILO estimates that more than 76 million children aged 10 to 14 were economically active in 1995. The greatest numbers were in Asia (44.6 million), followed by Africa (26.3 million) and Latin America (5.1 million). The incidence of economic activity in that age group was highest in Africa (26.3 percent), followed by Asia (13 percent) and Latin America (9.8 percent). The estimated incidence varied widely across Asia, for example, 45 percent in Nepal, 30 percent in Bangladesh, 18 percent in Pakistan, 16 percent in Thailand, 14 percent in India, 12 percent in PRC, 10 percent in Indonesia, 9 percent in Viet Nam, 8 percent in Philippines, and 3 percent in Malaysia. Trends over time have to be treated with caution; nevertheless, overall, developments based on ILO data have been encouraging in Asia, and the proportion of the world's child labor found in Asia has similarly declined sharply from more than 75 percent in 1980 to about 60 percent in 1995 (Basu and Basu 1996; ILO 1996b).

Although the profile of a typical child worker is difficult to draw because of wide situational variation across the developing world, surveys indicate that children are

of remittances by emigrant workers (Bloom and Noor forthcoming; Harrigan and Sumulong 1996). These remittances raise the standard of living of those receiving them, and by injecting external funds into the local economy can promote development. Emigration thus serves as an economic adjustment mechanism for these countries, some of which have not adopted effective policies for assimilating large numbers of new workers into the economy. However, labor migration also increases the stress on families and drains the human capital resources of poorer countries.

much more likely to work in rural than in urban areas. Child workers are generally employed in family labor, in small production units in rural or urban informal sectors, or as domestic servants in private households. The modern manufacturing sector employs relatively few children, although the inclusion of subcontracting to small, informal workshops or to homeworkers would result in more child labor being indirectly attributable to it. Given the above characteristics, most working children are unpaid family members. Gender differences in participation rates are not marked if one takes into account full-time housework performed by girls to enable their parents to work. In-depth, ILO-assisted surveys in the early 1990s in four developing countries (including India and Indonesia), found that 25 percent of children aged 5 to 14 were economically active. For one third, it was their principal activity; for the remainder it was secondary, additional to schooling. Although a great deal of international attention focuses on children employed in developing country export industries (such as textiles, garments, and carpets), evidently substantially fewer children are working in such industries than are working to meet domestic consumption requirements (ILO 1996a,b).

Some amount of child labor may be unavoidable in poor societies. Without child earnings or labor in the field and home, some families may face difficulty in subsisting. Poorly functioning adult labor markets may reinforce family dependence on child labor. Generally, child labor appears to take place outside the occupational status covered by labor market legislation. This is not to deny the legitimacy of action directed against more abusive forms of child labor that are detrimental to children's health and personal development. Employment in hazardous jobs (for example, match manufacturing), in bonded labor (for instance, carpet weaving in South Asia), and as prostitutes should be prime candidates for such action. In situations of low-quality education available to the poor, and given its implied cost, parents may perceive early entry into labor rather than schooling as more beneficial to themselves and to the future employability of their children. Broadly based growth that reduces poverty, along with increased, better adult employment opportunities, may, in the long run, be most conducive to alleviating the incidence of child labor. Propagating mass basic education of improved quality would bring further positive momentum to such a trend. In the meantime, the design of additional measures to mitigate the effects of child labor would be more effective with community participation.

Countries such as Brunei Darussalam, Japan, Singapore, and the Gulf states bring in immigrant laborers to help relieve the shortage of labor, particularly of unskilled labor. In these situations, labor flexibility takes the form of immigrants who respond to labor shortages. Some countries, such as Malaysia and Thailand, have a significant flow of workers both into and out of the country as they gradually shift from labor-exporting to labor-importing status.

Countries that receive labor treat unskilled migrant workers as temporary residents and often strictly regulate their occupations and access to social and other services. While the economic case for free migration is compelling, it often leads to friction within and between countries. Indeed, as demographic and other pressures push in the direction of increased labor migration, Asian governments will have to formalize agreements to monitor and set standards for the treatment of migrant labor and their families.

International labor standards have become a controversial aspect of both labor and trade policy in recent years (Bloom and Noor 1994). At the heart of the debate is the claim of a number of wealthy, industrial nations that many of Asia's developing countries, for example, Bangladesh, PRC, India, Pakistan, and Viet Nam, are securing an unfair advantage in international trade by allowing unfair wages, long hours, and inhumane working conditions. The lack of consistent labor standards across countries may promote a so-called "race to the bottom" mechanism, where all countries reduce their standards to compete in the trade arena. Industrial countries also argue for the adoption of international labor standards on humanitarian grounds, claiming that such standards would improve the welfare of workers in poorer countries. In response, many developing countries argue that labor standards are simply a form of protectionist trade policy.

In an integrated world economy, labor-related issues are as much matters of trade policy as they are of labor policy. For example, insofar as the imposition of labor standards increases production costs, it will reduce international competitiveness (disproportionately so in labor-intensive sectors of the economy). For developing Asian countries, this is equivalent to introducing an export tax, thereby undermining their natural comparative advantage. In this way, labor standards are a second-best option to tariff policies, whose use is highly restricted under the current world trading system. Thus, international pressure to invoke labor standards in Asia's developing countries are imbued with a conflict of interest between humanitarian concerns and economic self-interest (Noor 1996).

Overall, Asian economies tend to impose relatively few regulations on labor markets. The International Labour Organisation has established more than 120 conventions on government practices in relation to labor. These conventions cover such diverse areas as the right to organize, collective bargaining, forced labor, discrimination, equal pay, minimum working age, and many others. On average, the number of conventions ratified is 71 in high-income OECD countries, 50 in Latin American countries, 41 in Japan, 26 in sub-Saharan African countries, 25 in South Asian countries, and 14 in Southeast Asian countries. Thus according to this measure, Asian countries tend to have relatively few regulations. While no Asian countries have ratified the International Labour Organisation's convention on minimum working age, most do have laws preventing child labor, although these laws are difficult to enforce. Comparatively few Asian countries have ratified the convention on the right to organize. Whether this low level of labor market regulation has contributed to Asian economic success is subject to debate, but clearly rapid economic development has occurred in an environment where labor market regulation has generally not been extensive. As Asia's economies become more sophisticated, so the importance of appropriate labor market institutions will increase. Many of the old approaches to labor markets in Asia will not work in the future. In the past, political leaders often set the rules that defined labor market institutions and upheld them by force. This kind of approach will not work in Asia's increasingly pluralistic societies. Relationships between governments, employers, and employees have to become more consultative and open. The challenge is to ensure that this does not reduce the necessary flexibility.

To begin with, Asian governments will need to concentrate more on education and training. Flexibility in a more sophisticated economy demands a higher skill base. Second, they will need to develop new models of cooperation between employers and employees. Some Asian countries have experienced periods of sharp labor strife, and serious clashes are still occurring, but others have tended to recognize the value of cooperation between labor and management. Japan's case is instructive. The number of workdays lost to labor disputes fell from more than 8 million in 1975 to 145,000 in 1990 and 85,000 in 1994 (Asian Productivity Organization 1996). Formal consultation systems are an important part of this success. Productivity growth is promoted because decisions are made in advance and the gains will be divided between employers and workers (Asian Productivity Organization 1996).

Despite the increasing breadth and sophistication of many Asian economies, the large informal sector will continue to play an extremely important role in buttressing labor market flexibility for the foreseeable future. In many Asian countries, the informal economy encompasses activities ranging from scavenging, operating a pedicab, and selling small items to supplying a wide range of personal services. High taxes, bureaucratic impediments to formally establish legal businesses, inadequate municipal transportation and sanitation services, environmental regulations, minimum wages, and a desire to circumvent child labor laws have given impetus to this sector. Once established, informal enterprises often build quite successfully on their founders' energy and ingenuity to become significant economic and social forces in a community.

During the next few decades, most population growth in Asia will be in the cities. In many cases, employment growth in the formal sector will not be rapid enough to absorb the population influx from rural areas. The informal sector will serve as a buffer for rural to urban immigrants, supplying them with livelihood for considerable periods of time. As economies develop, workers in the informal sector will tend to move to the formal sector.

Although informal enterprises in the service and industrial sectors represent a thriving and important segment of the economy in many countries, the workers employed in such concerns typically lack even the most rudimentary protection. Long working hours, low pay, and dangerous working conditions are common, and child labor abounds. Countries that wish to improve labor standards will have to seek solutions to these problems without damaging the vitality of the informal sector. Development itself will help, although it offers no short-term relief to those currently laboring under difficult conditions.

Conclusion

This chapter has described a demographic transformation in Asia that is without parallel, both in terms of the number of people involved and the speed with which it is taking place. In a couple of generations, the region's population profile has been transformed. Mortality and fertility rates have plummeted and life expectancy has risen sharply. Although countries' progress through the demographic transition has differed dramatically within Asia, with East Asia being the most advanced and South Asia the least advanced, demographic characteristics throughout Asia are unrecognizable compared with only 50 years ago. This transition has been far faster than that of the industrial countries in the previous century, and much of the reason lies with massive health technology transfers to the region and family planning policies.

This demographic transition did not occur automatically, nor were its benefits reaped automatically. This chapter's central conclusion is that public policy is instrumental in stimulating a demographic transition, in capturing its benefits, and in coping with its costs.

First, government policy influenced both the timing and speed of Asia's population change. Dramatic improvements in public health programs in the immediate postwar years lay behind the initial drop in mortality rates—infant and child mortality rates in particular. The subsequent rise in life expectancy itself prompted a fall in fertility, as parents preferred to invest more resources in fewer children. Here, too, however, public policy made a difference. Government attitudes toward population policy, particularly family planning policy, had a major influence on how quickly birthrates fell. Public investment in education, especially for women, also did much to promote lower fertility.

Second, government policy determines whether a country captures or squanders the potential benefits of population change. This chapter has shown how a demographic transition causes a temporary bulge in the population that gradually works its way through the population's age structure. When the relative number of working-age people increases, demographic factors provide the potential for higher economic growth, but this potential will translate only into faster economic growth with appropriate public policies. East Asian countries have shown how large the benefits of harnessing demography with prudent policy can be. A strategy of market-based, export-led economic growth with flexible labor and product markets allowed these countries to maximize the potential that population change provided. Moreover, they invested heavily in education, which not only speeded up the demographic transition, but also helped maximize the benefits of growth.

With the wrong economic policies, however, East Asia's growing labor force could easily have resulted in growing ranks of unemployed. For countries such as those in South Asia, where the bulge in the working-age population is still to come, this possibility lies ahead. They can still boost economic growth, but can also fritter it away. Whether or not they will capture the benefits of demographic change will depend on the presence of appropriate economic policies.

Finally, the latter stages of a demographic transition provide new policy challenges. As the bulge generation ages, it no longer boosts growth. Elderly people work less and save less. As the share of dependent, elderly people in the population rises, so the demographic gift becomes a burden that public policy must try to minimize. In particular, policymakers must design provisions for pensions and health care in a way that ensures adequate provision without creating unsustainable financial commitments. East Asia is now facing these challenges.

As this chapter has shown, demography provides a powerful lens through which to view many future trends. Demographic change affects economic growth, employment patterns, consumption, and saving. Increased life expectancy and higher incomes create demands for more and higher quality education and health services that, in turn, contribute to future growth. Urbanization, functioning in tandem with more women working, reduces incentives to have children, changes women's role and status, and creates challenges for public health and the provision of local public services. Understanding these processes will help policymakers devise imaginative and bold initiatives that will facilitate economic growth, social equity, and a healthy environment.

Proposing policy solutions is one thing; implementing them is something altogether different. Asia's changing demographic profile implies a need for difficult political decisions. In increasingly pluralistic societies, governments cannot simply impose their decisions. From family planning approaches to pension policy, Asian governments will need to build consensus for the kinds of policies that bring the greatest benefits from demographic change and minimize its costs. This demands foresight and prudence. As future population trends are set by births that have already occurred, demographic trends can be foreseen well ahead of time. Thus Asia's governments have time to prepare themselves for demographic change. They cannot afford to ignore it.

References

Asian Productivity Organization. 1996. *Labor-Management Cooperation: From Labor Disputes to Cooperation.* Tokyo: Asian Productivity Organization.

Asher, Mukul G., and G. Shantakumar. 1995. "Financing Old Age Through the National Provident Fund Mechanism." Revision of the paper presented at the Seventh World Congress of Social Economics, The New World Order: Social Economies in Transition, 3-7 August, 1994, Verona, Italy.

Auerbach, Alan J., Laurence J. Kotlikoff, and Willi Leibfritz, eds. Forthcoming. *Generational Accounting Around the World.* Chicago: University of Chicago Press.

Basu, K., and A. Basu. 1996. "The Quality of Work Experience in Emerging Asia." Background paper for *Emerging Asia: Changes and Challenges*. Asian Development Bank, Manila.

Bercuson, Kenneth, Robert Carling, Aasim Husain, Thomas Rumbaugh, and Rachel van Elkan. 1995. *Singapore: A Case Study in Rapid Development*. IMF Occasional Paper. Washington, D.C.: International Monetary Fund.

Bloom, David E., guest editor. 1995. "Special Edition: AIDS in Asia." *Current Science* 69(10): 822-70.

Bloom, David E., and Richard B. Freeman. 1986. "The Effects of Rapid Population Growth on Labor Supply and Employment in Developing Countries." *Population and Development Review* 12(3):381-414.

_____. 1988. "Economic Development and the Timing and Components of Population Growth." *Journal of Policy Modeling* 10(1):57-81.

Bloom, David E., and Peter Godwin. 1997. *The Economics of HIV and AIDS: The Case of South and South East Asia*. New Delhi, India: Oxford University Press.

Bloom, David E., and Ajay S. Mahal. 1997. "Does the AIDS Epidemic Threaten Economic Growth?" *Journal of Econometrics* 77:105-24.

Bloom, David E., and Waseem Noor. 1994. "Labor Standards and the Emerging World Economy." Columbia University, New York.

_____. Forthcoming. "Is an Integrated Regional Labor Market Emerging in East and Southeast Asia?" In Duncan Campbell, Aurelio Parisotto, Anil Verma, and Asma Lateef, eds., *Regionalization and Labor Market Interdependence in East and Southeast Asia*. London: Macmillan.

Bloom, David E., and Francisco Rivera-Batiz. 1996. "Global Trends in the Financing of Higher Education: Prospects and Challenges for the Next Decade." Paper prepared for the Meeting on Higher Education and Development, 11 December, World Bank, Washington, D.C.

Bongaarts, John. 1994. "Population Policy Options in the Developing World." *Science* 263(February):771-76.

Boserup, Ester. 1981. *Population and Technological Change: A Study of Long-Term Trends*. Chicago: University of Chicago Press.

Boulier, Bryan. 1985. "Family Planning Programs and Contraceptive Availability: Their Effects on Contraceptive Use and Fertility." In Nancy Birdsall, ed., *The Effects of Family Planning Programs on Fertility in the Developing World*. Population and Development Series No. 2. Washington, D.C.: World Bank.

Brooks, Douglas H., and Myo Thant. 1996. "Health and Education Issues in Asian Transition Economies." Asian Development Bank, Manila.

Brown, T., and W. Sittitrai, eds. 1995. "The Impact of HIV on Children in Thailand." Research Report. Thai Red Cross Society Program on AIDS, Bangkok.

Caldwell, John, and Bruce Caldwell. 1996. "Asia's Demographic Transition." Background paper for *Emerging Asia: Changes and Challenges*: Asian Development Bank, Manila.

Card, David, and Alan B. Krueger. 1992. "Does School Quality Matter? Returns to Education and the Characteristics of Public Schools in the United States." *Journal of Political Economy* 100(1):1-39.

Coale, Ansley. 1986. "Population Trends and Economic Development." In Jane Menken, ed., *World Population and U.S. Policy: The Choices Ahead*. New York: Norton.

Coale, Ansley, and Edgar Hoover. 1958. *Population Growth and Economic Development in Low-Income Countries*. Princeton, New Jersey: Princeton University Press.

Collins, Susan. 1991. "Saving Behavior in Ten Developing Countries." In D. Bernheim and J. Shoven, eds., *National Saving and Economic Performance*. Chicago: University of Chicago Press.

Ehrlich, P. R. 1968. *The Population Bomb*. New York: Ballantine.

Freeman, Richard B., and Martin L. Weitzman. 1987. "Bonuses and Employment in Japan." *Journal of the Japanese and International Economies* 1(2):168-94.

Gannicott, Kenneth. 1996. "Education in the Asian Transition Countries." Asian Development Bank, Manila.

Gerdtham, Ulf-G., Jes Sogaard, Fredrik Andersson, and Bengt Jonsson. 1992. "An Econometric Analysis of Health Care Expenditure." *Journal of Health Economics* 11:63-84.

Gertler, Paul J. 1995. "On the Road to Social Health Insurance: Lessons from High Performing Asian Economies." Paper prepared for the International Conference on Financing Human Resource Development in Advanced Asian Economies, 17-18 November, Asian Development Bank, Manila.

Grootaert, Christiaan, and Ravi Kanbur. 1995. "Child Labour: An Economic Perspective." *International Labour Review* 134(2):187.

Harman, Grant, and M. Selin, eds. 1991. *Funding for Higher Education in Asia and the Pacific*. Bangkok: United Nations Educational, Scientific, and Cultural Organization, Principal Regional Office for Asia and the Pacific.

Harrigan, Frank. 1996. "Saving Transitions in Southeast Asia." Asian Development Bank, Manila.

Harrigan, Frank, and Lea Sumulong. 1996. "Aspects of Asian Macroeconomic and Structural Interdependence." Background paper for *Emerging Asia: Changes and Challenges*. Asian Development Bank, Manila.

Higgins, Matthew. Forthcoming. "The Demographic Determinants of Savings, Investment, and International Capital Flows." *International Economic Review*.

Hitiris, Theo, and John Posnett. 1992. "The Determinants and Effects of Health Expenditure in Developed Countries." *Journal of Health Economics* 11:173-81.

Hsiao, William. 1995. "Medical Savings Accounts: Lessons from Singapore." *Health Affairs* 14(2):260-66.

ILO (International Labour Organisation). 1996a. *Child Labor: What Is to Be Done?* No. 1TM/1/1996. Geneva.

———. 1996b. "Stop Child Labour!" *World of Work* (16):12-24.

Kang, Kenneth. 1994. "Why Did Koreans Save So Little and Why Do They Now Save So Much?" *International Economic Journal* 8:99-111.

Kelley, Allen C. 1988. "Economic Consequences of Population Change in the Third World." *Journal of Economic Literature* 27(4):1685-728.

Kelley, Allen C., and Robert M. Schmidt. 1996. "Saving, Dependency, and Development." *Journal of Population Economics* 9(4):365-86.

Khoo, Siew-Ean, and Chai Bin Park. 1978. "The Effect of Family Planning Programs on Fertility in Four Asian Countries." *International Family Planning Perspectives* 4(3):67-73.

Koswara, Jajah. 1996. "Capacity Building in University Research: The Indonesian Experience." In Erik W. Thulstrup, ed., and Hans D. Thulstrup, asst. ed., *Research Training for Development*. Frederiksberg, Denmark: Roskilde University Press.

Lee, Ronald, Andrew Mason, and Timothy Miller. 1997. "Saving, Wealth, and the Demographic Transition in East Asia." Paper presented at the Conference on Population and the Asian Economic Miracle, 7-10 January, East-West Center, Honolulu, Hawaii.

Leibfritz, Willi, Deborah Roseveare, Douglas Fore, and Eckhard Wurzel. 1995. "Aging Populations, Pension Systems, and Government Budgets: How Do They Affect Savings?" Working Paper No. 156. Organisation for Economic Co-operation and Development, Economics Department, Paris.

Lewin, Keith M. 1996. "Access to Education in Emerging Asia: Trends, Challenges, and Policy Options." Background paper for *Emerging Asia: Changes and Challenges*. Asian Development Bank, Manila.

Livi-Bacci, Massimo. 1992. *A Concise History of World Population*. Cambridge, Massachusetts: Blackwell.

Macro International, Inc. 1990-94. *Demographic and Health Survey*. Calverton, Maryland.

Mann, J., and D. Tarantola. 1996. *AIDS in the World II*. New York: Oxford University Press.

Mason, Andrew. 1987. "National Saving Rates and Population Growth: A New Model and New Evidence." In D. G. Johnson and R. Lee, eds., *Population Growth and Economic Development: Issues and Evidence*. Madison, Wisconsin: University of Wisconsin Press.

Meadows, D. H., D. L. Meadows, J. Randers, and W. W. Behren, III. 1972. *The Limits to Growth*. New York: Potomac Association.

Meltzer, David. 1995. "Mortality Decline, the Demographic Transition, and Economic Growth."

Mincer, Jacob, and Yoshio Higuchi. 1988. "Wage Structures and Labor Turnover in the United States and Japan." *Journal of the Japanese and International Economies* 2(2):97-133.

Mingat, Alain. 1995. "Towards Improving our Understanding of the Strategy of High Performing Asian Economies in the Education Sector." Paper prepared for the International Conference on Financing Human Resource Development in Advanced Asian Economies, 17-18 November, Asian Development Bank, Manila.

National Statistics Office of the Philippines and Macro International, Inc. 1994. *National Demographic Survey, 1993*. Calverton, Maryland.

Newhouse, Joseph P. 1977. "Medical Care Expenditure: A Cross-National Survey." *Journal of Human Resources* 12(winter):115-25.

_____. 1993. *Free for All? Lessons from the Rand Health Insurance Experiment: A RAND Study*. Cambridge, Massachusetts: Harvard University Press.

Noor, Waseem. 1996. "Labor Standards: A Guise for Protectionist Policy?" Columbia University, New York.

Pitayonon, Sumalee, Sukontha Kongsin, and Wattana S. Janjareon. 1997. "The Economic Impact of HIV/AIDS Mortality on Households in Thailand." In David E. Bloom and Peter Godwin, eds., *The Economics of HIV and AIDS: The Case of South and South East Asia*. New Delhi, India: Oxford University Press.

Psacharopolous, George. 1994. "Returns to Investment in Education: A Global Update." *World Development* 22(9):1325-43.

Robey, Bryant, John Ross, and Indu Bhushan. 1996. "Strategies for Meeting Unmet Demand." *Population Reports* Series J(43):1-43.

Rosovsky, Henry. 1990. *The University: An Owner's Manual*. New York: Norton.

Schultz, T. Paul. 1987. "School Expenditures and Enrollments, 1960-80: The Effects of Income, Prices, and Population Growth." In D. G. Johnson and R. Lee, eds., *Population Growth and Economic Development: Issues and Evidence*. Madison, Wisconsin: University of Wisconsin Press.

Sen, Amartya. 1994. "Population: Delusion and Reality." *The New York Review of Books* 41(15):62-71.

Silverman, Gary, and Trish Saywell. 1996. "Cramming Classes." *Far Eastern Economic Review* 159(46):26-8.

Simon, J. 1981. *The Ultimate Resource*. Princeton, New Jersey: Princeton University Press.

Summers, Robert, and Alan Heston. 1994. *Penn World Table*, Mark 5.6 (website version). Philapelphia: University of Pennsylvania.

Taylor, Alan. 1995. "Debt, Dependence, and the Demographic Transition: Latin America into the Next Century." *World Development* 23:869-79.

Taylor, Alan, and Jeffrey G. Williamson. 1994. "Capital Flows to the New World as an Intergenerational Transfer." *Journal of Political Economy* 102:348-69.

UN (United Nations). 1991. *Global Estimates and Projections of Populations by Age and Sex.* New York.

_____. 1994. "World Population Prospects 1950-2050 (The 1994 Revision)." *Demographic Indicators 1950-2050 (The 1994 Revision)*, electronic data. New York.

UNICEF (United Nations Children's Fund). 1996. *The State of the World's Children 1997.* New York: Oxford University Press.

Waldo, Daniel R., Sally T. Sonnefeld, David R. McKusick, and Ross H. Arnett, III. 1989. "Health Expenditures by Age Group, 1977 and 1987." *Health Care Financing Review* 10(4):111-20.

Williamson, Jeffrey G. 1993. "Human Capital Deepening, Inequality, and Demographic Events along the Asia-Pacific Rim." In G. Jones, N. Ogawa, and J. G. Williamson, eds., *Human Resources and Development along the Asia-Pacific Rim.* Oxford, U.K.: Oxford University Press.

Williamson, Jeffrey, and Matthew Higgins. 1996. "Asian Savings, Investment, and Foreign Capital Dependence: The Role of Demography." Background paper for *Emerging Asia: Changes and Challenges.* Asian Development Bank, Manila.

Wilson, Chris. 1996. "Understanding the Nature and Importance of Low-Growth Demographic Regimes." International Union for the Scientific Study of Population (IUSSP), Committee on Historical Demography and Academia Sinica Institute of Economics, *Proceedings of Conference on Asian Population History.* Liège, Belgium.

World Bank. 1984. *World Development Report 1984.* New York: Oxford University Press.

_____. 1995. "World Data 1995." *Socio-Economic Time Series Access and Retrieval System,* Version 3.0, electronic resource. Washington, D.C.

_____. 1996. *China Higher Education Reform.* Report No. 15573-CHA. Washington, D.C.

4

ENVIRONMENT AND NATURAL RESOURCES

During the past 30 years, Asia has lost half its forest cover, and with it countless unique animal and plant species. A third of its agricultural land has been degraded. Fish stocks have fallen by 50 percent. No other region has as many heavily polluted cities, and its rivers and lakes are among the world's most polluted. In short, Asia's environment has been under attack. While rapid economic development has created dynamism and wealth, Asia has at the same time become dirtier, less ecologically diverse, and more environmentally vulnerable.

This is not surprising. The environment also suffered during the industrialization of Western Europe, North America, and Japan: the London smogs of the 1950s, the decimation of Europe's forests, and the congestion and pollution in New York and Tokyo are legendary. Rising prosperity implies not only expanded economic activity, but also a changing economic structure: from low-impact subsistence agriculture to more intensive agriculture and industry. Because Asia's economic transformation has taken place so much more quickly than elsewhere, the environmental impact appears worse. Nature can accommodate resource exploitation and assimilate pollution to some extent, but when the rates of resource use or pollution rise beyond the levels the environment can assimilate, depletion and degradation are inevitable unless countries take specific steps to protect their environments.

Asia's environmental problems were not a result of the promotion of rapid rates of growth. Slower economic growth provides no guarantee of a better environment. For instance, slow growing South Asia suffers similarly profound environmental problems as fast growing East Asia. As Chapter 2 pointed out, rapid growth is the best way to alleviate poverty, which is itself related to the rate of environmental degradation. Moreover, higher incomes not only raise people's willingness to pay for environmental protection, but also generate the resources to finance it. Rather, Asia's mistakes lay in two separate areas.

First, for too long Asian policymakers ignored the environmental impact of rapid growth. Concern about pollution or degradation was simply not a priority. The prevailing government mentality was one of "grow now, clean up later." As popular demand for a cleaner environment responds only slowly to rising incomes, and even then private markets do not respond spontaneously, this lack of government concern was a problem. Clean air and water are, after all, public goods. Thus Asian governments should have been vigilant about the environmental impact of their rapid growth and designed public policy to keep pollution, congestion, and resource depletion within safe and manageable bounds.

Second, once governments did adopt environmental regulations, they were ineffectively designed and inadequately implemented. Too many approaches were simply copied from industrial countries, yet Asian governments did not learn from the industrial countries' mistakes. While Asian policymakers introduced sophisticated environmental standards and rigid regulatory regimes, all too often they neither monitored nor enforced these standards. In other words, Asia lacked the institutional capacity to implement its environmental policy.

This chapter's main conclusion is that a new approach toward environmental management will do much to arrest environmental degradation in Asia. The region needs a new model for environmental management, one based on greater reliance on incentives for compliance, on targeted government regulation, and on effective implementation. Policies for all economic sectors must take the environment into account and the flexible, market-based approach that underlay Asia's economic growth must now be applied to its environmental management. Asia can no longer afford to ignore its environment; however, it will not need to sacrifice growth to improve environmental quality. Asia's environmental failures are such that reforms could benefit both the economy and the environment.

The chapter begins with a description of the current state of Asia's environment. Next, it examines the causes of degradation and then estimates the costs of environmental damage. It moves on to offer an alternative vision of environmental management and looks at the possible situation during the next 30 years before concluding.

The Current State of Asia's Environment

Asia is the world's most polluted and environmentally degraded region; however, not all parts of Asia are equally polluted and the region does not fare worst in every environmental indicator. The range of environmental problems is huge—from the degradation of rural land to the pollution and congestion of the region's megacities. Some areas have unique difficulties, such as the danger that rising sea levels pose for the Pacific islands. Some environmental problems are created locally, such as the pollution of water resources, while others are involuntarily imported from abroad, for instance, acid rain in Japan and Korea comes largely from coal burning in the People's Republic of China (PRC). The following paragraphs summarize the main trends.

Air Pollution

The air in Asia's cities is among the dirtiest in the world. The levels of ambient particulates—smoke particles and dust, which are a major cause of respiratory diseases—are generally twice the world average and more than five times as high as in industrial countries and Latin America. Throughout Asia, lead emissions from vehicles are also well above safe levels. Lead causes blood poisoning and significantly impairs children's cognitive development. Finally, ambient levels of sulfur dioxide—an important cross-border pollutant that contributes to acid rain, which in turn damages crops and eats away at synthetic structures—are 50 percent higher in Asia than in either Africa or Latin America. They are, however, still only one third of the level in industrial countries.

Levels of air pollution substantially exceed the international standards for air quality set by the World Health Organization (WHO). Ten of Asia's 11 megacities exceed WHO guidelines for particulate matter by a factor of at least three, four exceed acceptable lead levels, and three exceed acceptable ozone and sulfur dioxide levels (WHO and UNEP 1992).[1] Among 41 cities ranked by the total range and average level of particulate pollution, 13 of the dirtiest 15 were in Asia (WHO and UNEP 1987).

While global energy consumption fell by 1 percent per year between 1990 and 1993, Asia's consumption grew by 6.2 percent a year. As Asia is

---

1. A megacity is defined by WHO and UNEP (1992) as an urban agglomeration with a current or projected population by the year 2000 of 10 million people. Using this definition, Asia has 13 megacities (including those in Japan). The study selected only 11 of the 13 megacities.

using more energy, especially energy with a relatively high carbon content such as coal and oil, so carbon dioxide emissions have risen rapidly. In particular, two of Asia's giant economies, the PRC and India, rely heavily on coal. As a result, Asia's share of greenhouse gas emissions, responsible for climatic change, is increasing fast. Asia's carbon dioxide emissions are growing four times as fast as the world average; but to date, carbon dioxide emissions per person are low, less than half the world average and only 15 percent of the level in countries of the Organisation for Economic Co-operation and Development (OECD). Nevertheless, since the 1970s, industrial emissions as a whole have grown 60 percent faster in Asia than anywhere else.

As concerns other pollutants, the situation is improving. The introduction of unleaded fuels is reducing average lead levels, although the rate of decline is slower in Asia than elsewhere and is from higher levels. Particulate pollution is also declining: between 1991 and 1995 particulate pollution in Asia was almost 40 percent below its level between 1971 and 1975. (Note, however, that the 40 percent drop cited could be a statistical anomaly.)

The extent of air pollution varies considerably (Table 4.1). Particulate levels are highest in South Asia, moderate but rising in Southeast Asia, and fairly low in East Asia. Lead levels are highest in Southeast Asia; moderate in South Asia; and low in the PRC, with the exception of a few eastern cities where they are rising rapidly. Sulfur dioxide pollution is most severe and rising in East Asia, although much of it originates from outside the region, and is moderate in PRC, India, and Southeast Asia (however, several hot spots exist in east PRC, northeast India, and Thailand). Most of the variation depends on the extent to which local power plants and industries use high-sulfur coal as the main energy source. In short, efforts to improve air quality should focus on particulates in South Asia and the PRC, lead in Southeast Asia, and sulfur dioxide in East Asia and eastern PRC.

Water Pollution

By virtually every measure, Asia's rivers are far more polluted than those in the rest of the world.[2] One kind of river pollution is the level of suspended solids (the amount of waste suspended in the water).

---

2. The Global Environment Monitoring System's Water Programme provided data on ambient water quality used in this section.

Table 4.1 Relative Severity of Environmental Problems in Asian Subregions

Pollutant	East Asia	Southeast Asia	South Asia	Pacific	PRC	India
Air pollution						
Sulfur dioxide	xxx	xx	x		xx	xx
Particulates		xx	xxx		xx	xx
Lead		xxx	xx		x	x
Water pollution						
Suspended solids		xx	xx		xxx	xx
Fecal coliforms		xxx	xx	xx	xx	xxx
Biological oxygen demand		xxx	xx			xxx
Nitrates	xx	x	xxx		xx	xxx
Lead	xx	xxx	x		x	x
Access to water and sanitation						
Lack of access to safe water		xxx	xxx	xx	x	xxx
Lack of access to sanitation		xx	xxx	xx	xxx	xxx
Deforestation						
Deforestation rate		xxx	xx		xx	xx
Land degradation						
Soil erosion		xxx	xxx		xxx	xxx
Waterlogging and salinization		xx	xxx		xx	xxx
Desertification			xxx			xx
Imperata spread		xxx				xx
Energy consumption						
Annual growth rate	xxx	xxx	xxx		xx	xx
Carbon dioxide emissions	xx	x	x		xxx	xx

xxx = very severe; xx = severe; x = moderate but rising
Source: Derived from data in Global Environment Monitoring System (1996a, b); World Bank (1995); World Resources Institute (1996).

According to the Global Environment Monitoring System, Asia's rivers typically have 4 times the world average of suspended solids and 20 times OECD levels.

Organic waste is a specific kind of water pollution. The more organic waste a river or lake contains, the more oxygen this waste uses up during decomposition. The extent of organic waste can be gauged by the biological oxygen demand: the higher the biological oxygen demand, the more polluted a river or lake is. In Asia's rivers the biological oxygen demand is 1.4 times the world average, 1.5 times OECD levels, and many times higher than in Latin America. Specifically, Asia's rivers contain three times as much bacteria from human waste (fecal coliform) than the world average and more than ten times OECD levels. The reported median fecal coliform count in Asia's rivers is 50 times higher than the WHO guidelines.

Finally, Asia's surface waters contain 20 times more lead than surface waters in OECD countries, mainly from industrial effluents. Only nitrate levels—which indicate the presence of human or animal waste or runoff from chemical fertilizers—are lower in Asia than in the rest of the world.

Within Asia the nature and severity of water pollution differs. Suspended solid levels are highest in the PRC, while fecal coliform counts are highest in India and Southeast Asia. Nitrates are a more serious problem in South Asia, including India, while lead is worst in Southeast Asia.

Water pollution has several sources. Untreated municipal sewage, industrial effluents, and runoff from urban and agricultural activity (especially from pesticides and fertilizers) are the main culprits in Asia. A further problem is the lack of wastewater treatment. In Beijing and Manila, for instance, only 10 to 15 percent of wastewater is treated, and that is considered high by Asian standards. The failure to treat urban wastewater means that surface water downstream from urban areas is full of pathogens, organic material, heavy metals, and other pollutants. Thus the extent of water pollution noted earlier, while extremely high, may understate actual pollution levels, because measuring stations tend to be upstream from major urban areas.

The trends in Asia's water pollution are also not encouraging. The levels of suspended solids have almost quadrupled since the late 1970s, even though they have remained unchanged or improved in the rest of the world; and even though Asia achieved some reduction in biological oxygen demand levels in the early 1980s, this did not continue into the 1990s.

Many of the potential health hazards posed by such polluted surface water can be reduced by providing access to safe water through municipal water supply and sanitation services. Yet here too Asia's record is poor. A far smaller proportion of people in Asia have access to safe drinking water than in any other part of the world except Africa. One in three Asians has no access to a safe water source that operates at least part of the day within 200 meters from the home. Even for those with access, supply is often interrupted and unreliable: in many cities it averages between 4 and 14 hours a day. Access to safe drinking water is lowest in Southeast Asia and South Asia, including India.

Access to sanitation is generally even lower than access to safe water. Almost one in two Asians has no access to sanitation services. Where services are available, sewage collection and treatment are usually lacking, so the effluent flows into surface or groundwaters. Thus, while slightly more than half of all Asians have access to some form of sanitation, only 10 percent of the sewage generated is treated at the primary level. The situation is worst in South Asia, the Central Asian republics, Indochina, and PRC. In rural India, for instance, only 16 percent of the population has access to sanitation, and in the PRC this figure is less than 10 percent.

Solid and Hazardous Waste

As people become richer, so they generate more rubbish. Income levels alter not only the quantity, but also the nature of consumption. The shift from own-grown to purchased food, the move from staple to meat-based diets, and the increasing use of less biodegradable packaging all mean that rising income tends to be associated with more municipal waste. One study (Beede and Bloom 1995) suggests that, on average, across countries, a 1 percent rise in income brings a 0.34 percent rise in municipal solid waste. Thus it comes as no surprise that Asia's rapidly rising incomes have brought about a dramatic increase in solid waste.

On average, municipal authorities in Asian cities spend between 50 and 70 percent of their revenues on municipal waste management. Nonetheless, collection services remain low, with only 50 to 70 percent of residents receiving any service (Cointreau-Levine 1994; UNEP 1993). In Gujranwala, for instance, a city of more than 1 million inhabitants in Pakistan, fewer than one in five residents has access to solid waste management services, with the figure standing at only one in ten among low-income households (DeShazo 1996).

Less visible, but potentially more dangerous, than ordinary municipal solid waste are the growing quantities of hazardous and toxic wastes that hospitals, certain factories, and households generate. Contrary to conventional wisdom, the production of hazardous waste decreases as a country becomes richer and its economic structure changes. For instance, the PRC, which generates 50 million tons of toxic waste a year, and India, which generates 40 million tons a year (ESCAP 1995) produce much more hazardous waste per person than Korea or Japan. In Asia 60 to 65 percent of hazardous waste is put in dumpsites or landfills, 5 to 10 percent is dumped in the ocean, and the rest is incinerated or chemically treated (UNEP 1993). In most cases proper safeguards are absent or largely ineffective.

Deforestation

Asia's forest cover is shrinking by 1 percent a year. This is particularly serious as Asia has relatively less forest cover than the rest of the world. With 13 percent of the world's forestland and half its population, Asia has just one third as much forest per person as the world average, and only one tenth as much forest per person as Latin America.

Deforestation can occur for several reasons: excessive fuelwood collection and logging; construction of infrastructure, especially roads and dams (which have been particularly important in Asia); or conversion of land to agricultural use. A great deal of deforestation has already occurred in South Asia, where it is partly responsible for increased desertification, soil erosion, flooding, and biodiversity loss, and is particularly acute in Southeast Asia.

Land Degradation

The amount of land per person is scarcer in Asia than in other parts of the world. In 1992 Asia had only 0.3 hectares of agricultural land per person, compared with 1.6 hectares in the rest of the developing world and 1.4 hectares in OECD countries. Asia's soil is also of poorer quality than elsewhere: less than 4 percent of Asian soil has no inherent soil constraints (that is, it can be used to grow a wide variety of crops), compared with 15 percent in Africa and 12 percent in Latin America.

Soil can be ruined in various ways. It can be eroded, salinized, waterlogged, and desertified. Deforestation, cultivation of steep slopes, poor drainage, and inadequate soil conservation have all contributed to soil degradation in Asia. Soil erosion is Asia's most widespread natural resource problem, and is equally severe in Southeast Asia, South Asia, PRC, and India. In India 27 percent of the soil suffers from severe erosion. The corresponding figure for the PRC is 6.4 percent. In Thailand the mean erosion rate for soil is 34 tons per hectare every year. This compares with a tolerance level for tropical soil of 13 tons of topsoil loss per hectare per year.

Salinization and waterlogging are also acute: 130 million hectares of Asian cropland (most of it in PRC, India, and Pakistan) are salinized and waterlogged because of poor irrigation practices. In the arid and semi-arid areas of South Asia, desertification is also a major problem. As many as 63 million hectares of rainfed land and 16 million hectares of irrigated land have been lost to desertification. The colonization of denuded forestland by imperata grass is another serious problem. Imperata is a type of grass that is of little use, is costly and difficult to eliminate, and prevents anything else from growing.

Biodiversity Loss

Asia accounts for about 40 percent of the world's species of flora and fauna. However, encroachment on wildlife habitats for agriculture and infrastructure, deforestation, land degradation, and water pollution have taken their toll on these biological resources and reduced their diversity. With a few exceptions, such as Bhutan and Malaysia, Asian countries have lost between 70 and 90 percent of their original wildlife habitats. Asia's high population density is a major factor in this, although the success of some countries in preserving a large proportion of their remaining habitats suggests that the population to land ratio may not be the only factor. About 1.3. million square kilometers, or some 7 percent of Asia's total land area (excluding the South Pacific countries and Central Asian republics), are protected. Relative to population, this is much less than in the rest of the world. None of Asia's developing countries are particularly effective at managing their protected areas. A country's relative wealth as measured by its gross national product (GNP) is not a good indicator of either the percentage cover of protected areas or the effectiveness of protected area management.

Asia's coastal and marine fisheries, and mangrove and coral reef systems are among the most diverse in the world. Approximately two thirds of the world's coral reefs are in Asia. More than 1,200 species of fish inhabit the waters surrounding the Maldives alone. Freshwater eco-systems in Southeast Asia are among the largest and best developed in the world; however, more than half of Asia's wetlands have been lost, and more than half of the mangroves in the Indo-Malayan realm have been cleared. Most wetlands of international significance are reportedly threatened. The proximate causes include hunting, drainage, pollution, destructive fishing practices, and conversion to other uses such as human settlement.

Priorities for Environmental Management

What type of pollution should governments worry most about? The answer varies depending on whom you ask. An approach popular among researchers in industrial countries gives top priority to problems that pose a high risk to human health, which include air pollution and unsafe drinking water. Those problems that pose high risks to ecosystems and aspects of human welfare (enjoyment of amenities, for instance), come second. These include the loss of species and natural habitat. Environmental problems that pose moderate risks to ecosystems and human welfare, including the contamination of surface waters and pesticide deposits, come third. Low-risk environmental concerns, such as ground-water contamination and thermal pollution, come last.

Another way to gauge priorities is to canvass public opinion. International surveys indicate that developing country respondents rank problems that affect their local communities higher than respondents in industrial countries (Bloom 1995). This is hardly surprising given that their local problems are generally worse. Poor sanitation and garbage disposal, poor water quality, and poor air quality were the top ranked environmental problems affecting local communities. Among national and global problems, air pollution, surface water pollution, and defor-estation came top of the list, followed by biodiversity loss and soil erosion.

Policymakers seem to have somewhat different priorities than researchers and the general public (Figure 4.1). In a survey prepared for this study, Asian environmental policymakers ranked water pollution and freshwater depletion as the region's top environmental problem, followed by deforestation and air pollution in second place, and solid waste running third. Developing a strategy to deal with these problems, however, means understanding their causes.

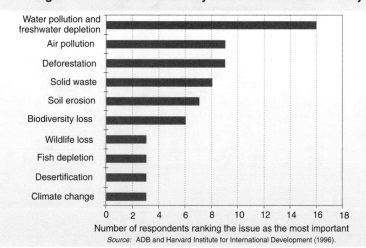

Figure 4.1 Ranking of Environmental Issues by Asian Environmental Policymakers

Number of respondents ranking the issue as the most important

Source: ADB and Harvard Institute for International Development (1996).

The Causes of Asia's Environmental Degradation

Explanations for Asia's environmental ills abound (Box 4.1). Some observers blame rising populations, taking a Malthusian view that a finite amount of natural resources cannot support ever larger populations. Others emphasize poverty as the underlying cause of environmental damage. The latter argue that without access to any other source of livelihood, the poor are forced to plunder the environment. Competition for open access resources such as firewood can also encourage the poor to have more children to help them gather the resources (Panayotou 1996). Higher fertility in turn exacerbates poverty. Another possibility is that environmental degradation is an inevitable by-product of economic growth. A final possibility is that environmental degradation is largely the result of institutional and policy failures. The following sections examine the validity of each of these arguments in the Asian context.

Population Growth and the Environment

At first sight, population growth and environmental degradation seem closely linked. A proliferation of people is highly correlated with deforestation, soil erosion, damage to the local ecosystem, and other forms of

Box 4.1 Environmental Degradation in the Central Asian Republics

The present state of environmental degradation in the Central Asian republics of Kazakstan, the Kyrgyz Republic, and Uzbekistan can be attributed largely to the inherent inefficiencies of a centrally planned economy and to environmental neglect. Natural resources—soils, minerals, water, gas and petroleum, forests—were exploited irresponsibly. State ownership of productive sectors that operated on the basis of quantitative production goals, coupled with central allocation of funds within a framework that lacked mechanisms to limit overexploitation or inefficient exploitation, did not encourage a rational use of resources. The results were often environmentally devastating.

Environmental issues in the Central Asian republics can be categorized at three levels: the first is areas of high ecological concern, the second is the significant urban and industrial pollution in major population centers, and the third is degradation in rural locations that cover widespread areas. The physical, social, and economic catastrophes associated with the desiccation of the Aral Sea and the residual harmful effects of past exposure to nuclear testing and uranium wastes are well known. But perhaps one that affects more people from a public health point of view, the most widespread environmental problem in the Central Asian republics is air pollution, which originates mainly from heavy industry (metallurgy, power, and chemical industries). Below cost pricing, in particular, for fuel and energy, and extensive recourse to subsidies did not favor investments in pollution control or abatement, adequate maintenance of existing plants, or recycling. Contamination of groundwater with heavy metals and industrial waste is also a major problem around industrial centers because of improper waste treatment. Massive areas of Central Asia have become unproductive as a consequence of desertification, salinization, and soil erosion caused by unwise agricultural policies. Despite a growing awareness of these issues and widespread availability of technical skills to address some of them, the financial dislocation the transitional economies of Central Asia are currently facing portends a slow process of environmental improvement.

environmental degradation. Closer inspection, however, reveals that things are not that simple. How a population behaves is more important than how fast it grows.

Some Asian economies, notably Korea and Taipei,China, successfully separated population growth from resource degradation. They did so through a combination of sustainable growth in agricultural productivity (based on favorable crop prices, secure land tenure, and credit availability) and job creation outside agriculture. But in other countries, notably India and the Philippines, agricultural growth was slow and government policies favored capital-intensive industry. Surplus labor was unable to move out of agriculture into alternative employment, and environmental damage was high.

Slower population growth, however, does not necessarily slow down the rate of environmental degradation. In Sri Lanka and Thailand, for instance, where population growth rates have declined rapidly, environmental degradation has continued as fast as in other countries with higher population growth rates. The critical factor seems to be whether or not the costs of environmental degradation are factored into individuals' decisionmaking. When property rights to resources, such as fodder or fuelwood, are not clearly defined, individuals are less likely to be concerned about degrading them.

Much of the empirical evidence of the relationship between population density and growth, and environmental degradation is based on studies of deforestation. Most of these studies find only a weak or no relationship between the two (Cleaver and Schreiber 1993). They only find strong statistical relationships between populations and environmental damage in the presence of poverty, ill-defined property rights, a lack of employment alternatives, or failed government policies. The interaction between population density and income levels per person, rather than population density alone, seemed to influence deforestation rates (Panayotou 1994; Tongpan and Panayotou 1990). Thus the combination of rapid population growth and poverty seems to be particularly damaging for the environment.

Five countries—PRC, Indonesia, Malaysia, Myanmar, and Thailand—account for 80 percent of Asia's deforestation. Yet most of these countries have reduced their population growth rates and are continuing to reduce them still further. For example, Indonesia's population growth rate is expected to fall below 1.5 percent by the year 2000, but even if this downward trend was to accelerate, it is unlikely to protect Indonesia's remaining forests. In contrast, a change in forest concession policies could make an enormous difference. Estimates suggest that the Indonesian government could increase its annual earnings from timber by $1 billion, while at the same time halving the area logged each year, if it awarded longer term logging concessions on a competitive basis, introduced area-based taxes, and relied less on export bans. In contrast, in countries such as Nepal, Pakistan, Philippines, and Viet Nam, which have high population growth rates, whose societies are still largely rural, and where the encroachment into forests for land and firewood remains high, population policies hold environmental promise.

The relationship between population growth and land degradation is equally hazy. Substantial research on the complex interactions between population growth and related food production on the environment has produced mixed results. Increasing population density can go hand in hand with improving or worsening land conditions. In countries with no unused land to be brought into cultivation, the intensification of agricultural production can result in environmental problems that are usually related to the increased use of chemical fertilizers and pesticides, but here too, much depends on the role of incentives, such as subsidies (Tiffen, Mortimore, and Gichuki 1994). Japan and the United States in the 20th century both stand as examples of countries where increasing population density has been accompanied by improved land conditions.

The situation with water resources is no different. Indonesia, with one of the world's highest freshwater endowments per person, faces water shortages. PRC, India, and Pakistan face severe water shortages that have much to do with water subsidization and little to do with population growth. For instance, if Pakistan's irrigation system increased its efficiency by 10 percent, the water saved could irrigate another 2 million hectares (World Resources Institute 1987), but as long as Pakistan's farmers do not have to bear the true cost of water, they are unlikely to appreciate its scarcity and likely to waste it.

In short, population growth and density alone do not imply environmental degradation. Because the environment does not have an infinite carrying capacity, further increases in population density beyond some threshold may imperil resources. Asia may not have reached this stage. The combination of population density and poverty is more likely to imperil the environment, and in the presence of institutional failures it is more likely still.

Poverty and the Environment

Almost 1 billion people in Asia live in poverty. Understandably, poor people focus on the present. Survival today is their most important concern. Moreover, their willingness and ability to pay for environmental protection are severely limited.

The poor have little or no access to financial resources (credit) or to information and technology. Most important, however, they often lack secure property rights. Natural resources, such as fuelwood, fodder, fish, game, and water, are all open access, and the poor must capture as much of them as they can. This leads to higher fertility, because children are an asset in the race to capture resources. But high fertility, in turn, leads to further impoverishment as resources are overexploited and degraded. This is the negative spiral of poverty and environmental degradation (Dasgupta 1995; Panayotou 1996).

The poor also tend to live in areas that are more prone to environment-related natural disasters, such as flooding and landslides, or near heavily polluting factories, dumps, and hazardous waste sites. Malnutrition and poor health make them more susceptible to infectious diseases. Lower incomes, less education, and less access to health care than those who are better off mean that they are less able to recover once infected. Thus environmental degradation reinforces poverty, which in turn reinforces environmental degradation in an endless vicious circle.

Poverty no doubt contributes to environmental degradation, but it is not an independent cause. Like population growth, poverty seems to exacerbate environmental problems in the presence of market, institutional, and policy failures.

Economic Growth and the Environment

As much of Asia's environmental degradation took place and accelerated during the region's rapid economic growth of the past 30 years, a reasonable question is whether growth has been its main cause. Do higher income levels imply a worse environment? Several researchers (Grossman and Krueger 1995; Panayotou 1995) have identified a relationship between income and the environment that displays an inverted U-shaped pattern known as the environmental Kuznets curve (Figure 4.2). This relationship implies that as a country gets richer, its environment will get worse before it gets better.

The logic behind this observation is as follows. As economic development accelerates, agriculture becomes more intensive, resource extraction increases, and industrialization takes off; thus the rates of natural resource depletion begin to increase, and the quantity and toxicity of waste rise. Eventually, as economies become richer still, their economic structure shifts toward industries and services that use natural resources less intensively. Greater prosperity brings with it increased environmental awareness and a willingness and capacity to pay for a cleaner environment. As a result, countries enforce environmental regulations

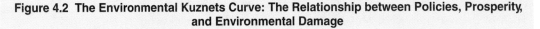

Figure 4.2 The Environmental Kuznets Curve: The Relationship between Policies, Prosperity, and Environmental Damage

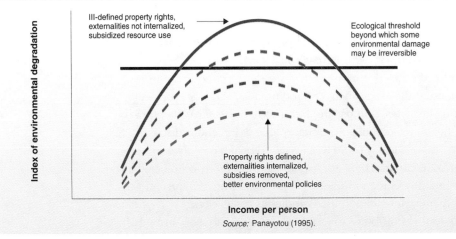

Source: Panayotou (1995).

more strictly and spend more money on the environment. Subsequently, environmental degradation levels off and gradually declines.

Casual observation suggests that this relationship applies to the urban as well as to the rural environment. For example, the cities of the newly industrializing countries, such as Bangkok, Seoul, and Shanghai are far more polluted than they were 20 or 30 years ago, and their pollution levels are rising at rates that match or exceed their rates of economic growth. Conversely, cities in the industrial countries are cleaner today than they were 20 or 30 years ago.

This study examined the relationship between the environment and growth with specific reference to Asia, and tested for a relationship of the Kuznets type between the rate of environmental degradation indicated by selected pollutants and the level of economic development. The analysis showed that for some pollutants Asia does indeed exhibit an inverted U-shaped relationship between environmental degradation and income, that is, environmental degradation first rises and then falls as income per person increases. These pollutants include sulfur dioxide, particulates in cities, and fecal coliform and arsenic (from industry) in rivers. The turning point at which the ambient levels of these pollutants begin to fall is an annual income per person of $5,000 to $7,000 (on a purchasing power parity basis) (Islam 1996). Panayotou (1995) obtained similar results for deforestation rates for a sample of tropical countries dominated by Asian countries. The turning point, however, was at a much lower level of annual income per person: approximately $1,000 (on a purchasing power parity basis).

These findings suggest that during the next 20 to 30 years, environmental quality will improve slowly in East Asia and in the higher-income countries of Southeast Asia, such as Malaysia, and will continue to deteriorate in South Asia and the lower-income countries of Southeast Asia.

For certain pollutants, such as sulfur dioxide, heavy particles, and fecal coliform in rivers, there appear to be important differences in the income-environment relationship between Asia and the rest of the world. In Asia certain types of pollution tend to rise more rapidly with higher income than they do elsewhere, but they also begin to fall more quickly. Higher initial population density together with more rapid industrialization may account for the rapid rise, while increased environmental awareness and the availability of new abatement technology permit pollution to be reduced at relatively lower income levels.

While this result provides grounds for optimism, it raises a question, namely, are these observed relationships between income and the environment inevitable? Must a worsening environment always accompany economic growth or can the environmental Kuznets curve be flattened? Substantial evidence exists that it can be. In the presence of policy distortions or policy failures the environment deteriorates more at low income levels than in their absence. Similarly, the improvement of the environment with income growth at higher income levels is not automatic, but depends on the policies and institutions in place.

Institutional, Policy, and Market Failures

People prefer a clean environment to a dirty one. As they gain more disposable income and leisure time, they tend to seek out unspoiled forests and recreation sites. Thus potential demand exists for clean air, clean water, and natural recreation areas such as national parks. Environmental degradation, however, means that this demand is not being met. That is due in large part to institutional, policy, and market failures.

Market failures can occur in several ways. For example, markets fail to price resources for which there are no secure property rights. Fuelwood taken from open access forest is free to the user, but inflicts social costs through the impact of deforestation on soils, water resources, and biodiversity and through the carbon dioxide released when fuelwood is burned. Even where property rights exist, the prices of goods often fail to reflect the environmental cost of their production. The environmental cost of a chemical factory's effluent, for instance, is not automatically reflected in the market price of its products.

Asia's policy and institutional failures also fall into several categories. First, the private sector has been largely excluded from providing environmental services. As in many other parts of the world, such services as water supply and sanitation, solid waste collection, watershed protection, biodiversity conservation, and wastewater treatment are considered to lie exclusively in the purview of the state. As a result, the private sector has been unable to respond to demand for environmental services. In other areas, governments have failed to define property rights, thereby constraining the private sector's response. The classic tragedy of the commons, whereby resources owned by none are overexploited by all, applies to many of Asia's forests, rivers, and other environmental resources.

Second, Asia's public sector has failed to fulfill the demand for environmental improvement. Although people want a better environment and are often prepared to pay for it, governments have been slow to respond. This is primarily due to a shortage of capital and operating funds. Some governments have been unwilling to charge users the full cost of environmental services, and others that did charge users channeled funds to purposes other than environmental clean-up. Without full cost recovery or adequate public funding, environmental services are inadequate in terms of both quantity and quality as evidenced by many of Asia's water supply and sanitation facilities, irrigation systems, waste collection systems, and protected areas.

Third, where Asian governments have implemented environmental policies, they have tended to be inappropriate. Too often they simply adopted policies from rich countries and implemented them inadequately.

To illustrate Asia's policy and market failures, this section analyzes three examples: water provision, pollution control, and forest resource management.

Water Provision

Inadequate access to safe drinking water and sanitation is responsible for high rates of infant and child mortality in many Asian countries, and causes millions of deaths every year and millions of dollars worth of losses to Asia's economies. It is often blamed on rapid population growth, urbanization (Box 4.2), and poor people's inability to pay the full cost of water supply. Governments view provision of a subsidized source of poor quality water to part of the population as the best they can achieve under the circumstances.

This approach is erroneous in a number of respects. To begin with, the growing competition between alternative water uses, such as for irrigation, fishing, waste disposal, and household and industrial use, belie the notion that raw water is abundantly and freely available. Nonetheless, raw water resources (and the ability to dispose of wastewater) remain as open access goods. This is a classic case of market failure and is

Box 4.2 Megacities and the Environment

By the year 2020, more than half of Asia's inhabitants will live in cities. Many of them will live in megacities, that is, cities whose population is greater than 10 million people. Today, 9 of the world's 14 megacities are in Asia. By 2015 the number will rise to 18 out of 27, including those in Japan (United Nations 1995).

Megacities have many attractions, especially to migrants from rural areas. As they contain a disproportionately high share of economic activity, they offer more job opportunities and provide relatively better social services and infrastructure. However, rapid urban expansion has come at a high cost. High population densities, heavy traffic and the associated air pollution, and slum proliferation characterize Asia's megacities and pose acute environmental problems.

Traffic congestion in Asia's megacities is legendary. Vehicle use has been rising exponentially, doubling every seven years in Southeast Asia. The development of roads and other infrastructure has not kept up. Transportation, especially traffic jams, contributes the largest share of air pollutants to the urban environment of Asia's megacities, although energy production and

industrial fuel emissions also add to the dirty air. In addition, traffic jams have high economic costs. The price of congestion in Bangkok, for instance, varies from $270 million to more than $1 billion per year, depending on the value imputed to time stuck in traffic.

Water pollution also plagues Asia's megacities. Domestic and industrial wastewater discharges and the disposal of solid waste into open drainage courses contaminate surface and groundwater. Industrial wastewater constitutes a large share of the total discharge, estimated at 25 percent in Bangkok and 35 percent in Manila. The effects of chronic water pollution and inadequate sanitation and sewerage can be dramatic. In the southern and eastern parts of Bangkok, for instance, the over-exploitation of fresh groundwater is causing the city to sink by 5 to 10 centimeters a year. The proportion of urban residents with access to potable water declined during the 1980s.

In all of Asia's megacities, the slum and squatter communities are the most severely affected by pollution. This group makes up a shocking 25 to 30 percent of Asia's urban population.

exacerbated by poor government policy. Not only do governments not establish well-defined, secure property rights over water (whether state, municipal, communal, or private), they also tend to subsidize water for irrigation and other uses, and in many cases supply it free of charge. In Bangladesh, Nepal, and Thailand, for instance, the total costs of supplying water are at least ten times greater than the revenues collected. The PRC has recently introduced volume-based irrigation fees to promote more efficient water use, but the rates are still too low to alleviate water scarcity.

The idea that poor people cannot or will not pay for water is equally mistaken, and reflects a policy failure. Surveys and observations of poor households suggest that the poor are willing to, and actually do, pay for water. They often pay more than the wealthy, both absolutely and relative to their incomes. Surveys of water provision in India, Lao People's Democratic Republic, Pakistan, Philippines, and Thailand suggest that the poor are willing to pay far more than current tariffs for water, and indeed, that they are often prepared to cover the full costs of supply (World Bank 1992a, b). Low-income households often do not benefit from subsidized public supply because they lack access to the service. Instead, they often pay a much higher price (three to eight times as much) to obtain water from vendors, or they pay a high cost in terms of foregone activities to fetch water from distant sources. Estimates suggest that some poor people pay as much as 10 percent or more of their incomes to gain access to safe water (World Bank 1992a). The wealthy, in contrast, are usually the main beneficiaries of subsidized public service. Their excessive consumption limits water availability for the poor.

Statutory restrictions and capital market imperfections worsen the problem. Municipalities are often unable to borrow for capital investments. This means that they must collect the capital costs of water and sewerage investments up front as the "development costs" of urban land. Poor localities cannot pay these costs up front and so remain cut off from water and sewage services. Moreover, many urban poor live in shanty towns and slums that encroach on public land, and municipalities are often loath to make large capital investments on such land.

The policy of subsidizing water for agriculture and industry is equally mistaken. Water accounts for less than 1 percent of the production cost of industry. Its availability, reliability, and quality are far more important than its cost. Even in irrigated agriculture, where water is a more important part of the production process, free or subsidized water is not an advantage if excess water use leads to waterlogging. Reliable water supply and control are much more important than price. Farmers who produce high-value horticultural crops, for instance, are willing to pay as much as 10 to 15 percent of the value of their crop for a reliable supply. Moreover, given the large percentage (more than 80 percent in most Asian countries) of water used in agriculture, a small reduction in agricultural water use would make large quantities of water available for household and industrial use. The political economy of addressing these failures is difficult, but as water becomes ever scarcer, the need to do so becomes more urgent.

Institutional failures exacerbate the problems of water management. Multiple government agencies with overlapping functions and poor coordination are responsible for water supply. For example, few Asian countries integrate the management of river basins, thus watersheds remain unprotected and effluent discharges into water are unregulated. Leakages in water supply systems often exceed 40 percent, and only 2 percent of wastewater, on average, is treated.

Pollution Control

Pollution control in Asia is based largely on a command-and-control approach. Some of the most common policy tools are end-of-pipe standards, licenses, fines, and specific government orders to cease pollution. Governments often impose a uniform pollution standard across an industry, but monitoring is almost always inadequate. The result is a proliferation of unimplemented regulations. Even though policymakers are beginning to experiment with incentive-based economic instruments, such as tax incentives, pollution charges, and deposit refund systems, these are still relatively rare. (The advantages and uses of market-based instruments in Asia are discussed in more detail later.)

In India, for instance, the 1986 Environmental Quality Standards Act provides minimum national standards that are binding for all industrial firms nationwide. State pollution control boards cannot relax the standards, but can make them even more stringent. As the national standards are framed in terms of maximum concentrations of pollutants in effluents and emissions, factories have an incentive to dilute their pollution, not necessarily to reduce it. In any case, the implementation of these standards is largely ineffective. Statistics from the Central Pollution Control Board show that during the 1990s only 7 percent of factories in polluting industries (117 of 1,641 medium and large factories) actually complied with the norms. Most measures of pollution in India have worsened in recent years (Markandya 1996).

Economic instruments to combat pollution in India are largely limited to accelerated depreciation allowances (which the Indian authorities raised from 30 percent in 1983 to 100 percent in 1993/94) for pollution reducing equipment, as well as reduced customs duties. These have not proved to be very successful. They do not provide firms with incentives to choose the cheapest antipollution options.

The PRC has a complex system of environmental responsibility contracts between factories and local governments that set targets for reducing pollution. Environmental authorities also impose a detailed system of pollution levies. Unfortunately, this system has not been effective, because the authorities set the effluent charges below the marginal cost of reducing pollution. It was therefore cheaper for factories to pay the charge than to stop polluting. Moreover, state-owned enterprises cared relatively little about maximizing their profits, and thus about minimizing their costs. This again limited the system's effectiveness.

In 1987, the PRC introduced a system of discharge permits at the firm level. To promote efficiency, the authorities took the costs of pollution reduction for each firm and its financial health into account when allocating the permits. Unfortunately, as in India, they issued permits on the basis of pollutant concentration, thereby encouraging dilution (however, this defect was recently remedied). Moreover, the new system was imposed on top of earlier regulations, causing confusion and inconsistencies.

The PRC also requires that 7 percent of new investment in factories' plant and equipment be devoted to environmental investments, such as waste treatment facilities. However, only 4 percent of new investment has actually been allocated to environmental facilities. In addition, waste treatment did not increase proportionately, because many factories did not use their waste treatment facilities to save on operating costs (Panayotou 1997).

As elsewhere in Asia, Southeast Asian countries also rely primarily on a command-and-control approach. Effluent and emissions standards are the most common regulatory tools. The Philippines, for instance, has ambitious air and water quality standards that apply to all industrial establishments and power generation facilities, regardless of their size and location. However, these standards are inefficient and are inadequately monitored and implemented. Moreover, the environmental regulatory regime often conflicts with other aspects of economic policy. The country's fuel price policy, for instance, even in the deregulated market, favors the use of diesel over gasoline for the transport sector. Malaysia's air pollution standards are measured in tons of pollution load. Water effluent standards are measured as concentration ratios, thereby encouraging dilution of pollutants as in the PRC and India. Malaysia, however, overcomes this problem in part with effective monitoring. In certain industries, such as palm oil and rubber that have only a few, clearly identifiable polluters, Malaysia has had greater enforcement success than other Asian countries.

Thailand, too, relies largely on standards, screening, licenses, land use zoning, and fees backed by the threat of fines or imprisonment to implement its environmental policy. Even though the government is beginning to experiment with economic instruments, the basic approach is one of command-and-control regulation. One problem is that the bulk of Thailand's antipollution regulations were put in place when the country had fewer than 500 factories and was struggling to industrialize. With more than 50,000 factories today, the approach is ineffective.

Forest Resource Management

The degradation of Asia's forests is another example of market, policy, and institutional failures combining to cause massive environmental damage. The lack of secure property rights, both of agricultural land and often of forest resources, aggravates deforestation. Without secure land tenure, people do not invest in soil conservation practices. Thus maintaining agricultural yields on existing land becomes impossible, and people clear new land from the edges of forests.

The situation is aggravated by forest management policies. Explicit and implicit subsidies and volume-based taxes on timber removal encourage destructive logging, especially of marginal and fragile forestlands. Forest concessions are typically too short to provide incentives for conservation and replanting. When concessions are awarded, the goods and services a forest provides other than timber are rarely priced. This results in excessive deforestation and in conflicts between logging companies and local communities.

Concern about the rapid rate of deforestation has prompted several Southeast Asian countries, including Indonesia, Philippines, and Thailand, to impose bans on the export of unprocessed timber. In the

Philippines and Thailand the idea was primarily to conserve forests; in Indonesia the main goal was to promote domestic processing. By raising the value added of exports, more revenues could be generated for forest conservation. As a means of conserving forests, these policies have not worked. In the Philippines and Thailand illegal logging and land clearing continue unabated, and in Indonesia the domestic log processing industry is so inefficient that logging rates have risen.

Costs of Asia's Environmental Degradation

Environmental degradation can impose large costs on the economy and on society. These costs come in several forms, including adverse impacts on human health, loss of productivity, and lower overall well-being. Some of the costs are economic, that is, they impinge directly on the growth of a country's gross domestic product (GDP), while others are noneconomic, that is, they do not show up in national accounts, but reduce the overall quality of life.

Estimates of the economic costs of environmental degradation in Asia range from 1 to 9 percent of a country's GNP, depending on the country and the impacts included in such estimates (Table 4.2). Noneconomic costs that affect welfare, but not GNP, are even larger, but are often difficult to value. As an illustration consider the case of Pakistan, where Brandon (1995) estimated the annual economic losses from environmental degradation at $1.7 billion, or 3.3 percent of GNP. This calculation did not include costly noneconomic damage, such as the long-term health effects of industrial hazardous waste, losses from unsustainable harvesting of coastal and marine resources, and biodiversity loss. Human health impacts alone account for between 60 and 75 percent of the estimated environmental damage. In the PRC, Smil's (1996) estimates suggest that environmental improvements could yield productivity and health benefits on the order of $20 billion to $36 billion.

Effects on people's health—from exposure to air and water pollutants and to heavy metals—constitute the largest share of all environmental damage in terms of welfare loss. For example, in Jakarta, particulates are a leading cause of premature death and lead emissions result in a significant loss of cognitive capacity among children. Ostro (1994) and DeShazo (1996) estimate that damage from these two pollut-

Table 4.2   Partial Estimates of the Economic Costs of Environmental Degradation, Selected Economies and Years

Economy	Source	Form of environmental damage	Year	Annual cost ($ million)	Cost as a percentage of GNP
PRC	Smil (1996)	Productivity losses caused by soil erosion, deforestation, and land degradation; water shortage, and destruction of wetlands	1990	13,900-26,600	3.8-7.3
		Health and productivity losses caused by environmental pollution in cities	1990	6,300-9,300	1.7-2.5
	Chinese Academy of Social Science, quoted in Smil (1996)	General environmental degradation and pollution	1989	31,000	8.5
Indonesia	Ostro (1994) and DeShazo (1996)	Health effects of particulates and lead above WHO standards in Jakarta	1989	2,164[a]	2.0
Pakistan	Brandon (1995)	Health impacts of air and water pollution and productivity losses from deforestation and soil erosion	Early 1990s	1,706	3.3
Philippines	World Bank (1993)	Health and productivity losses from water and air pollution in the vicinity of Manila	Early 1990s	335-410	0.8-1.0
Thailand	O'Connor (1994)	Health effects of particulates and lead above WHO standards	1989	1,602	2.0

GNP = gross national product
a.   Adjusted for purchasing power parity; it includes nonuse values affecting welfare but not GNP.

ants alone amounts to as much as $2.2 billion once economic and welfare losses are added together.

Water misallocation also incurs high costs. The overemphasis on agricultural irrigation results in water shortages for domestic and industrial use. The inadequate provision of water and sanitation services similarly comes at a huge price. The fact that poor people are willing to pay as much as 10 percent or more of their incomes to buy water from private vendors (World Bank 1992a) vividly highlights the welfare costs of today's underprovision.

Such partial calculations obviously have their limitations, but they do put the economic and broader welfare costs of environmental degradation into perspective. They also raise the question of why Asia is not investing more in environmental improvements. One reason it has not done so is because inadequate measures of the costs of environmental neglect and of the benefits of environmental improvements mean that policymakers are unaware of the full extent of the problem, and they are also unaware of the potential benefits of environmental investment.

Costs of Inadequate Environmental Infrastructure

Asia has subscribed to the conventional view that environmental infrastructure is a semiluxury that contributes to health and quality of life—and hence to welfare—but little to economic growth. According to this view, economic infrastructure should be a priority in the development process, especially in the earlier stages when the returns to productive investment are high. Only at later stages of development, when rates of return to investment fall and the contribution of economic infrastructure to growth declines, should environmental investments receive more attention. Traditional project appraisal suggests that environmental investments earn a relatively low rate of return. For example, a cost-benefit analysis of World Bank projects from 1983 to 1992 found rates of return of 29 percent for roads, 19 percent for telecommunications, and 11 percent for electric power, compared with only 6 to 9 percent for water supply, sewerage, and sanitation (World Bank 1994).

The conventional approach makes two mistakes, however. It ignores the environmental impact of economic investments such as building electricity generating capacity or roads, and thereby overstates their returns. For example, roads may contribute to soil erosion, drainage problems, and deforestation, while power stations contribute to air pollution. When the productivity losses associated with these environmental impacts are considered, the rate of return to economic infrastructure may be lower than conventionally thought (Box 4.3). For example, Panayotou (1994) found that a 10 percent increase in roads in northeast Thailand reduced the forest area by 1 percent. Kummer and Sham (1994) found similar results for the Philippines.

Moreover, conventional project appraisal underestimates the benefits that accrue to investment in environmental infrastructure, such as water supply and sanitation systems, wastewater treatment plants, and pollution abatement technologies. A survey of studies on the health benefits that result from water provision and sanitation reveals that adequate clean water and sanitation could prevent half of the deaths from diarrhea, around 3 million people a year worldwide (World Bank 1992a). Another

Box 4.3 The Future of Environmental Impact Assessment in Asia

The process of environmental impact assessment (EIA) was introduced in Asia in 1972. While it initially emphasized the protection of natural resources, EIA has evolved into a comprehensive evaluation of all aspects of a project, including its ecological, social, economic, and institutional features; the role of stakeholders; the equitable distribution of project benefits; and the quality of life.

Although it has had considerable success in promoting environmental protection, EIA has come under criticism in recent years for not being effective enough to avoid or sufficiently mitigate the impacts of major development projects, and many people have expressed doubts about its relevance to environmental protection in the 21st century. Certainly several challenges lie ahead. EIA requires a significant level of expertise that is still scarce in many Asian countries. Building such expertise takes time. In addition, even the most sophisticated and comprehensive EIA report will not ensure environmental protection unless effective monitoring and enforcement mechanisms are in place, and these mechanisms are still lacking in many

Asian countries. Finally, to be effective, EIA needs support at all levels, from senior decisionmakers to local communities.

Looking forward, several trends are likely. Long-term training will continue at the central level, and as capabilities at the center gain strength, emphasis will increasingly move to the local level. Economic valuation of environmental impacts will be increasingly incorporated in EIAs. The EIA process will become more people oriented, encouraging stronger participation by project stakeholders, particularly nongovernment organizations and affected communities. This participation will take several forms, from project community consultation during the earliest project stages to actual preparation of EIA studies by nongovernment organizations and other parties. Oversight of the EIA process will be stricter, including the establishment of independent third parties to monitor EIA preparation and implementation. The introduction of sectoral EIAs and of regional approaches will provide additional support to a stronger, more effective EIA process for development projects in the coming century.

study found that a 20 percent increase in clean water supply or sanitation could raise life expectancy (Canning 1996); and as noted in Chapters 2 and 3, higher life expectancy can raise economic growth rates. The strong link between environmental infrastructure, life expectancy, and economic growth suggests that environmental investment should be a priority even in the poorest countries. Unfortunately, project rates of return that include only financial revenues do not reflect this urgency.

Costs of Resource Depletion

Asia's spectacular economic performance could be undermined not only by environmental pollution, but also by natural resource depletion. The world's two largest tropical timber exporters, Indonesia and Malaysia, are in Asia, as are several oil producers, including Brunei Darussalam, Indonesia, and Malaysia, and, to a lesser extent, PRC and Viet Nam; many Asian countries are significant producers of coal and nonfuel minerals; and all Asian coastal states have substantial fish stocks.

Some of these natural resources are nonrenewable, while others are renewable only at a slow rate. In most Asian countries nonrenewable resources are being rapidly extracted and renewable resources are being harvested far more quickly than they can be replaced. This leads to an important question: can Asia sustain its development if it is running down its stocks of both nonrenewable and renewable resources?

The answer is no unless Asia invests enough in physical and human capital to offset the depreciation of its natural resource base. Vincent and Castañeda (1996) estimated the dollar value of the extraction of three categories of natural resources (fossil fuels, other minerals, and forest products [logs, pulpwood, and fuelwood]) as well as of agricultural soils in 14 Asian economies between 1970 and 1992.[3] They compared this to the amount of national saving these economies had generated. Gross domestic saving exceeded the value of resource depletion by a comfortable margin in all the countries throughout the period.

This finding, however, does not provide grounds for complacency. In most countries the pace of natural resource depreciation is rising exponentially. For example, in some South Asian countries the share of revenue that represents the scarcity value of the resource extracted rose

---

3. These economies are Bangladesh, PRC, Hong Kong, India, Indonesia, Korea, Malaysia, Myanmar, Pakistan, Papua New Guinea, Philippines, Singapore, Sri Lanka, and Thailand.

from less than 1 percent in 1970 to between 40 and 60 percent in 1992. This implies that the natural resources in question are becoming scarce, and that these countries will need to save and invest an increasingly larger share of the net proceeds from resource extraction in the future than they have in the past.

Costs of Insufficient Protection of Natural Areas

Asian policymakers often overlook domestic demand for environment-based recreation, such as swimming, boating, camping, and hiking. Throughout Asia the resource base to support such activities is shrinking. Asia has the lowest land area under protection when measured on a per person basis (Braatz and others 1992).

Between 1989 and 1990 (the latest year for which complete statistics are available), expenditures for protected areas in Asia ranged from $54,000 to $364,000 per park or $5 to $794 per square kilometer. Total expenditures were between $30 million and $35 million a year. This is almost certainly insufficient to ensure the survival of the existing stock of protected areas. Appropriate levels of expenditure for each area depend on its size, its management objectives, and its tourism potential. Experts estimate that to manage Asia's protected areas effectively, expenditures should be on the order of ten times what they are currently (Braatz and others 1992).

The quality of national parks and other protected areas, and hence the revenues derived from them, are being compromised for several reasons: inadequate protection, low-quality services, and underpriced admission. For example, protecting and improving Thailand's Khao Yai National Park would cost between $7 million and $14 million, but it could generate $35 million a year from higher entrance fees. Estimates of noneconomic benefits, such as arresting the loss of biodiversity, run to $85 million per year (Mingsarn and others 1995). For the supply of recreational facilities and amenities in Asia to increase in tandem with rising demand, the authorities must at least raise entrance fees. Privatizing the management of protected areas is another option. Park management can be competitively bid and awarded to private sector providers, with environmental and social concerns adequately safeguarded through regulation, environmental performance bonds, or bank guarantees.

Policy Approaches for an Improved Environment

The preceding sections suggest that Asia has paid heavily for its environmental mismanagement and negligence. They also suggest that the potential for improvement is abundant once Asian policymakers begin thinking about environmental policy differently. What should the central tenets of such a new environmental model be? First, environmental policy must be more flexible. Although some regulation will, of course, be needed, it must be more flexibly and effectively implemented than at present, with greater reliance on economic instruments. Second, environmental policy must do more to address specific market failures, particularly the problem of open access resources. Third, government policies that exacerbate environmental problems, such as subsidizing the extraction of scarce resources, should be gradually removed. Fourth, environmental policymakers should be aware of, and should concentrate on, policy reforms that benefit both economic growth and the environment. Fifth, environmental factors should be explicitly included in broader policymaking discussions. Environmental analysis should become an integral part of sectoral policy reforms. And sixth, Asia's environmental policymakers must improve the capacity of their institutions. Policies must not only become more sensible, they must also be implemented more effectively. This section describes the various facets of this approach in more detail.

Making the Case for Flexibility

As noted earlier, a rigid command-and-control approach characterizes Asia's environmental policy in most cases. In attempting to control air and water pollution in particular, Asian countries have favored emission or effluent standards over more flexible instruments. This inflexible approach has led to high compliance costs and widespread undercompliance.

In contrast, a flexible antipollution approach would use economic instruments to substitute for or complement regulatory standards. It would allow industry a much freer hand in setting its own means of compliance based on the cost of pollution to the polluting entity. Policymakers would achieve the same overall environmental objectives—cleaner air and cleaner water—but in a more flexible manner.

A first step toward greater flexibility is an understanding of the cost structure of environmental improvement. For a system of emissions or effluent standards to minimize total abatement costs across all polluters, the standards must be fixed separately for each polluter on the basis of equal marginal costs of abatement. This is not feasible, because regulators cannot have the necessary detailed information, and polluters would have incentives to misrepresent their true costs. Economic instruments, however, permit such cost saving without regulators having to possess such detailed information.

When pollution levels are high, and especially when the use of distorting subsidies (such as energy subsidies) promotes pollution, the marginal costs of controlling pollution can be negative or zero, and rise only slowly. However, as environmental quality improves, so additional improvements begin to cost more. Thus reaching a level of zero pollution, or even near zero pollution, becomes prohibitively expensive.

For example, a study of particulate pollution in the Philippines (Rufo and Delos Angeles 1996) showed that the marginal costs of reducing particulate levels by 70 percent was $5.8 per ton. The marginal costs of a 90 percent reduction, however, would be almost three times as much. Similarly, a study of water pollution by 260 factories in the PRC (Dasgupta and others 1996) showed that removing 88 percent rather than 58 percent of the suspended solids generated would cost about 10 percent more, but to reduce the level of suspended solids by 98 percent would cost about 55 percent more.

The costs of reducing pollution also vary substantially between pollutants and sources. For instance, Hartman, Wheeler, and Singh (1994) found that the cost of removing sulfur dioxide in textile production in developing countries was $67 to $535 per ton, while an Environmental Resources Management (1996) study of the machinery and transport sectors found that the cost of sulfur dioxide removal ranged from $245 to $1,563 per ton. A World Bank (1993a) study found that it was much cheaper to reduce sulfur dioxide pollution in coal-fired power plants by 95 percent through fluidized bed combustion than by end-of-pipe flue gas desulfurization. Similarly, the same study found that in the case of solid waste disposal, incineration costs six to ten times as much as sanitary landfill or tidal land reclamation.

It is usually more expensive for older factories with outdated technology and for smaller factories that cannot take advantage of economies of scale in waste treatment to control pollution. In the case of India's pulp and paper industry, as mill capacity rises from 10 to 115 tons per day, the cost of pollution abatement per ton of paper produced falls by more than 70 percent (Dasgupta and Murty 1985). A flexible system of pollution control would permit older and smaller plants to reduce their compliance costs by paying larger or newer factories with lower costs to overcomply on their behalf, reducing costs overall.

Flexibility in the mix of antipollution responses can also help reduce compliance costs. For instance, if a factory can choose between changing its product processes, inputs, or pollution abatement efforts; relocating; or paying charges for polluting rather than being forced to stick to a single technology or emissions standard, it will choose the cheapest option. Thus environmental policy should give polluters the flexibility to choose how to respond to environmental regulation.

Asian environmental policymakers can use a vast array of economic instruments to supplement or substitute their existing regulations. Box 4.4 describes the most common ones. Tables 4.3 and 4.4 provide a more complete list of market-based instruments for environmental protection and natural resource management, together with examples of countries that use them.

How much money can a more flexible form of pollution control save? The sums involved are enormous; compare, for example, the difference between the price of the PRC's existing combination of discharge permits and fines on excess emissions (a command-and-control system) with the cost of a full emission charge system (a market-based instrument). Based on a sample of 260 enterprises in Beijing and Tianjin with multiple water pollution sources, Dasgupta and others (1996) found that an emission charge that would achieve the current abatement rate for each pollutant would reduce abatement costs from $47 million to $13 million per year, a saving of $34 million from this group of enterprises alone, or a 70 percent reduction from the cost of the command-and-control system.

A comparison of the proposed command-and-control-based antipollution investment program for the PRC and India (ADB 1992b, 1995) with the least-cost alternatives (Markandya 1996) also demonstrates the inefficiency of Asia's current policies. The command-and-control approach consists of investments required in the power sector from 1992 to 2000 to achieve a certain percentage reduction in emissions of major pollutants. The least-cost policy consists of selecting least-cost technologies using a model that minimizes costs. The cost of the command-

Box 4.4 Examples of Economic Instruments

Pollution charges force polluters to pay for the environmental damage their economic activities cause. Examples include effluent charges for wastewater, emission charges for air pollution, and fees for noise pollution. Such charges are set per unit of pollutant, which means that pollution streams from individual sources must be monitored and measured. Occasionally, presumptive pollution charges are based on engineering estimates. Self-reporting with random inspections is another enforcement mechanism.

Product charges are imposed on the polluting input rather than on the pollution itself, for example, on the carbon content of fossil fuels rather than on the carbon dioxide they emit. Product charges are incorporated into a product's price, and hence do not require monitoring of emissions. This makes them especially attractive for developing countries. In addition, differential product charges can encourage a shift toward less polluting products. Thailand has used differential taxation of gasoline effectively as part of its policy to encourage a shift to unleaded fuel.

Deposit refund systems induce producers and consumers of polluting products to return waste products for recycling or treatment and safe disposal. Deposit refund systems can be used for many products, including batteries, beverage containers, and even pesticide or chemical containers. A particular advantage for Asia is that deposit refund systems promote waste collection, a labor-intensive activity.

Tradable emission permits create a market in air or water pollution. The authorities set an overall level of permissible pollution for a particular airshed or watershed. The permits divide this level between firms based on norms agreed by policymakers. As the permissible aggregate level of pollution is lower than the current level, this creates an artificial scarcity and the permits acquire market value. Thus producers who wish to expand, for instance, must either reduce the pollution from their existing factories or buy permits from other factories. The desired reduction in pollution occurs at least cost.

User charges include utility charges for water, electricity, garbage collection, and so on; road tolls; and fees for access to amenities, such as parks and beaches. User charges should reflect the marginal cost of providing a service. Their objective is to manage demand for the service and recover the cost of supplying it.

Fiscal and financial subsidies commensurate with the resulting benefits are justified in cases where private sector activities generate greater social than private benefits. One example is public subsidies for planting trees.

and-control approach is ten times larger than the least-cost alternative for the PRC and three times larger for India. Although a number of assumptions made in the study may overstate the cost differential, it is clearly substantial.

International evidence also suggests that countries can achieve large savings by moving away from command-and-control regulations. In the United States, for instance, most studies show a ratio of command-and-

Table 4.3 Market-Based Instruments for Environmental Protection

Type of instrument	Description and country examples
Effluent (emission) charges	
Air (intraboundary)	• Air pollution prevention fee (Taipei,China); emissions charge above a threshold value (Korea)
Air (transboundary)	• Greenhouse taxes (taxes on carbon, sulfur) (Sweden, United States)
Water	• Charges for discharges above a specified level (PRC, Malaysia)
Solid waste	• Charges on disposal of household waste (most OECD countries and several U.S. states)
Noise	• Tax on landing aircraft used as a part of noise abatement programs (Japan)
User charges	• Water effluent treatment (several OECD countries, Thailand); solid waste disposal (Hong Kong, Thailand [partly])
Product charges	• On lubricants, mineral oil and products, batteries, fertilizers, agricultural chemicals, food containers
Presumptive charges	• Hazardous waste
Administrative charges	• Permitting, licensing, product certification
Input taxes	• Sulfur content of coal (Sichuan province of the PRC)
Emissions trading (marketable permits, tradable permits, tradable pollution rights, "credit systems," "averaging schemes"), "bubbles," offsets ("netting"), "banking"	• Tradable permits for particles (Santiago, Chile; Almaty, Kazakstan) • Auctionable permits for import and use of ozone-depleting substances (Singapore); acid rain trading program for electric utilities under U.S. 1990 Clean Air Act
Deposit refund system	• Beverage containers (Japan, Korea, Philippines, Taipei,China); car batteries, tires, pesticide containers (Korea)
Performance (guarantee) bonds (also noncompliance fees)	• Clean-up of mining wastes (Australia, Malaysia); prevention of littering along tourist treks (Nepal)
Tax differentiation	• Leaded versus unleaded petrol (Thailand); gasoline versus diesel fuel (most OECD countries)
Tax concessions	• Duty free imports of pollution abatement equipment (most of ASEAN); corporate tax incentives for pollution control industry (Taipei,China)
Subsidies	• Subsidized credit for developing "clean" technology (Taipei,China, Thailand); subsidies for energy conservation (Korea, Thailand)
Location incentives / disincentives, access rights	• Access fees in urban areas (Chile, Singapore); relocation incentives to polluters (Japan); auctioning of street user rights (Chile)
Resource pricing	• Marginal cost pricing of water supply and sewage collection (Chile); energy pricing, auctioning of certificates of vehicle entitlement (Singapore)
Environmental auditing	• Hazardous waste
Environmental liability insurance	• United States, some countries of the former Soviet Bloc
Environmental funds	• Fund to compensate victims of pollution (Japan, Korea); funds to encourage investment in pollution control technology (Indonesia, Thailand); Abandoned Mine Reclamation Fund (United States)

ASEAN = Association of Southeast Asian Nations
Source: OECD (1989); ADB (1994); Panayotou (1990).

control cost to least-cost ranging from 2 to 22. The saving is greatest in the case of particulates, Asia's most serious and widespread air pollution problem. Even if a more efficient regulatory system meant that only two thirds of the current cost of environmental protection could be saved, the effect would be equivalent to tripling environmental expenditures under the existing system. By improving efficiency, a more flexible and effective regulatory regime can also enhance a country's competitiveness. For example, a survey of business executives in 50 countries reveals a strong correlation between the flexibility of environmental regulations and international competitiveness (Panayotou and Vincent 1997).

Table 4.4 Economic Incentive Instruments for Natural Resource Management

Type of instrument	Description and country examples
Property or use rights	Land titling, communal management agreements (used in many developing Asian countries)
Resource or product pricing and taxation	Forest or mineral royalties, pricing of irrigation water in line with its true marginal cost, reduction of price support for soil-damaging or water-intensive crops, reduction of fertilizer and pesticide subsidies (several Asian countries), auctioning of forest concessions, offshore oil/gas fields
Performance (guarantee) bonds	Sustainable management of tropical forests (Philippines)
Land use taxes	Higher tax for erodible areas (proposed in Thailand)
User charges, access fees, licensing fees	Park entrance fees, fishing licenses, hunting licenses
Subsidies, tax concessions	Afforestation
Tradable resource shares or quotas	Water capacity shares, transferable quotas in fisheries (Australia, New Zealand), transferable water use rights (Chile; Madras, India; Nepal)
Transferable development rights	Heritage assets, coastal resources, biodiversity conservation sites (Puerto Rico; Maine, United States)
Removing government barriers to market entry	Voluntary exchange of water rights (United States)

Source: OECD (1989); ADB (1994); Panayotou (1990).

Despite their incentive effects and cost-saving features, Asian policymakers cannot simply introduce emission charges, tradable permits, and other economic instruments overnight. To be effective, the more sophisticated instruments require effective monitoring and enforcement whereas many simpler economic instruments, such as product charges and deposit refund systems do not, because they are incorporated into the product price. Several Asian countries have begun to introduce market-based instruments for environmental management on an experimental basis. Their successes and failures highlight some of the limitations that must be taken into account in the Asian context.

Charges and permits for effluents, in particular, require effective monitoring. This is feasible for medium and large stationary sources (that is, easily identifiable polluting plants), but is less so for small-scale scattered pollution sources. In Malaysia, for instance, the introduction of charges on palm oil effluent in the late 1970s was remarkably successful. Here pollutants are easily identified. Despite a 50 percent increase in the number of palm oil mills between 1978 and 1982, the extent of water pollution as measured by the biological oxygen demand fell from 222 tons of effluent per day in 1978 to only 5 tons in 1984. These charges did not result in a loss of competitiveness for the palm oil industry or reduce production.

Economic instruments in general do not work well when profit motives do not dominate firms' decisionmaking. For example, the PRC introduced industrial pollution charges in 1982 in an attempt to reduce effluents and emissions, but the system was not successful because state-owned enterprises were not concerned about cutting costs.

Flexible environmental regulations are also not advisable in cases where even small quantities of pollutants can cause significant damage, such as toxic or hazardous waste. In such instances, strict enforcement of inflexible command-and-control regulations is appropriate. In developing Asian countries this applies mostly to infectious hospital wastes and heavy metals from some industrial processes.

These limitations, together with the differing institutional constraints in Asian countries, have several implications. For the foreseeable future environmental management will be based on a mixture of regulation and economic instruments. In some areas environmental policy by command-and-control will remain necessary, but Asian countries should reduce their reliance on this approach, and make regulations more flexible.

The move toward greater flexibility will increase efficiency and improve environmental management. The more economically advanced countries, especially in East and Southeast Asia, may possess the necessary monitoring and enforcement capacity, as well as the profit-oriented and competitive industries to use the most sophisticated economic instruments, including such market-based instruments as pollution taxes and tradable permits. The less advanced Asian countries should begin with simpler economic instruments, as some are already doing. These should include product charges, deposit refund systems, presumptive charges, and tax incentives. In the long run these countries should invest in improved monitoring and implementation capacity to allow a gradual shift to more efficient economic instruments. In the meantime, they should continue experimenting with such systems on a pilot project basis to acquire experience and to adapt them to local conditions and needs. Controlling pollution among small-scale scattered sources will always be a challenge, but group responsibility, community pressures, and incentives for relocation, change of practices, and waste delivery work best.

Clarifying Property Rights

The lack of secure property rights lies behind the biggest market failures in Asia's environment. Insecure property rights over land mean that people underinvest in land improvement and have no incentives to conserve biological resources; the lack of property rights over water encourages misuse and prevents efficient allocation of scarce supplies; and the lack of property rights over fisheries encourages overfishing.

Asian governments should address all these issues. Property rights do not have to be private. They can also be communal or public, that is, owned by the state, but they need to be well defined, secure, and transferable. Where traditional, customary, or communal rights exist, the best policy might well be to strengthen these rights, rather than to supplant them with private property rights. When a natural resource has a broad national impact, say a critical national watershed, then state ownership is probably optimal. If the impact is local, for example, a village forest or local fishery, communal property rights combined with private use rights (which are regulated by the local community) are the most appropriate. In other situations, private property rights usually make the most sense.

Issuing secure land titles to farmers with insecure ownership can double or triple the value of the land, while the costs of the necessary cadastral surveys, title registration, and other expenses amount to only 2 or 3 percent of the pretitle value (Feder and others 1988). Improved security of ownership over land can therefore be self-financed. Even though Asia has a long history of land titles and cadastral surveys, property rights are still poorly defined in many areas.

Promoting water rights is another priority. Parts of India have had systems of water rights in operation for centuries. They are gradually being introduced in other parts of the world. Water rights are defined for a fixed quantity per unit of time, and are awarded by the authority that owns the water. Such rights could be tradable. The idea is to promote an active market for water use rights. This allows water to flow from low-value uses to high-value uses, thereby benefiting both farmers and cities and promoting efficiency.

Phasing Out Distortionary Subsidies

In Asia, as elsewhere, subsidies have ostensibly served a number of purposes. They have been used to promote new technologies, for example, pesticide subsidies; to help the poor, for example, water subsidies; to alleviate capital constraints, for example, capital subsidies; and to satisfy political constituencies, for example, energy subsidies. Some of these interventions were ill-conceived at the outset; others, such as fertilizer and pesticide subsidies, have outlived their usefulness; yet others, such as energy subsidies, started small, but have now become major budgetary, social, and environmental burdens. Globally, the annual costs of subsidies detrimental to the environment (including water, energy, and pesticide subsidies) exceed $500 billion (Earth Council 1996; Roodman 1996). Asia accounts for about a third of this estimate.

Water Subsidies

Asian countries spend an enormous amount of money subsidizing water for irrigation. The Food and Agriculture Organization of the United Nations (FAO 1994) estimates that aggregate irrigation subsidies amount to $11.4 billion a year in Asia, or 60 percent of the developing world total. Because such subsidies encourage wasteful use, including overirrigation that leads to waterlogging and salinization, as well as reduced water coverage, their elimination is likely to bring both fiscal and economic as well as environmental benefits. Fewer dams will be needed, less land will need to be ruined, and more people might have access to water.

Agriculture in Asia uses 80 to 90 percent of all water withdrawals, compared with 70 percent in the world as a whole and 40 percent in OECD countries. Assuming that water demand falls in proportion to a rise in its price,[4] a 10 percent increase in the price of irrigation would double the amount of water available to residential and industrial users, and still leave Asian agriculture with the largest share of water withdrawals in the world.

Huge reductions in subsidies, and hence efficiency gains, are also possible in nonagricultural water supply. The World Bank (1994) estimated that water supply systems in developing countries only recovered an average of 35 percent of their costs. This imposed a fiscal burden of $13 billion a year, of which Asia's share was probably around 60 percent. Thus the subsidy enjoyed by nonagricultural water users in Asia amounts to some $8 billion a year. In addition, eliminating illegal connections could save another $3 billion a year. Raising water charges to reflect the full cost of supply would increase the efficiency of use and might raise an additional $2.5 billion annually. Thus with better pricing and demand management and only modest investments in repairing and expanding distribution systems, around 50 percent of the current water supply in developing Asian countries could be saved and used to supply those people currently without access to water.

Energy Subsidies

Asian governments, like those of the OECD and of other developing countries, intervene heavily in their energy markets through direct and indirect producer and consumer subsidies. OECD energy subsidies are estimated to be in the range of $60 billion to $75 billion (OECD forthcoming). Larsen and Shah (1994) found that energy subsidies in non-OECD countries added up to between $270 and $330 billion in 1991, equivalent to 5 to 7 percent of their total GDP.

Several Asian countries have recently taken steps to reduce their energy subsidies. The PRC has raised coal prices closer to world market levels, Indonesia has reduced its energy subsidies substantially, and the Philippines is moving in the same direction. In a recent survey of Asian environmental policymakers (ADB and Harvard Institute for International

---

4.   Calculated from the midpoint of price elasticity estimates. Bhatia, Cestti, and Winpenny (1993) report estimates in the range of -0.4 to -1.5.

Development 1996), almost half of the respondents reported reductions in energy subsidies during the past five years, primarily for electricity and gasoline.

Agrochemical Subsidies

Advanced economies subsidize their agriculture sectors, while developing countries tax theirs. Total OECD subsidies for agriculture amount to $182 billion a year, or 40 percent of the value of production (OECD 1996). In developing countries, agricultural production faces an average effective tax rate of 30 percent. To compensate farmers for these taxes, developing country governments subsidize agricultural inputs such as irrigation, fertilizers, and pesticides. Subsidy rates for pesticide use range from 20 to 90 percent, with an average subsidy of 50 percent (Repetto 1985). Farah (1994) estimated that developing countries used $4 billion worth of pesticides in 1990. Therefore, a rough estimate of the value of pesticide subsidies in developing countries is $2 billion per year, with Asia's share coming to more than 60 percent.

Asian governments also subsidize fertilizers. Fertilizer subsidies in Bangladesh, India, Indonesia, Korea, Nepal, Pakistan, Philippines, Sri Lanka, and Thailand totaled more than $3.5 billion between 1988 and 1990. India alone spent $2.8 billion to subsidize fertilizers. The cost of provision aside, excessive use of chemical fertilizers damages both the soil structure and water resources through higher toxicity and eutrophication. To their credit, in recent years Asian governments have moved toward reducing fertilizer subsidies. In response to the recent ADB survey (ADB and Harvard Institute for International Development 1996), in 40 percent of the responding countries, Asian environmental policymakers reported that they had reduced agrochemical subsidies in the last five years. However, much more remains to be done in reducing direct and indirect subsidies for unsustainable agricultural practices.

Making Win-Win Environmental Investments

Asia's neglect of environmental investment to date has left countless public investment opportunities unexploited, which at modest cost could yield large economic and environmental benefits. Finding these win-win investment opportunities, where there are both economic and environmental gains, should be among the top priorities of Asia's new environmental model. They exist in virtually all sectors of the economy, from water supply to pollution control to forest conservation.

One area with enormous potential is investments to improve the efficiency of energy generation and use. Table 4.5 provides an estimate of the potential cost savings. As the table shows, Asia could save between $9 billion and $13 billion per year by more efficient electricity generation and $26 billion to $39 billion per year by improving residential and commercial energy use. These estimates do not even include productivity gains from the improvements in people's health and reduced damage to agriculture that lower pollution implies.

Another area with great win-win potential is pollution control in megacities. Every Asian megacity would achieve both economic and welfare gains from small investments in pollution control. For example, a World Bank (1993a) study indicated that an investment of $20 million to reduce water pollution discharges from the top 100 polluters in the Metro Manila area would result in labor productivity gains and reduced risk to fisheries valued annually at about $150 million. Similarly, an investment of $35 million in fuel reformulation to reduce lead in gasoline and sulfur in diesel fuels would result in gains from avoided illness and reduced damage to forestry and agriculture annually of about $85 million to $160 million.

Soil conservation is another area with enormous potential. Low-cost soil conservation technologies applicable to Asia, such as planting vetiver grass and constructing earthen bunds, could increase crop yields by 35 to 50 percent and result in economic rates of return of 22 to 95 percent (World Bank 1993b). This calculation does not include the off-site

Table 4.5 Potential Gains from Improved Energy Efficiency

Type of energy	Total consumption	Potential efficiency savings	Cost of efficiency gains	Cost of energy	Savings
Electricity	1,080 TWh	20%	$0.02/kWh	$0.06-$0.08/ kWh	$9 billion to $13 billion
Residential and commercial energy	645 million toe	20%	$100/toe	$300-$400/ toe	$26 billion to $39 billion

kWh = kilowatt hours; TWh = terawatt hours; toe = tons of oil equivalent
Note: 1 terawatt = 1 billion kilowatts.
Source: Consumption: ADB (1992a); potential efficiency savings: Saunders and Gandhi (1994).

environmental benefits of reduced sedimentation of water bodies, irrigation systems, hydroelectric dams, and ports. Such benefits could add another 5 to 10 percent to these rates of return.

These examples illustrate the enormous potential that exists for win-win investments in Asia. With the right pricing policies and an adequate regulatory framework, each investment could be self-financed, and hence attractive to the private sector.

Implementing Environmentally Sound Sectoral Policies

Asia's new environmental model must not be confined to its environment ministries. Governments should pursue environmentally sound policies in every sector of the economy. This section highlights selected examples in three sectors to illustrate the approach recommended.

Forest Policy

Forest policy in Asia is frequently based on bans. Log export bans and logging bans are well-intentioned responses to the need to increase value added from a depletable resource (Indonesia), to the growing scarcity of forest resources (Philippines), and to ecological disasters (Thailand), but they often make things worse rather than better. The reason is simple. Both log export bans and logging bans depress rather than increase the value of wood, thereby inducing more waste and less conservation. Making a resource less valuable is usually not an effective way of saving it. Thus governments must revise their policies to encourage efficient harvesting and processing of forest products and to promote investments in forest regeneration and conservation.

A first step is to reclassify property rights. Governments should divide forestland into land available to individuals, land available to groups of individuals or communities, and lands over which the state retains ownership and control. Forestlands that have no significant impact on those beyond their borders can be safely distributed and securely titled to the dispossessed, such as landless farmers and shifting cultivators. Forestlands with localized externalities, such as local watersheds, can be made communal property, provided that a community small and cohesive enough to manage them effectively can be defined. Finally, forestlands that have a regional or national impact, such as major watersheds or nature reserves, should stay under state ownership, though there should be greater cooperation between the state and nongovernment organizations (NGOs) in their management. Management would be most effective over a limited area with reduced outside pressure. India, for example, has been experimenting with assigning responsibility for forestlands to small user groups. Smaller areas under state ownership face fewer pressures from encroaching communities and are easier to manage.

Environmental considerations suggest that the procedure for awarding logging and other concessions should also change: from a system based on negotiations with concessionaires, licensing, and nominal fees to one based on competitive bidding. Such an approach would maximize the government's share of rents from forest resources, would help prevent the logging of marginal lands, and would reduce the risk of renegotiation of concessional agreements. Concessionaires should be provided with financial instruments for accumulating equity through forest investments that are transferable and marketable to encourage them to invest in conservation and reforestation. Governments should increase the duration and scope of forest leases to encourage the production of nontimber forest products and services and the regeneration of forest resources for subsequent felling cycles. They should also reform their forestry tax systems to eliminate incentives for destructive logging. For example, a change in the tax base from the volume of timber removed to the volume of merchantable timber on the site would eliminate the incentive for "high grading" (taking only high-value logs) and forest "mining" (that is, unsustainable harvesting). Finally, governments must ensure that concessionaires practice environmentally responsible management by requiring commensurate environmental performance bonds or bank guarantees.

Governments can promote private forest investments that generate social benefits, such as tree planting, through fiscal incentives like tax exemptions and subsidies. For instance, the forest tax structure should favor natural forest management over plantations and single-species plantations over soil-damaging crops such as corn and cassava. Governments should also provide logging companies with incentives to set aside parts of their concessions as nature reserves for conservation purposes and to provide a reserve of nontimber forest products for extraction by local communities.

Recognition and protection of local communities' customary rights of access to and use of forests is central to any successful forest policy.

Their physical presence in the forest and their intimate knowledge of the local ecology can be of immense value in protecting and regenerating the forest and harvesting and using nontimber products. Policymakers should think of forest communities as suppliers of environmental services and give them incentives to provide more of these services. As a general rule, governments should pay greater attention to incorporating local communities into all stages of economic development planning when they are affected.

Surrounding populations frequently encroach on forest reserves and national parks in search of land, food, fuelwood, and building materials, as do illegal loggers. Buffer zones between areas of intensive land use (for logging or farming) and areas of strict conservation may help control encroachment if they offer employment opportunities that are more attractive than encroachment. For example, the buffer zones may be exploited for nontimber goods on a sustainable basis or developed into areas for recreation and tourism. For such buffer zones to be effective, the people living in the forest or along its perimeters (squatters and shifting cultivators) should benefit from the new activities, and the open access status of the buffer zones should be terminated to prevent new entrants from dissipating any benefits that the buffer zones would generate.

The most cost-effective way to accomplish this is likely to be to grant secure and exclusive territorial rights over buffer zones to the local communities that depend on the forest for their livelihood. As long as policymakers design the incentive structure so that it favors sustainable use over logging and slash-and-burn farming and allocate the property rights to communities with a functioning social organization, they can rely on self-enforcement to protect the buffer zone and the core area of the reserve from encroachment. When a large number of communities is involved, however, a higher local authority or the government may need to play a more active role in enforcing communal rights, arbitrating conflicts between communities, and providing additional protection to the core nature reserve.

Water Policy Reforms

Reforms in water policies must deal with both the management of the resource and the delivery of water services. Experience suggests, and regional consultations support this view, that such reform can only succeed if governments address water sector issues holistically and act decisively through a national action program. The program should reform policy, revise legislation, streamline institutions, increase public-private partnerships, foster consultation and public awareness, prioritize infrastructure investments, promote resource management and conservation, and strengthen the government's planning and regulatory capacity in the sector (Arriens and others 1996).

Resource management should respond to river basin boundaries, starting in the priority basins. It should promote the concept of integrated resource basin management. Service delivery in water supply and irrigation can, over time, be contracted to autonomous and accountable service providers. This will increase water use efficiency, introduce viable services that charge appropriate fees to recover financial and economic costs, and minimize environmental externalities. With increased consultation between agencies and other stakeholders, national water action programs can be designed to meet national economic and environmental objectives. This is badly needed in most Asian countries.

Reforms of water management policies must include overhauling irrigation policy to provide incentives for efficient water use, to increase cost recovery, and to generate funds for rehabilitating, maintaining, and improving existing irrigation systems. The first steps in such a reform should be to strengthen water user associations and to make structural modifications to existing irrigation systems. Intermediate water storage, for example, should be possible at the head of distribution channels, and meters should be introduced in secondary channels. Such modifications would allow bulk water sales through contracts with water user associations and cooperatives. Some irrigation agencies in the PRC and India already do this.

Bulk water sales to water user associations could help reduce metering and collection costs by leaving water distribution to local organizations, which can best monitor water use and prevent meter manipulation or damage through peer group pressure. When volumetric (marginal cost) pricing is not feasible or is prohibitively costly, the authorities could introduce low-cost approximations, such as area-based irrigation charges and land taxes. This may, for example, be the case with groundwater. The sacrifice of efficiency in this case may be justified by the savings in metering and collection costs. The evidence worldwide suggests that farmers are prepared to pay for reliable irrigation. The availability and reliability of supply is far more important to them than its cost.

The same principles that apply to irrigation water should, in general, apply to all other uses of water, including industry, energy, and household use. Water users should pay for the full costs of supply, delivery, depletion, and pollution treatment attributable to their use. The payment should be linked to the quantity and quality of use, and the link should be transparent enough to encourage users to use water efficiently, to conserve it, and to minimize waste.

Energy Policy Reforms

Improving the efficiency of energy use has long been identified as one of the most effective ways to conserve energy and achieve environmental goals. Policymakers can accomplish this in two complementary ways: by improving the efficiency with which energy is produced and transmitted and by removing subsidies and other price distortions.

Electricity is usually the costliest form of energy. At the point of delivery to the consumer, the ratio between the amount of energy delivered and the fuel energy required to produce it is some 25 to 30 percent. The main objective on the energy supply side is to develop power generation technologies that raise the efficiency of fuel combustion, while at the same time they improve the efficiency of existing power generation plants. Upgrading transmission and distribution facilities can also result in significant energy savings. Better metering systems, modern billing techniques, and more stringent collection of electricity charges would also improve matters. Price is a major determinant of electricity demand and end-use efficiency. Overall, however, policymakers' appreciation that prices below true opportunity costs lead to wasteful electricity consumption is inadequate.

In recent years, many governments in both industrial and developing countries have introduced reforms in their power sectors. Most East Asian countries have invited the private sector to invest in power projects. Participation by independent power producers is only an intermediate step, however. Power utilities themselves should shift to private hands. The privatization of electricity generation should be a critical goal for all Asian governments, but its success depends on effective regulation. The process must be transparent, enabling interested parties and the public to identify the basis for the regulator's decision. Effective regulation must also be insulated from political influence to prevent special interests from controlling government decisions. Such steps, together with maintaining a stable political climate, are essential if private financing of energy investments is to be maximized.

Privatization must be accompanied by the most important reform in the energy sector: the removal of subsidies, both explicit and implicit. Fuel subsidies and electricity rate structures that do not make consumers pay more for power during periods of peak demand or at remote locations lead to excessive and inefficient use. Policymakers should supplement the removal of energy price distortions by introducing fiscal policy reforms that encourage investment in renewable forms of energy (Box 4.5).

Improving Institutional Capacity

Asian policymakers are concerned about the state of their countries' environment and keen to do something about it. An overwhelming majority of both environmental and economic policymakers believe that environmental protection will contribute significantly to social development objectives (Table 4.6). Many policymakers are keen to experiment with a more flexible approach as outlined earlier. An equally important consideration, however, is improving Asia's institutional capacity to do so.

This demands change in several directions. At the strategic level, government involvement in environmental management must shift from top-down management to focused and strategic intervention. A huge regulatory bureaucracy that employs thousands of environmental inspectors is not the way to implement Asia's new environmental model. Instead, streamlined environment ministries must coordinate a more decentralized approach and must ensure that environmental considerations are taken into account in all areas of policymaking.

Thus environmental concerns must become central to other ministries. In some instances, an increasingly market-based approach will allow this to happen naturally, for instance, finance ministries already view environmental taxes as additional sources of revenue. The expanded use of such instruments can take place within the government's existing administrative machinery. In some cases, better environmental management will involve removing issues from the purview of certain government ministries, for example, some Asian countries have begun to move the responsibility for managing protected areas from their forestry departments—which have an acknowledged bias toward timber and extraction—into specific institutions that focus on preservation.

Box 4.5 Sustainable Energy Development in the PRC and India

The PRC and India have large deposits of coal and rely on it for most of their electric power generation. Coal use, however, causes a number of environmental problems: it worsens local and regional air quality, increases water pollution, and hastens global climate change. Thus the sustainable development of energy supplies in the PRC and India depends on increasing energy efficiency and encouraging the use of renewable energy technologies (RETs).

The PRC is pursuing a vigorous, two-pronged strategy for improving energy efficiency. It has given priority to investment programs that accelerate the adoption of more efficient, low-carbon technologies, and is building the institutional and human capacities needed to implement them. It has introduced projects to improve the urban environment in major cities, including Beijing, Chengde, Dalian, Hefei, Qingdao, and Tangshan. The PRC is also promoting the use of market incentives and regulatory controls to encourage energy efficiency and environmental conservation.

India has extensive experience in developing and disseminating RETs, which currently account for about 1,200 megawatts of India's energy supply capacity. By the year 2005, another 2,200 megawatts will likely be supplied by RETs, involving a capital investment of $1.9 billion. RET users and manufacturers often face difficulties accessing financing. This has been a major impe-

diment to the commercialization of RETs in India. To address this bottleneck, the Indian government has set up a special financing institution for RETs, the Indian Renewable Energy Development Agency.

RETs are particularly important for rural power supply. Electrification in India's rural areas is far from complete. Although 81 percent of Indian villages were classified as electrified in 1990/91, this meant that one or more households in the village were connected to the grid. In reality, only 27 percent of rural households actually had electricity.

The poor reliability of rural power supply is an additional argument for using RETs. While the natural primary energy flows for RETs (sunshine and wind) may vary, the extent of variation at a given location can be taken into account when designing the RET system. RETs can also be tailored closely to the scale of the end use. For example, solar or wind turbine power systems can range from a few (or even fractional) kilowatts to the megawatt range, which makes them highly suitable for decentralized use in rural areas.

Finally, standardized, decentralized RET systems can bring many economic advantages. They do not require large-scale organization, additional infrastructure, or substantial regulation. Hence they can be installed more quickly and more cheaply than standard forms of electricity.

More generally, central governments will need to devolve responsibility for environmental management to appropriate local and regional levels and enter into partnerships with the private sector, NGOs, and local communities. For this, the capacities of local governments, the private sector, and NGOs will have to be improved. For instance, NGOs may self-regulate their levels of competence through an umbrella registration body that would evaluate their standards. This has happened, for

Table 4.6 Asian Environmental and Economic Policymakers' Views on Environmental Protection

Question	Percentage of respondents answering "yes"		Percentage of respondents answering "no"	
	Environmental policymakers	Economic policymakers	Environmental policymakers	Economic policymakers
Do you feel that removal of subsidies (e.g., pesticide, fertilizer, energy) that may help better utilize the natural resource base and protect the environment is justified/feasible in your country?	53	50	40	42
Do you feel that market/incentive-based environmental regulatory instruments (license fees, pollution taxes, competitive bidding, tradable pollution permits) can widen the revenue base and increase fiscal revenues in your country?	40	83	20	17
Do you feel that increased emphasis on environmental protection may lead to reduced export competitiveness of your country's industries?	13	17	47	42
Do you feel that aggressive promotion of environmental protection in your country could lead to a more innovative, efficient, and competitive industry?	47	Not asked	0	Not asked
Do you feel that aggressive promotion of environmental protection in your country could lead to the development of a competitive export sector for environmental capital goods and services?	33	42	7	33
Do you consider that better natural resource management and conservation (e.g., forests, land, water, fisheries) can contribute significantly to your country's equity and social development objectives?	80	75	0	0
Do you consider that at your country's present stage of development, environmental protection is regressive (helps the rich, not the poor)?	13	0	40	92
Are you optimistic about the future of the environment in your country over the next ten years?	80	67	7	0

Source: ADB and Harvard Institute for International Development (1996).

example, in Bangladesh. The appropriate level of government for environmental management is that at which effective measures can be undertaken. For instance, for integrated river basin or airshed management, institutional arrangements may have to straddle the jurisdictions of several states. However, for regulating automobile emissions, standard setting and enforcement should be at the level of municipalities.

Civil society more broadly must also become involved. Environmental impact assessments are an important means for stakeholders to participate at the project level. In some countries, the preparation of national environmental action plans provided opportunities for civil society to establish environmental priorities at the national level. During the course of preparing these plans, consultation reached all the way down to village-level decisionmakers.

Greater decentralization and broader participation are prerequisites for Asia's new environment model to work successfully. The move toward devolution and pluralism in environmental issues mirrors a broader trend already evident in Asian societies.

The Next Thirty Years

Will Asia's environment improve or worsen in the next 30 years? The answer depends in part on the pace of economic and demographic change. It also depends on technological progress, that is, the kinds of environmental technologies that will become available. External factors will also matter. Changes in global environmental patterns, particularly in global environmental standards, will affect Asia's future. Most important, however, the state of Asia's environment will depend on Asia's own policy choices. To highlight the importance of making the right kind of policy choices, this section makes some tentative projections of Asia's environmental future and the financing requirements associated with different policy options.

Economic Growth and Demography

As this study has pointed out, economic growth influences the environment in several ways. Rising incomes raise the demand for environmental improvement, and economic development changes the economy's structure, which in turn determines the relative importance of rural and "green" environmental issues versus urban and "brown" ones. Asia is likely to become more industrialized during the next 30 years, but the share of heavy industry will decline and that of light industry will rise. The service sector will begin to dominate in East Asia and will increase its share throughout the region. The rate of growth will obviously determine the pace of this transition.

Asia's population is likely to increase by 50 percent during the next 30 years, to reach almost 5 billion people by the year 2025. As pointed out earlier, the rate of population growth will continue to decelerate, but the pace of urbanization will accelerate. With only 24 percent of the population currently living in cities, Asia is the world's least urbanized region; however, at the current rate of urban population growth, by 2020 half of Asia's population will live in cities.

Technology

Predicting technological progress is almost impossible. Nonetheless, new or emerging technologies are likely to affect the global and Asian environment in the next 30 years: cleaner and more efficient energy production, pollution abatement, and resource conservation technologies that will lower the costs of controlling pollution, treating waste, and conserving natural resources.

To fuel the rapid growth of Asian economies, electricity generation in the region is forecast to grow at an annual rate of 6.5 percent up to the year 2000 and at an annual rate of 5.3 percent between 2000 and 2010. Coal combustion is currently the main source of electricity production in the PRC and India, and together they account for 80 percent of Asia's coal consumption, which for the region as a whole is some 2 billion tons per year. Despite efforts to substitute cleaner fuels, coal use will continue to rise at an annual rate of 3.7 percent per year to reach 3.1 billion tons by 2010, because of its abundant availability and cost advantage (Huq 1996). However, coal combustion is the source of many pollutants, including sulfur dioxide, nitrogen oxides, and dust, and accounts for 80 percent of sulfur dioxide emissions and acid rain in Asia. Whether Asia succeeds in reducing sulfur dioxide emissions and other energy-related pollutants will depend critically on the availability and cost of clean coal technologies.

Clean coal technologies add about $0.01 per kilowatt hour to the cost of electricity. For Japan, which sells electricity at $0.11 per kilowatt hour, this implies a 9 percent increase, but for the PRC, which sells electricity at only $0.03 per kilowatt hour, this implies a rise of 33 percent. The typical price of electricity for the rest of Asia is between $0.05 and $0.08 per kilowatt hour. High-efficiency clean coal technologies add between 15 and 30 percent to the capital cost of power plants in Asia. Therefore a key factor in projecting emission levels during the next 30 years is the prospect for lower-income Asian countries to develop and adopt lower cost, clean technologies.

Another factor is the extent to which renewable energy sources will become competitive with fossil fuels. The cost of renewable energy, especially solar energy, with which Asia is richly endowed, has been declining at the rate of 3 to 5 percent a year. If this rate continues, solar energy would become competitive with fossil fuels for some applications between 2010 and 2020, provided that governments remove their subsidies on fossil fuels. Small-scale solar energy production is already competitive for rural electrification in remote areas. Biomass, wind, and geothermal energy provision will be competitive with conventional sources even earlier. By 2030 all renewable energy sources are likely to become competitive with conventional power technologies (Table 4.7).

Technological innovation is also influencing pollution control. A number of low-polluting technologies and practices are currently available for activities ranging from electricity generation and transport to manufacturing and industry. These technologies can be used to control local pollutants such as nitrogen oxides and particulates, regional pollutants such as sulfur dioxide, and even global pollutants such as carbon dioxide (the latter through fuel switching). Depending on the pollutant and the industry, alternative pollution abatement technologies can reduce emissions and effluents by factors of 10, 100, and even 1,000 or more (Anderson and Cavendish 1992). If the benefits are so high, a valid question is why Asian countries have not yet adopted these technologies. In some instances, it is because the financial costs are higher than those of the polluting technology. In other cases, the reasons are simply inertia, risk aversion, and a lack of information. Moreover, the failure to charge for the environmental damages caused by existing polluting technology acts as an implicit "tax" on cleaner technology.

**Table 4.7 Comparative Costs of Electricity Generation from Conventional
and Renewable Energy Technologies, Actual and Projected,
Selected Years, 1980-2030**
($/kilowatt hour)

Source	1980	1990	2000	2030
Conventional sources (oil, coal, etc.) with no pollution control	—	0.05	—	—
Conventional sources with control of sulfur dioxide, particulate matter, and nitrogen oxides	—	0.06	—	—
Wind	0.32	0.08	0.05	0.04
Geothermal (various technologies)	0.04-0.08	0.04-0.07	0.04-0.06	0.04-0.05
Photovoltaic	0.89	0.30	0.15	0.05
Solar thermal				
Trough with gas assistance	0.24[a]	0.80	-0.06[b]	—
Parabolic dish	0.85	0.16	0.08	0.05
Biomass	0.06	0.05	0.05	0.04-0.05

— = not available
a. 1984 cost figures.
b. 1994 cost projections.
Note: All costs are averaged over the expected life of the technology.
Source: World Bank Alternative Energy Unit data as quoted by Brandon and Ramankutty (1993); Finnel, Cabraal, and Kumar (1991).

External Factors

Just as environmental damage is not always confined within national boundaries, so environmental policy depends on international as well as on national developments. The following external factors will impinge on Asia's environment and environmental policy in the future.

International Conventions and Treaties

International environmental agreements have proliferated in recent years. By 1992, 870 international agreements included environmental obligations, including several major global treaties, for example, the Montreal Protocol on ozone depletors and the 1992 Rio Summit agreements on climate change and biological diversity. While Asian developing countries will increasingly face pressures from industrial countries to implement their commitments strictly, these arrangements also provide Asian developing countries with opportunities to obtain technologies and investments for sustainable development, and they will have to insist that the industrial countries also fulfill their own, differentiated commitments.

In addition to formal conventions and treaties, international environmental law is also developing through the use of norms and guidelines, such as the Non-Binding Statement of Forestry Principles adopted at Rio in 1992. Peer pressure will increasingly force compliance with these norms. In due course, they may also harden into formal treaties.

Cross-Border Cooperation

Asian countries already have several regional and subregional cooperation programs for the environment in place. In Northeast Asia, for instance, six countries—PRC, Japan, Korea, Democratic People's Republic of Korea, Mongolia, and the Russian Federation—have recently adopted a framework for environmental cooperation that will focus on reducing power plant emissions and building capacity for collecting environmental statistics. Environmental cooperation, particularly over water resources, is an important component of the Mekong subregion partnership. In addition to transboundary air pollution and water resource management, environmental issues that demand international cooperation include the protection of fisheries and coastal marine resources, the exploitation of offshore oil resources, and the movement of toxic waste.

Transfer of Environmental Technology

Environmental technologies, like all other technologies, are owned by their creators and are protected under laws governing intellectual property rights. Recent agreements under the Uruguay Round of the General Agreement on Tariffs and Trade have strengthened the international protection afforded to property rights considerably. Some developing countries worry that this could have adverse consequences on their ability to pay for technologies that improve environmental protection. This is unlikely. As already noted, recent international agreements explicitly mandate industrial countries to commit financial resources for technology transfer. Moreover, an effective regime for guaranteeing intellectual property rights will strengthen the market for environmentally sustainable technologies. The global market for environmental goods is already worth some $300 billion a year, and could reach $600 billion by 2000. It may also stimulate research and innovation in the developing countries.

Trade and the Environment

Environmental considerations are increasingly voiced during the course of international trade negotiations. Like other developing countries, Asian countries face the possibility that stringent environmental standards will not only make their products uncompetitive, but will also be used as nontariff barriers.

The two most commonly cited environmental standards in trade are product standards related to production methods and ecolabeling. These are particularly important for Asian exporters, because about 60 percent of the value of their manufacturing exports originates in sectors with potentially significant environmental impacts. Product standards can reduce market access: they can be formulated in such a way that domestic industries find it easier to conform to them. For example, recycling requirements for packaging materials in Europe may discriminate against jute bags from Bangladesh even though, overall, jute bags may be more environmentally sound. In general, the World Trade Organization has held that trade policies should not discriminate between identical products. Ecolabels are voluntary, and are intended to allow consumers to express their demand for environmental conservation by buying environmentally friendly products. Nonetheless, ecolabels can also be biased against imported goods.

The International Organization for Standardization (ISO) has formulated the ISO 14000 series, which focuses on environmental management methods used in production processes. These standards are intended to ensure that firms comply adequately with their own countries' environmental standards. The main motivation behind these standards is to limit liability for environmental damage on the part of importers. Firms' adherence to ISO 14000 standards is voluntary, and must be certified by accredited third parties. The dissemination of ISO 14000 may affect Asian firms in several ways. At one level they may promote efficient management, and so boost returns; however, they may also act as a barrier to trade by increasing production costs, although gradual implementation could minimize such cost increases. In the long-run improved environmental performance should lead to competitive advantages. Firms that do not obtain such certification may find themselves facing a considerable international marketing disadvantage in the future.

Policy and Institutional Environment

Policy and institutional reforms are the critical components of Asia's environmental future. Without a conducive policy environment and a favorable incentive structure, few innovations will take place and substitutions from existing to cleaner technologies will be rare, especially when they involve increased costs. Until policymakers price scarce natural resources and environmental assets more realistically, the efficiency with which they are used will not improve.

Environmental policy in Asia could follow three directions. It could continue in its present form, characterized by overly ambitious, uniform, and inflexible pollution standards; technology specification; subsidized provision of water, sanitation, and waste treatment; inadequate monitoring; weak and erratic enforcement of environmental regulations; and weak environmental institutions.

It could move further in the direction of environmental policy in North America and Western Europe, characterized by strict command-and-control regulations rigorously enforced by a large environmental bureaucracy, and thereafter by the court system. This approach is economically inappropriate for Asia, which lacks the necessary enforcement capacity and has insufficient financial resources for large-scale investment in environmental protection unless other public and private investments are crowded out. Nonetheless, many environmental regulators in Asia, who are frustrated with the current weak and ineffective enforcement, favor a move in this direction.

Finally, Asian environmental policy could move in the direction outlined in the previous section, that is, it would be characterized by an eclectic combination of flexible regulatory, economic, and voluntary instruments that promote least-cost solutions and by gradual compliance schedules with predetermined escalation rates that would allow time for adjustment. Policymakers would phase out environmentally harmful subsidies; define property rights more clearly; and increasingly privatize the provision of water supply, sanitation, waste treatment, protected area management, and transport infrastructure, which would be financed through user charges that increasingly reflect the long-run marginal cost of supply.

Pollution in the Future

The importance of moving in this latter direction can be gauged from several perspectives. One way is to look at the likely path of pollutant emissions with or without policy reforms.

Electricity

With unchanged policies and technologies, emissions from electricity generation and transportation in developing countries will grow exponentially. Projections indicate that by 2030 they will be between five and ten times higher than during the 1990s. Improved policies could cut the rate of emissions by about 20 percent from their projected 2030 levels. Policy reforms, together with investments in low-polluting technologies, can more or less stabilize emissions at their 1990 levels. Policymakers would obtain the greatest reduction in emissions by focusing on particulates. Economic benefits alone are highest if policies are reformed, but no new investments are made. When reform is combined with investment, emissions fall precipitously, but the incremental net benefits shrink because of the high investment cost, although they continue to be positive. Thus reforming policies, for example, removing subsidies and introducing full-cost pricing, is beneficial for both GDP and welfare. When investment in control technologies is combined with reform, the effect on GDP is significantly reduced, although it is still positive, at least in later years. This suggests that policy reform should be the first priority, followed by investment in selected low-polluting technologies.

Transport Emissions

The picture is similar for transport-related emissions. Policymakers would obtain the lowest levels of emissions by undertaking energy price reforms, implementing pricing policies for roads that reduce congestion, and investing in the deleading of gasoline and the control of particulates. The highest net benefits are obtained by pricing reforms alone. Hence energy price reform and road pricing ought to be the first priority for action, followed closely by deleading of transport fuels. Pricing reforms would help both to improve energy efficiency and to reduce congestion, thereby reducing particulate emissions.

Sulfur Dioxide Emissions

Current growth paths suggest that sulfur dioxide emissions in Asia will rise from their 1990 level of about 40 million tons to 110 million tons by 2020. Introducing basic emission control technologies in PRC, India, and Pakistan and advanced technologies in other countries would cut emissions in 2020 by 40 percent. Introducing advanced technologies in all countries would cut sulfur dioxide emissions by 50 percent, but will still leave them 30 percent above their 1990 level. Emissions could only be reduced below their current levels if all countries used the best technology available, but the costs would be huge: more than $90 billion by 2020.

Slower economic growth would reduce the levels of sulfur dioxide in Asia's environment. Based on the relationships found in the environmental Kuznets curve discussed earlier, sulfur dioxide levels were projected for PRC, India, and Thailand under alternative growth and policy scenarios. Slower growth does result in lower ambient levels, especially in later years, because sulfur dioxide as a stock pollutant tends to accumulate when its rate of generation exceeds the environment's dispersion and assimilation capacity. Better policy, in this case more efficient regulatory institutions, result in lower emissions in later years even with faster growth. Sulfur dioxide emission disperses widely across the region and is deposited as acid rain, especially in East Asia.

Biodiversity Conservation in the Future

Prospects for an immediate improvement in biodiversity conservation are dim, and more species and ecologically sensitive areas will be lost in the coming decades. The process of changing toward more sustainable use of biological resources will depend on longer-term integrated policy formulation, institutional innovation, incentives, research, and resource inventorying. New challenges will emerge, particularly in relation to the mining of biological resources for their genetic material. Management of protected areas will remain the primary, though by no means the only, strategy for biodiversity conservation in the coming decades. If the status quo is maintained, we can expect to see a trend toward further encroachment of protected areas by governments (through approved economic development projects) and local residents (through hunting and gathering), which will lead to increasing fragmentation of protected area systems. Forestry departments will continue to struggle unsuccessfully with their dual and contradictory roles of forest exploiter and forest protector. Whether protected areas are under the control of forestry departments or other government agencies, the losing struggle to provide enough funds and human resources to manage protected areas adequately will continue. Opportunities for biodiversity conservation outside protected areas will be lost because of poor public awareness and anemic research programs, but above all by poor policies.

However, not all is doom and gloom. If nascent, but promising, efforts to pursue new approaches to biodiversity continue, Asia can expect to slow down, and eventually reverse, the most disturbing trends in the loss of biological resources. NGOs and communities are likely to continue their remarkable push for meaningful involvement in conservation and management, with a corresponding move toward more sustainable forms of resource use. Essential to stable financing and effective management of protected areas is their sustainable use for ecotourism, scientific and educational tourism, bioprospecting, carbon storage and other low-impact uses with efficient pricing, and widespread benefits to local communities. Concurrently, governments' role will shift toward regulation, monitoring, and evaluation, with NGOs and the private sector taking a greater share of management responsibility.

Expected demographic changes during the next 30 years may also work in favor of biodiversity conservation, although not necessarily of the quality of life, as rural residents continue to move to urban areas. Phasing out perverse incentives that encourage overexploitation of coastal and marine fish resources or of terrestrial resources such as forests will dampen the alarming projections for fish and forest losses caused by commercial operations, and will further encourage replacement of lost resources through reforestation and aquaculture.

Environmental Infrastructure Requirements

A second way to assess the importance of environmental policy reforms is to gauge the financial consequences of continuing business as usual. Infrastructure provision is a function of population growth and of growth in GDP per person. Because policymakers tend to view environmental infrastructure as unproductive, the relationship between growth and infrastructure provision is lower than for productive infrastructure. For example, a 10 percent increase in GDP per person results in only a 3 percent increase in water supply and a 2 percent increase in sanitation (Canning 1996). Moreover, provision of environmental infrastructure in urban areas costs three times as much as in rural areas, with the rate of urbanization adding another dimension to cost estimates.

Using simple extrapolation of urban and rural populations and assuming urban water supply costs of $200 per person and rural supply costs of $60 per person, annual net investments in water supply are projected to range between a low of less than 0.2 percent of GDP for Malaysia and Thailand to more than 0.7 percent for Nepal and Pakistan. For most Asian countries to achieve water supply coverage of 100 percent in the next ten years, their annual net investment must at least double or triple, but will nevertheless remain at less than 1 percent of GDP. The most important exceptions are Bangladesh, Myanmar, Nepal, and Pakistan, for which investment requirements rise to between 2 and 4 percent of GDP per year, which is obviously excessive for poor countries. PRC, India, and Indonesia are intermediate cases (1 to 1.5 percent of GDP), but in absolute terms they face the greatest demands, because they have by far the largest populations and high rates of urbanization.

Estimates of the net investment requirements for sanitation are of a similar order of magnitude, assuming average urban costs of $100 per person and rural costs of $30 per person. To maintain existing levels of service, annual net investment costs will be less than 0.5 percent of GDP for most countries, with a high of 0.8 percent of GDP for the PRC. To achieve 100 percent coverage in the next ten years under current pricing and managerial policies, annual net investment costs will rise above 1 percent of GDP for most countries, but are particularly excessive for poor countries, ranging from 2.6 percent of GDP for India to 5 percent of GDP for Bangladesh. It is thus not advisable for poor countries to attempt to achieve 100 percent coverage within ten years. A longer time horizon of 20 to 30 years is more realistic. However, these countries are also the ones that can expect the largest GDP and welfare dividends from increased coverage from their current extremely low levels of less than 15 percent. A quadrupling of access to sanitation services in Bangladesh, India, and Viet Nam is likely to boost the rate of GDP growth by almost half a percentage point. The accompanying health and welfare benefits would, of course, be much larger.

The aggregate costs of 100 percent coverage in water supply and sanitation during the next ten years for all of developing Asia are approximately $30 billion per year, compared with $10 billion per year to maintain the current level of service in the face of population growth.

Table 4.8 presents estimates of environment-related funding needs for the Asian and Pacific region for 1991-2025, based on the assumption that environmental policies will not change. The estimates for water supply and sanitation are based on an average annual growth rate that is consistent with full coverage over 30 (rather than 10) years. The aggregate funding needs for all sectors rise from less than $40 billion in 1995 to almost $250 billion in 2025, an average annual growth in expenditures of 7.2 percent, or twice the projected average growth rate of GDP. If such an enormous investment requirement were to be funded wholly by the public sector, this would pose intolerable fiscal burdens.

Table 4.8 Environment-Related Funding Needs for the Asian and Pacific Region, Selected Years, 1991-2025
(1990 $ million)

Field	1991	1995	2000	2005	2010	2015	2020	2025	Average growth rate per year (percent)
Water supply	5,941	6,919	8,924	10,306	11,840	13,291	14,689	16,017	3.0
Sanitation	3,008	3,340	4,187	4,762	5,404	6,010	6,595	7,150	2.6
Population	4,233	4,568	5,027	5,421	5,818	6,194	6,555	6,899	1.4
Education	—	2,249	2,486	2,993	3,394	3,774	4,140	4,487	3.4
Agriculture	—	1,738	2,537	2,995	3,553	4,232	5,059	6,065	8.6
Transportation	—	1,875	8,817	13,390	14,806	16,096	17,499	19,054	15.0
Industrial waste	—	1,564	9,039	20,781	26,616	32,460	39,482	48,026	19.5
Biodiversity	67	67	67	67	67	67	67	67	0.0
Forestry	3,701	3,701	3,701	3,701	3,701	3,701	3,701	3,701	0.0
Electric power	—	6,679	19,376	40,969	63,216	82,521	102,979	5,550	12.9
Acid rain	407	512	684	887	1,140	1,447	1,822	2,278	5.2
Global climate	5,365	5,365	5,365	5,365	5,365	5,365	5,365	5,365	0.0
Total	22,723	38,577	70,212	111,637	144,921	175,160	207,953	244,660	7.2

— = not available

Note: Asian and Pacific region refers to a sample of 30 countries in Asia plus Fiji and Papua New Guinea.
Source: 1991-2000: ADB (1994); 2001-2025: Nomura Research Institute as cited in Kato (1996).

Alternative policy approaches that involve pricing reform and improved management would reduce the burden considerably. Full-cost pricing of water, for instance, would achieve nearly full coverage without supply expansion in most Asian countries. Of course, this is not the case for every environmental good, and Asia will face investment needs. However, with an improved approach to environmental policy, the private sector could meet a large part of these investment requirements. Privatizing, introducing better pricing policies, removing adverse subsidies, and implementing other sensible policy reforms will ensure that Asia can afford to improve its environment.

With improved policies, Asia could keep its environmental expenditures to less than 2 percent of GDP or thereabouts, with the public sector providing less than half this amount. As public expenditures on the environment in developing Asia are currently just under 1 percent, this scenario will not involve a substantial increase in public expenditures on the environment, but a significant redeployment of existing resources toward a more targeted and strategic portfolio, and one that leverages additional capital from domestic and foreign private sources. The environmental outcome of this policy scenario is likely to be reduced environmental degradation as income levels rise, and hence less risk that ecological thresholds will be crossed. At the same time, the risks in fiscal discipline and economic growth are minimized, while welfare and sustainability gains are maximized.

Conclusion

The findings described in this chapter suggest that Asia will pay even more dearly for environmental negligence in the future than it has in the past. Without better policies, environmental degradation will worsen in most of the region during the next 30 years. Only in East Asia will things begin to improve, as income levels there have reached the point at which popular demand for an improved environment is forcing policy shifts. Elsewhere, income-induced demand will be too weak to offset the increase in pollution and resource degradation that rapid economic growth implies. Without conscious shifts in environmental policy, most of Asia will become dirtier, noisier, more congested, more eroded, less forested, and less biologically diverse.

Fortunately, the analysis has also provided grounds for optimism. Continued environmental degradation is not inevitable. This chapter has outlined the components of a new policy model that would do much to improve Asia's environmental future. Characterized by a strong, but limited, governmental role; by effective management and oversight; by an efficient pricing policy; by secure property rights; and by a prominent role for the private sector and civil society, this model would permit Asia's environmental policy to meet the challenges ahead.

Much depends, however, on how soon—and how effectively—Asian policymakers adopt this model. There is consensus in Asia that environmental degradation has reached unprecedented levels and is likely to get worse, and increasingly raise the price their countries are paying in terms of productivity, health losses, and human suffering. They recognize the need for new institutions, new approaches, new legislation, and better enforcement. All this gives grounds for optimism.

However, environmental problems are long-term ones that require long-term solutions. Countries must take action today to ensure a better environment a generation hence. The time profile of reform will vary between countries depending on their stage of development, political economy, and institutional capacity; nevertheless, they should initiate certain actions, such as phasing out environmentally damaging subsidies, without delay. They can adopt other measures, such as pollution taxes and full-cost pricing, gradually as they build up the capacity to do so and seek public consensus. The most profound reforms—privatizing environmental infrastructure and decentralizing environmental management—may take longer still. No single blueprint can be designed. Each Asian country will inevitably move toward a better set of environmental policies at its own pace. Far more important is that the goals are clearly articulated and the process started.

In contemplating the choice between action today and action tomorrow, Asian policymakers should note that time is not on their side. Everyday more children are poisoned by lead, more money is lost to traffic jams in megacities, more tons of productive soil are eroded, and more unique environmental assets are lost. The economic and welfare costs of environmental damage are already staggeringly high in Asia. When one takes into account the rising emission rates for most pollutants, the increasing speed with which pollution and resource degradation levels are building up, the growing number of people being affected, and the growth in environmental values relative to other values, the economic and welfare costs of further neglect are staggering. If Asia does not take the appropriate measures immediately, at a minimum the gains derived from growth would be eroded and support for growth-oriented policies could be undermined. The sustainability of Asia's prosperity could be threatened. Thus the time for action is now.

References

ADB (Asian Development Bank). 1992a. *Energy Indicators of Developing Member Countries of ADB*. Manila.

_____. 1992b. *Integrated Energy-Environment Planning*. Manila.

_____. 1994. *Financing Environmentally Sound Development*. Manila.

ADB and Harvard Institute for International Development. 1996. "Survey of Environmental and Economic Policymakers." Prepared for *Emerging Asia: Changes and Challenges*. Manila, Asian Development Bank.

Anderson, D., and W. Cavendish. 1992. "Efficiency and Substitution in Pollution Abatement." Discussion Paper No. 186. World Bank, Washington, D.C.

Arriens, Lincklaen W., J. Bird, J. Berkoff, and P. Mosley, eds. 1996. *Towards Effective Water Policy in the Asian and Pacific Region*. Vol. I. Manila: Asian Development Bank.

Beede, D., and D. Bloom. 1995. "The Economics of Municipal Solid Waste." *The World Bank Observer* 10(2):113-50.

Bhatia, Ramesh, Rita Cestti, and James Winpenny. 1993. *Policies for Water Conservation and Reallocation: Good Practice Cases in Improving Efficiency and Equity*. Washington, D.C.: World Bank.

Bloom, D. 1995. "International Public Opinion on the Environment." *Science* 269(July):354-58.

Braatz, S., G. Davis, S. Shen, and C. Rees. 1992. *Conserving Biological Diversity: A Strategy for Protected Areas in Asia-Pacific Region*. Asia Technical Department Series No. 1993. Washington, D.C.: World Bank.

Brandon, C. 1995. "Valuing Environmental Costs in Pakistan: The Economy-Wide Impact of Environmental Degradation." Background paper for *Pakistan 2010 Report*. World Bank, Washington, D.C.

Brandon, C., and R. Ramankutty. 1993. "Towards an Asian Environmental Strategy for Asia." Discussion Paper No. 224. World Bank, Washington, D.C.

Canning, D. 1996. "Productive and Environmental Infrastructure in Emerging Asian Economies." Background paper for *Emerging Asia: Changes and Challenges*. Asian Development Bank, Manila.

Cleaver, K. M., and G. A. Schreiber. 1993. *The Population, Agriculture, and Environment Nexus in Sub-Saharan Africa*. Agriculture and Rural Development Series No. 1. Washington, D.C.: World Bank.

Cointreau-Levine, Sandra. 1994. "Private Sector Participation in Municipal Solid Waste Services in Developing Countries." Urban Management Program Discussion Paper No. 13. World Bank, Washington, D.C.

Dasgupta, Ajit K., and M. N. Murty. 1985. "Economic Evaluation of Water Pollution Abatement: A Case Study of Paper and Pulp Industry in India." *Indian Economic Review* 20(2):231-67.

Dasgupta, P. S. 1995. "Population, Poverty, and Local Environment." *Scientific American* 272(2):40-46.

Dasgupta, Susmita, Mainul Huq, David Wheeler, and Chonghua Zhang. 1996. "Water Pollution Abatement by Chinese Industry: Cost Estimates and Policy Implications." World Bank, Washington, D.C.

DeShazo, J. R. 1996. "The Level of and Demand for Environmental Quality in Asia." Background paper for *Emerging Asia: Changes and Challenges*. Asian Development Bank, Manila.

Earth Council. 1996. "Economic Incentives for Sustainable Development." Draft. Institute for Research on Public Expenditure, The Hague.

Environmental Resources Management. 1996. *Revision of the EC Emission Limit Values for New Large Combustion Installations*. London.

ESCAP (Economic and Social Commission for Asia and the Pacific). 1995. *State of the Environment in Asia and the Pacific*. Bangkok, Thailand.

FAO (Food and Agriculture Organization of the United Nations). 1994. "Water Policies and Agriculture." In *State of Food and Agriculture 1993*. Rome.

Farah, J. 1994. "Pesticide Policies in Developing Countries: Do They Encourage Excessive Use?" Discussion Paper No. 238. World Bank, Washington, D.C.

Feder, Gershon, Tongroj Onchan, Yongyuth Chalamwong, and Chira Hongladarom. 1988. *Land Policies and Farm Productivity in Thailand*. Baltimore, Maryland: The John Hopkins University Press.

Finnel, J., A. Cabraal, and D. Kumar. 1991. "Renewable Energy Technologies: A Practical Solution to Providing Clean Electricity under Increasingly Stringent Environmental Requirements." Paper presented to the Third Annual Energy and Environment Conference, Meridian Corporation (Alexandria, Virginia), Denver, Colorado.

GEMS (Global Environment Monitoring System). 1996a. *Airs Executive International Programme* (http://www.epagov/airs/aeint). World Health Organization.

_____. 1996b. *Water Programme* (http://cs715.cciw.ca/gems/atlas-gwq/gems2.htm/). United Nations Environment Programme and World Health Organization.

Grossman, Gene M., and Alan B. Krueger. 1995. "Economic Growth and the Environment." *Quarterly Journal of Economics* 110(2):353-77.

Hartman, R. S., D. Wheeler, and M. Singh. 1994. "The Cost of Air Pollution Abatement." Policy Research Working Paper No. 1938. World Bank, Washington, D.C.

Huq, A. 1996. "Energy and Environment: The Asian Outlook." Background paper for *Emerging Asia: Changes and Challenges.* Asian Development Bank, Manila.

Islam, Nazrul. 1996. "Income-Environment Relationship: Is Asia Different?" Background paper for *Emerging Asia: Changes and Challenges.* Manila, Asian Development Bank.

Kato, S. 1996. "Emerging Asia and the Future of the Environment: Perspective and Agenda." Background paper for *Emerging Asia: Changes and Challenges.* Manila, Asian Development Bank.

Kummer, D., and C. H. Sham. 1994. "The Causes of Tropical Deforestation: A Quantitative Analysis and Case Study from the Philippines." In K. Brown and D. W. Pearce, eds., *The Causes of Tropical Deforestation.* London: University College of London Press.

Larsen, Bjorn, and Anwar Shah. 1994. "Global Climate Change, Economic Policy Instruments, and Developing Countries." Paper prepared for the 50th Congress of the International Institute of Public Finance, 22-25 August, Harvard University, Cambridge, Massachusetts.

Markandya, A. 1996. "Environmental Control Costs, Policy Options, Instruments, and Abatements." Background paper for *Emerging Asia: Changes and Challenges.* Manila, Asian Development Bank.

Mingsarn, Kaosa-ard, Theodore Panayotou, J. R. DeShazo, and others. 1995. *Green Finance: A Case Study of Khao Yai Natural Resources and Environment Program.* Cambridge, Massachusetts: Harvard Institute for International Development and Thailand Development Research Institute.

O'Connor, D. 1994. *Managing Environment with Rapid Industrialization: Lessons from East Asian Experience.* Paris: Organisation for Economic Co-operation and Development.

OECD (Organisation for Economic Co-operation and Development). 1996. *Subsidies and Environment: Exploring the Linkages.* Paris.

_____. Forthcoming. *The Environmental Implications of Energy and Transport Subsidies.* Paris.

Opschoor, J. B., and H. B. Vos. 1989. *Economic Instruments for Environmental Protection.* Paris: Organisation for Economic Co-operation and Development.

Ostro, B. 1994. *Estimating the Health Effect of Air Pollution: A Method with an Application to Jakarta.* Policy Research Paper WPS 1301. Washington, D.C.: World Bank.

Panayotou, T. 1990. "Economic Incentives in Environmental Management and Their Relevance to Developing Countries." In D. Erocal, ed., *Environmental Management in Developing Countries.* Paris: Organisation for Economic Co-operation and Development.

_____ (with Somthawin Sungsuwan). 1994. "An Econometric Analysis of the Causes of Tropical Deforestation: The Case of Northeast Thailand." Development Discussion Paper No. 284. Harvard Institute for International Development, Cambridge, Massachusetts. Also in K. Brown and D. W. Pearce, eds., *The Causes of Tropical Deforestation*. London: University College of London Press.

_____. 1995. "Environmental Degradation at Different Stages of Economic Development." In I. Ahmed and J. Doelman, eds., *Beyond Rio: The Environmental Crisis and Sustainable Livelihoods in the Third World*. London: Macmillan Press.

_____. 1996. "An Inquiry into Population, Resources, and Environment." In D. A. Ahlburg, A. C. Kelley, and K. O. Mason, eds., *The Impact of Population Growth on Well-Being in Developing Countries*. Berlin and New York: Springer-Verlag.

_____. 1997, "The Effectiveness and Efficiency of Environmental Policy in China." Environmental Discussion Paper, Harvard Institute for International Development, Cambridge, Massachusetts.

Panayotou, T., and J. Vincent. 1997. "Environmental Policy and International Competitiveness." Environmental Discussion Paper, Harvard Institute for International Development: Cambridge, Massachusetts.

Repetto, R. 1985. *Paying the Price: Pesticide Subsidies in Developing Countries*. Research Report No. 2. Washington, D.C.: World Resources Institute.

Roodman, D. M. 1996. *Paying the Piper: Subsidies, Politics and the Environment*. Worldwatch Paper No. 133. Washington, D.C.: Worldwatch.

Rufo, L. S., and M. Delos Angeles. 1996. "The Philippine Environmental Quality Indices Project." Harvard University and Asian Development Bank Environmental Quality Index Project. Harvard University, Cambridge, Massachusetts.

Saunders, Robert J., and Sunita Gandhi. 1994. *Global Energy Paths: Energy Policy Prescriptions for Sustaining the Environment*. Washington, D.C.: World Bank.

Smil, V. 1996. *Environmental Problems in China: Estimates of Economic Cost*. East-West Center Special Reports No. 5. Honolulu, Hawaii: East-West Center.

Tiffen, M., M. Mortimore, and F. Gichuki. 1994. *More People, Less Erosion: Environmental Recovery in Kenya*. Winchester, U.K.: Wiley and Sons.

Tongpan, S., and T. Panayotou. 1990. *Deforestation and Poverty: Can Commercial and Social Forestry Break the Vicious Circle*. Bangkok, Thailand: Thailand Development Research Institute.

UNEP (United Nations Environment Programme). 1993. *Environmental Data Report 1993-94*. Oxford, U.K.: Blackwell.

United Nations. 1995. *World Urbanization Prospects: The 1994 Revision*. New York.

Vincent, J., and B. Castañeda. 1996. "Sustainability and the Economic Depreciation of Natural Resources in Asia." Background paper for *Emerging Asia: Changes and Challenges*. Asian Development Bank, Manila.

WHO (World Health Organization) and UNEP (United Nations Environment Programme). 1987. *Global Pollution and Health*. London: Yale University Press.

_____. 1992. *Urban Air Pollution in Megacities of the World*. Oxford, U.K.: Blackwell.

World Bank. 1992a. "Water Resources Management." Policy Paper. World Bank, Washington, D.C.

_____. 1992b. *World Development Report 1992*. New York: Oxford University Press.

_____. 1993a. *Philippines Environmental Sector Study: Towards Improved Management of Environmental Impacts*. Washington, D.C.: World Bank, East Asia and Pacific Region, Industry and Energy Division.

_____. 1993b. "Watershed Development Sector Study: Towards Improved Management of Environmental Impacts." World Bank, East Asia and Pacific Region, Industry and Energy Division, Washington, D.C.

_____. 1994. *World Development Report 1994: Infrastructure for Development*. New York: Oxford University Press.

_____. 1995. *World Tables Diskette 1995*. Washington, D.C.

World Resources Institute. 1987. *World Resources 1987*. New York: Basic Books.

_____. 1996. *World Resources 1996-97: A Guide to Global Environment*, electronic database. New York: Oxford University Press.

5

THE QUALITY OF LIFE

The basic goal of development is to improve the quality of people's lives. Human well-being, however, is difficult to measure. The components of a long, healthy, and fulfilling life do not always lend themselves to statistical comparison. The most common indicator of development progress, gross domestic product (GDP) per person, provides a crude gauge of one, albeit important, aspect of human well-being. A more complete understanding of how the quality of life has changed demands a broader analysis. Some additional indicators, such as poverty rates or educational improvements, lend themselves to rigorous numerical comparisons. In other cases, the analysis is by definition more qualitative. The structure of the family and other social institutions, the nature of the work environment, and the relative position of women all influence the quality of life, but in ways that one cannot easily measure. The purpose of this chapter is to combine quantitative and qualitative approaches to document changes in Asia's quality of life and to try to understand why these changes have occurred. Once equipped with such an analysis, it becomes possible to project likely trends in Asia's quality of life, and to indicate future policy challenges.

What Happened to Asia's Quality of Life?

Life in Asia has changed remarkably during the last 30 years, and mostly for the better. On average, all standard indicators of the quality of life, such as poverty and mortality rates, have improved sharply. In the 1960s, poverty in most of Asia was as severe as in sub-Saharan Africa. Today, extreme poverty is virtually absent in Hong Kong, Korea,

Singapore, and Taipei,China, and is less severe throughout the region. All Asians now live longer and are better educated than their parents and grandparents.

These changes have not been uniform. More striking than the improvements in Asia's quality of life are the region's disparities. Differences between countries, between regions within countries, between rural and urban areas, between ethnic groups, and between the sexes are large. In many instances they have increased during the last 30 years. Life expectancy and other indicators of health and nutrition, for instance, were already higher in East Asia than South Asia in the early 1960s. Although they have improved in both subregions, East Asia has achieved more. Hence on many counts human well-being within Asia is diverging rather than converging. Within many countries the story is similar: the situation in many of the inland provinces of the People's Republic of China (PRC) is less favorable than in the coastal provinces. In South Asia especially, women's well-being lags far behind that of men.

In large part, this diversity in the quality of life has economic causes. The countries, especially in East Asia, that grew faster saw more rapid improvements in health, education, and poverty reduction. But economic growth does not explain all of Asia's diversity. Some countries and regions with relatively low incomes per person have disproportionately high standards of health, education, or nutrition. Sri Lanka, for instance, has a high standard of health and education in relation to its income per person. Social, cultural, and ethnic factors have all influenced changes in Asia's quality of life, particularly in terms of who benefits most. So, too, has public policy. The state of Kerala in India, for instance, has a low income per person, but a high level of publicly provided services. Understanding this diversity and its causes is central to explaining the changes in Asia's quality of life.

Poverty

One can measure the incidence of poverty in several ways (Box 5.1). One approach is to identify a threshold level of consumption based on a person's minimum calorie requirements plus a provision for other essentials. This is called the poverty line. The share of the population below this threshold is the share living in poverty. One problem with this method is that it is not always feasible to define such minimum consumption thresholds consistently across countries, which limits the scope for international comparisons. An alternative approach that makes international comparison easier is "dollar-a-day" poverty. According to this definition, all people living on less than $370 a year—measured in purchasing power parity (PPP)-adjusted 1985 dollars—are defined as poor. The incidence of poverty is the share of the total population that falls below the poverty line.

Based on the dollar-a-day benchmark, about 1.3 billion people in developing countries were poor in 1993, almost a third of the total population (Table 5.1). Their average income was about 10 percent below the dollar-a-day threshold. Almost three quarters of the world's poor live in Asia, in large part because most of the world's people live in this region. In 1993, 446 million people living in East Asia, including 372 million persons in the PRC, existed on less than a dollar a day. This means that about 25 percent of the population was poor, about the same proportion as in Latin America. A further 515 million people, or 43 per-

Box 5.1 Measuring Poverty

To compare the incidence of poverty between different places or over different times, analysts must fix absolute poverty lines. There are two frequent choices.

The food poverty line. This is the level of private consumption per person (or, if available, per adult equivalent) at which minimum calorie requirements, plus a small allowance for nonfood consumption, are just met.

The dollar-a-day poverty line. This defines an internationally comparable minimum level of private consumption. It is typically $1 per person per day in 1985 dollars, adjusted for purchasing power parity.

The *incidence* of poverty is the share of a country's population that falls below such poverty lines. It is also called the headcount ratio.

The *depth* of poverty is the proportion by which the average private consumption of poor people falls below the poverty line.

The *intensity* of poverty is the depth of poverty multiplied by its incidence. This is the same as counting the number of poor people, multiplying the result by their proportionate shortfall below the poverty line, and expressing the total as a proportion of the total population. This is also called the poverty gap index.

The *severity* of poverty is increased not only by the incidence and depth, but also by more unequal distribution of private consumption among the poor. For instance, if a rupee is taken from a poor person and given to a much poorer person, then the severity of poverty falls, even though its incidence, depth, and intensity are unchanged. Mathematically, the severity of poverty is commonly calculated by taking the square of each poor person's proportionate shortfall below the poverty line, adding up the total for all poor people, and expressing it as a proportion of the total population.

cent of the population, lived in poverty in South Asia. This was similar to a poverty incidence of 40 percent in sub-Saharan Africa.[1] On average, the poverty gap index was about 13 percent relative to the dollar-a-day poverty line in South Asia, compared with 9 percent in East Asia, or 3 percent if the PRC is excluded (Table 5.1).

Not only is the incidence of poverty lower in East Asia, but its decline has quickened in recent years.[2] Absolute food poverty seems to have disappeared in Hong Kong, Singapore, and Taipei,China and almost disappeared in Korea and Malaysia. Other countries have also made substantial progress. In Indonesia, for instance, the incidence of poverty was halved from 60 to 29 percent during the 1970s. By 1990 it dropped by half again to 15 percent. Moreover, Indonesia is one of the few Asian countries that succeeded in sharply reducing the regional disparities of its poverty rate in the 1980s. Malaysia's official data show a sharp reduction in the incidence of poverty: from 49 percent in 1970, to 21 percent in 1980, to 9 percent in 1995. It reduced food poverty significantly, from 18 percent in 1970 to 2 percent in 1990 (Johansen 1993). Other countries in Southeast Asia, such as the Philippines and Thailand, made less spectacular progress. In Thailand, for instance, poverty declined rapidly in the 1970s, but rose in the first half of the 1980s. In the Philippines it fell slowly in the 1960s, but remained stagnant until the mid-1980s. In both cases, the downward trend has now resumed.

Poverty in the PRC fell sharply after liberalizing reforms began in 1978. Land redistribution to family farms, sharply rising agricultural productivity, and the growth of labor-intensive township and village enterprises reduced poverty rapidly. In 1978, 28 percent of the PRC's population faced food poverty; by 1988 it was only 8 percent, although 29 percent of the population still lived on less than a dollar a day in 1993. Regional disparities within the PRC are enormous. The incidence of food poverty in Beijing, Guandong, and Shanghai, for instance, is virtually zero, while it is more than 20 percent in Inner Mongolia and Qinghai (World Bank 1992a).

---

1. Note, however, that poverty incidence by this measure may differ considerably from that derived from official national data. In some countries, the PRC for instance, it may be substantially above the official national poverty incidence estimate. In others, poverty incidence measured using national data is higher, for example, in Pakistan and Sri Lanka.

2. The dollar-a-day poverty measure is not available for the period prior to 1985. Comparisons over 15 to 20 years are possible for some individual countries, based on alternative country-specific estimates (Lipton, de Haan, and Yaqub 1996; Pernia and Quibria 1995; UNDP 1996; World Bank 1990). References to dollar-a-day poverty for individual countries are derived from World Bank (1997).

Table 5.1 The Incidence of Poverty, Selected Regions and Years

Region	Year	No. of poor (millions)	HCR (percent)	PGI (percent)
East Asia and Pacific	1987	464.0	28.2	8.3
	1990	468.2	28.5	8.0
	1993	445.8	26.0	8.7
East Asia and Pacific, excluding the PRC	1987	109.2	23.2	3.8
	1990	89.3	17.6	3.1
	1993	73.5	13.7	3.1
South Asia	1987	479.9	45.4	14.1
	1990	480.4	43.0	12.3
	1993	514.7	43.1	12.6
East Europe and Central Asia	1987	2.2	0.6	0.2
	1990	—	—	—
	1993	14.5	3.5	1.1
Latin America	1987	91.2	22.0	8.2
	1990	101.0	23.0	9.0
	1993	109.6	23.5	9.1
Middle East and North Africa	1987	10.3	4.7	0.9
	1990	10.4	4.3	0.7
	1993	10.7	4.1	0.6
Sub-Saharan Africa	1987	179.6	38.5	14.4
	1990	201.2	39.3	14.5
	1993	218.6	39.1	15.3
Developing countries	1987	1224.9	33.1	10.8
	1990	1261.2	32.9	10.3
	1993	1299.3	31.8	10.5

— = not available; HCR = headcount ratio of poverty incidence; PGI = poverty gap index
Note: These regions depart somewhat from those used in other places.
Source: World Bank (1996a) and calculations based thereon.

In South Asia the reduction of poverty has been much slower. Between 1950 and 1975, India made no visible progress in reducing poverty, although since then a downward trend has been evident. In the mid-1970s more than half of India's people lived below the food poverty line. By 1990 the share had fallen to 34 percent, although on a dollar-a-day basis, one in two Indians was still poor in 1992. Like the PRC, India has huge and persistent regional differences in the incidence of poverty. The mass of South Asian poverty is still concentrated in Bangladesh, the states of east and central India, and Nepal. Here well over half the population consume commodities worth less than a dollar a day (Lipton, de Haan, and Yaqub 1996).

Education

Educational performance in Asia has been mixed. East and Southeast Asian countries have long had an impressive record of primary education. As early as 1965, almost nine out of ten children of primary school age attended school (Table 5.2). Today primary school attendance is universal in East Asia. The primary enrollment rate is 117 percent, the highest in the developing world (it can be over 100 percent because some children in primary school are above or below standard ages). Enrollment rates are similar for boys and girls.

In South Asia primary school enrollment rates have also been rising.[3] Today, nine out of ten children go to primary school, compared with only seven out of ten in 1965. This average, however, hides large disparities between countries. Pakistan and Afghanistan have by far the lowest access to primary education in Asia. In Pakistan just four out of every ten children go to primary school. In Afghanistan it is only three out of ten. The dislocations of civil war contributed to a fall in Afghanistan's school enrollment rate during the 1980s. Regional averages also mark huge disparities within countries. In India, for instance, the state of Kerala has virtually universal enrollment in primary education, while others such as Bihar, Orissa, Rajasthan, and Uttar Pradesh lag 40 to 60 percent behind national averages. With the exception of Sri Lanka, the education of girls falls far below that of boys in South Asia.

Large school enrollment rates are a necessary, but not sufficient, condition for good education. Truancy, child labor, class repetition, inad-

---

3. However, see Drèze and Sen (1996) on the poor quality of enrollment data in India, which they reject as being quite unreliable.

Table 5.2 Changing Education Outcomes

Region	Primary enrollment rate (percent)[a]				Secondary enrollment rate (percent)		Primary pupil-teacher ratio		Adult illiteracy rate, 1995 (percent)
	Total		Female						
	1965	1992	1965	1992	1965	1992	1965	1992	
Sub-Saharan Africa	41	67	31	60	4	18	43	40	43
East Asia and Pacific[b]	88	117	—	113	—	52	33	23	17
South Asia	68	94	52	82	24	39	42	59	50
Europe[c]	102	99	97	—	45	—	31	—	—
Middle East and North Africa	61	97	43	89	17	56	38	26	39
Latin America and the Caribbean	99	106	97	105	20	45	34	26	13

— = not available
a. The enrollment rates are gross enrollment rates. For some countries with universal primary education, the gross enrollment ratios may exceed 100 percent because some pupils are younger or older than the country's standard primary school age.
b. Includes all of Southeast Asia, East Asia, and the Pacific.
c. Includes Europe and Central Asia for 1992 data.
Source: World Bank (1992b, 1995, 1996b).

equate resources, and unmotivated teachers can all mean that high primary enrollment rates do not result in good educational outcomes. On average, 80 percent of children reach grade four of primary school in developing Asia, but there are wide variations between countries. In South Asia, Cambodia, and Lao People's Democratic Republic (Lao PDR), children stay in school the shortest time, and in South Asia class repetition rates are also the highest.

Class sizes are another indicator of the quality of education. The more children a teacher must cope with, the more an individual child's education may be negatively affected. In the mid-1960s the typical class in East Asia had 33 pupils, about the same as in Latin America. Over the last 30 years this rate has fallen considerably to 23 pupils per teacher in 1992. In contrast, the typical pupil-teacher ratio in the mid-1960s in South Asia was 42. By 1992 it had risen to 59, more than double that of East Asia.

At higher levels of education the differentials between Asian countries are even larger. On average, 52 percent of children in East and Southeast Asia were enrolled in secondary school in 1992, while in South Asia the ratio was somewhat lower at 39 percent. But in a few economies—Kazakstan, Korea, Mongolia, and Taipei,China—secondary school enrollment has reached 90 percent. Virtually all children continue to secondary school and complete most grades. At the other extreme, in countries such as Afghanistan, Bangladesh, Cambodia, and Pakistan, fewer than 25 percent of children attend secondary school.

Asia's literacy rates reflect the disparities in access to education between countries and between sexes. In East Asia, one in ten adult males, at most, is illiterate; however, almost a quarter of adult women are illiterate, as compared with, say, 14 percent in Latin America. In South Asia the situation is worse than in sub-Saharan Africa. More than a third of adult males and almost two thirds of adult females remain illiterate.

Health

Standards of health and nutrition in Asia have improved substantially over the past two or three decades, as they have throughout the developing world (Table 5.3). But here, in particular, divergence rather than convergence is the pattern within Asia. A child born in East Asia today, for instance, can expect to live to about 70, almost 45 percent longer than a child born in 1960. In South Asia life expectancy has risen from 44 in 1960 to 61 today. This is comparable with life expectancy in the Middle East and North Africa and is substantially higher than life expectancy in sub-Saharan Africa. Nonetheless the gap between East and South Asia is larger than it was 30 years ago. These subregional averages hide even bigger differentials between individual countries. In Afghanistan, for instance, life expectancy in 1993 was 43 years, well below the average for sub-Saharan Africa, while in Hong Kong life expectancy was 79 years, just above the average for industrial countries.

One of the biggest influences on rising life expectancy rates has been a sharp drop in infant mortality rates. The infant mortality rate is the number of babies out of every 1,000 live births that die before their first birthday. In East Asia this rate fell from 95 in 1965 to 36 in 1993. In South Asia it fell from 147 in 1965 to 84 in 1993. Again, East Asia's improvement has been relatively larger. Here, too, regional averages hide impor-

Table 5.3 Health and Nutrition Trends, Selected Years

Economy	Life expectancy at birth (years)		Infant mortality rate (deaths per 1,000 live births)		Daily calorie supply (per person)	
	1960	1993	1965	1993	1965	1989
Bangladesh	39.6	55.9	144	106	1,970	2,021
India	44.0	60.7	150	80	2,021	2,229
Nepal	38.4	53.8	171	96	1,889	2,077
Pakistan	43.1	61.8	149	88	1,773	2,219
Sri Lanka	62.0	72.0	63	17	2,171	2,277
Cambodia	42.4	51.9	134	117[a]	2,292	2,166
PRC	47.1	68.6	90	30	1,929	2,639
Lao PDR	40.4	51.3	148	95	2,135	2,630
Myanmar	43.8	57.9	122	82	1,897	2,440
Viet Nam	44.2	65.5	134	41	2,041	2,233
Indonesia	41.2	63.0	128	56	1,791	2,750
Malaysia	53.9	70.9	55	13	2,353	2,774
Philippines	52.8	66.5	72	42	1,875	2,375
Thailand	52.3	69.2	88	36	2,138	2,316
Hong Kong	66.2	78.7	27	7	2,486	2,853
Japan	—	79.6	18	4	2,668	2,956
Korea	53.9	71.3	62	11	2,178	2,852
Singapore	64.5	74.9	26	6	2,285	3,198

— = not available.
a. 1990 data.
Source: UNDP (1996); World Bank (1992b, 1995).

tant intercountry differences. In Hong Kong, Korea, Malaysia, Singapore, and Sri Lanka, fewer than 20 babies per 1,000 die before their first birthday, an infant mortality rate comparable with that in industrial countries. In contrast, infant mortality rates in Afghanistan, Bhutan, and Cambodia are more than 100.

Variations in mortality rates in turn reflect differences in nutrition and in access to health care, safe water, and sanitation. Standards in all these areas have improved significantly over the past 20 or 30 years, but in South Asia especially, they remain low compared with the rest of the developing world. Overall calorie consumption per person in South Asia is marginally higher than in sub-Saharan Africa, but child nutrition is much worse. In 1990 approximately six out of ten children in South Asia had stunted growth because of malnutrition, compared with only four in ten in sub-Saharan Africa. One in three babies in South Asia is born underweight, compared with one in six in sub-Saharan Africa. In contrast, the incidence of child malnutrition in East and Southeast Asia is almost the lowest in the developing world, bettered only by Latin America.

Throughout Asia official measures of access to health care, safe water, and sanitation often overestimate access, and therefore must be interpreted with caution. Nonetheless, in general, access to all these services is far greater in East Asia than in South Asia. On average, over 90 percent of the population in East Asia has access to health care; although large variations that occur between countries are not necessarily related to income. In several low- and middle-income countries, including the PRC and Viet Nam, the access rate is 80 to 90 percent. In Cambodia and Thailand, it is between 50 and 60 percent. In South Asia, national data showing that about 75 percent of the population have access to health care need to be treated with caution.

According to national estimates, over 90 percent of East Asia's population has access to safe water, and about 25 percent has access to sanitation. The latter share rises to over 90 percent if the PRC and other transitional economies are excluded (UNDP 1996). In South Asia, official national estimates suggest that about 71 percent of people have access to safe water, with 30 percent having access to sanitation. But given the region's enormous water pollution problems (Chapter 4), these access rates are almost certainly overestimated.

Urban and Rural Asia

Thirty years ago, Asia was largely rural. In 1965 only one in five Asians lived in an urban area. Today about one third of Asians live in towns or cities, which is still low by international standards. In North America, Europe, and Latin America more than seven out of every ten people live in towns or cities. While Asia's level of urbanization is about the same as that of Africa, it has been heavily concentrated, with 40 percent of city dwellers in East Asia living in cities with 1 million inhabitants or more. Some Asian countries reflect a high degree of urban primacy; a number of megacities with a population of 10 million people or more have emerged.

Some of the biggest disparities in living standards are between rural and urban areas. Typically, incomes per person are far lower and the incidence of poverty far higher in rural areas. In some countries, such as Bangladesh, Kyrgyz Republic, Nepal, Philippines, Sri Lanka, and Thailand, such rural-urban disparities are particularly marked. In others, such as India and Pakistan, they are lower, but even there the incidence of poverty is higher in rural than in urban areas. The only exception is Indonesia, where the statistics may be distorted by the use of large rural-urban price differentials.

Unequal access to essential services such as safe water or health care reinforces income disparities. Typically between a third to a half of the rural population has access to safe water in the poorer Asian countries, compared with more than 50 percent in urban areas. Rural access to health care is generally better in East Asia than in South Asia, but is still substantially worse than health care in its cities. Child mortality rates, for instance, are between 50 and 100 percent higher in rural areas than in urban areas in many Asian countries. Access to adequate shelter is also a problem in some rural areas, particularly in South Asia.

Dangers of air pollution also exist in rural Asia, largely because of reliance on wood fuels for cooking and the resultant indoor wood smoke. Access to electricity varies widely, but is lower than in urban areas. Again there are large disparities between countries. In the early 1990s, over 50 percent of the rural population had access to electricity in PRC, Malaysia, Philippines, and Thailand, while in Bangladesh, Myanmar, Nepal, Sri Lanka, and Viet Nam, only one in five or fewer people in rural areas had access to electricity.

Although the quality of life in urban areas is generally higher, Asia's cities face severe and growing problems. Rising air and water pollution pose dangers to public health; and waterborne infections or parasitic diseases lead to many extra deaths from periodic outbreaks of cholera, hepatitis, and other epidemics. The access to sewerage systems is limited in urban areas, with many cities not having centralized systems. Heavy traffic congestion has economic costs, increases the stress of urban life because of long commute times, and raises the levels of air pollution. (Chapter 4). Inadequate shelter is also a problem. One recent study (Nijkamp 1994) estimates that for some urban areas between 30 and 60 percent of residents live in slums; another 25 to 30 percent live in illegal squatter settlements on or off the streets. In some cases, as few as 15 to 20 percent of urban residents live in normal shelters. Rapid escalation of property values and rents has adversely affected the access of even the white collar worker to housing in some urban housing markets. As

Asia's megacities continue to expand, these problems are likely to intensify. Thus far, measures to alleviate these problems have been hard to come by.

The Asian Family

Large changes in Asia's social institutions, such as the family, have accompanied the region's dramatic economic transformation. Average household size has declined as fertility has fallen, and the custom of multiple generations living together in extended families has declined. In Thailand the average household size fell from 5.7 in 1970 to 4.4 in 1990. In Hong Kong the decline was from 4.6 in 1970 to 3.7 in 1986. International comparisons reveal a strong negative relationship between household size and income, a pattern confirmed over time in individual countries. Poorer households are usually larger than richer ones. In India, for instance, the average household size for the poor is 5.7, while for the nonpoor it is 4.9.

Economic, demographic, social, and technological changes have all altered the nature of family life in Asia. New household technologies make full-time household work less necessary. Women are better educated and increasingly hold jobs outside the home. This encourages them to delay or forego marriage, to have fewer children, and to dissolve marital unions they deem unsuccessful. Marriage that traditionally took place at an early age in Asia, now takes place later. The proportion of women married by age 20 declined dramatically from the early 1960s to the late 1980s in Indonesia, Sri Lanka, and Thailand, for example. Kinship networks are becoming more dispersed as families have fewer children and people move more frequently. Family cohesion is also coming under pressure as education gaps between parents and children increase.

Conventionally recorded divorce rates in Asia are rising. The crude divorce rate—the number of divorces annually per 1,000 people—was 1.5 in Asia in the early 1990s, up nearly threefold from the 1950s. Apart from reflecting family stress, higher divorce rates may also reflect the increased freedom women have attained to improve their situations via divorce, an option that often did not previously exist.

In short, Asian family structure has changed. Many lament the demise of the "traditional" Asian family with its strong intergenerational links. Aside from the question of whether such an ideal Asian family ever existed, the diversity in family structure makes it difficult to judge whether change has improved or worsened family well-being.

Role of Women

Throughout the developing world women are worse off than men. They have less access to education, fewer employment opportunities, less control over household resources, and less personal freedom. Asia is no exception, although the social and economic positions of women vary enormously across countries. By many measures, South Asian women are among the most deprived in the world. In contrast, the relative position of East Asian women is quite favorable.

Overall, women's status and opportunities have improved in Asia, largely because of rising income, demographic change, better education, and better household technologies. These forces have partly liberated women from childbearing, have increased their relative productivity outside the home, and have increased their voice in household spending decisions. Nonetheless, Asian women still face enormous social pressures to fulfill traditional responsibilities, such as bearing and raising children or caring for the elderly.

The most striking illustration of women's disadvantage is the issue of millions of "missing women" in South Asia and the PRC (Drèze and Sen 1989). These countries have far fewer women relative to men than other parts of the world. This indicates discrimination in the form of gender-selective child nutrition and health care.

Women's disadvantage can also be seen in educational achievement. Although progress in female education has been substantial, female illiteracy is much higher than male illiteracy in all countries with low levels of education. In South Asia, adult female literacy rates rose from 17 to 35 percent between 1970 and 1993, while in East Asia they rose from 55 to 72 percent. In several Asian countries, including Bangladesh, India, Nepal, and Pakistan, women's illiteracy exceeds men's by 20 percentage points or more. The PRC also has substantial differences, though at a relatively high level of literacy: 89 percent for men and 71 percent for women. Overall East Asia has a far better record of female education than South Asia (Table 5.4). Female primary school enrollment rose from 39 to 80 percent in South Asia between 1960 and 1992, and from 85 to over 100 percent in East Asia and the Pacific.

In many parts of Asia, intrahousehold discrimination in food provision, health care, and education further depresses women's quality of life, especially their survival chances. In industrial countries, for instance, female life expectancy exceeds male life expectancy by about six years.

Taking this six-year gap as the standard, the degree of female disadvantage in other societies can be gauged by the extent to which the gap falls short of six years—the smaller the gap the greater is the likely degree of female disadvantage. According to this criterion, female disadvantage is worse in South Asia than elsewhere in developing Asia. There is hardly any excess of female life expectancy over males in Bangladesh, India, and Nepal, and only a slight gap of two years in Pakistan. Health discrimination also exists in other Asian countries (as in most other developing countries), albeit to a lesser degree. This is true of such diverse countries as the PRC, Indonesia, Lao PDR, Malaysia, Mongolia, Myanmar, and Philippines, where life expectancy for females exceeds that for males by only two to four years.

In contrast, in the most advanced economies of Asia—Hong Kong, Korea, and Singapore—female life expectancy is comparable with that of the industrial world. Thailand and Viet Nam have achieved a similar differential at a much lower level of income; Kazakstan and the Kyrgyz Republic, reflecting their past experiences in the former Soviet Union, show a differential that even the industrial countries find hard to match (UNDP 1996).

Table 5.4 Gender Disparities, 1993

Region	Life expectancy at birth (years) Female	Male	Adult literacy rate (percent) Female	Male	Gross enrollment rate, all educational levels (percent) Female	Male	Earned income share (percent) Female	Male
Sub-Saharan Africa	52.5	49.3	45.4	64.7	37.2	45.9	35.6	64.4
East Asia and Pacific[a]	70.8	66.8	71.9	89.1	55.0	61.0	37.5	62.5
South Asia	60.5	60.1	35.0	61.7	43.2	59.6	23.9	76.1
Eastern Europe and CIS	74.2	64.2	98.7	98.9	76.5	72.4	40.2	59.8
Middle East and North Africa[b]	64.1	61.5	40.4	65.6	51.0	63.4	20.0	80.0
Latin America and the Caribbean	71.2	65.9	84.2	87.0	68.2	68.9	26.1	73.9

CIS = Commonwealth of Independent States
a. Includes all of Southeast Asia, East Asia, and the Pacific.
b. Excludes Iran, Israel, Syrian Republic, West Bank, and Gaza.
Source: UNDP (1996).

The situation in the Central Asian republics, however, is unique because the welfare of women is worsening. Policies under the former Soviet Union allowed all individuals free access to health care and education. These policies reduced a traditional bias against women. In addition, women participated heavily in the labor force, thereby increasing their economic power and enhancing their role in the household. During the present economic transition, these policies are being reversed (Box 5.2). Thus as with child care, the number of children attending kindergarten in 1995 was less than half that in 1991 for both Kazakstan and the Kyrgyz Republic. Women are increasingly unemployed, and access to health and education is based more on the ability to pay. In conjunction with generally worsening economic conditions, these changes are likely to lead to a resumption of gender bias and lower expenditures on women and girls.

Progress for women has been greatest in Southeast Asia, both in absolute terms and in terms of equality with men. For example, in Thailand the gap in female-male literacy rates narrowed between 1980 and 1990, whereas in the Philippines the literacy rate of women is comparable with that of men. The overall favorable economic environment in this subregion suggests that these improvements can be extended further. But even in Southeast Asia, improvements in the quality of life for rural women have been slim, because higher incomes are still accompanied by extremely long working days.

Violence and physical pressure against women persists throughout Asia. It takes many forms, including sex-selective abortion, female infanticide, child marriage, child and adult prostitution, domestic violence and abuse (including dowry-related incidents), and poor treatment of elderly women (especially widows).

Work Environment

Economic and demographic transformation has profoundly altered the working environment in Asia. In 1960 three out of four working Asians were employed in agriculture. By 1990 the share had fallen to 62 percent of the labor force. The share of people working in industry rose from 10 to 17 percent, while the share employed in services grew from 15 to 21 percent (ILO 1996). Not surprisingly, these shifts were sharpest in the fastest-growing countries of East and Southeast Asia, but the trend is similar throughout the region.

Box 5.2 Social Transition in the Central Asian Republics

At independence, the Central Asian republics were characterized by the social protection systems of the former Soviet Union, broader in nature than those normally associated with industrial market economies. Programs included low administered prices supported by an array of budgetary subsidies, housing and public utilities at nominal prices, and a wide range of social services, often provided at the enterprise level, free, or at a minimal fee. A significant proportion of labor compensation was in the form of nonwage benefits. Well-developed education and health care delivery systems meant that at independence, for the most part, various social indicators, life expectancy, literacy, and so on were high, particularly compared with countries of similar per person income.

Economic and fiscal crises following the disintegration of the Soviet Union placed severe pressure on the capability to deliver social services. At the same time, socioeconomic deterioration was giving rise to a more complex situation and set of problems, including that of single-company townships. The previous system was not fiscally sustainable, even as living standards eroded severely and poverty incidence rose, in some cases dramatically. Appropriate remedial and targeted measures became necessary so that past achievements would not be eroded. For these countries—unlike the experience in much of Asia—the 1990s have seen an onset of deterioration in social indicators, particularly the incidence of poverty. Facilities have been extensively run down or even closed, even as many assets and services have been transferred from enterprises to local governments. Given the inadequate fiscal resources of local governments, broadly based fiscal reform will need to support social sector reform.

An adequate social safety net has a key role to play in societal transformation for those accustomed to an extensive range of generous social support. Social protection measures as formerly designed were not focused to provide adequate targeted relief

Demographic changes have altered the composition of the labor force as more women began working relative to men. Between 1960 and 1990, the proportion of men between the ages of 15 and 65 who worked fell from 83 to 77 percent, while that of women remained constant at around 54 percent. The drop in the share of working males is largely a result of more adolescents (aged 15 to 20) continuing their education. In the case of females, this effect is offset by more women entering the workforce for the first time. Hence the participation rates of men and women are converging. Nonetheless, the extent of female participation in the formal workforce differs substantially between countries in the region. The lowest rates are found in South Asia and by far the highest are in the former communist countries.[4]

---

4. This remains true despite the known underestimation of female workforce participation rates in official data from South Asia. For further details on these and other statistics related to work, see Basu and Basu (1996).

to the poorest in compensation for the adverse effects of the transition on them. The general reduction or elimination of universal consumer subsidies that has been widely effected gives added importance to targeted social assistance that is fiscally sustainable. Providing an adequate social safety net requires surmounting a twofold challenge. First, support has to be tailored to resource availability. Undertaking this is likely to require the sensitive task of withdrawing benefits that appear generous by more conventional international standards, targeting support at the most vulnerable groups, and reducing access to benefits for those above socially acceptable levels. Second, a more systematic assessment of need is required, thereafter ensuring benefit protection in real terms for the most vulnerable groups (elderly, children, and people increasingly in open and hidden unemployment).

Governments are endeavoring to realize potential cost savings through institutional changes as well as through administrative practices and organizations that improve efficiency and effectivity. An early reform, for instance, was the privatization of the bulk of the housing stock. Innovative approaches will also be necessary. Thus, in Uzbekistan the government has established new forms of targeted social assistance to those with low incomes using traditional community associations. It also seeks to rationalize the health delivery system, by such means as developing outpatient health care and strengthening primary health care units, particularly in rural areas. In the Kyrgyz Republic the government, in accordance with its limited resources for social assistance, has designed a more narrowly focused program for the poor. Assistance is more equitably distributed by region and is aimed at reducing the number of people entitled to benefits by as much as 35 percent. In Kazakstan, the government has considered such actions as unifying the welfare benefits system, raising the retirement age for men and women, and simplifying unemployment registration.

While increasing participation in the workforce is transforming the working lives of women and enabling them to earn a better livelihood, not all aspects of their quality of life are improved as a result. Those who cannot afford to hire domestic help—the vast majority—are obliged to combine domestic work with economic activity and suffer the burden of the double day. Many also face discrimination in the workplace.[5] In Korea, for instance, a country with an average Asian rate of female labor force participation, discrimination against women is strong: they have jobs of lower status; and the gender wage differences are large (Mazumdar 1994). Where legislation provides for the protection of women's rights, as in India's large-scale industries, for instance, women are often not hired,

---

5. Wage gaps, for instance, arise mainly because women get a poorer education and hence do less well-paid jobs and tasks. Wage discrimination by gender for the same task and productivity seldom exceeds 10 percent (Lipton 1983).

and there have been clear cases of employer policies to dismiss women because they were thought to be too expensive. Nonetheless, women's situations in the formal sector are better than in some informal sector activities—especially work as domestic servants, both at home and abroad. Increasing numbers of women, especially from India, Indonesia, Philippines, Sri Lanka, and Thailand, migrate temporarily to work as domestic help in the richer countries of East and Southeast Asia, the Middle East, and Europe. While poor Asian women gain economically from this expanding source of livelihood, they often have to endure degrading conditions of work, quite apart from the suffering caused by the disruption of their family life.

Inadequate protection against inhospitable conditions of work, such as long hours or low health and safety hazards—affects both men and women in much of Asia. Some of the richer countries in East Asia have introduced effective legislation to improve these conditions. Notably, Taipei,China introduced the Labor Standards Law in the mid-1980s to protect female workers' rights. Other countries have legislation on paper, but it is seldom effective, and affects only the small proportion of workers who belong to the formal or registered sector. Most still work in the informal sector, whose share of the workforce was roughly estimated at 60 to 80 percent in South and Southeast Asia (ILO 1992). A large and growing proportion is not self-employed, but hired. There is no protection for this multitude of workers.

Interpreting Asia's Changing Quality of Life

Why have improvements in Asia's quality of life been so diverse? Why has poverty retreated faster in some countries or regions than in others, and why have the health, education, and overall living standards improved more for some Asians than for others? No simple answers exist. Asian countries vary not only in their initial economic conditions (as discussed in Chapter 2) and in their policy choices, but also in their social and cultural traditions. All of these factors influence changes in the quality of life.

Nonetheless, a careful analysis across countries suggests a number of broad conclusions. First, economic growth is the main determinant of improvement in human well-being. Although the quality of life can, in principle, be improved by a better allocation of existing resources, it is the accumulation of new resources (through economic growth) that allows for rapid and sustainable improvements in the quality of life.

Second, not all economic growth brought improvements in the quality of people's lives. The inward-oriented, capital-intensive growth that occurred through much of the developing world in the 1950s, for instance, did little to combat poverty. South Asian countries that followed import-substituting, capital-intensive growth strategies saw relatively little reduction in the incidence of poverty. Labor-intensive manufactures and agricultural growth were the key underpinnings of poverty reduction in Asia.

Third, even if higher economic growth brings people more resources, they may not be able to convert these into improvements in their quality of life because of the failure of market or nonmarket institutions. In the patriarchal societies of South Asia, for instance, families often "fail," because they transfer insufficient food, schooling, or health care to females.

Fourth, public policy can exacerbate or mitigate this effect. Public spending that subsidizes expensive health care and higher education to an urban elite, and that neglects basic health and education for the rural poor, will worsen diversities in the quality of life. In contrast, policies that explicitly target the poor or disadvantaged can help minimize such differentials.

Growth and Poverty Reduction

Globally, rapid poverty reduction has been much more likely to occur in countries and periods with rapid economic growth (Chen and Ravallion 1994; Deininger and Squire 1996a, 1996b).[6] Asia is no exception. Those Asian countries that achieved the most spectacular reductions in poverty in recent decades—such as the PRC, Hong Kong, Indonesia, Korea, Malaysia, and Singapore—also grew the fastest.

The strategy of export-led growth, based on labor-intensive manufactures, which lay behind East Asia's spectacular economic performance, was particularly conducive to poverty alleviation. Rising demand for

---

6. Rapid growth in East Asia, and in global cross-country regressions has, however, been associated with prior spread of access to education and land (Birdsall, Ross, and Sabot 1994; Bruno, Ravallion, and Squire 1996; Deininger and Minten 1996; Deininger and Squire 1996a), and hence with prior improvements in the quality of life. Drèze and Sen (1989) show a similar sequence of quality of life improvements preceding and stimulating growth in the PRC after 1963.

workers in export industries absorbed surplus labor and eventually led to real wage rises. Quite rightly, therefore, outward orientation is widely cited as the main determinant of East Asia's poverty reduction. Other factors, however, also mattered. Mass basic education, for instance, not only influenced the rate of economic growth, but helped ensure that it was widely shared, by easing the transition of workers from employment in agriculture to employment in labor-intensive exports. In the fast-growing East Asian economies, the rapid growth of labor-intensive production across a wide front, led by exports, accounted for much of the massive reduction in poverty.

The structure and growth of the agriculture sector also influenced East Asia's success at reducing poverty. Several East Asian economies—including Korea and Taipei,China—undertook egalitarian land reforms in the immediate postwar period, which laid the foundations for intensive family farming. The PRC began similar land reform oriented toward family production in the late 1970s with the introduction of the "household responsibility system." In countries such as Indonesia and Malaysia, land reforms were not introduced,[7] but land distribution was already fairly equal, at least compared with South Asia. International comparisons suggest strong relationships between land inequality and subsequent slow growth and high poverty (Binswanger, Deininger, and Feder 1995; Bruno, Ravallion, and Squire 1996; el-Ghonemy 1990; Lipton 1993; Tyler, el-Ghonemy, and Couvreur 1993). Hence, a relatively equal distribution of land probably boosted East and Southeast Asian agriculture.

More important was the effect of the Green Revolution in the 1960s and early 1970s. The introduction of new locally adapted rice and wheat varieties that were responsive to fertilizer inputs and extremely high yielding changed Asian agriculture completely. Rising yields dramatically increased the productivity both of agricultural labor and land. This helped reduce poverty in several ways. A growing food surplus ensured a more reliable and cheaper food supply for rural people and the growing industrial workforce. Cheaper food prices by themselves helped reduce the incidence of poverty. Rising agricultural production also created employment opportunities in agriculture and in other nonfarm rural activities. These were significant in such high-performing Southeast Asian economies as Indonesia and Malaysia, and in the Punjab states of India and Pakistan.

---

7. Malaysia, however, settled over 2 million mostly poor people on farms through Federal Land Development Authority schemes.

Initially, the rapid growth of high-yielding crops depended on public agriculture research and on access to water, mainly from large public sector irrigation schemes. Hence, sensible public investments lay behind some of Asia's early agriculture-led poverty reduction. So did the presence of appropriate property rights and incentives that motivated farmers to increase productivity. In some countries, such as the PRC and Indonesia, poverty reduction from agricultural growth preceded export-led growth. Even in those countries that eschewed export-led growth, rises in agricultural productivity helped reduce poverty. South Asian countries that saw little export-led growth continued to have an overall high incidence of poverty. But even there, periods of rapid agricultural growth—and the associated fall in the relative price of food—were typically periods of much lower poverty incidence. Conversely, when crops failed and the price of food rose, so too did the incidence of poverty (Datt and Ravallion 1995; UNDP and ILO 1993).

In short, the clue to East Asian success in combining rapid growth with poverty reduction lies in the adoption of policies, institutions, and technologies that fostered broad-based growth: an outward orientation, labor-intensive growth, egalitarian and productivity-enhancing land arrangements and investments in irrigation, agricultural research and extension, rural infrastructure, and rural industries. The relative importance of these elements varied between countries and over time within the same country, but the basic constituents were the same.

This basic mechanism was also influenced by other policy decisions. Improvements in health or women's education, for instance, helped alleviate poverty by promoting smaller families. As Chapter 3 noted, higher life expectancy and lower mortality eventually lead to a drop in fertility. Poverty and fertility are closely linked. Poor families are typically larger than rich ones, as children are useful, for instance, for gathering firewood. But since large families save less and invest less in human capital, poverty is transmitted from generation to generation (Pernia and Quibria 1995). Hence policies that promote smaller families also help to reduce poverty.

While necessary, these ingredients do not guarantee poverty-reducing growth. In Thailand in the 1980s, for instance, poverty remained stagnant, although economic growth accelerated after liberalizing reforms. Unlike most other high-performing countries of Asia, which combined rapid growth with improving (or at least unchanged) income distribution, Thailand saw its income distribution worsen so much that even rapid growth did not dent poverty. While poverty probably began to fall in the 1990s, its persistence in the 1980s warns against drawing simple conclusions about the relationship between poverty and growth.

Beyond reducing poverty through growth, most low-income Asian countries with a high incidence of poverty have tried to alleviate poverty through specific poverty-reducing government programs. Direct food transfers and food subsidies to the poor have been used in times of dire need. In general, however, sizable, inefficient, and expensive government-run systems of food storage and distribution have not evidently been an effective method of stabilizing food prices for the poor. Moreover, they tend to be urban-biased and are as likely to benefit the rich as the poor. Sri Lanka, for instance, spent about 10 percent of GDP on untargeted food subsidies in the late 1970s before replacing them with targeted food stamps (Gunatilleke and others 1994).

Governments have sometimes tried to alleviate poverty with formal subsidized credit programs or credits that are subsequently converted to grants. Lack of access to credit is one of the biggest constraints facing the poor. Unfortunately, these programs are often poorly targeted and end up supporting the nonpoor. Moreover, they often prove financially unsustainable. A well-known example is India's Integrated Rural Development Program. Not only was this scheme poorly targeted, it also proved financially unsustainable. Beneficiaries often used loans for consumption rather than asset creation. Many reviews suggest that the program's effectiveness at reducing poverty has been dubious (UNDP and ILO 1993). Sri Lanka's experience in the late 1960s and early 1970s also illustrates the point. The New Agricultural Credit Scheme, and the Comprehensive Rural Credit Scheme, introduced to combat poverty, achieved loan recovery rates of only 50 to 60 percent (Gunatilleke and others 1994).

Microlending is an alternative and more successful approach. About 85 percent of Asian farmers, and an even higher proportion of poor farmers, lack access to credit. Microfinance programs target credit to the poor. Although these loans are not tied to collateral, loan recovery rates are high, often well over 90 percent. The effectiveness of the schemes depends on group liability for default and a gradual escalation from small initial loans that cannot be renewed without repayment. Some, but not all, microlenders charge market interest rates. Although most microfinance programs begin with subsidized or grant funds, the most successful ones graduate to full cost recovery relatively quickly. Some of the most successful microfinance programs have been developed by non-government agencies.

By the end of the 1980s, Asia had at least five national-level microfinance programs with more than 100,000 clients: Indonesia's Badan Kredit Kecamatan, Badan Kredit Desa, and Kupedes programs; the Grameen Bank in Bangladesh; and Thailand's Bank for Agriculture and Agricultural Cooperatives (BAAC). Other important programs include Bangladesh Rural Advancement Committee (BRAC) and Proshika in Bangladesh, and Mysore Resettlement and Development Agency (MYRADA) in India. There are also a number of large provincial level programs and many smaller ones. All together about 10 million poor Asians probably have access to microcredit. Compared with the requirements, the scale of access to microfinance programs is still limited, but the approach is promising.

A third approach to poverty alleviation is transfer payments in the form of small wages for public works programs. These programs have been used quite effectively in India to support landless agricultural workers during the off-season when there is no work in the farms, or during periods of drought. Hence they have managed to reduce the incidence of poverty in periods when it normally goes up (UNDP and ILO 1993). The Maharashtra Employment Guarantee Scheme is a good example of such a program (Acharya 1990). Effective targeting of these programs is achieved by a hard physical labor requirement. Only the desperately needy are prepared to do so much work for so little pay. These make-work schemes are often criticized for not being productive, or creating durable assets. But since their main purpose is to provide transfers, this is a misplaced criticism.

Thus growth-mediated strategies and direct support-led strategies for poverty alleviation can be mutually reinforcing with the right policies and institutions in place. This appears to have been most important where the improvements in the quality of life started from a low base.

Understanding Educational Achievements

Education benefits from economic growth. Greater prosperity allows both individuals and governments to pay for more and better education. A fast growing economy also boosts the return to investment in education, and so raises the demand for it. But comparative experience both across and within countries shows that educational achievement is not entirely dependent on income. PRC, Myanmar, Sri Lanka, and Viet Nam have achieved much higher levels of education than most other countries at their income levels. The currently advanced East Asian countries all had high levels of educational achievements compared with their levels of income before they entered their high growth phases (ADB 1996). Considerable diversity also exists between different states and provinces within Asian countries, even at comparable income levels. In 1989, for instance, rural female literacy rates in 18 provinces of the PRC ranged from 11 to 75 percent, although rural income per person varied only from 400 to 600 yuan (Drèze and Saran 1995). Nor is the incidence of poverty directly related to educational achievement. In rural India, for instance, female literacy varies from 12 percent in Rajasthan to 85 percent in Kerala, two states with roughly similar levels of poverty.

Differences in public commitment and private values go some way toward explaining this diversity. Prejudice may drive down the actual or perceived return to education, especially for girls. The very low female literacy rates in Afghanistan and Pakistan and in rural areas of several Indian states, such as Bihar and Madhya Pradesh, have much to do with traditional perceptions of women. Public provision of education is essential to correct this. In Pakistan, half the variation in female literacy rates is accounted for by the presence or absence of a girls' primary school (Alderman and others 1996). A public commitment to basic education also lay behind East Asia's remarkable success in education. In the early 1960s, when most East Asian countries were no richer than the rest of the region, governments (as well as parents) spent larger shares of GDP on mass primary schooling than most low-income countries do today. Widespread literacy resulted. The transitional countries of Central Asia and Mongolia successfully followed a similar strategy. To varying degrees, so did the state of Kerala in India, PRC, Myanmar, Sri Lanka, and Viet Nam. Education in these places far outstrips that of other countries and regions with comparable incomes.

Incentives also play an important role in the effective use of educational resources. Poor parents need incentives to send their children to school, thereby foregoing the immediate economic benefit of child labor. Teachers need incentives to deliver high quality education. Incentives can be improved in a variety of ways. In the south Indian state of Tamil Nadu, for instance, the free noon meals program introduced in the 1980s has led to a remarkable expansion in school enrollment, by giving parents the incentive to forego the benefit of child labor (though this program was not necessarily an optimally targeted antipoverty strategy). In the state of Kerala in India, grassroots activism has played an important role in making sure that the poor are in a position to claim their rights to education. In high-performing East Asian countries, teachers were typically paid higher salaries compared with average national wage levels than elsewhere (though, at least to begin with, costs per student remained low as class sizes were much larger than in other developing countries). Furthermore, allocative efficiency was ensured by conserving public resources, mainly for primary education. It is only more recently, as fairly high per person incomes were attained, that public resources were allocated to higher levels of education (Mingat 1995).

Why Health and Nutrition Improved

More affluent people can afford better standards of nutrition and health care. That is why countries with healthier and better fed populations tend to be richer. Nonetheless, just as with education, income is not the sole determinant of health and nutrition. Sri Lanka's population, for instance, has a standard of health that is normally associated with much richer countries. Between 1960 and 1994, PRC, Hong Kong, Korea, Malaysia, Singapore, Sri Lanka, Thailand, and Viet Nam all reduced the mortality rate of children under five by between 80 and 90 percent. Yet these economies' rates of economic growth varied enormously. In Hong Kong, Korea, and Singapore annual income per person rose by more than 6 percent; in Sri Lanka it grew by less than 2 percent. Hence it is possible to improve health and nutrition without fast growth.

One factor is the importance placed on primary health care facilities, especially the prevention of communicable diseases and maternal mortality, rather than on sophisticated treatment of noncommunicable diseases. By emphasizing primary care, some poorer countries, such as the PRC and Viet Nam, have rivaled richer countries in terms of universal health care coverage. The emphasis on primary care boosts overall health outcomes in two ways. First, it is cheaper than secondary or tertiary medical care, thereby enabling limited resources to reach a larger number of people. Second, the same level of primary care can be achieved more cheaply in a poor country than a richer one. Primary care is labor-intensive, and labor is cheaper in poorer countries.

Health services were also used more widely in Sri Lanka and other "healthy" poor countries. While the availability of health services is necessary for improving health outcomes, it is by no means sufficient. Much depends on how people actually use the services. In practice, this usually means how much use women make of the services (because it is mothers, and women in general, who typically take care of health and nutrition within the family). That in turn depends on women's awareness of the importance of health care, their self-confidence to demand and obtain the necessary services, and their ability to interact with the providers of health services.

The level of maternal education determines much of this. A number of microlevel studies show that maternal education has a profound impact on nutritional status and survival chances (for example, see World Bank 1980). Household surveys in India, Pakistan, Sri Lanka, and Thailand show that the incidence of undernutrition falls steadily as maternal education improves. Several microsurveys indicate that this relationship holds true between households with comparable levels of poverty. In fact, the level of maternal education does not have to be particularly high before nutrition and health improve. Even women who have completed primary school typically have up to 20 percent less undernutrition among their children than illiterate mothers (Bhargava and Osmani 1996).

Countries that extend primary health care and female literacy up to near universal levels, and close the food gap of the poor either through redistributive measures or targeted food distribution programs, can improve the health outcomes of their people sooner than others. Such policies also boost health further in two indirect ways. Better education by itself promotes economic growth, which in turn allows greater expenditure on health. Better educated women also tend to marry later and have fewer children, both of which bring lower rates of child and maternal mortality.

Given this relationship, social and cultural norms that discriminate against the health and nutrition of women impoverish the quality of life for the community as a whole. That is why South Asia has the largest prevalence of undernourished children in the developing world. Statistical analyses show that although low income, inadequate food, and low female literacy contribute to childhood stunting or wasting, these factors alone cannot explain the special disadvantage of South Asia (Bhargava and Osmani 1996). Where South Asia really differs is in the incidence of low birth weight babies. In South Asia, 33 percent of all babies are born underweight, as compared with 19 percent for the developing world as a whole. As these babies grow up, they tend to be physically more retarded and more susceptible to infections. Hence a society with more low birth weight babies will tend to be one that suffers from more child and adult undernutrition.

The main explanation for low birth weight babies is poor maternal nutrition. The variation of low birth weight across countries can be linked to factors that affect maternal nutrition, such as income per person, female literacy, female labor force participation, and age at first marriage. South Asia scores low in all of these variables, but even that does not fully account for the exceptionally high incidence of low birth weight babies (Bhargava and Osmani 1996).

Cultural factors, such as the status of women within the family, seem to be at least partly responsible. In Bangladesh, northern India, and Pakistan, evidence abounds of selective underfeeding and health care deprivation of small girls. Such factors are absent in other countries (Harriss 1990; Svedberg 1990). Pregnant women in South Asia often lack iron-rich foods. According to recent estimates, 78 percent of pregnant women in South Asia suffer from anemia, compared with 43 percent in sub-Saharan Africa.

In short, the poor health and nutrition outcomes in much of South Asia are the result of a vicious intergenerational circle. Malnourished mothers give birth to low birth weight babies. Low birth weight makes such children vulnerable to infections. That, together with food inadequacy (especially for girls) leads to a high share of stunted and malnourished people, especially women. These produce low birth weight babies, and the circle is complete. Economic growth will eventually improve the situation; maternal education can accelerate the improvement.

Looking Ahead:
Prospects and Policy Challenges

Predicting the future is perilous, particularly the future of something as complex as the quality of life. As previous sections have explained, Asia's quality of life has been influenced by the complex interactions of economic growth, demographic shifts, policy decisions, and cultural norms. Developments in all these areas will profoundly affect how life in Asia changes. Any predictions are, at best, rough indications of future change.

Nonetheless, some underlying trends that will affect Asia's future quality of life can be easily identified. As Chapter 2 explained, economic growth is likely to speed up in those countries where quality of life is now lowest or most threatened, such as South and Central Asia and the PRC. It will slow down most in the higher-income countries of East Asia. These growth patterns suggest that the quality of life within countries in Asia may converge in the future, unlike the experience of 1965 to 1990. However, faster national convergence does not necessarily imply convergence between regions or groups within countries. Remote communities, minority groups, and women could fall ever further behind.

Demographic changes discussed in Chapter 3 suggest that the balance between age groups within Asia will shift dramatically. In South Asia, the number of workers will rise relative to the number of children. In Bangladesh, for instance, the share of people under 15 will fall from 40 to 25 percent of the population over the next 25 years. In the richer countries of East Asia, the share of the elderly will rise. In Korea, for instance, the share of those aged 65 or older will rise from 5 to 14 percent of the population. These demographic shifts will alter the needs and costs of education, health, and social security, as well as the profile of poverty and affluence.

The nature of Asia's economic transformation also implies that urbanization will proceed rapidly. In India, the share of the urban population will rise from around 25 to 40 percent by 2025; in the PRC it will rise from 26 to 51 percent. The share of urban dwellers who live in cities with more than 1 million residents will also rise sharply. This continuing rural-urban shift means that urban-based problems in the quality of life (such as congestion or urban pollution) will increase in importance. It also means that political influence will slip ever further away from rural people, whose overall quality of life will remain much worse than that of people in towns and cities.

Poverty in the 2020s

If the future relationship between economic growth and poverty resembles that of the past, then poverty in Asia will continue to fall. Future poverty trends can be estimated by gauging the historical responsiveness of poverty to GDP growth from international statistical comparisons, and combining this with projected future rates of GDP growth. Chapter 2 estimated Asia's future rates of GDP growth under two scenarios: one in which policies continue unchanged, another in which Asian countries adopt the high-growth East Asian policies. Future rates of poverty are estimated under both scenarios.

Estimates of the poverty-growth relationship based on international comparisons must, however, be interpreted with care. The initial distribution of people below the poverty line—which varies between countries—is critical in determining how growth affects poverty. The farther people are below the poverty line, the more difficult it is to bring them above it. Moreover, the relationship between economic growth and poverty can vary over time. To take these factors into account, the projections of dollar-a-day poverty at the year 2025 (see Figure 5.1) are calculated on the following basis: first, the distribution of consumption as reflected in household surveys (including some unpublished data made available by Klaus Deininger); second, the projected growth of GDP per person around 2025; and third, estimated conversions of extra GDP into extra private consumption.[8]

Despite these refinements, the estimates should be treated as indicative of trends rather than as specific projections. Many variables, such as demographic change, that are incorporated in the GDP estimates, affect poverty independently of their impact on growth. Second, direct anti-poverty policies could make a difference not accounted for in these projections. Third, the estimates refer only to national averages; groups and areas may diverge significantly. These caveats aside, however, the estimates below shed considerable light on the future of Asian poverty.

As Figure 5.1 shows, South Asian countries are likely to see dramatic reductions in poverty incidence. Under baseline policies, for instance, India's incidence of dollar-a-day poverty could fall from around 50 percent of the population in the early 1990s, to below 20 percent by about 2025. With East Asian style economic policies, poverty rates could be brought closer to 10 percent. Despite these potential improvements, Asia's core poverty will still be concentrated in South Asia around 2025, specifically in Bangladesh and some parts of India. Over the next quarter

---

8. Methods are explained in Lipton, de Haan, and Yaqub (1996). These estimates allow for the fact that "national-accounts" private consumption exceeds the survey estimate, by different proportions in different countries. It is assumed that growth increases expected value of consumption at the same rate for each position in the consumption hierarchy—approximating the finding that growth is distribution neutral (Chen, Datt, and Ravallion 1994; Deininger and Squire 1996b; Bruno, Ravallion, and Squire 1996). The analysis also shows, however, that the impact of growth on the share of the poor in income or consumption varies over time for some countries. However, the consumption share of the poor may not decline at the same rate as the average income rises.

Figure 5.1 Poverty Incidence Projections

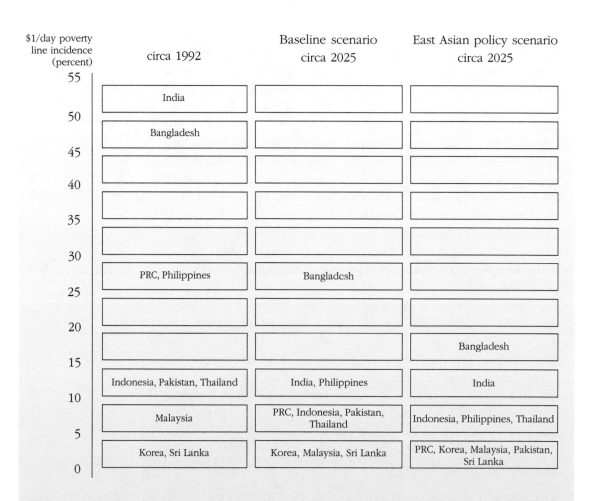

Note: Data for Bangladesh, Korea, and Thailand refer to food poverty incidence based on national poverty lines derived from minimum calorie intake requirements. These estimates are not comparable across countries or with $1/day poverty incidence estimates which are typically somewhat higher than food poverty estimates.
Source: Lipton, de Haan, and Yaqub (1996)

century, dollar-a-day poverty in Pakistan and Sri Lanka will have ceased to be a major problem.

One threat to rapid poverty reduction in India, as in other low-income Asian countries, is that of faltering growth in agricultural production or employment. The farm sector remains the main income source for over two thirds of India's people, including over three quarters of the poor. The growth projections emphasize the links of overall growth to poverty. But so far India's poor—urban as well as rural—have gained most from growth in agriculture, and hardly at all from industrial growth (Datt and Ravallion 1995). East Asian policies and resulting higher industrial labor intensity might change that, but a slowdown in agricultural growth or its employment potential bodes ill.

If the relationship between growth and poverty that existed in the PRC between 1970 and 1990 continues to hold, dollar-a-day poverty in the PRC could fall to less than 10 percent by about 2025, but this relationship has historically been highly variable. During the land reforms between 1978 and 1984, poverty fell rapidly as growth rose. In the late 1980s, the responsiveness of poverty to growth weakened, as income distribution worsened and growth shifted to urban areas, especially in the southeast of the PRC.

More recently, overall poverty reduction has resumed, but regional and urban-rural inequalities are increasing in the PRC. Millions of unregistered migrants moving from rural to urban areas and usually denied the normal safety nets create a new type of poverty. In the north and west, and among minority ethnic groups—traditionally poor groups and areas—poverty remains severe. Future poverty reduction depends on accelerating food output and employment growth in leading rice and wheat areas; attracting capital for nonfarm activities, especially township and village enterprises, to the northern and western poverty belts; and allowing townward migrants equal access to available urban social services.

The Southeast Asian transitional economies have prospects for sustained high growth. However, for this to translate into comparable poverty reduction, it will be necessary for policy analysts to take account of the heavy dependence of the poor upon progress in, and access to, food staple production. The Central Asian republics and Mongolia are beginning to recover from sizable output falls, but growing inequalities in their early market development will require attention to social safety nets if poverty is to decline. These countries, however, are constrained because they are landlocked and far from markets. More than elsewhere, the future of poverty in Central Asia will depend on developing new international economic and political relations that permit a redirection and burgeoning of trade and exchange.

In several East Asian countries conventional dollar-a-day poverty has already all but disappeared. By around 2025 this will be the case for others, such as Indonesia and Malaysia. The continuing pursuit of labor-intensive growth will remain the key long-term strategy of poverty alleviation. Given the limitations of labor absorption possibilities in agriculture, the rural poor will increasingly need to turn to off-farm rural activities. These will be helped by the development of rural infrastructure, which may also induce more rural and small town industrial development. Nonetheless agricultural growth will remain important for rural poverty alleviation. In Southeast Asia, for instance, increased investment in rice research and improved rice yields will do much to ameliorate rural poverty. Similarly, targeted poverty alleviation policies will remain important.

Education in the 2020s

As discussed earlier, educational outcomes depend on income levels, government policy, and private values. Projecting the development of each of these factors is clearly impossible. Considerable insight can be gleaned by examining the relationship between education and income alone. Remember that better education can stimulate economic growth, while greater prosperity in turn increases the demand for education, as well as creating the resources to finance it.

A study of 48 low- and middle-income countries shows that each 1 percent rise in GDP per person is associated with a 0.87 percent fall in the rate of illiteracy among people aged 15 or more. For example, if a country with a 50 percent illiteracy rate doubled its GDP per person, it could expect illiteracy to fall to 27.3 percent. The links between higher GDP per person and illiteracy also account for the links between lower poverty and higher educational spending; for instance, these second factors have no statistically significant links to illiteracy once differences in GDP have been taken into account (Anand and Ravallion 1993; Lipton, de Haan, and Yaqub 1996). Figure 5.2 projects illiteracy rates in Asian countries based on this historical relationship with GDP per person.

Figure 5.2   Illiteracy: Crude Projections

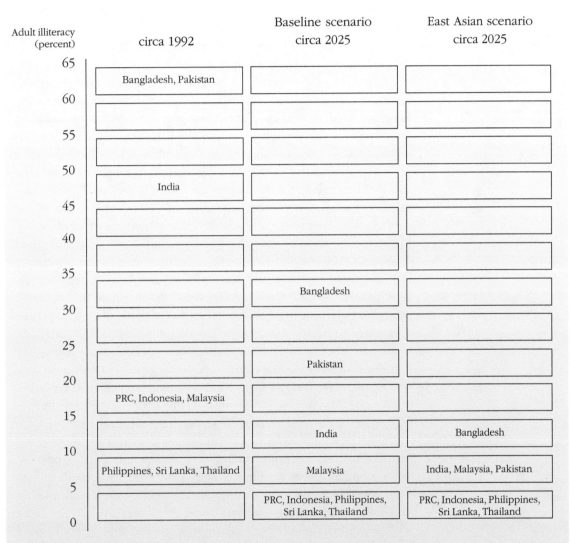

Adult illiteracy (percent)	circa 1992	Baseline scenario circa 2025	East Asian scenario circa 2025
65	Bangladesh, Pakistan		
60			
55			
50	India		
45			
40			
35			
30		Bangladesh	
25			
20		Pakistan	
15	PRC, Indonesia, Malaysia		
10		India	Bangladesh
5	Philippines, Sri Lanka, Thailand	Malaysia	India, Malaysia, Pakistan
0		PRC, Indonesia, Philippines, Sri Lanka, Thailand	PRC, Indonesia, Philippines, Sri Lanka, Thailand

Source: Anand and others (1993); Lewin (1996); Radelet, Sachs, and Lee (1996); UNESCO (1992).

Though a useful overall indicator, these projections are likely to be overestimates, because demographic changes are not factored in. Many Asians will be too young to be counted as literate adults. However, many Asians in 2025 will be too old—having finished school more than 25 years earlier—to have gained from more, or better, schooling in the interim. Figure 5.2 excludes these demographic effects. It assumes that future economic growth will affect literacy as it did in the past. But as the age structure of Asian populations is shifting, so adult literacy in the 2020s depends, much more than in the past, on a shift of resources into efficient adult education. Thus Figure 5.2 should be interpreted as the maximum attainable levels of adult literacy around 2025. Nonetheless, it seems reasonable to expect that illiteracy will have become a minor problem in Asia by about 2025, except in Bangladesh, India, and Pakistan.

Universal enrollment in primary education is a necessary, but not sufficient, condition for producing rapid rises in literacy. Schools also need to retain pupils to complete courses. In 1993, for instance, of the children who entered primary school, India only retained 66 percent up to grade four; Bangladesh retained 55 percent; and Pakistan retained 53 percent (Lewin 1996). Improving retention rates—in part by shifting state resources toward better quality basic schools—will help convert GDP growth into the literacy levels projected in Figure 5.2. In South Asian countries that tend to devote a smaller share of GDP to public spending on primary education than do countries with similar GDP per person in other developing regions, more government spending on primary education is particularly important. Some countries must also concentrate on redressing gender imbalances and reaching out to backward areas. Maximizing literacy also means concentrating on primary education for girls and for those from remote rural areas.

Both the PRC and India are typical of countries at their levels of income per person, with gross primary enrollment rates of more than 100 percent, and secondary gross enrollment rates around 40 to 50 percent.[9] At these levels, future economic growth will yield much smaller rises in enrollment rates than past growth (Lewin 1996). Both the PRC and India must concentrate on reaching lagging regions and groups, but beyond this, Asia's two giant economies face rather different educational futures.

In the advanced areas of the PRC—notably urban centers and the coastal belts—children have access to between six and nine years of

---

9. Note however that Drèze and Sen (1996) reject the statistic for India as being unreliable and exaggerated compared to alternative and more reliable survey information.

schooling. Here the agenda is to raise quality, efficiency, and achievement. In poorer areas and for national minorities, low enrollment, high dropout, and substantial repetition remain a problem. However, high economic growth, low population growth, and a helpful change in age structure will mean that the PRC can finance radical equalization of educational access—if that is where the political priorities lie.[10]

India's starting point is different. The gaps between the best and worst areas for schooling, say Bihar and Kerala; between the best and worst universities and schools; and between girls and boys are greater than in the PRC. Illiteracy is much higher. India's absolute population growth, even of school students, will be well above the PRC's for some decades. However, rising incomes will create demand for more, better, and longer education. Secondary enrollment ratios will continue to rise, with specialization reflecting shifting market demand. For the basic cycle to be available to all, some of these improvements will have to be privately financed, and the relative costs of primary and basic secondary education per child may have to fall.

Bangladesh and Pakistan share India's problems in a more severe form. However, Bangladesh has an advantage to set against its greater problems in financing education: it is at a later stage of the demographic transition than Pakistan, with slower population growth, and the prospect of a much faster fall in the ratio of school-age children to workers and taxpayers. Pakistan has recently embarked on a major program, partly funded internationally, to expand primary education and redress gender disparities. It is at present an outlier, with educational quality far below what would be predicted from its levels of real income. Catching up will be a long haul; and only if the gender gap is addressed, as planned, will Pakistan make much progress by 2025.

In the poorest countries of Asia, much greater access to basic education is clearly the highest priority. In the past, the allocation of public education resources in South Asia, for instance, was grossly misallocated in favor of higher levels of education at the cost of primary education. This is in sharp contrast to the high-performing East Asian economies, which before they entered their high growth phase, gave much greater emphasis to primary education, largely leaving higher education to the private sector.

---

10. PRC's ratio of under 15-year-olds to prime-age adults will fall from 41 percent in 1990 to 30 percent in 2020 (in India it will fall from 61 to 36 percent).

Public resource allocations to education in the poorest countries are likely to rise, but rapid improvement from a very low base will also require reassignment of subsidies from tertiary to primary education. Whether this is politically feasible is not clear. It may prove too tempting for cash-strapped governments to leave large areas of educational outreach to nongovernment organizations. These organizations are playing an innovative role in testing educational methods and delivery systems, but cannot substitute for government commitment to primary provision. Moreover, governments will have to concentrate especially on reducing biases—regional, rural, and above all gender—in the provision of education. Here too, nongovernment organizations can help—the Bangladesh Rural Advancement Committee exemplifies the role that nongovernment organizations can play in reducing the bias against the education of girls. Fortunately, all over Asia, except in Nepal, Pakistan, and Papua New Guinea, a sharp pending fall in the proportion of under 15-year-olds will reduce the cost of universal primary schooling and accelerate the economic growth that pays for it. East Asian policies can further accelerate growth.

In the middle-income countries, as primary education and literacy approach complete coverage, the quality of secondary and tertiary education must become a priority. In tertiary education, both high costs and high private returns will mean that educational demand will increasingly be met through the market, probably with student loans. Even in better-off countries this will involve problems of access for poor and rural students, which will call for imaginative schemes to combine equitable access with financial viability of the higher education system. An equitable solution is not easy to find. A number of different approaches may have to be applied: earmarked graduate taxes, student loans, merit-tested scholarships, corporate funding for potential future employees, and so on. (See Chapter 3 for a discussion of the financing of higher education in Asia.)

The benefits of educational investment become evident with a long lag. That is why it is important for governments in both low- and middle-income Asian countries to take anticipatory actions now, to ensure adequate educational outcomes in the 21st century.

Health and Nutrition in the 2020s

Future health and nutrition standards in Asia are based on the International Food Policy Research Institute's (IFPRI's) projections for food and nutrition, along with the World Bank's projections for survival and mortality (Rosegrant, Agcaoili-Sombilla, and Perez 1995; World Bank 1993). The projections run to 2030, and some of the underlying assumptions differ from those used in the rest of this study. IFPRI has projected food availability per person up to 2020 in a multicountry framework. Food prices and quantities are determined by supply and demand, with countries linked through trade. The baseline projection is based on IFPRI's best estimates of future income, population, trade protection, and farm technology. IFPRI also constructs four other scenarios based on lower population growth, lower investment, higher investment, and the complete removal of agricultural protection all over the world.

With baseline policies that project lower per person GDP growth than the projections used in Chapter 2, South Asia will increase the number of daily calories available per person by 13 percent to 2,600 kilocalories a day, more than the current level in Southeast Asia. Bangladesh will lag, with only 2,127 kilocalories per person. The PRC, in contrast, will gain strongly, increasing calorie availability per person from 2,667 in 1990 to 3,373 in 2020. In Southeast Asia, calorie intake will rise much more slowly as incomes grow.

IFPRI also projects future rates of child malnutrition using a model in which malnutrition depends on calorie availability, the extent of female education, the percentage of the population with access to safe water, and the share of public expenditure on social services. Under the baseline scenario, the share of malnourished children under five will fall to 43 percent in South Asia (down from 59 percent in 1990). Bangladesh shares in this improvement almost equally with its neighbors, underlining the fact that average calorie availability alone is a very imperfect guide to malnutrition. The PRC and Southeast Asia improved from around 23 percent in 1990 to 15 percent in 2020. As with food availability, the high investment scenario, corresponding also to higher savings and per person GDP outcomes, results in the lowest child malnutrition incidences. Low population growth, implying a more rapid demographic transition, also results in reduced child malnutrition for Asian countries.

Under all IFPRI's scenarios South Asia will still have a larger share of undernourished children in 2020 than any other part of the developing world. Even under the best of IFPRI's scenarios, one in three South Asian children under five will remain malnourished. This chapter previously emphasized that malnutrition in South Asia was mainly due to cultural practices related to maternal health care and nutrition. IFPRI's projections assume the persistence of such practices. However, with greater material prosperity, urbanization, and more female education, they may begin to change. If so, malnutrition among under-fives might be cut to the 20 percent projected for sub-Saharan Africa; nevertheless South Asia will still have pervasive child malnutrition three decades from now.

How is this projected persistence of child malnutrition consistent with the large projected reduction in poverty? First, the incidence of child malnutrition is typically much higher today than the incidence of poverty. Hence, even a proportionate reduction in both poverty and child malnutrition would still leave a much higher incidence of child malnutrition than poverty incidence in 2020. The incidence of child malnutrition tends to be higher than poverty incidence for at least two self-reinforcing reasons. Poor families tend to have more children. Hence, the proportion of poor—and therefore undernourished—children in the total number of children tends to be higher than the proportion of the poor in the total population. Furthermore, girls suffer greater deprivation than boys in the intrafamily distribution of food and nutrition. Even though the average consumption of family members may be just above the poverty line, girls within the family may still be suffering from malnutrition. This implies a higher incidence of child malnutrition compared to poverty incidence.

The World Bank (1993) has projected mortality and survival chances for the year 2030 on the basis of likely demographic changes, expected developments in disease patterns, and possible advances in disease control. Their analysis suggests that life expectancy at birth will either equal or exceed 70 in the PRC, India, and the rest of Asia by 2030 (Table 5.5). Young people will see relatively greater improvements in life expectancy, because the analysis assumes that the infectious diseases of childhood will be conquered with much greater success than the degenerative diseases of the old. While this assumption is generally valid, there are important exceptions.

First, the growing danger of AIDS (often combined with tuberculosis) will have serious implications for health throughout Asia, and especially in countries such as India, Myanmar, and Thailand, where 1.75, 0.35, and 0.7 million people, respectively, are currently infected (WHO 1996). Second, with increasing urbanization and population growth, competition for water will intensify. One effect may be reduced availability of clean water, especially in urban slums. Urban access to clean water is superior to rural access, but is constrained by lack of sewerage and solid waste disposal. In densely populated urban areas, up to

Table 5.5 Mortality Risk and Life Expectancy, Selected Years

Economy/region and age range (years)	Probability of dying (percent)			Life expectancy (years)		
	1950	1990	2030	1950	1990	2030
PRC						
0-4 years	31.5	4.3	1.6	38	69	77
5-14 years	6.3	0.8	0.3	47	67	73
15-59 years	53.4	17.5	9.7	40	58	63
60-75 years	65.2	41.5	23.0	12	18	20
India						
0-4 years	30.4	12.4	4.5	42	58	70
5-14 years	5.0	2.7	1.0	54	61	68
15-59 years	38.5	25.0	15.1	47	53	59
60-75 years	61.1	48.9	33.8	14	16	18
Other Asia						
0-4 years	23.4	9.7	3.8	44	62	72
5-14 years	4.9	1.7	0.6	52	63	70
15-59 years	45.0	21.2	13.9	44	54	60
60-75 years	59.3	44.9	31.4	13	16	19
Developing economies						
0-4 years	28.6	10.6	4.9	40	63	71
5-14 years	5.7	2.2	0.8	50	64	69
15-59 years	46.7	23.5	15.3	43	55	60
60-75 years	60.3	43.8	32.6	13	17	19
Industrial economies						
0-4 years	6.0	1.1	0.6	65	76	81
5-14 years	1.0	0.3	0.1	65	72	77
15-59 years	20.7	10.7	6.4	55	62	67
60-75 years	43.1	27.6	16.5	17	20	22

Source: World Bank (1993).

90 percent of the food cooked and sold on the streets is contaminated with fecal matter. If present trends continue, urban morbidity and mortality from gastrointestinal diseases will increase, offsetting some of the gains from improving clean water availability in rural areas.

Communicable diseases also pose other threats. Malaria is resurgent globally. The problem is worst in Africa, but some regions in Asia (India, in particular) are also affected. Emerging antibiotic-resistant tuberculosis threatens the poor everywhere. The transitional economies of Central

Asia and Mongolia face special health problems, as economic transition has contributed to the breakdown of social safety nets and worsened health provision.

In middle-income Asian countries, the main health policy issues concern the financial implications of an aging population and their demands for sophisticated curative health care. Lifestyle changes associated with higher incomes can influence the pattern of disease. In the fast-growing East and Southeast Asian economies, for instance, consumption of fat per person has doubled in the past two decades (FAO 1996). Obesity is becoming an acute problem in the richer parts of Asia. Substance abuse—alcoholism, drug addiction, and cigarette smoking—are all on the rise. These will increase the likelihood of chronic noncommunicable diseases, such as cancer or cardiovascular disease.

Chapter 3 discusses health care financing and options for health insurance, particularly in more affluent East Asia, in more detail. In poorer Asian countries, the clear priority should be to focus on preventive care in rural areas. However, as in the case of education, actual spending patterns are quite distorted. Too many public resources are diverted to expensive curative care in modern, urban hospitals, where rich, urban residents are treated at highly subsidized rates. A second problem involves negligence, carelessness, and the poor quality of treatment, and patient care, especially for women. Here again, poor services stem from centralized administration and lack of accountability to the patient. Predictably, there is a high incidence of patients privately paying doctors to get proper treatment even in public facilities. The challenge of health policy is to radically alter the patterns of public resource allocation for health and health administration, despite anticipated resistance from articulate and influential urban lobbies—including the official health establishment itself. The path to better policies is obvious but the political barriers to reform are formidable.

Changes in Work Experience

As Asia's economic structure transforms, so too will the nature of employment. The proportion of workers in agriculture will continue to fall sharply. Even in the PRC and India, less than half the labor force will be involved in agriculture by the 2020s. Far more people will depend on others for food and work than they do today. At the same time, formal contracts of employment will become more prevalent.

The quality of formal sector employment should improve in the coming decades. Greater economic prosperity will help reduce the tradeoffs between employment opportunities and job quality. In early East Asian development, employment grew rapidly, at some cost to workers' other rights, such as the right to bargain, and appropriate conditions of health and safety in the workplace. In contrast, job security and workers' rights in South Asia were safeguarded in public and large private firms, but overall employment grew slowly. As East Asian countries grow more affluent and labor becomes more skilled, such tradeoffs will become less harsh. This has already started to happen. East Asian workers are acquiring ever more legally sanctioned job security and other benefits. The tactic here is to ensure that these sanctioned improvements in working conditions do not compromise labor flexibility. In richer Asian countries, labor scarcity will also drive improvements in the quality of work. As populations age over the next 25 years, the pressures of labor scarcity will be felt increasingly in other areas too. This may result in a higher incidence of international labor migration within Asia (discussed in Chapter 3).

Economic growth, particularly outward-oriented growth, will also improve other aspects of the quality of work, such as child labor, but only extremely poor parents, with few adult employment opportunities supply child labor despite atrocious conditions. Global experience confirms that as economic growth brings and requires higher wages and more employment for skilled adults, both the supply of and demand for child labor falls (Box 3.3, Chapter 3). An outward orientation also provides women with greater opportunities to join the formal labor market. Many labor-intensive manufactured exports, such as textiles and electronics, tend to be intensive in female labor.

Increasing international integration also brings challenges to the labor market. Competition for low-skilled jobs is likely to increase, as employers increasingly relocate to lower-wage countries (as shoe manufacturers, for instance, have already relocated from Northeast to Southeast Asia). To remain competitive, workers will have to become increasingly educated and skilled to move into higher value-added occupations. Provided such skill increases occur, Asian workers should enjoy higher real wages and improved working conditions in the future. Equipping students and workers with better information technology skills will be a challenge for Asian governments and firms.

Future Urbanization and Rural Development

In the coming decades, Asia will become a predominantly urban society. Economic transformation promotes urbanization as the concentration of industry leads to a concentrated demand for labor in urban agglomerations. Worldwide, the urban population is likely to double from about 2.5 billion to about 5.1 billion by the year 2025. Three out of five of these people will be living in Asia, or about 55 percent of the Asian population. In industrial countries, urbanization tends to stabilize when about 75 to 85 percent of the population lives in towns or cities. This implies that Asia's urban population is likely to grow well beyond 2025 (Table 5.6).

Southeast Asia and the PRC will see the fastest rates of urbanization up to 2010. Thereafter the growth of towns and cities will rise fastest in South Asia. Excluding Japan, most of Asia's new urban residents will live in five countries: Bangladesh, PRC, India, Indonesia, and Pakistan. Large differences will exist between Asian countries. By 2025, nine out of ten people in Korea will live in towns or cities, while in Bhutan over 80 percent of the population will still live in rural areas.

Asia's new urban population will mainly concentrate in existing towns and cities. By 2015, Asia will have 272 cities with more than 1 million inhabitants, up from 118 in 1990. The number of megacities with over 10 million inhabitants will rise from 9 in 1995 (Bombay, Beijing, Calcutta, Jakarta, Osaka, Seoul, Shanghai, Tianjin, and Tokyo) to 20 in 2025. Bangalore, Bangkok, Dhaka, Delhi, Hyderabad, Karachi, Lahore, Madras, Manila, Shenyang, and Yangon will by then all have over 10 million inhabitants apiece. Altogether 400 million Asians will live in megacities in 2025, about half of them in South Asia. Nonetheless, the trend toward urban primacy, that is the dominance of one major metropolis in a country, may well decline in several Asian countries (Table 5.7).

Managing Asia's urbanization process will not be easy. Recent exercises undertaken at the Asian Development Bank (Stubbs and Clarke 1996) indicate that trillions of dollars of investment will be needed to develop urban infrastructure over the next 25 years. The major investment needs will be for urban transport, water supply, and sanitation. Those urban centers that can attract more investment through better planning and management will be able to afford the greatest improvements in the quality of life of their residents.

Table 5.6 Level of Urbanization, 1995 and 2025
(percent)

Economy/region	1995	2025
East Asia		
PRC	30.3	54.5
Hong Kong	95.0	97.3
Korea	81.3	93.7
Mongolia	60.9	76.5
Central Asia		
Kazakstan	59.7	74.8
Kyrgyz Republic	38.9	57.2
Southeast Asia		
Cambodia	20.7	43.5
Indonesia	35.4	60.7
Lao PDR	21.7	44.5
Malaysia	53.7	72.7
Myanmar	26.2	47.3
Philippines	54.2	74.3
Thailand	20.0	39.1
Viet Nam	20.8	39.0
South Asia		
Bangladesh	18.3	40.0
Bhutan	6.4	19.0
India	26.8	45.2
Maldives	26.8	45.8
Nepal	13.7	34.3
Pakistan	34.7	56.7
Sri Lanka	22.4	42.6
World total	45.2	61.1
More developed regions	74.9	84.0
Less developed regions	37.6	57.0

Source: United Nations (1995).

Urban management must progress along several dimensions. Governments can take the lead in improving the market for urban land. Broad guidance on urban expansion and land use planning is important, as is the dissemination of information on land availability and land prices. Some elements of land use regulation need to be liberalized: land titling and registration, for instance, can be simplified. Governments must also support the access of low-income households to affordable land, in

Table 5.7 Urban Primacy: Percentage of Urban Population Residing in the Largest Urban Agglomerations, Selected Years

Subregion/city/economy		1960	1980	1995	2015
East Asia					
Shanghai	PRC	7.1	6.0	4.1	3.5
Seoul	Korea	34.1	38.2	31.8	27.3
Central Asia					
Almaty	Kazakstan	10.9	11.7	12.4	11.9
Southeast Asia					
Jakarta	Indonesia	19.1	17.9	16.4	15.6
Kuala Lumpur	Malaysia	15.9	15.9	11.5	10.1
Manila	Philippines	27.2	32.9	25.3	22.5
Bangkok	Thailand	65.1	59.3	55.7	48.8
Ho Chi Minh	Viet Nam	25.9	26.5	23.0	19.6
South Asia					
Dhaka	Bangladesh	24.5	32.2	35.5	33.8
Bombay	India	5.1	5.1	6.0	5.8
Yangon	Myanmar	22.6	27.3	31.6	28.3
Karachi	Pakistan	16.7	21.0	20.2	17.7
Latin America					
Buenos Aires	Argentina	44.6	42.5	36.1	31.5
Rio de Janeiro	Brazil	15.1	10.9	7.8	6.3
Mexico City	Mexico	28.6	31.2	22.2	18.2
North America					
New York	Unites States	11.2	9.3	8.1	7.0
Africa					
Nairobi	Kenya	35.8	32.3	26.6	24.6
Lagos	Nigeria	12.5	22.5	23.4	23.4
Johannesburg	South Africa	14.4	11.1	8.8	7.9

Note: An urban agglomeration is defined as a city with 750,000 or more residents in 1990.
Source: United Nations (1995).

particular by providing credit for low-income housing and greater security of tenure of land. Urban transport planning also needs careful attention, because the extent of a city is defined by its transport network.

Overall, the improvement of living conditions in Asia's urban areas will depend on a successful collaboration between government, community, and private sector resources for the provision of services. Decentralization of urban finances is an important component of this. Local public sector institutions need strengthening; they need independent access to financial markets and discretion to raise taxes and levy charges. Local governments need greater flexibility to enter into contracts with private providers of services. This requires sophisticated contract and regulatory services. The public sector's role should be one of facilitator rather than the direct provider of urban services. Full cost pricing, where possible, should ensure that the private sector assumes a greater proportion of investments in urban infrastructure, such as water provision or public transportation.

As Chapter 4 of this study discussed, Asia's cities will need to adopt a more integrated approach to environmental management in particular. In the past, investments in urban water supply have been much higher than in wastewater and solid waste management. In the years ahead this imbalance will need to be corrected, although with rapid urbanization access rates may not improve in some countries (Pernia and Alabastro 1996). In the 21st century integrated water resource management to meet the competing demands for water will become an urgent priority. To cater for increased urban demands for water, cities will have to tap resources ever further away through huge water resource development projects. In doing so, careful attention must be paid to the water requirements of rural inhabitants.

More broadly, there is a danger that Asia's future urbanization comes at the expense of rural development. Even in 2025 almost one in two Asians will still live in rural areas. Although there too, absolute increases in the quality of life—better education, health, and access to safe water and sanitation—are likely, disparities between rural and urban areas will remain large. Aside from an increased need for investment in primary education and basic health care, rural Asia faces a massive backlog in improving access to safe water and sanitation. As rural areas become relatively less important, both economically and politically, Asian countries must ensure that they do not get left behind.

Rural environmental problems will remain acute. Biomass fuels are likely to remain the predominant energy source for the poor in rural Asia for the next 30 years. Thus medium-term energy goals in rural areas should concentrate on making biomass fuels less damaging to human health and to the environment. Less polluting stoves could be designed, produced, and marketed through the private sector, with the assistance of community-based organizations. Ensuring secure property rights would create the incentive for improved biomass resource management.

In rural areas too, decentralization of decisionmaking will be an important prerequisite for increased empowerment. Rural Asia then may have better prospects for its pressing physical and social investment needs gaining recognition. In some Asian countries, rural communities may be better placed to organize self-help groups together with nongovernment organizations than less cohesive urban areas. Microfinance schemes, for instance, should be replicated throughout rural communities in Asia. Policies that help to improve the welfare of women are an important component of improving overall rural welfare in many parts of Asia.

While the failure to improve Asia's urban environment will increasingly detract from the quality of life, the failure to improve Asia's rural environment could threaten the livelihood and habitat of rural people. Asia's problems of water availability, land degradation, and deforestation are discussed in Chapter 4.

Future of the Asian Family

Asia's continuing economic transformation will precipitate further social change. Greater urbanization, demographic shifts, and rising female participation in the labor force will continue the transition from the extended to the nuclear family. As discussed earlier, the incidence of divorce is increasing. Official recorded divorce rates are positively correlated with per person income, both within Asia and for a broader cross section of countries. As a result, projected income growth also suggests an increase in divorce rates. By 2025, divorce rates are expected to reach roughly 2.6 per 1,000 in Hong Kong, Korea, and Singapore, a figure about 2.5 times the level of current divorce rates in these economies, and roughly equal to the rate prevailing in Canada today.

Thus the Asian family is unlikely to provide the social safety net that it used to. Public institutions will be increasingly called upon to provide services such as day care for children, welfare assistance for single mothers, and general child support. Care for the elderly will become a more serious issue for Asian society and the family, particularly East Asia (Box 5.3). The decline of traditional family structures will also increase demand for public health insurance, unemployment compensation, disability insurance, and public pensions.

Although Asia need not follow the path of other advanced industrial economies directly, such social problems as crime, drug abuse, broken homes, and neglected children that are common in Western society, will probably rise in Asia too. The incidence of crime is still low in Asia compared with other parts of the world, but it is rising, and drug abuse is more widespread than authorities commonly acknowledge.

Future Role of Women

In some parts of Asia, women's status has improved considerably during the past three decades. Nonetheless, women still face many barriers and imbalances. They are less educated, less healthy, and treated unequally in the labor market. Asian policymakers face important decisions when deciding how far to address these issues. First, countries must decide whether they wish to equalize opportunities or outcomes for men and women. The philosophical underpinnings and practical implications of these two choices differ significantly. Because the starting line for women and men is not the same, simply aiming for equality of opportunity implies that past discrimination limits women's ability to benefit from a new regime of equal opportunity. This suggests that affirmative action is needed. But, conversely, affirmative action can lead to costly inefficiencies and contribute to political tension.

Increasing equality of opportunity means removing long-standing laws and practices that have either explicitly or effectively discriminated against women. These include laws and practices that restrict women's rights to own or inherit property or to secure credit, that make it difficult or impossible for women to enter certain occupations, that restrict women's access to education, or that make women financially dependent on men. This is not easy. Often the social consensus on which such discriminatory laws are based is unchanged. Moreover, it is especially difficult to pass legislation that aggressively seeks to overturn traditional practices in the absence of women's active support for such measures. In many cases such support is missing, at least on any widespread basis.

The best prospects for short-term improvements in the status of women involve the removal of laws that most egregiously violate women's basic opportunities to move toward equality with men. India's efforts to ban dowries and Thailand's prohibitions on prostitution are both notable in this regard, although their limited effects show how difficult it is to reverse long-standing and deep-seated practices.

Gender equality can also be approached more positively by implementing policies intended to equalize outcomes between men and women. This might take a variety of forms. Girls' secondary and tertiary education could be subsidized more than that of boys. Women could be hired preferentially in certain occupations. Institutions such as the Grameen Bank, which provides credit mainly to women in rural areas, could be specifically fostered. Women's legal ability to seek divorce and retain half of a family's assets could be bolstered. Mechanisms to finance old-age security could be developed to target women, who tend to outlive men. In all of these cases the benefits from targeting women would have to be weighed against the distortionary costs of preferential policies.

A third approach is to introduce specific policies designed to assist women who are combining the roles of worker and household manager. Among Asian couples, women are not often viewed as the primary

Box 5.3 Care of the Elderly

Asia's population is aging. The proportion of people aged 65 and older is likely to increase from 5 percent in 1995 to 9 percent in 2025. In East Asia the share of old people will rise from 7 to 13 percent. In South and Southeast Asia, where the demographic transition began later, the share of old people will rise from 4 to 7.5 percent and from 4.5 to 8 percent, respectively (UN 1994).

These averages hide sharp disparities between countries. In Hong Kong, for instance, people aged 65 and older will make up 24 percent of the population in 2025, compared with only 10 percent today. In Singapore the relative size of the elderly population will almost triple, from 7 to 20 percent. PRC, Korea, Sri Lanka, and Thailand will all have between 10 and 15 percent of their population aged 65 or older by 2025. In absolute terms, the increase will be largest in the PRC and India, where 180 million and 115 million people, respectively, will be older than 65 by 2025.

Traditionally the care of the elderly has rested with the family in Asia, but the region's demographic transition has profoundly altered the structure of families. Fertility has declined and average household size has fallen. This implies that the care of a larger number of elderly is spread across a smaller number of family members. As people marry later, the chances that adult couples must care for both young children and elderly parents increase.

Socioeconomic change has also affected intergenerational relationships. Industrialization and urbanization, together with greater access to education, have all brought women (the traditional caregivers within the family) greater employment opportunities outside the home. The shift from family enterprise to wage-based employment is likely to remove control of productive resources from the elderly, in turn undermining their authority over younger family members. As rural to urban and international migration physically separate genera-

breadwinner, but they are still considered to have primary responsibility for managing the household. Hence they face the so-called double day of a formal job and housework. Western societies have attempted to address these issues in a variety of ways, including through flexible working hours, the expansion of sick leave to cover parents' needs to attend to sick children, on-site child care centers, job sharing, provisions for maternity and paternity leave, and child care tax credits. These practices make it easier for women to combine work and family responsibilities and are likely to prove as beneficial to women in Asia as elsewhere.

In short, public policy has an important role to play in alleviating gender inequality. History suggests that economic growth alone promotes some measure of gender equality. But the persistence of labor and credit market discrimination and of violence against women in many

tions, the obligation to support the elderly weakens. All these factors contribute to a weakening of family cohesion.

Asian society will therefore have to cope with relatively more old people in an environment of eroding family commitment to support them. A possible indicator of this is the Maintenance of Parents Act of 1995 in Singapore. One response, prevalent in industrial countries, is increased pressure for public sector provision of substitutes for family care (such as community-based support services; publicly provided welfare, pensions, and health benefits; or homes for the aged). Such support can be expensive, especially given advances in health care that further prolong life expectancy. In Japan, for instance, health expenditure for the elderly is likely to increase by 30 percent from 1980 to 2025 (UN 1988).

The developing countries of Asia would be well advised to consider more innovative approaches to these problems. An interesting approach is to use economic incentives to combat the forces that are weakening the traditional family commitment to care for the elderly. Hong Kong, Korea, and Singapore for example, have developed housing policies centered around providing family incentives to care for the elderly. Urban housing is designed to include the specific needs of the elderly as well as the coresidence of different generations. Specific incentives include tax allowances and priority access to house purchases for families with multiple generations living together.

Other approaches encourage the active and productive participation of the elderly in the community through innovative employment opportunities that cater to older people's capabilities and experience. Japan has successfully introduced such approaches. As Asian countries begin to seriously consider whether to adopt widespread public social security provision for the elderly, they will need to review the level of benefits and traditional age of formal retirement in the face of longer life expectancy.

wealthy industrial countries suggest that gender inequality is not purely a stage of development problem. The future well-being of Asia's women thus depends in large part on future public policy decisions.

Conclusion

In general, future prospects for Asia's quality of life look more favorable than past trends. Not only will most indicators of well-being, such as educational achievement, health, and nutrition, continue to improve across Asia, they will improve most quickly in the poorer parts of the region. Convergence rather than divergence could become more typical of Asia's quality of life. Nonetheless, certain groups of people, certain regions, and particular components of quality of life are at risk. Many Asian women still face the prospect of a considerably worse life than men. Rural Asians will not see life improve as much as urban dwellers. Unless steps are taken to redress policy and institutional failures, the environment will come under increasing strain for urban and rural Asians alike.

By 2020, today's middle-income Asian countries, primarily in East Asia, will face second-order quality of life problems. They will need to reduce moderate and relative poverty, achieve universal secondary education, expand tertiary education, improve urban and rural amenities, affordably handle old age and chronic disease, and reconcile labor market flexibility with job security.

In today's low-income Asian countries, these same problems will preoccupy a largely urban middle class. By 2020 this group will include as many as 30 percent or more of the population, compared with about 20 percent now. At the same time, however, these countries will still have a smaller, and so politically weaker, hard core of very deprived people. At least 10 percent, perhaps 20 percent of the people in Bangladesh, PRC, and India will face one, probably several, of the following: food poverty, illiteracy, malnutrition, high child mortality, inadequate access to water, poor sanitation, and lack of access to land. Asia's low-income countries thus face a "telescoped transition," where the problems of affluence and poverty coincide. Coping with this telescoped transition and ensuring that the disadvantaged do not get left behind will demand innovative and farsighted public policy.

This chapter has shown that improvements are closely associated with economic growth, particularly poverty reduction. The lesson, however, is that success lies in adopting policies, institutions, and technologies that foster broad-based growth. In addition to growth-mediated strategies, direct support efforts followed by some governments at particular times have been important. Experience shows that public resources can be directed more productively at primary education and basic health care, as well as improving access to safe water and sanitation, particularly in rural areas.

Specific country economic, social, cultural, and historical circumstance will continue to influence further success. Thus, the impact of demographic change on quality of life will vary across countries and within countries across time. Although the bulk of Asians presently reside in rural areas, in the future the scale of urbanization will pose a serious challenge to Asian governments. Failure to cope adequately with this could result in a less optimistic prospect than that presented here. Urban services more amenable to cost recovery are increasingly likely to involve private sector participation. Local government will need greater financial and administrative empowerment, in both urban and rural areas. In coping with future urbanization, however, Asian countries must ensure that problems of rural development do not get neglected.

Government intervention will be needed where gross inherited inequalities or other institutional failures impede the provision of such benefits as gender-neutral education, health care, and access to credit. Even then, such intervention need not always take the form of direct government supply of services and goods. Creating an appropriate institutional base for mass sharing in market development and in human fulfillment will be important. Disadvantages such as poverty, ill-health, and poor education often operate jointly, mutually reinforce each other, and especially affect lagging regions and groups. Those affected may lack the capabilities to take advantage of opportunities created by economic growth. The pursuit of inclusive public policies may be needed to overcome such disadvantages. It is also evident that complementarities in outcomes can be harnessed by a focus on key deficiencies. Thus improving the well-being and status of women will have a positive impact on other quality of life indicators, such as child nutrition and health, education, and literacy.

References

Acharya, S. 1990. *Maharashtra Employment Guarantee Scheme: A Study of Labor Market Intervention*. New Delhi: International Labour Organisation, Asian Regional Team for Employment Promotion.

Alderman, H., J. Behrman, D. Ross, and R. Sabot. 1996. "Decomposing the Gender Gap in Cognitive Skills in a Poor Rural Economy." *Journal of Human Resources* 31(1):229-54.

Anand, S., and M. Ravallion. 1993. "Human Development in Poor Countries: On the Role of Private Incomes and Public Services." *Journal of Economic Perspectives* 7(1):133-50.

Asian Development Bank. 1996. *Financing Human Development: Lessons from Advanced Asian Economies*. Manila.

Basu, A., and K. Basu. 1996. "The Quality of Work Experience in Emerging Asia." Background paper for *Emerging Asia: Changes and Challenges*. Asian Development Bank, Manila.

Bhargava, A., and S. R. Osmani. 1996. "Health and Nutrition in Emerging Asia." Background paper for *Emerging Asia: Changes and Challenges*. Asian Development Bank, Manila.

Binswanger, H., K. Deininger, and G. Feder. 1995. "Power, Distortions, Revolt and Reform in Agricultural Land Relations." In J. Behrman and T. N. Srinivasan, eds., *Handbook of Development Economics*. Vol. 3B. Amsterdam: Elsevier Science Publications.

Birdsall, N., D. Ross, and R. Sabot. 1994. "Inequality and Growth Reconsidered." St. Anthony's College, Oxford, U.K.

Bruno, M., M. Ravallion, and L. Squire. 1996. "Equity and Growth in Developing Countries: Old and New Perspectives on Policy Issues." World Bank Policy Research Department, Washington, D.C.

Chen, S., G. Datt, and M. Ravallion. 1994. "Is Poverty Increasing in the Developing World?" *Review of Income and Wealth* 40(4):359-76.

Datt, G., and M. Ravallion. 1995. "Why Have Some Indian States Done Better than Others at Reducing Poverty?" World Bank Policy Research Department, Washington, D.C.

Deininger, K., and B. Minten. 1996. "Does Asset Distribution Make a Difference? New Evidence from Data on International Land Distribution." World Bank, Washington D.C.

Deininger, K., and L. Squire. 1996a. "A New Dataset Measuring Income." *World Bank Economic Review* 10(3):565-91.

_____1996b. "New Ways of Looking at Old Issues: Inequality and Growth." World Bank, Washington D.C.

Drèze, J., and M. Saran. 1995. "Primary Education and Economic Development in PRC and India: Overview and Two Case Studies." In K. Basu, P. Pattanaik, and K. Suzumura, eds., *Choice, Welfare and Development: A Festschrift in Honour of Amartya K. Sen*. Oxford, U.K.: Clarendon Press.

Drèze, J., and A. K. Sen. 1989. *Hunger and Public Action*. Oxford, U.K.: Clarendon Press.

_____. 1996. *India: Economic Development and Social Opportunity*. India: Oxford University Press.

el-Ghonemy, M. 1990. *The Political Economy of Rural Poverty*. London: Routledge.

FAO (Food and Agriculture Organization of the United Nations). 1996. *The Sixth World Food Survey*. Rome.

Gunatilleke, Godfrey, Myrtle Perera, R. Waniganatre, R. E. Fernando, W. D. Lakhsman, J. K. Chandriasini, and R. D. Wanigaratne. 1994. "Sri Lanka." In M. G. Quibria, ed., *Rural Poverty in Developing Asia*. Vol. 1. Manila: Asian Development Bank.

Harriss, B. 1990. "The Intra-family Distribution of Hunger in South Asia." In J. Drèze and A. K. Sen, eds., *The Political Economy of Hunger*. Vol. 1, *Entitlement and Well-being*. Oxford: Clarendon Press.

ILO (International Labour Organisation). 1992. *The Urban Informal Sector in Asia: An Annotated Bibliography*. Geneva.

_____. 1996. *Economically Active Populations: Estimates and Projections, 1950-2010*. Geneva.

Johansen, F. 1993. "Poverty Reduction in East Asia: The Silent Revolution." Discussion Paper No. 203. Washington D.C.: World Bank.

Lewin, K. 1996. "Access to Education in Emerging Asia: Trends, Challenges and Policy Options." Background paper for *Emerging Asia: Changes and Challenges*. Asian Development Bank, Manila.

Lipton, M. 1983. *Labor and Poverty*. Staff Working Paper No. 616. Washington, D.C.: World Bank.

_____. 1993. "Land Reform as Unfinished Business: The Case for Not Stopping." *World Development* 21(4):641-57.

Lipton, M., A. de Haan, and S. Yaqub. 1996. "Poverty in Emerging Asia." Background paper for *Emerging Asia: Changes and Challenges*. Asian Development Bank, Manila.

Mazumdar, D. 1994. "The Republic of Korea." In S. Horton, R. Kanbur, and D. Mazumdar, eds., *Labor Markets in an Era of Adjustment*. Vol. 2. *Case Studies*. Washington, D. C.: Economic Development Institute of the World Bank.

Mingat, A. 1995. "Towards Improving Our Understanding of the Strategy of High Performing Asian Economies in the Education Sector." Paper presented at the International Conference on Financing Human Resource Development in Advanced Asian Countries, 17-18 November, Asian Development Bank, Manila.

Nijkamp, P. 1994. "Improving Urban Environmental Quality: Socio-economic Possibilities and Limits." In Ernesto M. Pernia, ed., *Urban Poverty in Asia: A Survey of Critical Issues*. Hong Kong: Oxford University Press.

Pernia, E. M., and S. L. F. Alabastro. 1996. "Aspects of Urban Sanitation and Safe Water in the Context of Rapid Urbanization." Background paper for *Emerging Asia: Changes and Challenges*. Asian Development Bank, Manila.

Pernia, E. M., and M. G. Quibria. 1995. "Poverty in Developing Countries." Asian Development Bank, Manila.

Rosegrant, M., M. Agcaoili-Sombilla, and N. Perez. 1995. *Global Food Projections to 2020*. Food, Agriculture, and the Environment Discussion Paper No. 5. Washington D.C.: International Food Policy Research Institute.

Stubbs, J., and G. Clarke. 1996. *Megacity Management in the Asian and Pacific Region*. Vols. I and II. Manila: Asian Development Bank.

Svedberg, P. 1990. "Undernutrition in Sub-Saharan Africa: Is There a Gender Bias?" *Journal of Development Studies* 26(3):469-86.

Tyler, G., M. el-Ghonemy, and Y. Couvreur. 1993. "Alleviating Rural Poverty through Agricultural Growth." *Journal of Development Studies* 29(2):358-64.

United Nations. 1988. *Economic and Social Implications of Population Aging: Proceedings of the United Nations International Symposium on Population, Structure and Development*. New York.

_____. 1994. *The Sex and Age Distribution of the World Population: The 1994 Revision*. New York.

_____. 1995. *World Urbanization Prospects: The 1994 Revision*. New York.

UNDP (United Nations Development Programme). 1996. *Human Development Report*. New York: Oxford University Press.

UNDP and ILO. 1993. *Employment, Poverty, and Economic Policies*. New Delhi: Asian Regional Center for Employment Promotion.

UNESCO (United Nations Educational, Scientific and Cultural Organization). 1992. *Statistical Yearbook*. France: Imprimerie Jean Lamour, Maxeville.

WHO (World Health Organization). 1996. *The World Health Report 1996*. Geneva.

World Bank. 1980. *Health*. Sector Policy Paper. Washington, D.C.

_____. 1990. *World Development Report 1990: Poverty*. New York: Oxford University Press.

_____. 1992a. *China: Strategies for Reducing Poverty in the 1990s*. Washington, D.C.

_____.1992b. *World Development Report 1992: Development and the Environment*. New York: Oxford University Press.

_____. 1993. *World Development Report 1993: Investing in Health*. New York: Oxford University Press.

_____.1995. *World Development Report 1995: Workers in an Integrating World*. New York: Oxford University Press.

_____. 1996a. *Poverty Reduction and the World Bank: Progress and Challenges in the 1990s*. Washington, D.C.

_____. 1996b. *World Development Report 1996: From Plan to Market*. New York: Oxford University Press.

_____. 1997. *World Development Indicators*. Washington, D.C.

APPENDIX

This appendix describes the specification and estimation of the statistical model of cross-country economic growth used in Chapter 2 and parts of Chapter 3. Further details can be found in Radelet, Sachs, and Lee (1996).

The basic approach is as follows. Let g_i be the instantaneous growth rate of per person income in country i between 1965 and 1990, adjusted for purchasing power parity (PPP). Y_i is the PPP-adjusted level of income per working-age population in 1965. Let $Z_{1i}, Z_{2i}, Z_{3i}, \ldots, Z_{ni}$ be a list of additional variables that potentially explain the growth rate in country i. These variables are suggested by various theories of growth. For example, they describe trade policies, geography, the quality of market institutions, demographic change, and other dimensions of an economy that might affect long-term growth rates. It can then be expected that in a sample of developing and industrial countries, the rate of growth of each country should be explained by the initial level of income per working-age person of the country as well as by the other variables.[1] In mathematical terms the growth equation can be represented as follows:

$$g_i = \alpha\, Y_i + \beta_1 Z_{1i} + \beta_2 Z_{2i} + \beta_3 Z_{3i} + \ldots + \beta_n Z_{ni} + \gamma + \varepsilon_i$$

where γ is a constant term and ε_i is a random disturbance for country i. Such an equation helps us to compare the three main approaches to growth. For example, the neoclassical theory predicts that poorer countries will grow faster than richer countries, holding other influences on

---

1. Note that in the underlying equations of the model, the growth rate is expressed as the growth in output per worker. To explore the impact of demographic variables on economic growth, the difference in the growth rates of the total population and the working-age population is added to both sides of the equation. These variables appear as two of the Z_i variables on the right-hand side of the equation. This addition transforms the left-hand side of the equation to the growth rate of output per person. The theory predicts that these variables should enter with coefficients of 1 (on growth of working-age population) and -1 (on growth of overall population). We could not statistically reject these hypothesized values. See Radelet, Sachs, and Lee (1996) for further details.

growth constant. This suggests that α (the coefficient on initial income per worker) will be *negative*: the higher the initial income per worker, the lower the growth rate. The endogenous growth theory, in contrast, predicts that α will be zero, or even positive: poorer countries will not grow more rapidly than richer countries, and may even grow more slowly (for example, if their poverty reflects their smaller stock of knowledge and pace of innovation). The statistical equation also tells us which of the other *"Z"* variables—geography, government policy, demography, and so on—help to account for differences in growth rates.

Box A-1 presents the definitions and sources of each of the key variables, and Table A-1 reports descriptive statistics on these variables. The sample includes 78 countries from around the world, corresponding to the complete group of countries for which all the necessary data could be obtained. The underlying theory suggests the correct specification of each of the *Z* variables. In some cases, the variables are most appropriately expressed as period averages, such as with government saving and openness. For quality of government institutions, the 1981 value is used as an approximate midpoint of the sample, because earlier observations are not available. For the human capital variables (life expectancy and schooling), the correct specification is the base year observations, as used in previous studies of convergence. The population change variables (growth rate of population and growth rate of the working-age population) are expressed as the average annual log differences between 1965 and 1990, as the underlying theory suggests (see Radelet, Sachs, and Lee 1996 for more discussion). For these population change variables, instrumental variable equations were also used to control for possible reverse causation. Instruments included indicators of national population policies, religious composition of the population, and population growth rates prior to 1965. The results, although not presented here, were similar to those of the basic model.

Basic Results

The results from the basic specification are shown in column 1 of Table A-2. All the estimated coefficients are of the expected sign, and all but two are statistically significant at the 5 percent level. The estimated growth rate of the total population is significant at the 7 percent level, and the coefficient on average years of schooling at the 13 percent level. In most cases, the standard errors of the estimates are quite small (as shown by the high t-statistics), indicating well-determined statistical relationships. The results provide strong evidence for conditional convergence, with α estimated to be -1.98 with a standard error of 0.21 (and a t-statistic of -9.42). This indicates that the 95 percent confidence interval on the estimated coefficient is between -2.40 and -1.56. The two population change variables are each of the expected sign. In theory, the estimated coefficients for the growth rates of the working-age population and the total population should be 1 and -1, respectively. The empirical results do not permit rejection of these hypotheses.

The second and third columns of Table A-2 show the results when dummy variables are added for countries in East and Southeast Asia, South Asia, Latin America, and sub-Saharan Africa. In each case, these variables are statistically insignificant. These results indicate that the basic set of explanatory variables accounts for most of the differences in growth rates between these regions and the full sample.

Of course, these results represent the "average" relationships across countries, rather than a precise explanation applicable to all countries across time. Some individual countries undoubtedly differ in terms of the strength of the relationships. Nevertheless, the basic specification captures the broad relationships that influence economic growth across countries quite well. These variables explain about 87 percent of the variation in growth rates across the sample, a strong result for this kind of analysis. In particular, the basic specification tracks the actual growth performance of Asian countries very well. The "fitted" growth rates for each country (calculated by multiplying the estimated coefficients by the actual value for each variable for each country, and adding these terms together) correspond closely with the actual growth rates in most cases. For example, India's fitted growth rate for 1965-90 is 2.16 percent, compared with the actual rate of 2.03 percent, and the PRC's fitted growth rate is 5.30 percent, compared with the actual rate of 5.09 percent. The largest single difference for the 14 Asian countries in our sample was in Malaysia, where the fitted growth rate of 3.53 percent fell below the actual rate of 4.49 percent by about 1 percentage point.

Variations in Sample Size and Included Variables

The robustness of the results was tested by eliminating some of the countries in the sample in two ways (Table A-3). First, one fourth of the countries in the sample was randomly dropped (by eliminating every fourth observation). The estimation results were broadly similar to those from the full sample. Moreover, the fitted values for economic growth for the omitted countries matched the actual values with a 92 percent correlation. Second, the 14 Asian countries were eliminated from the sample. Once again, the estimation results did not change substantially. In this case, the fitted values for economic growth for the omitted Asian countries matched the actual values with a 93 percent correlation.

A wide variety of other explanatory variables were tested, many of which have been included in other analyses of economic growth. Because of space limitations, the results from the full list of variables cannot be reported here, but a sample of these results is shown in Tables A-4 and A-5. Column 1 of Table A-4 includes primary school enrollment rates rather than average years of education, with slightly weaker results than the base specification. Column 2 uses adult literacy rates as the education indicator. The results are similar, and perhaps a bit stronger, than in the base specification, but data on literacy rates in 1965 are available for only 60 countries. Column 3 replaces government saving with national saving, which conceptually is a preferable specification. However, there is a strong simultaneous relationship between national saving and growth, making the interpretation of the results more problematic. Moreover, national saving may be measured with substantial error. One way to treat the issue of simultaneity would be to employ a two-stage estimation procedure using instruments for the national saving variable. The results from this technique, however, were not wholly satisfactory, perhaps because of measurement errors, or simply because of an inadequate theory of private saving. The basic specification therefore remained preferable (see Radelet, Sachs, and Lee 1996 for more details). The final column of Table A-4 shows the results with total government expenditure rather than with government saving. The results are somewhat weaker than in the base case, and the estimated coefficient on government expenditures is statistically insignificant.

Table A-5 shows the results with the addition of inflation, initial income distribution (measured by the gini coefficient), political instability, and political rights, some of the more common variables other analysts use. In each case, the additional variable is insignificant and adds little to the total explained variance. The same was true when other variables were added (with results not shown here), including initial levels of debt, prevalence of malaria, components of government spending, and so on. Including the gini coefficient (column 2 of Table A-5) required eliminating 31 countries from the sample. We also included measures of gender equality, urbanization, birth rates, and death rates (both overall and for different population age groups).

Of course, a wide range of other specifications are possible, allowing for nonlinear relationships between the variables and economic growth and interactions between some of the independent variables. One such nonlinear relationship was detected between life expectancy and growth. Both life expectancy and life expectancy squared are included in the base specification, and the results indicate that the positive impact of longer life expectancy on growth tapers off and becomes negative at higher levels of life expectancy (specifically, after 68 years). Many other possible relationships were explored without improving the results.

Growth Projections

The projected growth rates for the 14 Asian countries in the sample are estimated by multiplying 1995 values (or the closest year possible) for each of the "Z" variables by the estimated coefficients, and adding the resulting terms (including the originally estimated constant term). For Malaysia, which was the largest outlier of the Asian countries, we added the difference between the fitted and actual growth rates for 1965-90 (about 1 percentage point) to the projected growth rate. This change reflects the subjective judgment that the model's relatively large underprediction of Malaysia's past growth suggests the strong possibility of an important underprediction of the future growth as well. A likely reason for Malaysia's strong performance in the past (relative to the model's prediction) has been its ability to manage the challenges arising from natural resource abundance better than most other resource-abundant countries, rendering Malaysia an outlier for natural-resource abundant countries. Assuming that this strong management continues, adding the error term to the projected growth rate seems reasonable. The adjustment was not made for any other country.

Data Quality

As with any empirical investigation in developing countries, some of these data are probably somewhat weak. For example, the data on life expectancy at birth (World Bank 1995) are, in some cases, based on indirect estimation rather than on direct measurement. Nevertheless, this variable is probably the best single indicator available that captures the broad dimensions of the population's health in the base year. It is used extensively in other research, such as in the United Nations Development Programme's human development index. Similarly, the data on average years of schooling (Barro and Lee 1994) is based on long historical data on school enrollments, rather than on direct survey methods. It also does not take into consideration the quality of schooling. Despite these issues, this measure is superior conceptually to either current enrollment rates (which provide little information on the working-age population already out of school) or literacy rates (which tell us little beyond the achievement of a basic level of education). Also, some analysts question the suitability of using PPP-adjusted income data from Summers and Heston (1994), because for some countries the data are estimated rather than measured directly. Of course, the PPP-based income data used here are conceptually superior to data based on official exchange rates. As a test, income data based on official exchange rates (World Bank 1995) were substituted for both initial income levels and income growth rates in our sample. The results were broadly similar to those from the base specification. Similarly, for other variables, a range of alternative measures and sources was considered. The data ultimately chosen were those judged to be the best of the available choices. As improved data become available in the future, more precise estimates of the relevant parameters will become possible.

References

Asian Development Bank. 1996. *Key Indicators of Developing Asian and Pacific Countries*, electronic data. Manila.

Barro, Robert, and J. W. Lee. 1994. "Sources of Economic Growth." *Carnegie-Rochester Conference Series on Public Policy* 40(2):1-46.

Brassey's Incorporated. 1996. *World Factbook 1996-1997.* Washington, D.C.

Gang, Fan, Dwight Perkins, and Lora Sabin. 1996. "China's Economic Performance and Prospects." Background paper for *Emerging Asia: Changes and Challenges*. Asian Development Bank, Manila.

Knack, Stephen, and Philip Keefer. 1995. "Institutions and Economic Performance: Cross-Country Tests Using Alternative Institutional Measures." *Economics and Politics* 7(3):207-27.

Radelet, Steven, Jeffrey Sachs, and Jong-Wha Lee. 1996. "Economic Growth in Asia." Background paper for *Emerging Asia: Changes and Challenges*. Asian Development Bank, Manila.

Sachs, Jeffrey, and Andrew Warner. 1995. "Economic Reform and the Process of Global Integration." *Brookings Papers on Economic Activity* 0(1):1-95.

Summers, Robert, and Alan Heston. 1994. *Penn World Table,* Mark 5.6 (website version). Philapelphia: University of Pennsylvania.

UN (United Nations). 1994. "World Population Prospects 1950-2050 (The 1994 Revision)." *Demographic Indicators 1950-2050 (The 1994 Revision)*, electronic data. New York.

World Bank. 1995. *World Data 1995*. Socioeconomic Time Series Access and Retrieval System, Version 3.0, electronic resource. Washington, D.C.

Box A-1. Definitions and Sources of Data Used in the Growth Regressions

Growth in gross domestic product (GDP) per person is calculated as the difference in the natural log of GDP per person in 1990 and the natural log of income per person in 1965, divided by 25. GDP data are drawn from Summers and Heston (1994). The last year for which data in this data set are complete is 1990, which determines the end of the period of analysis. For the PRC, the growth rate is based on data in Gang, Perkins, and Sabin (1996).

GDP per worker in 1965 is taken from Summers and Heston (1994). Data on the size of the working-age population is from UN (1994). For the PRC, the 1965 level is extrapolated based on the 1990 level and the growth rate from Gang, Perkins, and Sabin (1996) as noted above. The data are expressed as a share of U.S. GDP per worker in 1965.

Average years of secondary schooling of the adult population (age 15 years and older) in 1965 is from Barro and Lee (1994).

Life expectancy at birth is taken from World Bank (1995).

Natural resource abundance is measured as the share of primary product exports in GDP in 1971 (the earliest year for which complete data were available), taken from World Bank (1995).

The ratio of coastline distance to land area is taken from The World Factbook, 1996-97 (Brassey's Inc. 1996).

Openness to the global economy is drawn from Sachs and Warner (1995). This index is the fraction of years between 1965 and 1990 that the country was considered to be open to trade. A country is considered to be open if it meets minimum criteria on four aspects of trade policy: average tariffs must be lower than 40 percent, quotas and licensing must cover less than 40 percent of total imports, the black market premium on foreign exchange must be less than 20 percent, and export taxes should be moderate.

Government saving/GDP is defined as the difference between the central government's current revenues and current expenditures, divided by nominal GDP. All data are taken from the World Bank (1995). For some Asian countries for which data were unavailable from World Bank, data were taken from ADB (1996).

Institutional quality is based on the index created by Knack and Keefer (1995), which is itself an average of five indicators of the quality of public institutions, including (a) the perceived efficiency of the government bureaucracy, (b) the extent of governmental corruption, (c) efficacy of the rule of law, (d) the presence or absence of expropriation risk, and (e) the perceived risk of repudiation of contracts by the government. Each country is scored on these five dimensions on the basis of surveys of business attitudes within the countries. The subindexes on the five measures are then summed to produce a single, overall index that is scaled between 0 and 10.

Growth of the working-age population is defined as the growth rate of the population aged between 15 and 64 years. Data are taken from UN (1994).

Growth of the total population is taken from UN (1994).

Table A-1. Summary of Key Variables by Region
(unweighted averages)

Variable	All economies	East Asia	South Asia	Southeast Asia	Sub-Saharan Africa	Latin America
Growth rate of GDP per person, 1965-90 (percent)	1.90	6.70	1.70	3.80	0.60	0.80
Initial conditions						
Real per person GDP in 1965 (1985 prices)	3,163	2,010	996	1,161	826	2,611
Average years of secondary schooling in 1965	0.80	1.50	0.50	0.50	0.20	0.60
Resources and geography						
Natural resource intensity (primary exports as a percentage of GDP in 1971)	0.11	0.01	0.05	0.17	0.16	0.16
Tropics	0.53	0.63	0.40	1.00	0.91	0.79
Landlocked	0.17	0.00[a]	0.00[a]	0.00[a]	0.47	0.10
Ratio of coastline distance to land area	0.29	2.83	0.07	0.43	0.02	0.17
Policy and choice variables						
Openness	0.43	0.97	0.06	0.73	0.08	0.17
Government saving rate (percent of GDP)	1.60	5.60	1.00	3.50	3.00	1.20
Quality of institutions	5.99	7.79	4.23	4.95	4.72	4.37
Demography						
Life expectancy in 1965 (years)	57	63	49	52	41	56
Growth of the working-age population (annual average between 1965 and 1990, percent)	2.23	2.68	2.51	2.90	2.85	2.60
Growth of total population (annual average between 1965 and 1990, percent)	1.96	1.68	2.26	2.35	2.92	2.20

a. The landlocked countries in these regions could not be included in the analysis.
Source: see Box A-1.

Table A-2. Cross-Country Growth Regressions, Base Specification
Dependent variable: growth of real GDP per person,
1965-90 (78 countries)

Independent variable	Coefficient		
Initial output per worker (log)	-1.98	-1.98	-2.14
	(-9.42)	(-8.78)	(-8.34)
Schooling (log)	0.21	0.20	0.21
	(1.53)	(1.43)	(1.43)
Natural resource abundance	-2.43	-2.44	-2.22
	(-2.36)	(-2.31)	(-2.04)
Landlocked	-0.61	-0.61	-0.55
	(-2.28)	(-2.27)	(-2.01)
Tropics	-1.26	-1.34	-1.12
	(-4.29)	(-4.42)	(-3.03)
Ratio of coastline distance to land area	0.26	0.25	0.27
	(2.37)	(2.18)	(2.30)
Government saving rate	0.12	0.12	0.12
	(4.94)	(4.81)	(4.83)
Openness	1.97	1.87	1.67
	(6.20)	(5.61)	(4.58)
Quality of institutions	0.25	0.24	0.29
	(3.47)	(3.28)	(3.22)
Life expectancy	0.34	0.33	0.31
	(3.47)	(2.72)	(2.55)
Life expectancy squared	-2.0E-3	-2.0E-3	-2.0E-3
	(-2.23)	(-2.14)	(-2.01)
Growth of the working-age population	1.13	1.08	0.98
	(2.86)	(2.61)	(2.20)
Growth of the total population	-0.77	-0.73	-0.60
	(-1.83)	(-1.64)	(-1.22)
East and Southeast Asia		0.20	-0.21
		(0.51)	(-0.42)
South Asia		-0.40	-0.82
		(-0.95)	(-1.58)
Latin America			-0.35
			(-0.82)
Sub-Saharan Africa			-0.84
			(-1.59)
Adjusted R^2	0.87	0.86	0.86

Note: t-statistics in parentheses. Constant term not reported. R^2 is the percentage of the variation in the dependent variable explained by the independent variables.
Source: Radelet, Sachs, and Lee (1996).

Table A-3. Cross-Country Growth Regressions, Smaller Sample Size
Dependent variable: growth of real GDP per person,
1965-90

Independent variable	Coefficient	
	Dropping every 4th observation	**Dropping Asia**
Initial output per worker (log)	-1.96	-1.89
	(-8.18)	(-6.94)
Schooling (log)	0.09	0.21
	(0.47)	(1.30)
Natural resource abundance	-1.78	-2.97
	(-1.53)	(-2.45)
Landlocked	-0.89	-0.49
	(-2.71)	(-1.69)
Tropics	-1.33	-1.36
	(-3.56)	(-3.62)
Ratio of coastline distance to land area	0.39	0.55
	(1.52)	(1.24)
Government saving rate	0.10	0.12
	(3.11)	(4.20)
Openness	1.96	1.34
	(5.25)	(3.27)
Quality of institutions	0.32	0.27
	(3.62)	(3.29)
Life expectancy	0.37	0.32
	(2.65)	(2.50)
Life expectancy squared	-3.0E-3	-2.0E-3
	(-2.07)	(-1.94)
Growth of the working-age population	1.09	0.90
	(2.29)	(1.89)
Growth of the total population	-0.53	-0.54
	(-1.07)	(-1.05)
Number of countries	59	64
Adjusted R^2	0.86	0.78

Note: t-statistics in parentheses. Constant term not reported. R^2 is the percentage of the variation in the dependent variable explained by the independent variables.
Source: Radelet, Sachs, and Lee (1996).

Table A-4. Cross-Country Growth Regressions, Variations on Education and Government Saving

Dependent variable: growth of real GDP per person, 1965-90

Independent variable	Coefficient			
Initial output per worker (log)	-1.90	-1.67	-1.92	-2.01
	(-9.11)	(-6.60)	(-8.59)	(-8.38)
Secondary schooling years (log)			-0.07	0.02
			(-0.50)	(0.15)
Primary schooling ratio (log)	0.38			
	(1.01)			
Literacy		0.46		
		(1.91)		
Natural resource abundance	-2.16	-1.82	-1.89	-2.79
	(-2.12)	(-1.54)	(-1.72)	(-2.02)
Landlocked	-0.69	-0.65	-0.72	-0.57
	(-2.64)	(-1.91)	(-2.62)	(-1.89)
Tropics	-1.32	-1.30	-1.62	-1.64
	(-4.51)	(-3.87)	(-5.20)	(-4.73)
Ratio of coastline distance to land area	0.29	0.15	0.44	0.53
	(2.68)	(1.08)	(3.71)	(2.11)
Government saving rate	0.11	0.11		
	(4.77)	(4.18)		
National saving rate (including transfers)			0.04	
			(2.81)	
Total government expenditures				0.96
				(0.89)
Openness	2.03	2.24	2.41	2.60
	(6.40)	(6.15)	(6.48)	(6.72)
Quality of institutions	0.26	0.28	0.22	0.27
	(3.64)	(3.18)	(2.80)	(3.48)
Life expectancy	0.28	0.27	0.21	0.35
	(1.89)	(1.81)	(1.61)	(2.58)
Life expectancy squared	-2.0E-3	-2.0E-3	-1.0E-3	-3.0E-3
	(-1.52)	(-1.08)	(-1.25)	(-2.16)
Growth of the working-age population	1.23	1.45	1.34	1.45
	(3.12)	(3.00)	(3.33)	(3.37)
Growth of the total population	-0.86	-1.12	-0.75	-0.78
	(-2.02)	(-2.19)	(-1.67)	(-1.64)
Number of countries	77	60	76	73
Adjusted R^2	0.86	0.86	0.86	0.83

Note: t-statistics in parentheses. Constant term not reported. R^2 is the percentage of the variation in the dependent variable explained by the independent variables.

Source: Radelet, Sachs, and Lee (1996).

Table A-5. Cross-Country Growth Regressions, Additional Variables

Dependent variable: growth of real GDP per person,
1965-90

Independent variable	Coefficient			
Initial output per worker (log)	-1.97	-2.32	-1.98	-2.04
	(-9.25)	(-6.95)	(-8.63)	(-9.36)
Secondary schooling years (log)	0.18	0.10	0.16	0.23
	(1.24)	(0.48)	(1.13)	(1.65)
Natural resource abundance	-2.52	-1.73	-2.67	-2.61
	(-2.36)	(-1.29)	(-2.49)	(-2.49)
Landlocked	-0.66	-1.81	-0.62	-0.63
	(-2.44)	(-1.89)	(-2.27)	(-2.30)
Tropics	-1.25	-1.01	-1.23	-1.36
	(-4.23)	(-2.42)	(-4.01)	(-4.54)
Ratio of coastline distance to land area	0.26	0.29	0.27	0.44
	(2.35)	(2.54)	(2.47)	(1.89)
Government saving rate	0.13	0.12	0.13	0.13
	(4.95)	(2.96)	(4.70)	(5.02)
Openness	2.02	2.09	1.89	2.00
	(6.22)	(4.40)	(5.57)	(6.32)
Quality of institutions	0.24	0.54	0.27	0.21
	(3.18)	(4.56)	(2.72)	(2.81)
Life expectancy	0.31	0.54	0.33	0.35
	(2.49)	(3.27)	(2.65)	(2.92)
Life expectancy squared	-2.0E-3	-5.0E-3	-2.0E-3	-3.0E-3
	(-1.94)	(-2.91)	(-2.10)	(-2.38)
Growth of the working-age population	1.14	0.29	1.06	0.99
	(2.84)	(0.49)	(2.60)	(2.49)
Growth of the total population	-0.78	0.09	-0.72	-0.63
	(-1.83)	(0.14)	(-1.69)	(-1.23)
Inflation	0.30			
	(0.48)			
Initial Gini coefficient		0.02		
		(1.20)		
Political instability			0.47	
			(0.38)	
Political rights				-0.09
				(-1.23)
Number of countries	77	47	74	76
Adjusted R^2	0.86	0.88	0.87	0.86

Note: t-statistics in parentheses. Constant term not reported. R^2 is the percentage of the variation in the dependent variable explained by the independent variables.
Source: Radelet, Sachs, and Lee (1996).

BIBLIOGRAPHICAL NOTE

A large number of people have contributed to the *Emerging Asia: Changes and Challenges* study. The Asian Development Bank (ADB) commissioned a number of focused background papers. These papers and their authors are identified at the end of this note. The citations in the body of the report refer to materials that have been drawn on directly.

The following people contributed directly to one or more chapters of the report: David Bloom, Jeffrey Sachs, Michael Lipton, Siddiqur Osmani, Theodore Panayotou, Steven Radelet, Jeffrey Williamson, and Arjan de Haan. Staff of ADB who directly contributed were Piyase Abeygunawardena, Indu Bhushan, V. V. Desai, David Edwards, Prodipto Ghosh, Frank Harrigan, Rajiv Kumar, Bindu Lohani, Elisabetta Marmolo, Sudipto Mundle, and Sultan Hafeez Rahman.

The following ADB staff provided valuable comments, advice, and inputs: Edvard Baardsen, John Boyd, Douglas Brooks, Dieter Bucher, Elisabetta Capannelli, Guangzhe Chen, Charles Currin, Dilip Das, Robert Dobias, J. Warren Evans, Jesus Felipe, Dagmar Graczyk, M. Riyaz Ul Haq, Edu Hassing, Edward Haugh, Sophia Ho, Aminul Huq, Peter King, John Kuiper, Jeffrey Liang, Benjamin Loevinsohn, Riccardo Loi, Srinivasa Madhur, Mark Mitchell, Rita Nangia, Gene Owens, Ernesto Pernia, Stephen Pollard, Nikhilesh Prasad, S. Tahir Qadri, Pradumna Rana, Narhari Rao, Sermpol Ratasuk, Asad Ali Shah, Toru Shibuichi, Ricardo Tan, Arjun Thapan, Steven van der Tak, Etienne van de Walle, Graham Walter, Christine Wong, and Sadiq Zaidi.

At the Harvard Institute for International Development, the following people provided especially valuable comments and assistance in the preparation of this work: John Gallup, Larry Rosenberg, Donald Snodgrass, and Jeffrey Vincent.

Many other people provided key inputs and useful advice: Steven Anderson, Wasim Azhar, Nirupam Bajpai, Neil Bennett, Eric Bettinger,

Alok Bhargava, Tim Brown, David Canning, Tod Cowen, Klaus Deininger, J. R. DeShazo, Robert Faris, Gary Fields, Sherry Glied, Morley Gunderson, William Hsiao, Mumtaz Hussain, Taku Imagawa, Donald Johnston, Roy Kelly, Gerald Keusch, Nathan Keyfitz, Laurence Kotlikoff, Ronald Lee, Anil Markandya, Andrew Mason, Matthew McGuire, Lysander Menezes, Jacob Mincer, Jonathan Morduch, Karthik Muralidharan, Sharmila Nanda, Joseph Newhouse, Waseem Noor, Andrew Noymer, Hui Pan, Dilip Parajuli, Kristen Phelps, Sze-Tien Quek, Martin Ravallion, Amulya Reddy, Francisco Rivera-Batiz, Michael Roemer, Henry Rosovsky, Amartya Sen, Jonathan Simon, Saurabh Sinha, Lyn Squire, Robert Stavins, Sachi Takeda, C. Peter Timmer, Myriam Vellia, Staci Warden, Andrew Warner, Inger Weibust, Shahin Yaqub, Xiang Yu, and Richard Zeckhauser.

The following people reviewed the background papers and provided comments: Jere Behrman, Francois Bourguignon, Ricardo Cospedal, Gary Fields, Junichi Goto, Burkhard Heer, Klaus Leisinger, Marc Nerlove, Naohiro Ogawa, I. G. Patel, T. Paul Schultz, T. N. Srinivasan, and Erik Thorbecke.

Background Papers

Bardhan, Kalpana, and Stephan Klasen. "Women in Emerging Asia."

Basu, Alaka Malwade, and Kaushik Basu. "The Quality of Work Experience in Emerging Asia."

Bhargava, Alok, and Siddiqur Osmani. "Health and Nutrition in Emerging Asia."

Bloom, David, John Gallup, and David Beede. "Energy and Poverty."

Brooks, Douglas. "Challenges for Emerging Asia's Trade and Environment."

Caldwell, John, and Bruce Caldwell. "Asia's Demographic Transition."

Canning, David. "Productive and Environmental Infrastructure in Emerging Asian Economies."

Chatterjee, Shiladitya. "Recent Experience in the Private Financing of Infrastructure in Asia: An Analysis of Related Issues."

Das, Dilip. "Asian Exports: Past Trends and Future Prospects."

DeShazo, J. R. "The Level of and Demand for Environmental Quality in Asia."

Gang, Fan, Dwight Perkins, and Lora Sabin. "China's Economic Performance and Prospects."

Glaeser, Edward. "Information Technology and the Future of Asia."

Goldman, Richard. "Agriculture and Growth in Asia."

Gunderson, Morley. "Labor Market Institutions and Flexibility in Asia."

Harrigan, Frank, and Lea Sumulong. "Aspects of Asian Macroeconomic and Structural Interdependence."

Henderson, Vernon. "Urbanization in Asia."

Hughes, Anthony Vernon. "Issues in Development and Dependence in the Pacific Islands."

Huq, Aminul. "Energy and the Environment: The Asian Outlook."

Islam, Nazrul. "Income-Environment Relationship: Is Asia Different?"

Joshi, Vijay, and I. M. D. Little. "India: Reform on Hold."

Kato, Saburo. "Emerging Asia and the Future of the Environment— Perspective and Agenda."

Kumar, Rajiv. "Globalization, Economic Restructuring, and Role of Government: Prospects for Asian Economies."

Lall, Sanjaya. "Coping with New Technologies in Emerging Asia."

Lewin, Keith. "Access to Education in Emerging Asia: Trends, Challenges, and Policy Options."

Lipton, Michael, Arjan de Haan, and Shahin Yaqub. "Poverty in Emerging Asia."

Mangahas, Mahar. "The Quality of Home and Habitat in Asia."

Markandya, Anil. "Environmental Control Costs, Policy Options, Instruments, and Abatements."

Mazumdar, Dipak. "Labor Markets and Their Evolution in Asia."

Park, Yung-Chul. "Financial Liberalization and Market Opening in Asia: The Implications for Economic Development and Integration."

Pernia, Ernesto, and Stella Luz Alabastro. "Aspects of Urban Sanitation and Safe Water in the Context of Rapid Urbanization."

Prasad, Nikhilesh. "Governance and Other Nonmarket Factors in Asian Development."

Radelet, Steve, Jeffrey Sachs, and Jong-Wha Lee. "Economic Growth in Asia."

Snodgrass, Donald, Bong-Min Yang, Zainal Aznam Yusof, and Tatsuo Hatta. "Human Resource Development in Asia."

Vincent, Jeffrey, and Beatriz Castañeda. "Sustainability and the Economic Depreciation of Natural Resources in Asia."

Williamson, Jeffrey, and Matthew Higgins. "Asian Savings, Investment, and Foreign Capital Dependence: The Role of Demography."

Wong, Christine. "Transition Economies of Asia."

The following contributed country background notes: Naved Hamid, Yun-Hwan Kim, Srinivasa Madhur, Chris Manning, Min Tang, and Nguyen Van Quy.

INDEX